ALL THE KING'S WOMEN

Hans Holbein: Portrait of an Unknown Man
Rothschild – A Story of Wealth and Power
England in the Age of Thomas More
Sweet Robin: Robert Dudley, Earl of Leicester
A Tudor Tapestry: Men, Women and Society in Reformation England
The World Encompassed: Drake's Great Voyage, 1577–1580
Reformation: Christianity and the World 1500–2000
(with Felipe Fernández-Armesto)
The King and the Gentleman:
Charles Stuart and Oliver Cromwell 1599–1649
In the Lion's Court: Power, Ambition,
and Sudden Death in the Reign of Henry VIII

All the King's Women

Love, Sex and Politics in the Life of Charles II

Derek Wilson

HUTCHINSON
LONDON

First published in the United Kingdom in 2003 by Hutchinson

The Random House Group Limited
20 Vauxhall Bridge Road, London SW1V 2SA

Random House Australia (Pty) Limited
20 Alfred Street, Milsons Point, Sydney
New South Wales 2061, Australia

Random House New Zealand Limited
18 Poland Road, Glenfield
Auckland 10, New Zealand

Random House (Pty) Limited
Endulini, 5a Jubilee Road
Parktown 2193, South Africa

The Random House Group Limited Reg. No. 954009

www.randomhouse.co.uk

A CIP catalogue record for this book is available
from the British Library

Papers used by Random House
are natural recylable products made from wood grown in
sustainable forests. The manufacturing processes conform to
the environmental regulations of the country of origin

ISBN 0 09 179379 3

Typeset by SX Composing DTP, Rayleigh, Essex
Printed and bound in Great Britain by Clays Ltd, St Ives Plc

'Go among those women? Not unless I can wear blinkers!'

Lady Anne Clifford

CONTENTS

LIST OF ILLUSTRATIONS

1st section

The five eldest children of Charles I, Sir Anthony Van Dyck, 1637. (The Royal Collection © 2003, Her Majesty Queen Elizabeth II (photo: A.C.Cooper))

Henrietta Maria appearing in a court masque, detail from *Apollo and Diana* by Gerrit van Honthorst. (The Royal Collection © 2003, Her Majesty Queen Elizabeth II (photo: A.C. Cooper))

Histoire de l'Entrée de la Reyne Mère, by Jean Puget de la Serre, 1639. (By permission of The British Library (C.37.I.9))

Chalk drawing of *Charles II*, Samuel Cooper, *c.*1660 (The Royal Collection © 2003, Her Majesty Queen Elizabeth II (photo: A.C. Cooper))

*Jane (née Lane), Lady Fisher, c.*1660, artist unknown. (By courtesy of the National Portrait Gallery, London)

Charles II and Jane Lane riding to Bristol, Isaac Fuller, 1660s. (By courtesy of the National Portrait Gallery, London)

The Royal Escape in a Breeze, Willem van der Velde the Elder, *c.*1651. (The Royal Collection © 2003, Her Majesty Queen Elizabeth II (photo: Dominic Brown))

Charles and Mary of Orange dancing at The Hague, Hieronymus Janssens. (The Royal Collection © 2003, Her Majesty Queen Elizabeth II (photo: A.C.Cooper))

Charles II miniature, David Des Granges, after Adriaen Hanneman, *c.*1648. (By courtesy of the National Portrait Gallery, London)

Somerset House from *Britannia Illustrata*, L. Knyff. (Mary Evans Picture Library)

Illustration showing a stage set with ships from *The Empress of Morocco*, by Elkanah Settle, 1673 (By permission of The British Library (644.i.8))

English tin-glazed earthenware dish showing Charles II and Catherine of Braganza, *c.*1662-85. (Victoria and Albert Museum (photo: © V&A Picture Library))

A plan of the Palace of Whitehall, unattributed engraving, 1680. (Mary Evans Picture Library)

An orange seller, from *Cries of London,* unidentified series, 18th century. (Mary Evans Picture Library)

2nd section

Charles II and Nell Gwyn, Edward Matthew Ward, 1854. (Victoria and Albert Museum (photo: © V&A Picture Library))

Barbara Villiers, Countess of Castlemaine, Samuel Cooper, *c.*1660-1. (The Royal Collection © 2003, Her Majesty Queen Elizabeth II (photo: EZM))

Catherine of Braganza, Jacob Huysmans, *c.*1664. (The Royal Collection © 2003, Her Majesty Queen Elizabeth II (photo: EZM))

Frances Teresa Stuart, later Duchess of Richmond and Lennox, in a riding habit, Samuel Cooper, *c.*1663. (The Royal Collection © 2003, Her Majesty Queen Elizabeth II (photo: EZM))

Henrietta Anne, Duchess of Orléans, Sir Peter Lely, *c.*1662. (By courtesy of the National Portrait Gallery, London)

Louise de Keroualle, Duchess of Portsmouth, Sir Peter Lely, *c.*1671-4. (The J. Paul Getty Museum, Los Angeles (photo © The J. Paul Getty Museum))

Hortense Mancini, Duchess de Mazarin, attributed to Jacob-Ferdinand Voet, *c.*1670. (By kind permission of Althorp)

Mary Davis, possibly by William Pawlett, *c.*1673. (By kind permission of His Grace The Duke of Buccleuch and Queensberry KT)

Lucy Walters, Nicholas Dixon. (By kind permission of His Grace The Duke of Buccleuch and Queensberry KT)

Nell Gwyn, Simon Verelst, *c.*1680. (By courtesy of the National Portrait Gallery, London)

3rd section

Illustration from *The Works of His Grace George Villiers Duke of Buckingham in Two Volumes,* 1715. (By permission of The British Library (12271.c.33))

St. James's Park in the time of Charles II, Johannes Kip, *c.*1720. (Guildhall Library, Corporation of London)

Man being robbed in a brothel, Richard Gaywood. (Ashmolean Museum, Oxford)

The home of Nell Gwyn in 1820, unattributed engraving in 'Old and New London', *c.*1650-87. (Mary Evans Picture Library)

The Compleat Auctioneer, artist unknown. (By permission of The British Library (MS Harley 5947, f. 2))

A pope-burning procession, unattributed illustration, 1679. (Mary Evans Picture Library)

A London Coffee House, contemporary engraving by unknown artist, *c.*1700. (Mary Evans Picture Library)

Horseguards Parade with King Charles II, Hendrick Danckerts, *c.*1630-80. (By permission of the Duke of Roxburghe)

Gold medal to commemorate the Peace of Breda, Jan Roettier, 1667. (© copyright The British Museum)

Henrietta Maria as a widow, William Faithorne. (By courtesy of the National Portrait Gallery, London)

INTRODUCTION

'All' – it is a tiny word with infinite pretensions, so its use in the present context demands careful definition. First, let me make clear what this book is *not*: it is not a *catalogue raisonné* of Charles II's sexual conquests. Even if it were possible to compile such a list it would have little value. Kiss-and-tell revelations about living celebrities sell tabloid newspapers but distort the images of their subjects and provide few clues to their place in the great scheme of things. When we look back at some of the men and women of past ages who really *were* important, over-zealous attention to contemporary salacious tittle-tattle similarly distorts our understanding. Of no one is this truer than Charles II, the supposedly libidinous 'merry monarch'. The received myth presents him as a carefree and accomplished seducer who, when he was not doing it, was thinking about it. Novelists, filmmakers and even some biographers have tended to take as their starting point the verdict of the diarist John Evelyn:

> An excellent prince, doubtless, had he been less addicted to women . . . his too easy nature resigned him to be managed by crafty men and some abandoned wretches, who corrupted his otherwise sufficient parts . . .[1]

Or of Gilbert Burnet, Bishop of Salisbury:

> His love of pleasure and his vast expense with his women, together with the great influence they have had in all his affairs both at home and abroad is the chief load that will lay on him; for not only the women themselves have great power, but his court is full of pimps and bawds, and all matters in which one desires to succeed must be put in their hands.[2]

The picture apparently painted by such high-minded, scandalised observers is vivid and easily recognised: it is the portrait of a debauched king set against the background of a decadent court. It inspired writers of romance and Hollywood costume drama to present tales of lecherous milords in full-bottomed wigs pursuing hapless maidens in low-cut gowns through the teeming streets and gilded salons of Restoration London. Historians and biographers, taking seriously the volume and venom of contemporary criticism, have felt obliged to analyse coolly what manner of man this royal womaniser was – weak or wily, manipulator or manipulated, an indolent hedonist who went with the flow or a canny mover and shaker of people and events – and the roué's cynical smile leers through their careful prose.

What writers have so often failed to take full account of is that such disapproving judgements as those most commonly quoted say as much, if not more, about prevailing male attitudes to women as they do about the king's character. Why should it have been considered reprehensible for a ruler to enjoy female company or even to discuss important matters of state with people he trusted simply because they were not men? Everyone at court was scrambling for influence, wealth and power. Why should that have been accepted (if not approved) behaviour for courtiers but not for courtesans?

The answer is fear. In a male-dominated society women were regarded as a lower order of creation. The pious John Milton racked his brain to try to understand,

> ... why did God,
> Creator wise, that peopled highest heaven
> With spirits masculine, create at last
> This novelty on earth, this fair defect
> Of nature ...[3]

For the proper ordering of society women had to be kept in subjection. But that was easier said than done precisely because this 'defect' was 'fair'. Women were possessed of a sexual magic that made them irresistible to men. Once their spell had been cast, poor, hapless males could be reduced to debilitating servitude. As if that was not bad enough, in post-Restoration society all manner of women were asserting and exercising new kinds of authority.

The Civil War and the politico-religious revolution which accompanied it had spread social chaos. All major upheavals inevitably impact on gender roles. The wars of the twentieth century which plucked women from the kitchen and deposited them in munitions factories and the armed services rapidly accelerated the speed of female emancipation. What happened in the mid-seventeenth century was even more revolutionary. It was, in the words of Professor Christopher Hill, 'the most turbulent, seditious and factious [period] of recorded English history'.[4] Therefore its impact on the position of women was profound. Deprived of husbands or fathers, many found themselves running family estates and businesses. Some were caught up in sects like the Quakers or Ranters which denied the assumptions undergirding male dominance and allowed them to assume the roles of prophets, preachers and religious leaders. But while these took on 'holy' lives some of their less fortunate sisters were driven into high-class prostitution. Girls of good family cast adrift in a turbulent world had to accept the 'protection' of footloose royalist officers or exploit the gifts nature had bestowed on them to attract members of the Prince of Wales' itinerant court in exile. Then there were the educated women who, in an age of unprecedented vigorous political comment, saw no reason not to enter the debate and who published their own pamphlets and books.

Once the monarchy was restored the nation's leaders in court and parliament assumed that the unfortunate innovations of the last two decades could be swept away and pre-war stability restored. It did not happen. Suddenly women achieved even greater prominence in society. Their most obvious showcase was the stage. Within months the king and the Duke of York had given their patronage to two theatre companies and Charles, personally, decreed that the female roles were to be played by women. The idea was new. It was French. It was shocking. The influence of actresses and parts that were written for them transformed the drama. Evelyn was appalled. He explained that he seldom went to the theatre,

> . . . as they were abused to an atheistical liberty, fowl and undecent, women now (and never till now) permitted to appear and act, which, inflaming several young noblemen and gallants became their whores and to some their wives . . . and another greater person . . . fell into their snares . . .[5]

It was not long before women were actually writing for the stage. And not only for the stage. Female authors actually had the audacity to venture into print alongside their male counterparts with poems, essays and observations on politics and philosophy. Women were soon among the celebrities of the day. Crowds flocked to see the eccentric Duchess of Newcastle when she came to town to observe experiments being conducted by members of the Royal Society. (She was only admitted after a heated debate by members of the governing body.) And as for the king's mistresses, they never failed to cause a stir when they travelled abroad. Lady Castlemaine seated in her carriage bedecked with jewels and drawn by no fewer than eight horses was a sight to behold.

This new prominence gained by some members of the opposite sex was seen by the leaders of society as a threat. Evelyn confined his comments to his diary. Others did not. On this topic there was a curious alliance between Puritan preachers and dissolute court rakes. There appeared a vigorous sub-genre of anti-feminist poetry and satire, much of which was violent and pornographic in its denunciation of women.

Men-about-town who, like the Earl of Rochester, led utterly debauched lives readily dipped their pens in bile to libel individual ladies or to inveigh against the sex as a whole. They did not hesitate to lay all the blame for the decadence of the age on women and in terms that make disgusting reading even in our liberal age. Restoration satirists used language that no postmodern novelist or media writer would be able to get away with today.

And this invective merged with criticisms of the king. For Charles revelled in female company. He was rarely seen without at least one woman in attendance and his daily ritual included supper in the chambers of one of his lady friends. They formed almost a protective shield and men who had petitions or matters to discuss with the king, including, on occasion, his ministers, frequently had to make their approaches through one of these attendants. So, they became obvious targets for criticism. It was they who distracted the monarch from affairs of state and who used their influence to drain the royal purse.

Satirists inevitably lampooned Charles' sexual activity. Yet, contrary to the received mythology, it was not his bedroom antics that provoked the greatest disapprobation. To have a mistress, even a bevy of mistresses, was not something to be ashamed of: quite the reverse. In the prevailing dual morality, pretty women existed to be enjoyed and there was scarcely a nobleman or gentleman in the land that did not boast the possession of such a desirable status symbol. Charles was not a byword for sexual athleticism. He is known to have sired about thirteen bastards and his name can be linked definitely with a dozen or so women. There were undoubtedly scores more of whom no trace has been left in record or rumour. By seventeenth-century royal standards that was not a prodigious record. Nor was Charles reckoned a master of seduction. Most of his 'conquests' were either acquired for him by courtiers eager to win his favour or they very willingly jumped into his bed for the obvious perks that could bring. When he did set himself to woo a woman he was by no means always successful. We must tear our imaginations away from the royal bedchamber to understand just what it was about Charles and his women that people really objected to.

It was the Duke of Ormonde, one of Charles' longest-serving ministers, who referred to his 'effeminate conversation'. By that he meant that the Prince of Wales (as he then was) was far too fond of female company, that he was unmanly, 'soft', more interested in silly gossip than in the serious, male business of politics. This was the behaviour that later critics readily picked up on. Instead of using women and exercising mastery over them he treated them almost as equals. Indeed, he often allowed them to dominate him. Charles was, therefore, going against the grain of what others believed should be the policy of the restored monarchy. Instead of reversing all the disastrous trends of the previous two decades, he was actually endorsing some of the more unwelcome changes. He was seen to be soft on many of the rebels. He wanted to exercise toleration of religious minorities. He readily danced to the tune piped by Louis XIV. And he appeared to be giving royal assent to the topsy-turvydom of female emancipation.

It is this and not the narrow discussion about sexuality that makes Charles' relationships with the opposite sex so fascinating and which helps us to take in more facets of his character and reign. It is what I have set out to explore in the following pages. From his earliest days he was in the company of strong women. His mother, Henrietta Maria, was the dominant influence in the royal family. His sister Mary, with whom he spent much time during the years of exile, was the wife of the Prince of Orange and had to fight political battles with the republican members of the States-General. Of all his siblings Charles was closest to his younger sister, Henrietta, and she became his intermediary and adviser in clandestine dealings with the French court during the first ten years of his reign. But relatives and mistresses were not his only close female companions. During his precarious existence after the military defeat of his father the dispossessed prince was dependent on several women. To these years date his great adventure with the shadowy Jane Lane and his passionate love affair with Lucy Walter. Better known are the 'great' mistresses of the Restoration court – Barbara Villiers, Nell Gwynn, Louise de Keroualle and Hortense Mancini. And there is also Frances Stuart, 'the one that got away'. Each of them was a forceful personality. Each in her own way had had to overcome formidable obstacles to achieve the relative security of being a king's 'friend'. The woman who had to find a *modus vivendi* with the mistresses was Charles' longsuffering wife, Catherine of Braganza. She, too, had to be strong to endure, not only childlessness and her husband's philandering, but the taunts of satirists and the schemes of politicians who wanted to put an end to the royal marriage in the interests of securing a legitimate heir to the throne. Each of these women contributed something different and something important to the life of Charles II. The influence they exercised over his development and, thus, the character of his reign was both positive and negative. However, beyond the twelve individuals I scrutinise in the following pages there lie those millions of female subjects who also were the king's women. Those who were close to Charles were in some sense representatives of that wider constituency. If we want to understand them we have to set their stories against those of the majority in the post-war years of dramatically changing perceptions.

One of the political satires which catalogued the ills of the Restoration asked the question, 'Canst thou divine when things shall be mended?' and provided the answer, 'When the reign of the line of the Stuarts is ended'. Charles' failure to look beyond his own security to that of the dynasty helped to seal its fate and in his attitude towards women we can see just how far he was out of touch with contemporary ideas about relationships between the sexes. Women had played a major role in the way Charles thought, felt and reacted. They had made his life tolerable both before and after his restoration. They boosted his self-esteem and supported him in his kingly role. Yet they also weakened his authority and thus contributed to the downfall of the House of Stuart. To understand Charles' intimate relationships we have to view them individually, rejecting over-simplification and sexual stereotyping. We have to recognise in Charles II a man in many ways at odds with the conventions of his age – conventions which demanded the complete subordination of women.

If this book says anything fresh and interesting it is only because I have been enthused, inspired and helped by the reflections and insight of other scholars and the endeavours of those who, in libraries and archive offices, are dedicated to facilitating the exchange of information and ideas. Most of the books I have consulted over the years of this project's slow maturation are acknowledged in the notes and bibliography but I would like to render my special thanks for access to Dr Sonya Wynne's unpublished PhD thesis and for the unfailing courtesy of staff at the British Library, Cambridge University Library, Exeter University Library, the National Portrait Gallery and the Devon Local Studies Centre.

PART ONE

THE ADVENTURES AND MISADVENTURES OF YOUTH

All you that do desire to know
What did become of the King of Scots,
I unto you will truly show.
After the flight of northern rats
'Twas I did convey
His highness away,
And from all dangers set him free,
In women's attire,
As reason did require,
And the king himself did wait on me.

He of me a service did crave
And oftentimes to me stood bare,
In women's apparel he was most brave,
And on his chin he had no hair.
Wherever I came
My speeches did fame
As well my waiting-man to free.
The like was never known
I think by anyone,
For the king himself did wait on me.

My waiting-man a jewel had
Which I for want of money sold.
Because my fortune was so bad
We turned our jewel into gold.
A good shift indeed
In time of our need.
Then glad was I and glad was he
Our cause it did advance
Until we came to France.
And the king himself did wait on me . . .

The Last News from France, Being a true relation of the escape of the King of Scots from Worcester to London and from London to France, who was conveyed away by a young gentleman in woman's apparel . . .[1]

CHAPTER 1

Paradise Lost

He stands foursquare, centre canvas, looking straight out at the viewer in the pose reserved for kings. Elegant in silk and lace, self-assured with one hand resting on the head of a boarhound, symbol of strength, the seven-year-old Charles Stuart is flanked by the four younger royal siblings who were alive in 1637 when Van Dyck painted this idyll of privileged childhood. It is a masterful group portrait of children (notoriously difficult to paint) and we admire it. It is charming and we are charmed by it. It is also our first real glimpse of the boy destined to become the third and penultimate Stuart king. (In earlier depictions of the infant prince he is little more than a sumptuously dressed doll.) Does it tell us anything about the child already being groomed to inherit the pleasures and burdens of monarchy?

We see, as courtiers and visitors to court saw, that Charles is more like his mother, Henrietta Maria, than his father. The dark eyes, the full lips and the luxuriant hair framing the podgy features bespeak his Medici-Bourbon inheritance. There is a marked contrast with the thin face and wary eyes we encounter in pictures of Charles I at about the same age. A stiffness, a nervous tension hover about the images of the father created by an earlier generation of portraitists which is decidedly absent from the relaxed pose of the son.

Most responsible parents try to avoid the errors and replicate the virtues they perceive in their own upbringing and Charles I and Henrietta Maria were responsible parents. Charles had passed a miserable childhood. Even by the standards of the day he was brought up remote from his father and mother and was starved of affection. King James and Queen Anne were often at loggerheads and sometimes used their children as weapons in their domestic feuds. James was a pompous political theorist with an exalted view of kingship which he imposed on his heir. He wrote treatises, *Basilicon Doron* and *The True Lawe of Free Monarchies*, for Charles, in which he set out the virtues and responsibilities of a semi-divine ruler and he entrusted his son's education to a succession of pious clerics. The boy tried desperately hard to live up to his father's theories. What made that more difficult was that James did not practise what he preached. He was addicted to hunting and gave himself over to pleasures, often of a coarse and very ungodlike nature, when he should have been attending to affairs of state. As a result of all this Charles emerged into adolescence as a devout, serious, refined young man, determined, when the time came, to be a responsible, respected Christian king, presiding over an elegant court where the highest moral and cultural standards would prevail. As a father he found physical demonstrations of love well-nigh impossible. There was nothing 'touchy-feely' about Charles I. His wife was altogether different.

Charles I's marriage to a French princess in 1625, when he was twenty-four and she fifteen, was a mismatch. He was painfully reserved; she was an extrovert. He was serious; she was frivolous. He was wholly committed to the Protestant Church of England; she was an ardent French Catholic. He believed that queens should be submissive creatures dedicated to producing heirs and appearing in public as graceful and decorative consorts. She had been reared in a royal tradition which alowed wives and mothers considerable influence. The couple were, therefore, locked together in emotional dependence and had to find a *modus vivendi*. That they did so, after an initial period of tumultuous strife, is to their mutual credit. The fact that, under the pressure of civil war, their harmony broke down, is no matter for surprise.

Henrietta Maria was brought up in a court where luxury, corruption, Catholic devotion and intrigue fed off each other. She was the youngest child of Henry IV of France, 'Henry the Great' as he was fondly remembered by many of his countrymen, but never knew her father, who was assassinated by a Catholic fanatic within six months of her birth. Her mother, Marie de Medici, thus became the dominant influence in her life. Marie was a veritable *femme formidable*. Regent of France during the minority of her son Louis XIII, she refused to be prised away from power when he came of age. With the aid of her creature, Armand-Jean du Plessis, later Cardinal Richelieu, she continued to dominate a faction-ridden court. Before Henrietta Maria left Paris in 1625 she had witnessed her mother's incredible self-glorification in the series of narrative paintings celebrating her life commissioned from Peter Paul Rubens for the walls of her new Luxembourg palace. (Ten years later this became the inspiration for the same artist's glorification of James I, which Charles I had commissioned for the Banqueting Hall in Whitehall. Charles II thus had two grandparents immortalised by the leading Flemish artist of the age.)

What stories about Henry IV, one wonders, were passed on to his grandchildren? It is an interesting speculation because Charles II shared certain characteristics with his illustrious grandsire. Both were pragmatists who had to cope with bitter religious strife. Both converted to Catholicism. Both were notorious womanisers. Marie was appalled at her husband's infidelities. She may even have shared the view of many Catholics that his conversion from Calvinism in order to stifle political opposition was something less than wholehearted. Certainly the queen regent was passionate in her allegiance to Rome and brought up the pampered baby of the family to share this commitment. Henrietta Maria believed that her marriage to the King of England was part of a crusade to bring that nation back into the Roman fold and was petulantly disappointed when Charles remained doggedly loyal to his national Church.

By the time the heir to the English throne was born Marie de Medici's ace had been trumped. The man she had placed at young Louis' right hand no longer needed her. Richelieu was ready and able to run France by himself. When her intrigues failed, the queen mother was dismissed from the court and, early in 1631, fled to the Spanish Netherlands. In 1638 Charles I was obliged to play unenthusiastic host to his mother-in-law when she arrived for a visit which dragged on for two and a half years. His eldest son would long remember the wet, windy October day when he was lined up with his siblings in the courtyard of St James's Palace to greet this truly overpowering royal exile. She arrived with a modest retinue of six coaches and seventy horses but still managed to dominate the wintry scene. Throughout her stay she preserved a haughty mien to every member of the host country who approached her. She immediately began to take charge of her own family and, though she bestowed an austere affection on her grandchildren, they must have found her a rather frightening old lady.

Marie de Medici also exacerbated the religious divisions within the court. In their ardour to deliver their family and the lands ruled by their family from the sins of heresy and schism, Charles' mother and grand-mother took every opportunity to achieve his conversion. He was taken to mass in the baroque exuberance of Henrietta Maria's chapel at Somerset House and was made much of by the Capuchin priests in her entourage. The king, whose personal convictions and political awareness combined to create the certainty that any desertion from the Church of England would be disastrous for the dynasty, deliberately countered these influences. He admonished his son to honour his mother and obey her in all things, save in matters of religion. As he listened to the theological discussions and arguments between his parents and various of their chaplains and friends, doctrinal and ecclesiological niceties will have passed well above the boy's head but certain associations will have become lodged in his unconscious.

It was not only in matters of their children's *religious* upbringing that king and queen differed. Henrietta Maria was concerned about her husband's personality and style of kingship. The protocol of the English court was stiff and formal, more like that of Spain than France. Not only did she find it hard to accommodate herself to it, she was convinced that it created unnecessary problems. Monarchs should never condescend too far but neither should they appear stiff and unapproachable. Bishop Burnet reflected towards the end of Charles II's reign on the influence of his mother:

The queen mother observed often the great defects of the late king's breeding and the stiff roughness that was in him, by which he disobliged very many and did often prejudice his affairs very much; so she gave strict orders that the young princes should be bred to a wonderful civility.[2]

Henrietta provided most of the parental warmth the royal children received and especially was this true for Charles. For him and his siblings visits to their mother's quarters were fun. Henrietta Maria was surrounded by dwarfs, dogs of all shapes and sizes, jesters and monkeys. She was always devising all sorts of entertainments. Charles was the queen's favourite child and, in the gaiety of her household, moral restraints were not severe. Flirtations, affairs and gossip about those flirtations and affairs were part of the daily routine and, if adulterous liaisons were not officially approved of, everyone knew they happened. The sexual implications of life in the queen's suite must only have dawned slowly on the growing child but he enjoyed being with these courtiers who were always devising games, jokes and diversions into which he entered with enthusiasm. The queen's women adored dressing the royal children in beautiful costumes and rehearsing with them their lines and dance movements for the sumptuous plays and masques which were a feature of court life in the 1630s. It was from Henrietta Maria's side that most of the initiatives came that created the extraordinary cultural hothouse of the Stuart *beau monde*.

But Henrietta Maria and her awesome mother were not the only formidable women who dominated Charles' early years. They had other concerns more pressing than the day-to-day nurture of tiny princes and princesses. The woman with whom Charles spent most of his time was his nurse, Christabella Wyndham. No less than Charles' mother and grandmother, Christabella was a strong, determined woman. In the Civil War she would show herself to be a veritable Amazon (see below pp. 39–41). She was also a great beauty. Clarendon, who heartily disapproved of her and her influence over the heir, commented acerbically that there was 'nothing of woman in her but her body', and that her distinguishing marks were 'great rudeness and a country pride'.[3] But Clarendon was not alone in this opinion. Years later one of Samuel Pepys' informants recollected that Mrs Wyndham 'was nurse to the present king, and one that while she lived governed him and every thing else . . . as a minister of state',[4] and her CV provides ample evidence that she was, indeed, an overbearing and ambitious matriarch who, if she did not govern her grasping husband, certainly urged him up the ladder of royal favour.

She was the daughter and sole heiress of Hugh Pyne, a successful lawyer of Lincoln's Inn, who had invested heavily in property in Somerset and who married her to Sir Edmund Wyndham, one of the leading gentlemen of the county who also had strong court connections. From the beginning of Charles I's reign the young couple set about courting the monarch's favour and extracting the maximum material advantage. They importuned for several lucrative offices, for some of which they were locked in legal combat with other claimants. Edmund, a seventeenth-century 'fat cat', was involved in whatever moneymaking scheme was going. He extracted profit from the manufacture of soap, the re-use of wine barrels by the brewing industry and mineral rights in Wales. The Wyndhams were typical of the grasping courtiers who provoked the indignation of those outside the charmed royal circle. In 1640 parliament adjudged Edmund guilty of peculation and deprived him of his seat as MP for Bridgwater. Despite, or perhaps because of, being so pushy he *and* his wife advanced in royal favour and received several marks of royal esteem. By 1635 Christabella was in her mid-twenties and the full flush of her beauty. This was the year in which she was appointed nurse to the infant Charles. Whatever her initial responsibilities and privileges may have been, she immediately set about adding to them and was soon insisting on being addressed as 'Lady Governess'. She and her husband were close to the king and queen. When one of their daughters was baptised the king attended the ceremony and Prince Charles stood sponsor for the baby. Christabella was the first woman who demonstrated love to Charles *physically*. It was to his nurse that the toddler turned for kisses and cuddles and for comfort when he had hurt himself. The boy developed and retained a strong attachment to Christabella, who became the archetype of many of the women who were to feature in his life – pretty, domineering, emotionally demonstrative and grasping.[5]

The ravishing fairyland of Charles I's court during the 'golden years' (1629–40) when he ruled without a parliament was a deliberate creation; the work of painters such as Rubens, Van Dyck and Gerrit van Honthorst, poets and playwrights of the stature of Ben Jonson, William Davenant and James Shirley, and the master of stagecraft, Inigo Jones. It was a sumptuous, self-conscious, introverted, highly élitist little cosmos. Charles and, more specifically, his queen had something to prove to their dull, boorish subjects. Stuart kingship was a glorious semi-divine gift from God. Charles and Henrietta Maria were the mother and father of a fortunate people, the epitome of harmony and wedded bliss,

> Charles the best husband, while Maria strives
> To be, and is, the very best of wives.[6]

Their glittering court rivalled those of France and Italy, hitherto regarded as the trend setters of fashion and sophistication. The denizens of this court looked down from the kaleidoscopic sinuousness of their baroque palaces on the dour, drab world of ordinary mortals. James I had adumbrated that a king and a subject were different in kind and the assertive luxuriousness of his son's court proclaimed that arrogantly to the world.

Yet another marked difference between Charles I and his wife was that never for a moment did he think that splendid display was the be-all and end-all of kingship. He had a profound sense of duty. Every day was lived to a nice schedule of private devotion, work, public audience and recreation. Though he entered happily into court entertainments, he was concerned not to give the impression that the pleasure principle was all-embracing. He frequently urged courtiers to go back to their shires and employ at least some of their time in care of their estates.

Charles and Henrietta Maria were, by the standards of the day, devoted parents. They spent quite a lot of time with their children, perhaps, in part, because neither of them had received much affection in their own early years. Both had been denied the care of loving fathers. Henrietta Maria had never known Henry IV; Charles had experienced James I as more of a schoolmaster than a father. The royal family were often seen walking together in their palace parks, and courtiers and ambassadors remarked that the princes and princesses passed many evenings with their parents playing games or being amused by fools and hired entertainers. As he grew up, young Charles was taken riding and hunting by his father. He was also gradually initiated into the formal aspects of court life.

From about 1638 he was provided with his own household and apartments and from this time he was less involved with either the queen and her women or his nurse. Now began his induction into a man's world and he was provided with guides whom the king considered best qualified to prepare him for his sacred future. The king's choice of mentors provides clear evidence of his concern to wean the boy away from the Catholicising, flippant self-indulgence of his mother and her friends.

The king took seriously his responsibility to train his heir, not by writing long, windy treatises such as he had been subjected to by James, but by personal instruction and example. He was, himself, the book from which he wished his heir to learn – pious beyond the standard of many who called themselves 'Puritan' and encased in the eggshell of royal mystique. Thus, from the age of about seven, the boy stood beside his father to receive ambassadors and, even earlier, he had had his first experience of the long, elaborate Garter ceremony which the king so much loved. Around the time of his eighth birthday he was made the central figure of a scarcely less grand ritual when he was invested as Prince of Wales. We know that the king was, above all contemporary monarchs, a stickler for the most pernickety details of court etiquette and ensured that he and his family were attended with the utmost deference. There exists a painting by van Honthorst of the prince dining formally with his parents. They sit in a vast hall attended by scores of servants, watched from a respectful distance by privileged sightseers.

Yet, alongside this steady process of induction went very careful protection of the heir. Charles I had vivid memories of his own unhappy childhood – the lone hours of careful study, the parental reprimands, the painful self-discipline as he tried to meet James' exacting standards, the embarrassment of being expected, as a shy, stammering boy, to make speeches and debate publicly with clever theologians. By contrast, he was indulgent and spared his son such miseries. Thus, the lively royal youngster was brought up in an atmosphere of sharp contrasts – family informality at the heart of rigid ceremonial; regular devotional exercise without over-zealous exposition to personal holiness; an educational regime which placed emphasis on exercise and did not make great intellectual demands.

We can deduce much about the boy's tutoring from a letter written by his governor which set out the philosophy behind his training. The man given the job of supervising the prince's education was William Cavendish, Earl of Newcastle. The earl, in his mid-forties at the time of his appointment, was a seasoned courtier-diplomat who had faithfully served the dynasty all his adult life. He was a man of many parts; a substantial and efficient northern landowner, a sportsman who sat a horse better than most of his contemporaries, an effective military leader, a munificent host whose entertainments of the court at Welbeck and Bolsover were, in the words of Clarendon, such as 'had scarce before ever been known in England',[7] a patron of the arts, lionised as a veritable Maecenas by the literary establishment, who enjoyed the company of talented men such as Ben Jonson, Dryden, Davenant, Thomas Hobbes and, during his exile, René Descartes, but who was also, in his own right, a poet and a playwright with several stage productions to his credit (though Pepys was contemptuously dismissive of his lordship's dramatic talents). Newcastle was an ambitious man, who understood the ways of the court and the peccadilloes of the Stuart monarchs and successfully exploited both in his own interests. He was essentially a pragmatist, as Clarendon, who was far from being an unqualified admirer of Newcastle, more than hinted:

> He was a very fine gentleman, active and full of courage, and most accomplished in those qualities of horsemanship, dancing and fencing, which accompany a good breeding; in which his delight was. Besides that, he was amorous in poetry and music, to which he indulged the greatest part of his time; and nothing could have tempted him out of those paths of pleasure which he enjoyed in a full and ample fortune, but honour and ambition to serve the King . . .
>
> He loved monarchy, as it was the foundation and support of his own greatness; and the Church, as it was well constituted for the splendour and security of the Crown; and religion as it cherished and maintained that order and obedience that was necessary to both; without any other

passion for the particular opinions which were grown up in it and distinguished it into parties . . . as he detested whatsoever was like to disturb the public peace.[8]

This urbane, highly cultured nobleman was a man at peace with himself and consequently easy in his relationships with others. After the Restoration he would have no qualms about withdrawing from court life to devote himself to horse racing and *belles-lettres*, and his wife, one of the most eccentric creatures in Carolean London, would then describe Newcastle's demeanour as 'courtly, easy, civil and free, without formality or constraint, and yet have something in it of grandeur, that causes an awful respect for him'.[9] The verdict is scarcely unbiased but, taken with everything else we know about Cavendish, has a strong ring of truth. Certainly Charles maintained a lifelong affection for his old governor who, during the brief time that Cavendish had charge of the prince's welfare, studied to make himself agreeable to his pupil, especially fostering in the young man a love of horseflesh and imparting something of his own skill in the saddle. The contrast between this avuncular figure and Charles' prim, intense father was very obvious and cannot fail to have had its effect on the boy's impressionable mind.

Newcastle wrote a mini-treatise of advice for his royal charge which is instructive about both the intentions of his mentor and the receptivity of his pupil.[10] It takes little reading between the lines to discover that young Charles was no scholar. Newcastle observes frankly, 'Sir, you are in your own disposition . . . not very apt to your book.' But the earl does not write this in a spirit of carping criticism. On the contrary, he counsels, 'I would not have you too studious, for too much contemplation spoils action, and virtue consists in that.' Moreover, 'the greatest clerks are not the wisest men, and . . . the greatest captains were not the greatest scholars; neither have I known bookworms for great statesmen'. The wise ruler will concentrate on studying men. The only kind of literature Newcastle did advocate was histories, 'that so you may compare the dead with the living' (advice which an as yet obscure Cambridgeshire gentleman, Oliver Cromwell, also gave to his son). With this caveat, the governor recommends those subjects to which Charles *should* apply his mind:

> Sir, it is fit you should have some languages, though I confess I would rather have you study things than words, matter than language; for seldom a critic in many languages hath time to study sense . . . at best he is or can be but a living dictionary . . .

Eight years later, when the prince paid his first visit to France, it was a matter of comment that he could not speak the tongue of his maternal ancestors. It is something of a surprise that the boy who had often been in

16

the company of his mother and grandmother and their modish friends had learned so little French. He simply had not made the effort and Newcastle's easygoing regime had not inculcated the discipline of study.

Another of the earl's recommendations Charles had no difficulty following related to religion:

> Beware of too much devotion for a king, for one may be a good man but a bad king; and how many [examples] will history represent to you that, in seeming to gain the Kingdom of Heaven, have lost their own.

Could any words have been more prophetic? In little more than a decade King Charles would become the Church of England's foremost martyr. Unable to relinquish or modify his religious principles he had lost both his kingdom and his head. In 1638, when the very idea of civil war would have appalled court and people, did Newcastle see where the king's pious intransigence might lead? At the very time that he wrote his advice, irate Scots were uniting behind the National Covenant, signifying their resistance to the imposition of an English prayer book. Newcastle, the northern magnate, understood well the feelings aroused by religion over the border. Newcastle, the courtier, knew how determined the king was to have his way in the matter. Though he could not be specific, he warned the prince about following his father's lead. What Cavendish advocated was a statesman's religion, a grafting of willow on oak. He would have been failing in his duty if he had not addressed what was, in fact, the burning issue of the day. For twenty years continental Europe had been plunged into bloody chaos by the clashes of Reformation and Counter-Reformation armies. For five years Archbishop Laud had been stirring strife within England by enforcing the spread of what many regarded as covert Catholicism. The pragmatic earl well judged the danger of hardline religious politics.

Yet, while he steered Prince Charles away from his father's bigotry, he also tried to buttress him against a temptation to which he was more prone – apathy:

> ... if you have no reverence at prayers, what will the people have, think you? They go according to the example of the prince. If they have none, then they have no obedience to God; then they will easily have none to your Highness ... [By contrast] if any be Bible mad, over much burned with fiery zeal, they may think it a service to God to destroy you ... Thus one way you may have civil war, the other a private treason.

Towards the end of his brief discourse this worldly-wise councillor extolled *noblesse oblige*: 'be courteous and civil to everybody'. Smiles and tokens bestowed by princes bought better allegiance than disdain.

Above all, a king in training should be gracious towards women, who especially appreciate little marks of favour. And let him always be calculating as to his own advantage: 'the king must know at what time to play the king and when to qualify it'. He must use the trappings of monarchy to his own ends:

> For what preserves you king more than ceremony? The cloth of estate, the distance people are with you, great officers, heralds, drums, trumpeters, rich coaches, rich furniture for horses, guards, marshall's men making room . . . their staff of office and [crying] 'now the king comes;' . . . this is the mist cast before us and [dazzles] the commonwealth . . . In all triumphs whatever or public showing yourself you cannot put upon you too much King . . .

Yet – and these are the most remarkable words in the letter – 'I would not have you so seared with majesty as to think you are not of mankind, nor suffer others, or yourself, to flatter you so much.' James I had urged his successor always to remember that the Almighty 'made you a little god to sit on his throne and rule over other men'.[11] Newcastle realised the corrosive power of such megalomania. The earl never wavered in his loyalty to the Stuart cause but, like many royalist politicians, he did not buy into divine right extremism.

The elegant, charming and perceptive letter was obviously the distillation of the advice which the Earl of Newcastle offered by word and personal example during the two years that he had charge of the Prince of Wales. It urged Cavendish's own practical and practicable principles while, at the same time, responding to his charge's strengths and weaknesses. It well judged the differences between the two Charleses, father and son, and, therefore, offers us a glimpse of the boy who would become king – intellectually lazy and unlikely to become the slave of high principle, affable, not especially devout, equally easy in the company of male and female companions. These, at least, were the traits Newcastle wished to foster, and the young prince, at an impressionable age, allowed himself to be guided.

One attribute that came naturally to Charles, and that Newcastle had little need to stress, was chivalry towards women. From his earliest years he enjoyed female company. In the prevailing culture of the day it was unquestioningly accepted that women were inferior to men, that they existed for the use and support of their husbands and for their physical necessity as baby-making machines. But that did not square with Charles' experience. The women in his early life were forceful, fun-loving and sympathetic. Nor did the king present an obvious counterbalance. Most boys learn from their fathers how to develop the macho, sexually aggressive aspects of their character but the aesthetic, refined Charles I presented a model of stylised courtesy, constancy, consideration and genuine affection (if stilted in its emotional expression) for his wife, daughters and female companions. The prince was developing into a 'ladies' man' in the full sense of that expression and it is not difficult to see why.

But there were other influences also at work during his early years. The king ring-fenced his son's education with good, sound Church of England clergy. The boy's nominated tutors were Brian Duppa, John Earle and Richard Steward. They were all academics who came from the same school of Oxford theologians and were what we would today call high churchmen. They were committed supporters of Archbishop Laud's determination to make the Church of England hierarchy a major power in the state and they shared his intolerance of 'free' spirits who demurred at following in every particular the rites ordained by the establishment. It was their task to impress upon the heir to the throne the essential, divinely decreed and, therefore, indissoluble link between crown and mitre. Charles was never fully convinced.

Brian Duppa, Bishop of Chichester (he was translated to Salisbury in 1641), was an ecclesiastic of stately bearing who was specifically charged by the king with being the guardian of his son's conscience. He was a frequent visitor to court, having at an early stage in his career won the patronage of the Earl of Dorset, lord chamberlain to the queen, whose wife was governess to the royal infants. More significantly, Duppa's career was advanced by George Villiers, Duke of Buckingham, the royal favourite whose family was closely (and disastrously) bound up with the Stuarts for much of the century. The bishop seems to have been able to combine the almost mutually exclusive arts of the courtier and the man of God (his published works include, as well as sermons, a book of valedictory poems on the death of Ben Jonson), or, at least, so the prince thought. Duppa was a party man who stuck firmly to his convictions when, during the Commonwealth and the Protectorate, they were politically incorrect. The religious certainties he sought to inculcate in his pupil stemmed from his belief in the episcopal system which he understood to have behind it the weight of 1,600 years of tradition. Like the king, like Newcastle, like many who within a few years took up the royalist cause, Duppa regarded Church and State as inextricably bound together, so that any attempt to loosen the bond or assert the primacy of individual conscience was both sinful and criminal and could only bring about the collapse of an ordered society. As James I had succinctly put it, 'No bishops, no king.'

The sour Bishop Burnet regarded Duppa's appointment as a disaster. Acknowledging that Salisbury was 'a meek and humble man and much loved for the sweetness of his temper', he yet thought that he was quite unfit – presumably because of the extreme nature of his opinions – to have a formative influence over the heir.[12] Newcastle was, however, satisfied with the tutor. He reported that the bishop wore his scholarship lightly so as not to bore a lively boy who had very little interest in doctrinal or ecclesiastical disputes. As for the future king, he held his teacher in awe – later, if not at the time. Charles always had a genuine respect for men who exhibited a sanctity he had no desire to emulate himself. He remained a lifelong friend of Duppa and was present at his deathbed.

John Earle's personality can hardly have been more different. Of him Burnet wrote, 'He was the man of all the clergy for whom the king had the greatest esteem. He had been his subtutor, and had followed him in all his exile with so clear a character, that the king could never see or hear of any one thing amiss in him. So he, who had a secret pleasure in finding out anything that lessened a man esteemed eminent for piety, yet had a value for him beyond all the men of his order.'[13] The reasons are not difficult to understand. Clarendon found Dr Earle to be

> a man of great piety and devotion, a most eloquent and powerful preacher; and of a conversation so pleasant and delightful, so very innocent and so very facetious [i.e. elegant], that no man's company was more desired and loved. No man was more negligent in his dress, and habit, and mien; no man more wary and cultivated in his behaviour and discourse . . . He was amongst the few excellent men who never had nor ever could have an enemy.[14]

Though a skilled disputant with Puritans, Earle was firmly opposed to persecuting them for their sincerely held views. One might say that he represented the acceptable face of high Anglicanism. Perhaps it was for this reason – as a foil to Duppa – that he was chosen to be the bishop's understudy. It certainly seems that Charles' love of toleration had its tap root in the gentle, lively teaching of this amiable man.

Earle formed a connection between the court and what we might call the 'Bloomsbury Set' of the 1630s. Great Tew, on the edge of the Cotswolds, was the seat of Lucius Cary, Viscount Falkland, one of the most attractive characters of a troubled age. He turned his house into what was almost an open university college. Scholars, courtiers, politicians, poets and wits came to Great Tew from Oxford and London to discuss with a freedom impossible elsewhere the burning political and religious issues of the day. The atmosphere generated by Cary seemed to dissipate the bitter partisanship which was dragging the country towards civil war. Here were to be found scholarly discussion and the creative exchange of ideas. John Earle, one of the bright young men of the day, was a *habitué* of this learned clique and claimed to have gained more from the Cary circle than from his studies at Merton. His writings, as well as the good opinion of his contemporaries, show him to have been a scholar of wit and moderation. In 1641 Earle succeeded Duppa as senior tutor to the princes. The royal children cannot have felt the furious clash of ideas and emotions that, during the years of their father's personal rule, were raising some men to places of distinction in the Church, incarcerating some in prison, and driving still others to seek refuge beyond the seas. Yet, through their tutors, they will have become aware of some of the issues of the day and of different ways of confronting them. Prince James' temperament inclined him to take his stand on principle. His brother was ever disposed to seek eirenical solutions.

However, it is not sufficient simply to label the future Charles II as a 'tolerant' monarch. Very different attitudes to life parade under the banner of 'toleration' and men hold those attitudes as a result of combined life experience and intellectual conviction. For detached seventeenth-century scholars mutual acceptance came from a close study of the conflicting issues and a realisation of their complexity. John Earle had a deep respect for sincere partisans of a cause he could not himself subscribe to – and went on arguing with them. A man like Lucius Cary was impelled by Christian charity. He longed to see people of dramatically opposed opinions living and letting live or striving for compromise. So depressed was he at the drift into war that, at the battle of Naseby, he deliberately led a suicidal charge. Others, and there must have been many such in these islands in the 1630s, could not or would not see what all the fuss was about. Lacking deep religious convictions of their own, they were impatient with the devotees of theological and political abstractions who foolishly believed that breaking heads and burning houses somehow proved their points. Charles II's concept of 'toleration' was of this last order. He hated conflict, wanted contending parties to agree and found it difficult to understand why they would not.

These attitudes and various permutations of them were present in the upbringing of young Charles Stuart. Since he was too young to form mature judgements and since, anyway, he was not of a scholarly disposition, he responded more to personalities than to abstruse arguments about episcopacy, divine right, uniformity in religion, and the privileges of parliament.

It may have been the prince's lack of passion for the Church of England that prompted King Charles, at the height of the war, to appoint Richard Steward, his clerk of the closet, to his son's entourage, with the strict injunction that he was to guide the heir in all matters pertaining to the Church. Steward was an ecclesiastical politician who had entered the royal court in 1633 and had, ever since, been an intimate of the household and a trusted adviser. He was a fierce controversialist frequently put up by the Laudians to defend the honour, power and privileges of bishops. Clarendon gives us a picture of him in oratorical spate during one of the many debates that took place during the war years. The Church of England, Steward insisted, was the body 'to which God had vouchsafed the most perfect reformation' of all the Protestant churches. It had retained episcopacy, without which there could be 'no ordination of ministers, and consequently no administration of sacraments, or performance of the ministerial functions'.[15] It was men like Steward who steeled Charles I to that unyielding commitment to those principles that brought him to the block.

Peer pressure among older children and adolescents is always a powerful factor, though it counted for less in an age which held elders in greater respect than does our own. Charles had his circle of intimate friends, with whom he indulged in boisterous escapades and shared secrets. Prominent among them were the Villiers boys. George and Francis were the sons of the first Duke of Buckingham, the widely hated royal favourite who had gained such a mastery over Charles I before his accession and had dominated policy in the early years of the reign. When Buckingham was struck down by an assassin's dagger in 1628, the king, prostrate with grief and guilt, pledged himself to look after his friend's orphaned children. They were brought up with his own, and young Charles, therefore, never knew a time when he did not have two slightly older 'brothers' (Francis was senior by a year and George by two and a quarter years). It would have been natural for the prince to idolise and emulate George Villiers and they were, indeed, throughout youth very close. The influence of the young duke a few years later was, according to the straitlaced Burnet, deplorable:

> . . . he was wholly turned to mirth and pleasure: he had the art of turning persons or things into ridicule beyond any man of the age: he possessed the young king with very ill principles, both as to religion and morality, and with a very mean opinion of his father, whose stiffness was with him a frequent subject of raillery.[16]

The bishop was writing from hearsay several years after the event. What is interesting about his verdict is that it coincides with observations made by other contemporaries about Charles' attitude towards his father. As a young man the prince and later king cast aside the mantle handed down by the serious, conscientious, pernickety monarch, and writers were obliged to find some reason for his unfilial behaviour. Naturally, they looked for the explanation to Charles' more boisterous companions. But the roots of his cynical, worldly-wise approach to life and his rejection of his father's style ran deep into his earliest years.

Such, then, were some of the influences that went to the making of Charles, Prince of Wales. He was brought up in a closed environment by parents committed to their family and to the principle of monarchical power. The king and queen differed both in personality and in their understanding of what it meant to rule the Stuart dominions but both impressed upon the heir the need to prepare himself for his divinely ordained destiny, and his education and training for his future role had already begun. Of course, to a child the prospect of actually being king lay in the far, hazy future. His father might live another twenty, thirty or more years. Meanwhile, he could concentrate on enjoying himself and in the hothouse atmosphere of his parents' court there was much to enjoy – including amorous adventures.

Love and sex were everyday topics in palace chambers and no stories were considered as having an '18 rating', unsuitable for juvenile ears. Courtiers boasted of their conquests and the queen's women gossiped about the latest affairs. While courtly love was the dominant subject of fashionable poets, more basic tales formed the subject matter of popular ballads bought on London streets and eagerly learned by the amateur musicians of the royal household.

There is no doubt that Charles I and his queen tried to set a high moral tone at the centre of national life. The importance of personal example had been impressed upon the king by his own father:

> ... this glistering worldly glory of kings is given them by God, to teach them to press so to glister and shine before their people in all works of sanctification and righteousness that their persons, as bright lamps of godliness and virtue may, going in and out before their people, give light to all their steps.[17]

Much has been written about the rarefied atmosphere of Stuart court dramas and the pure, exalted sentiments they expressed. Similarly, the libertinism of the Restoration theatre is well known. However, we must be careful not to make too stark a contrast between the dramatic art of the 1630s and that of a generation later. Charles II was a great lover of the stage and its people – especially actresses – and it is important to understand how his enthusiasm developed.

Charles I was a martinet, concerned as much for the morals of his people as for their religion. Just as he sought to control the worship in parish churches through Archbishop Laud, so all places of entertainment were kept under scrutiny by his master of the revels, Sir Henry Herbert, brother of the priest-poet George Herbert. This official performed his work diligently – some would have said officiously. He licensed every kind of public game and show from billiards to the display of elephants and other 'savage beasts' and even attempted to extend his mandate to cover the publication of books.

Herbert's first responsibility was the supervision of stage pieces presented at court, of which there were over 400 between 1625 and 1640. He and the king ensured that virtue was the theme of everything presented to the household. This emanated from Charles himself who laboured conscientiously to be a model of piety, courtesy, taste and culture and who impressed upon all members of his creative team the need for his court to be a school of morality. It followed that a strict censorship governed all stage performances. Masques were elaborate conceits featuring gods and goddesses, heroes and heroines, which identified the life of Olympus with that of the Stuart court. Plays might treat of more down-to-earth subjects but they, too, were vetted in accordance with a well-defined set of moral guidelines.

A contemporary referred to one element of the prevailing royal cult as 'a love called Platonic . . . abstracted from all corporeal gross impressions and sensual appetite'.[18] In music, stage productions, poetry and painting the king and queen were represented as the emblems of chaste marital fidelity and the leaders of a court society which had forsworn the vulgarity of the merely carnal.

Such high-mindedness was less easily asserted outside the walls of royal palaces but every play presented in the London theatres had to be licensed by Herbert (for a fee) and we know from one incident how assiduously he went through submitted manuscripts. In 1633 he took objection to certain lines in William Davenant's new play *The Wits* and excised such expletives as 'faith' and 'death'. The author complained to the king, and Charles carefully went over the piece with his master of the revels. He it was who decided that the offending words were 'asseverations not oaths' and sanctioned their reinstatement, much to Herbert's disgruntlement. In 1639 Charles approved a bolder initiative when his wife brought over a troupe of actors from Paris – which included women. Pious citizens were scandalised but the earth did not open up to swallow the perpetrators of such impudence. Clearly, the king was more broadminded than the religious extremists (he and the queen both sponsored companies of actors) but he shared their concerns and the culture clash in the capital should certainly not be seen in over-simplified terms as a war between Puritans and players.

One cause of royal anxiety was the fact that the worlds of court and capital overlapped. Writers for the popular stage met the demand for bombast, rumbustious action, bawdy, salacious innuendo, satire and comedy based on observation of real London life. A dramatist like Richard Brome, whose smash hit *Sparagus Garden* (1635) was a roistering comedy of unredeemed coarseness, openly boasted that his plays sought only to make his audiences laugh, unlike the 'classicising poet-bounces' favoured by cultural snobs. Gentlemen and ladies of the royal household were eager followers of fashion and that included keeping up with the latest productions at the Cockpit, the Curtain, the Globe and other venues where plays were performed for public or private audiences. While court revels apostrophised the establishment, these pieces all too often poked fun at authority. Whereas masques upheld Christian values, popular plays chronicled the triumphs of low cunning and basic passions. The disparity between the two strands of drama is well illustrated by the queen's attendance at *The Triumphs of the Prince d'Amour*, a relatively inoffensive offering presented at the Middle Temple. It was noted that Henrietta Maria came clothed in 'citizen's habit'.

The artistic set pieces presented at court had a strong didactic element aimed at counteracting that lewdness which was inevitable in a velvet-wrapped enclave where young men and women were thrown together with little to occupy their energies but the pursuit of pleasure. The courtier-versifier, Thomas Carew, virtually gave the game away in adulatory lines written for Henrietta Maria:

> Thou great Commandress, that dost move
> Thy sceptre o'er the crown of Love,
> And through his empire, with the awe
> Of thy chaste beams, dost give law;
> From his profaner altars we
> Turn to adore thy deity.
> He only can wild lust provoke;
> Thou those impurer flames canst choke;
> And where he scatters looser fires
> Thou turnst them into chaste desires.[19]

The 'impurer flames' were being regularly fed, not only by popular stage productions, but by bawdy songs, ribald stories and popular ballads such as the tale of Peg and Kate, two good-time girls who spent the night at an inn carousing with a generous benefactor who feasted them well in return for their favours only to leave them with the bill in the morning; and ditties with such self-explanatory titles as 'A Good Throw for Three Maidenheads' and 'This Maid Would Give Ten Shillings for a Kiss'. In their efforts to assert and maintain high standards the royal trend setters were, therefore, up against the formidable obstacles of everyday life in an enervating world of wealth and luxury. The royal court has never existed which lived out the ideals represented by Stuart propaganda. Moreover, the privileged denizens of Charles' entourage rejected the kinds of restraints urged by earnest preachers and Puritan pamphleteers. Fashionable élites always scorn conventional morality. Like money, style and privilege, libertarianism is part of the insignia which sets them apart from the 'common herd'. Thus, while Charles and his queen and their more sober attendants were adumbrating chaste refinement, their younger, less restrained followers were setting a tone of modish hedonism.

Outside their charmed circle growing resentment was shown to the behavioural norms of the favoured few. Among royal watchers there is always a mix of responses – veneration, envy, resentment, irritation – on display to the pampered, highly publicised lifestyle of the top family.

Among the severe critics of the regime the most vitriolically outspoken was William Prynne, lawyer, pamphleteer and militant Puritan. His book, *Histriomastix*, was a 1,000-page indictment of the theatre and one third of Prynne's invective was kept for the bad example set by the court, which the author castigated for

> effeminate mixed dancing, stage plays, lascivious pictures, face painting, health drinking, long hair, love locks, periwigs, woman's curling, powdering and cutting of their hair, bonfires, New Year's gifts, May games, amorous pastimes, lascivious effeminate music, excessive laughter, luxurious, disorderly Christmas-keeping, mummeries, with sundry suchlike vanities . . .[20]

The book is interesting, not for its hysterical overstatement of the case, but for the equally exaggerated response it provoked. Charles saw the book as a personal attack and a complete distortion of the highly moral tone he believed that his court was setting. He was stung into using the full weight of the law to crush the impudent Prynne. The offender was incarcerated in the Tower for a year before his case came to trial and when it did he was sentenced to life imprisonment, a stupendous £5,000 fine, deprivation of his Oxford degree, and the loss of both his ears. When he refused to be chastened by this treatment he was subjected to further punishments, including being branded on both cheeks and confined in Jersey's Mount Orgueil Castle, where, it was hoped, he would be far removed from any sympathisers.

It was not just Prynne's presumption that angered the king. *Histriomastix* claimed that he was failing to set a Christian moral tone even within his own household. It was not only fanatical Puritans who regarded as unseemly much that passed for normality at court. Crowds congregated at the trials of Prynne and his fellow prisoners to shout their support. As soon as Charles was forced to summon parliament one of the assembly's first acts was to order the release of the miscreants and to denounce their persecution as 'bloody, wicked, cruel, barbarous and tyrannical'.[21] Prynne re-entered London as a hero, accompanied by 2,000 horsemen, 100 coaches and a multitude of pedestrian supporters who cheered him all the way. The rarefied culture of the court and the king's increasingly draconian methods of dealing with opposition were different facets of the same asserted reality: monarchs and subjects are clean different things and it is presumptuous to refuse the 'mystical reverence that belongs unto them that sit in the throne of God'.[22]

These were some of the background elements to the life of the young Prince of Wales. Much of that life was given over to games and pocket adventures in St James's Park and the familiar but fascinating corridors, passages and cheek-by-jowl buildings of Whitehall Palace. But, by gradual degrees, he became aware of events and feelings outside his own highly protected environment. As his young mind embraced the existence of a wider and potentially more exciting world beyond the confines of royal residences he grew curious about that world. He cannot have been kept in ignorance of the more stirring and intriguing affairs eagerly discussed about the court. His early love of dressing up, acting and everything to do with the magic, fantasy world of the players' companies gave him an interest in the performances taking place within a couple of miles' radius of Whitehall. Did he ever manage to sneak away to one of the disreputable London theatres or was he obliged to remain content with second-hand reports of the latest stage successes? As he approached adolescence with its resentment of control and its inevitable questioning of parental attitudes and values he may well have found the restraints of court life irksome. But he comprehended little in detail of the darker forces moving outside Eden. For as long as possible his parents tried to shield their children from the unpleasant realities closing in on them like the inexorable jaws of some slow-moving trap but Charles could sense the growing tension between his mother and father and the increasing anxiety among their friends and confidants.

It was in May 1641 that the implications of being heir to the throne began to come home to the young Charles. His father despatched him to the House of Lords with a letter vainly pleading for the life of his friend and minister, the Earl of Strafford, hoping that the youth and innocence of the emissary might move the hearts of those determined to make an example of the agent of royal absolutism. The ploy failed. The parliamentary leaders now began to take a close interest in the Prince of Wales. If the father proved obstinate, the son, if properly reared during his formative years, might be made more amenable to sharing power with the representatives of the people. The main obstacle to be overcome was the Earl of Newcastle:

They liked not that he should have the government of the Prince, as one who would infuse such principles into him as would not be agreeable to their designs and would dispose him to no kindness to their persons, and that they would not rest till they saw another man in that province; in order to which they would pick all quarrels they could, and load him with all reproaches which might blast him with the people, with whom he had a very good reputation.[23]

The king who had signed Strafford's death warrant was in no position to stick up for Newcastle so the earl saved him the embarrassment by resigning. The prince thus said goodbye to this exuberant mentor and friend with whom he had delighted to ride and fence and saw him replaced by the elderly Marquis of Hertford of whom it was said, 'He was of an age

27

not fit for much activity and . . . was wedded so much to his ease that he loved his books above all exercises'.[24] A few weeks later Charles also lost his grandmother. The symbol of French autocracy was another irritant in the relations between king and parliament. So, much to Henrietta Maria's distress, she went once more on her travels and died a year later, an exile to the last.

As politics encroached more and more on the gay world of the court, and specifically on the routine and personnel of the prince's immediate environment, he began to share his parents' insecurity and anxiety. His father was plunged into black despair at his guilt over Strafford's death and his mother, increasingly irritated by the king's seeming inability to stand up to his presumptuous subjects, was constantly trying to stiffen his backbone. In the autumn, as the mood in the City grew ugly, the king sent his family away to Oatlands, a royal manor in Surrey. But he could not bear to be parted from them for long and they returned to the capital within weeks. Early in the New Year, goaded mercilessly by his wife, Charles made a rapid descent on the House of Commons to arrest five of his most outspoken critics. He returned empty-handed and humiliated. Six days later, amidst hasty bustle and confusion, the royal siblings were told to make ready for a journey. The Stuart family were unceremoniously fleeing their fragile paradise.

On 10 January 1642 King Charles took his wife and children away from Whitehall and up the Thames to Hampton Court. It was a hasty, ill-prepared departure. The crisis at Westminster had boiled up rapidly. Parliament had won its tactical battle with the king. A showdown was inevitable. The City was triumphantly *en fête*, confident of seeing the royal power further curbed. Charles, against the advice of his council, decided to distance himself from further humiliation and also to give himself more freedom of manoeuvre. At Hampton Court all was at sixes and sevens. Charles and his siblings found their usual quarters unprepared and they had to spend their first night sleeping in makeshift beds in their parents' room.

Six weeks later the family was split up, never to be reunited. The king sent his wife and daughter Mary to the continent for their safety and in order to buy foreign support in the armed conflict which was becoming inevitable. The excuse offered to parliament was that the ten-year-old princess, recently married to the Prince of Orange, had to be escorted to her husband's home. The leave-taking at Hampton Court was tearful and it marked a turning point in Charles' life. Now the boy was to be plunged into a man's world, and a rough world at that.

CHAPTER 2

Love and War .

Like his father, Charles had his life turned upside down when he was on the verge of adolescence. It was in 1612, days before his twelfth birthday, that the future Charles I lost his elder brother and became, unexpectedly, heir to the Stuart throne. His son was approaching the end of his twelfth year when the train of events began which would prevent him succeeding to that throne. By the standards of the day he was now tall for his age. He had a mass of curling dark hair and would, within a few years, be described by a connoisseur at the French court as 'swarthy, with fine black eyes and a wide, ugly mouth'. His well-learned court manners were elegant and he had learned something of his father's imperious bearing in dealing with subordinates. The child about to be thrust into militant manhood already possessed a physical magnetism which, combined with his status and his future prospects (no one in 1642 was seriously canvassing the abolition of monarchy), made him very attractive to both men and women, a prince to be courted out of mingled loyalty, admiration and self-interest.

We must be careful to avoid undue sentimentality when envisaging this pampered child who would, within months, be facing the real terrors of battle. Childhood was brief in the seventeenth century and affective relationships different from those of our own day. Princes and princesses had their own households and spent most of their time with companions and attendants away from their parents. They were prepared for the grown-up world from an early age and often married before puberty. Knowing nothing else, boys and girls looked forward to having their own husbands, wives, children and adult responsibilities. Charles was excited to be measured for real as opposed to ceremonial armour, to take part in military manoeuvres, to play his part in preserving the dynasty and to hear his parents' plans for marriage alliances. He knew that men were comparing and contrasting him with his father and he was already able to look critically at the way the king handled national affairs. The phrase 'When I am king' must have thrust itself into his thinking with increasing frequency.

All that said, the Stuarts were by the standards of the time a close family. Writing to his sister, Mary, three weeks after her departure, Charles reported that his father was 'very much disconsolate and troubled' at the loss of his wife and daughter. 'We are as much as we may merry, and more than we would sad,' he declared with a wistfully elegant turn of phrase.[25] But the family was fractured and Prince Charles was no longer swaddled in affection, comfort and luxury. He was entering the phase of life when emotions and basic attitudes are most subject to change and harsh new realities would frame his outlook on life.

He spent the crucial years of twelve to fifteen with his father in a world of tumult and stress. He experienced the clangour and awfulness of battle. He witnessed bloody death. He saw the bodies of boys no older than himself shattered by shot and slashed by sabre. He became a party to arguments about strategy and tactics. He heard the king's decisions questioned and criticised and began to form his own objective opinions on the practicalities of kingly rule. It may have been Bismarck who succinctly observed that politics is the art of the possible but many national leaders before him had learned pragmatism the hard way and Charles II was one of them. His father had worked to a pious blueprint of kingship, seeking to shape people and events to a pre-formed ideal. His motivations had been Christian commitment and an emotional drive to prove himself to James I. But neither spiritual nor filial devotion had taken deep root in Charles by the time other forces came into play. War is no nursery of fine sensibilities.

Parliament had approved the appointment of the Marquis of Hertford as Charles' tutor because they thought him a 'safe' man for the job. William Seymour was the brother-in-law of the Earl of Essex, leader of the parliamentary forces, and the more extreme members of the anti-court party hoped, through his agency, to detach the prince from his father. They miscalculated. On his return from Dover to see his wife and daughter safely aboard their ship, the king sent to Hertford to bring the other children to Greenwich. A hanger-on at court, disappointed at not gaining preferment, hurried to Westminster with the news and embellished his story with information about a plot to smuggle the heir out of the country. Parliament's leaders immediately sent instructions to the marquis to keep the Prince of Wales at Hampton Court. Seymour, however, chose to obey the king and swiftly reunited father and son. Now it was alarmingly obvious that the anti-royalists were intent on using the Prince of Wales as a hostage, and King Charles was more than ever determined to keep his son close by him as he moved northwards to link up with powerful magnates on whose loyalty he could depend. Days later he thwarted an attempt to snatch the boy at the royal hunting lodge of Theobalds by hurrying to Newmarket. From there he and his entourage rode to York, putting themselves beyond the reach of an enraged parliament. Charles was accompanied by his brother, James. Their younger siblings were left behind, their destinies in the hands of parliament.

Five months later, the Prince of Wales was at his father's side when he unfurled his standard at Nottingham. He was given nominal command of a troop of life-guards and, though he was, for the most part, kept out of real danger, he did see active service in the early engagements of the war. To the twelve-year-old 'officer' the conflict was exciting and he entered into it with bravura. At the first battle of Edgehill he and his brother James were almost captured, Charles having to be restrained from rushing towards the enemy brandishing a pistol and shouting defiance. In the aftermath of the carnage, when a dispirited king, overwhelmed by the appalling loss of life, declined to follow up the military advantage before him, his son's bravery was one of the few factors which provided any cheer. Immediately on retiring to Oxford, where he set up his court, he commissioned from his sergeant-painter, William Dobson, a portrait of Charles in elaborate armour with a depiction of the battle in the background.

There was an air of unreality about the royal establishment at Oxford. While troops drilled in college quadrangles and cellars became munitions arsenals, the household officers tried to keep up a pretence of normality; the idea that the court had simply moved its location and that its rituals and routines remained unchanged. The king and his attendants went hunting while ladies of fashion paraded their finery through the streets. Loyal courtiers and their families jostled with each other to find cramped accommodation in the university city and there was the usual competition for places close to the king and his children. But nothing could dispel the anxiety which brooded over those who waited eagerly for the latest news from London, knowing that they would be hazarding their lives again as soon as the campaigning season opened.

The mythic splendours of the 1630s could not be recreated. In particular King Charles was unable to sustain the illusion of piety and decorum among followers who were living with the uncertainties and excitements of war. Hedonism now cast off restraint, in part because boring, drab self-control was associated with the king's enemies. Fornication became fashionable and was trumpeted by the court poets.

> Let us use time whilst we may;
> Snatch those joys that waste away!
> Earth her winter coat may cast,
> And renew her beauties past;
> But, our winter come, in vain
> We solicit spring again:
> And when our furrows snow shall cover,
> Love may return but never lover.

So wrote Sir Richard Fanshawe, soon to be appointed to Prince Charles' council. Braggarts swaggered the Oxford streets in their sashes and plumes. They bonded together in the camaraderie of the bottle and the gaming table. They settled their scores in duels or with the aid of hired thugs.

Amidst all this brave-faced confusion the prince's position was ambiguous; part vulnerable child, part heir to be protected at all costs, part soldier. And, also, there was his continuing education and training to be considered. Clarendon later lamented that young Charles had never been subjected to intellectual discipline and was 'very little conversant with business, nor spent his time so well towards the improvement of his mind and understanding as might have been expected from his years and fortune'.[26] Now he experienced yet another change of governor. The Marquis of Hertford having been appointed lieutenant-general of the western counties, the post of tutor to the royal children became vacant. It was filled by Thomas Howard, Earl of Berkshire, imperiously dismissed by Clarendon with the words, 'his affection for the crown was good; his interest and reputation less than anything but his understanding'.[27] The king it seems had resolved that the tutorship should now be little more than a sinecure, since he intended to assume personal responsibility for his eldest son's upbringing. There seemed to be no reason, in 1642, why Charles should ever be separated from his father or his mother (who arrived in Oxford the following summer).

In fact, little consistent control was exercised over the rapidly developing adolescent from this time on. When on campaign he was in the company of soldiers and he enjoyed the rude companionship of the camp. This was the first sustained contact he had had with his father's subjects and he enjoyed it. For their part, they must have noted the difference between the king's austere, iconic bearing and the heir's 'common touch'. Another dissimilarity growing up between father and son was in their attitude to the conduct of the war. The king was cautious, vacillating, ever willing to listen to councillors urging peace. Henrietta Maria, by contrast, was as always impatient. She returned to France in July 1644 but, whether at her husband's side or writing letters from Paris, she kept up a barrage of entreaty. He must show his enemies no quarter. He must, at all costs, retain his crown and the powers that attended it. Whether by military success or negotiation or duplicity he must ensure the survival of the dynasty. Not for nothing was she her mother's daughter and her influence weighed heavily with the prince.

The military command was made up of hawks and doves and the younger element was prominent among the latter. Less concerned about political subtleties than the king's more cautious councillors, they felt passionately about 'honour' and 'loyalty' and held in deep contempt the mere 'shop-keepers and cobblers' who had the effrontery to oppose their sovereign. Like the scions of secure county families who hastened to the colours to fight 'Boney' or 'Kaiser Bill' in later conflicts, these young blades never for a moment doubted the righteousness of their cause or the inferiority of their foes. Thus morally and intellectually blinkered, they clamoured for action. The 'Cavalier Poets' mingled sex, glory and political naïvety in their verses:

My dear and only love, I pray
This noble world of thee
Be governed by no other sway
But purest monarchy;
For if confusion have a part,
(Which virtuous souls abhor),
And hold a Synod in thy heart,
I'll never love thee more . . .

But if thou wilt be constant then,
And faithful to thy word;
I'll make thee glorious by my pen
And famous by my sword,
I'll serve thee in such noble ways
Were never heard before!
I'll crown and deck thee all with bays,
And love thee evermore.

So James Graham, Marquis of Montrose, the Stuarts' headstrong Scottish champion, one of the many brash, rash cockalorums who died in their service. Even their enemies recognised the military value of these death and glory boys. Cromwell, deploring the quality of many parliamentary recruits, asked, 'Do you think that the spirit of such base and mean fellows will ever be able to encounter gentlemen that have honour and courage and resolution in them?'[28]

The Prince of Wales was much in the company of this dashing élite corps. His heroes were men of the stamp of his cousin, Rupert of the Rhine. This flamboyant cavalry commander in his mid-twenties was a much more attractive role model for Charles than the greybeards with whom his father surrounded him. Another influential figure who now re-entered his life was George Villiers, Duke of Buckingham, returned with his brother from Cambridge university to serve in the royal army. It is, therefore, not surprising that Charles should have been easily weaned from commitment to his father's attitudes and policies or that Clarendon should have looked back on the Oxford period as one during which the prince's filial duty and affection were being undermined.

In March 1645, Charles came into close contact with the man who was to have an enormous influence over him for the next twenty-two years. The king decided to send his eldest son into the West Country to take over nominal command of the royalist forces in those parts and he appointed a council to guide him. Its leading figure was Sir Edward Hyde (later Earl of Clarendon). At thirty-six, Hyde had behind him a spectacularly rapid career as lawyer, parliamentarian and royal confidant. Two years previously he had been made chancellor of the exchequer, with responsibility for raising finance for the continuation of the war. He was an astute politician and a man of independent mind upon whom the king relied implicitly. More significantly from Charles' point of view, Hyde was a man who thought clearly, adhered firmly to the Church of England and upheld high moral principles. The king, ever on the watch for suitable mentors for his son, recognised in Sir Edward yet another worthy to join the succession of the heir's virtuous guardians.

The military situation had deteriorated alarmingly since Charles had resolved to exercise personal supervision of his son's upbringing. By the end of 1644, the turning-point battle of Marston Moor had been fought and lost, leading to the surrender of York, Newcastle and other important centres in the northern counties. The North might be abandoned but the situation elsewhere was more ambiguous. Oxford remained secure, even though the royalist forces had been forced out of Abingdon, not seven miles away, and the king enjoyed considerable support in the lands to the south and west of his temporary capital. In Scotland there was some cause for hope provided by victories gained by Montrose but the royalists were faced with an impossible logistical problem of uniting into one formidable army their forces in various parts of the realm. A fundamental weakness of the royalist cause was that it relied on county gentry rallying their tenants and neighbours. But most of these rural squires were more concerned about their local rivalries than about wider political realities and their followers were usually reluctant to fight far from home.

Increasingly Charles' moods swung back and forth. Sometimes, in deep despair, he faced the prospect of defeat. At others, he cajoled and encouraged his generals to greater efforts and more inventive stratagems which would bring that victory that he felt sure God would grant him. He considered making peace with the rebellious Irish lords and bringing a Catholic army over the western water. Through the efforts of Henrietta Maria and other agents abroad he hoped for material aid from brother monarchs. The Prince of Wales was one of the factors in these calculations. In the early months of 1645 his possible marriage to the Portuguese infanta was discussed, her father, John IV, promising both troops and a million-pound dowry.[29] When that came to nothing, the prince was offered in marriage to his sister-in-law, one of the daughters of William of Orange. However, the House of Stuart's situation was too precarious and the exigencies of war did not allow of those delicate and sensitive negotiations necessary to conclude a royal match – something for which the heir to the throne may well have been grateful.

One thing that was quite clear amidst the confusion of fluctuating fortunes, desperate plans and frustrated hopes was that the risk of both the sovereign and the heir falling into parliamentary hands must be avoided. It was thus that the king decided to make his son general of the Western Association. He entertained the fond hope that the appearance of the prince in the West might put fresh heart into the fractious royalist commanders and provide them with a figurehead behind whom they could unite. As for young Charles himself, the king intended that the experience should 'unboy' him. His father knew full well how impressionable and how essentially irresponsible young Charles was and was aware that some of the prince's friends and companions were encouraging him to an undesirable independence of view. The king went as far as sending at least one of his son's intimates abroad. Thomas Elliott was despatched to France at the same time that the prince went to Bristol for the express purpose of keeping the two young men apart and strict orders were given that, if Elliott should return and try to make contact with Charles, he was absolutely to be denied access. The king hoped that a measure of authority, under the watchful eye of one of his most trusted and mature servants, might, as far as the exigencies of war allowed, stimulate that growth of character necessary for the performance of Charles' future role. Hyde, according to his own later testimony, protested that he was needed in Oxford, but was overruled when the king told him 'with some warmth' that the entire scheme depended on Hyde's acquiescence.[30]

In all probability the minister's instinct was correct. Charles I, like all the Stuart rulers except Charles II, was a hopelessly inadequate judge of character. A large ingredient of his tragedy was his inability to know which of his bevy of councillors and generals was giving him wise, carefully calculated and disinterested advice. Had Hyde remained at his right hand, some of the king's rash decisions over the next three and a half years might have been avoided. But the father's loss was to prove the son's gain, both in exile and during the early years of his reign. It was also to prove of inestimable benefit to future historians. Hyde wrote a detailed account of the troubled mid-century years and in his prose we obtain for the first time a clearer impression of the prince, his new master.

The picture he creates is of a boy ineffectually tackling a man's job and all too easily allowing himself to be distracted. Young Charles failed totally to do what his father expected of him. In fairness it must be acknowledged that the task he had been assigned was impossible to accomplish and that the resources available to him were laughably inadequate. He fell back on charm and appeals to his followers to remain loyal to the regime. But he lacked the necessary charisma to inspire the kind of sacrifices that would be necessary to pluck victory from the jaws of defeat and when he was under pressure he too readily sought diversion in his own pleasures. The events of the next few months were important in forming Charles' self-concept. Had he emerged from them with a sense of having succeeded in his first experience of independent command, he might have learned lessons about vision, self-sacrifice and discrimination in the choice of friends which would have stood him in good stead as king. Instead, his adventures only tutored him in the arts of survival and seeking out pleasure even in the most trying circumstances.

On a wet 4 March 1645, Charles took his leave of Oxford, excited at the prospect of being able to spread his wings and escape the cage of parental supervision. His enthusiasm would have been dashed if he could have looked into the future and known that he would never see his father again. This was the moment when the prince's fifteen years of travels began, and they began as inauspiciously as they were to continue. His 'court' was impoverished, his troops were demoralised and his senior officers were at odds with each other. The soldiers had little confidence in the generals appointed by the king and they blamed their leaders for the defeats they had suffered, not without some justification. They were ill-equipped and poorly fed. Hyde reckoned them 'a dissolute, undisciplined, wicked, beaten army'. Their cavalry, supposedly the cream of society, constituted a force 'their friends feared and their enemies laughed at; being only terrible in plunder, and resolute in running away'.[31] As for the prince's own provision, this was so inadequate that he was obliged to borrow from members of his suite in order to furnish his table.

The plan was for the prince to set up his headquarters in Bristol, the second city in the realm and the most important in royalist hands. From here the campaign in the West could be organised and contact made with loyalist elements in Wales. The port could be held for the reception of Irish troops and, possibly, reinforcements from the continent. The strategy, which doubtless sounded impressive when drawn up in the king's council of war, was nothing more than a pipe dream. None of the resources that had been promised materialised and the western leaders who had petitioned for the prince to come had their own agendas.

> they who had been so confident, instead of forming and pursuing any design for raising men or money, were only busy in making objections and preparing complaints, and pursuing their private quarrels and animosities against others. And so they brought every day complaints against this and that governor of garrisons, for the riots and insolences of the lord Goring's soldiers, that those parts of the county which were adjacent to Sherborne and Bridgwater were compelled to work at those fortifications, and a world of such particulars . . .[32]

The young general, instead of bravely rallying eager supporters of the cause, found himself trying to smooth ruffled feathers and pleading for assistance. What was even more humiliating was that, while his father's subjects listened courteously to his appeals, they did nothing about them.

Prince Charles' authority was an illusion. He knew it and everyone around him knew it. His tutors were present to keep him on the straight and narrow path mapped out by his father. His council made all the decisions and often met without him. Clarendon recorded that his highness was occasionally 'persuaded' to attend, which suggests a certain reluctance, but that, when present, he did apply himself to the work in hand. To the prince's adolescent mind these deliberations may well have appeared not only tedious but pointless. Decisions reached could be and sometimes were overruled by higher powers, for the tentacles of ruinous division and conflicting opinions reached out over the land from Oxford. Once courses were agreed upon they were not infrequently frustrated by the unco-operativeness of field commanders. In addition to these checks upon Charles' independence of action there came messages from his father. The king, notwithstanding his stated desire to have the Prince of Wales stand upon his own feet and establish the dignity of his position, could not refrain from sending him advice and instructions which altered with the changing exigencies of war: he must pay close attention to his council; he must not leave Bristol without permission; if need be, he must seek refuge in Denmark: no, France would be better for there he could be guided by his dear mother – 'in all things, save religion'.

When some of the king's correspondence fell into the hands of the enemy they made great play with it and what, they claimed, it revealed about his effete and ineffectual government. Thus, in July 1645, *Mercurius Britannicus* gleefully published a letter from Charles to his queen about an addition the prince wished to make to his household. The young man wanted to have Sir John Greenfield as a gentleman of the bedchamber. He sought his father's permission but had, in fact, already made the appointment. The king passed the information on to Henrietta Maria: 'I have refused the admitting of him until I shall hear from thee. Wherefore, I desire thee first, to chide my son for engaging himself without one of our consents, then, not to refuse thy own consent, and, lastly, to believe that, directly or indirectly, I never knew of this till yesterday.' The editor delighted to point out that the king was so much under his wife's thumb that he was afraid to cross her (she had apparently promised the post to another) and was at pains to excuse himself from blame in the matter. 'Now let all men consider,' he concludes, 'what a necessity lies upon this nation, in defence of their own safety . . . when no affairs (of concernment or frivolous) are transacted but according to the will and pleasure of the queen.'[33]

There was one very compelling reason for the king to keep young Charles on an extended leading rein, one that his politically aware advisers at Oxford were not slow to urge in their own interests as well as the monarch's: they feared the establishment of a rival court. Those controlling the prince might take it into their heads to do a separate deal with parliament. The heir might become the tool of councillors and generals opposed to the strategies agreed upon at Oxford. And, of course, should anything happen to the father, the son would become the fount of all patronage. Those who shared these apprehensions knew the prince well enough to realise that the bastion of his filial duty was not impregnable and events over the next few weeks were to show how right they were to be worried.

Most of the individuals and factions spiralling round the prince during the summer of 1645 wore their royalism as a loose cloak to cover personal ambition and private feuds. At the end of April, Charles was persuaded to leave Bristol and set up his headquarters further west. One reason for this was an outbreak of plague in the overcrowded city but the move suited various parties who wanted to widen the gulf between the prince and the government. One of the promoters of this challenge to the king's instructions was George Goring, 'the best company but the worst officer that ever served the king'.[34] Goring was one of the most voracious members of the cormorant court, a man who had a well-trained eye for the main chance and intended to turn the troubled times to his own advantage. By April 1645, he had already governed Portsmouth for parliament, turned the port over to the king, surrendered it after a brief siege, fought with distinction in the North under Newcastle, spent nine months as a prisoner in the Tower, contributed by his rash cavalry leadership to the defeat at Marston Moor, failed to raise his own region of Sussex and Hampshire for the king, captured but speedily lost Weymouth, and failed to oust parliamentary forces from the vital strategic centre of Taunton. Throughout all these exploits he had campaigned for a major military command and his rivals firmly believed that his reluctance to commit his troops too heavily and his encouragement of their scandalous plundering of the countryside were designed to build up a formidable force, loyal to himself alone, which would put him in a commanding political position. Among the many rumours that were rife about Goring was that he had been heard to boast that, as soon as he had a sufficient force at his back, he would hand over the prince to his father's enemies. Clarendon's ringing condemnation indicates how dangerous he thought this adventurer to be:

> Goring . . . would without hesitation have broken any trust, or done any act of treachery, to have satisfied an ordinary passion or appetite; and, in truth, wanted nothing but industry (for he had wit and courage and understanding and ambition, uncontrolled by fear of God or man) to have been as eminent and successful in the highest attempt in wickedness of any man in the age he lived in or before. And of all his qualifications dissimulation was his masterpiece; in which he so much excelled, that men were not ordinarily ashamed, or out of countenance, with being deceived but twice by him.[35]

This was the plausible rogue who presented himself to Prince Charles at the end of April.

But Goring was not the only fly in the ointment for Edward Hyde and those members of the prince's council who were trying to realise the king's wishes regarding the training of his son. Charles' establishment had moved to Bridgwater and there he saw a familiar and much-loved face. Christabella Wyndham greeted her former charge – literally – with open arms. Clarendon complained that she behaved towards the prince with unseemly familiarity: sometimes 'she would run the length of the room and kiss him'.[36] It is not clear what irritated Hyde more – these vulgar displays or the fact that Charles welcomed them. Mrs Wyndham wasted no time in cultivating the prince, trying to wheedle favours out of him and generally (in Hyde's opinion) making herself a confounded nuisance.

For her the coming of the princely court to Bridgwater was a fortuitous event that she and her family were determined to take full advantage of. At the outset of the war, she and her husband had returned to their own county to help organise the royalist forces. It was in very truth a *joint* endeavour for, while Sir Edmund had done sterling work in the early months and been appointed high sheriff of Somerset and governor of Bridgwater, his wife had proved herself a veritable Boudicca in the royalist cause. She constantly urged her husband and his officers to sterner efforts and, when Bridgwater was later under siege she very nearly made a major impact on the outcome of the war by almost removing one of its leading protagonists. From the battlements she fired a musket at the parliamentary general, Sir Thomas Fairfax, which came very close to hitting its mark. Having failed, this Amazon immediately sent her trumpeter to the enemy commander with the taunt that, if he were a real courtier, he would return the compliment. It can scarcely be doubted that this grasping and ambitious woman would have preferred to be with the royal court at Oxford instead of being banished to the unfashionable and unprofitable West. Now that her darling boy had come to her she was determined to make the most of it.

Charles' initial stay in Bridgwater lasted only a week but that was more than long enough for Christabella to reassert her influence over him. We can see in this first 'relationship' of Charles' sexually mature years all the ingredients which were to mark so many of his subsequent dealings with women. He was very attracted to his old nurse. Hyde's first indignant assessment of their behaviour (slightly modified later) was that his young master felt 'fondness, if not affection' for Christabella. Some have inferred from this that Mrs Wyndham initiated Charles into the pleasures of the bedroom and that she was his first known sexual partner. She was around thirty, had not lost her looks and was perfectly capable of using her physical attributes to strengthen her hold on the prince. The prudish Clarendon would not have allowed himself to refer explicitly to princely adultery. Regrettably, the slender evidence does not allow us to assert that Charles engaged in immoral acts with a woman twice his age, but that is not really the important point. However close their intimacy in private and whether it was based upon the child–nanny or adolescent–whore relationship, Christabella made the most of it in public: 'she valued herself much upon the power and familiarity which her neighbours might see she had with the Prince of Wales, and therefore upon all occasions in company, and when the concourse of the people was greatest, would use great boldness towards him'.[37]

Charles cheerfully indulged her and this had three serious consequences. First, she diverted him from the serious business to which his council wished him to attend. It is significant that the scapegrace Thomas Elliott now turned up again. Having slunk away from France without permission, he made straight for Bridgwater where he enjoyed the protection of Christabella (he would later marry one of her daughters) and where he aided and abetted those whose energies were most directed towards keeping the prince amused – much to the chagrin of his conciliar greybeards. With the war going badly and the factionalism prevalent which made it prodigiously difficult to devise and pursue a common military/political policy, Charles' advisers might reasonably have hoped for a greater degree of attention from him to the crises which cropped up on a daily, and at times an hourly, basis.

Second, Christabella was guided by nothing more elevated than her own self-interested agenda. 'She had . . . many private designs of benefit and advantage to herself and her children, besides the qualifying her husband to do all acts of power without control upon his neighbours, and laboured to procure grants or promises of reversions of land from the prince.'[38] She was accustomed to the politics of the royal court, where direct access to the king was the means of gaining favours. But Charles had neither the authority nor the means to bestow largesse upon Christabella and her circle and to play the generous monarch, able to reward his friends at will.

Christabella's third and most serious offence was to exacerbate divisions among the prince's followers. '. . . she laboured to raise jealousies and dislike between them, and kindled such a faction in the [prince's entourage] as produced many inconveniences'.[39] She played upon the ill-defined relationship between the prince's council and his court, particularly exploiting the insecurities of the Earl of Berkshire, Charles' governor. This, too, was no more than she had learned at Whitehall. But she went further: 'she affected in all companies (where she let herself out to any freedom) a very negligent and disdainful mention of the person of the king'.[40] She deliberately encouraged Charles to throw off parental control and act with that independence that his father had been so apprehensive about. The prince should display that firmness of purpose of which the king was manifestly incapable. For example, when a Bridgwater man was arrested for attending a Presbyterian service Christabella urged summary royal justice: let the rogue be strung up forthwith from the sign outside the George Inn. Small wonder that the council rushed him back to Bristol – plague or no plague.

But there he could have no abiding city. The moves available to the royalists on the chessboard of war were diminishing rapidly and with them the options open to the prince. While the king headed northward with the main army, Goring was given the western command he had longed for. But, when Fairfax threatened Oxford and orders were given for all available royalist forces to unite for a major confrontation with the enemy, Goring refused to budge, intent on keeping control of all the loyal troops in Somerset, Devon and Cornwall. Prince Charles' councillors, equally determined to keep their charge out of the general's clutches, moved the court westwards along the Bristol Channel coast, reaching Barnstaple by mid-May.

Here, once again, the scheming of the Wyndhams came under scrutiny. Sir Hugh, the son of Edmund and Christabella, had a quarrel with another young man by the name of Wheeler. In the course of it Wheeler laid information against his enemy: Wyndham had boasted that he would join with the Prince of Wales to depose his father and that he, personally, would cut the king's throat. Sir Hugh, of course, denied this treason and demanded that Wheeler be examined. Witnesses were summoned but 'seemed prepared beforehand on the behalf of Wyndham' and mysteriously could remember nothing of the rash words supposedly spoken by the accused. Wheeler was banished from the prince's presence and the Wyndhams were celebrating their little triumph when they learned that Sir Hugh was to share Wheeler's fate until such time as the king, himself, had looked into the matter. Wyndham rode to Bridgwater where, with his parents, he was soon defending the town against a parliamentary siege. The family's enmity against Hyde was sealed. It would not be the last time he fell foul of Prince Charles' favourites.[41]

Sir Edmund Wyndham was no less inactive militarily than George Goring. Having been charged by the king with the recovery of Taunton, he preferred to stay in his own town and wait for the worst. Given the intense distaste for the war which now gripped the western counties and the difficulty of recruiting troops whose prospects of being paid were negligible, there was little more that he could do. On 10 June he wrote an ingenuous letter to the king, putting the best possible interpretation on a desperate situation. It is worth quoting at length because of what it reveals about Wyndham's concern to have the prince remain in the West Country:

Our endeavours here have not been to make conquests but to preserve the West under obedience . . . and to raise an army worthy of the command of the prince . . . When your Majesty considers the forces we found about Taunton . . . together with the weakness of your Majesty's foot, not above 1,500 in the army, and the garrisons very ill manned; and the other notorious defects of your magazines and garrisons, as likewise the aversion of the affections of the people from your service and their inclination to comply with the rebels. And when you shall compare the then condition of the West with the present and the strength and posture of your army and that of the rebels then and now, we hope your Majesty will conclude that the prince's presence in these parts has not been unhappy to your service and that the only error of that counsel was that he was not hither sooner.[42]

Two weeks later came the disaster of Naseby, lost, perhaps, because of the self-interested Gorham's disobedience. It was a defeat from which the royalists did not recover. Fairfax and Cromwell swept southwards and westwards and, with no enemy field army to face, had only to take out garrison after isolated garrison. Despite Wyndham's optimistic words, Bridgwater surrendered on 23 July.

Charles, moved to ever remoter locations by his minders, received a confusion of conflicting orders and suggestions about his future. His local supporters were divided. Some urged him to remain in Cornwall and use it as a base for a renewed offensive and daily looked for the arrival of promised French troops who never materialised. Others wanted the prince to come to terms with his foes and put a swift end to all the suffering imposed on the nation. Henrietta Maria imperiously demanded his removal to France, a move resisted by Hyde and his companions who blenched at the prospect of the heir coming under papist influence. They counselled Charles to move his court to Ireland and thereby to demonstrate that he was not quitting his father's realm. The king, vacillating as ever, could not decide which haven might be the most appropriate for his son. However, he did know the young man well enough to realise that he would always tend to take the easiest available option and thus wrote to him, after Naseby, in a tone intended to stiffen his backbone:

My late misfortunes remember me to command you that which I hope you shall never have occasion to obey; it is this: if I should at any time be taken prisoner by the rebels, I command you (upon my blessing) never to yield to any conditions that are dishonourable, unsafe for your person, or derogatory to regal authority, upon any considerations whatsoever, though it were for the saving of my life; which in such a case, (I am most confident,) is in greatest security by your constant resolution, and not a whit the more in danger for their threatening, unless thereby you should yield to their desires. But let their resolutions be never so barbarous, the saving of my life by complying with them would make me end my days with torture and disquiet of mind, not giving you my blessing, and cursing all the rest who are consenting to it. But your constancy will make me die cheerfully, praising God for giving me so gallant a son, and heaping my blessings on you; which you may be confident (in such a case)

will light on you. I charge you to keep this letter still safe by you,
until you shall have cause to use it; and then, and not till then, to shew
it to all your council; it being my command to them as well as you;
whom I pray God to make as prosperously glorious as any of the
predecessors ever were of

Your loving father,
Charles R.[43]

By the end of February 1646 the royal party had reached Pendennis
Castle, perched high above the Fal estuary. Behind them parliamentary
forces were steadily advancing. Before them lay the changeable waters of
the Channel. The council, fearful as much of the king's friends as his
enemies, and knowing that even within their stony refuge plots were being
laid to seize the prince, devised a desperate plan to spirit Charles away. At
dead of night on 2 March they smuggled him aboard a ship which took him
to the Scilly Isles. But that could only offer him a brief respite. There was
not enough food for Charles and his entourage and the available accommodation was far from princely. Besides these discomforts there was the
growing threat of a naval blockade. After six weeks the party sailed on to
Jersey.

What a reversal of his circumstances met him there! Instead of moving
uncertainly round a ravaged country, living on short commons and
surrounded by people whose loyalty was suspect, Charles was now
greeted warmly by a cheering populace and entertained by a host who
could afford to indulge him with luxury and splendour. George Carteret,
the lieutenant-governor, was an ardent royalist and an extremely able
administrator who had added to his inherited wealth the proceeds of
privateering and confiscating the property of parliamentarian supporters.
He made Elizabeth Castle available to his royal guest, gave him a present
of £1,500 and catered lavishly for all his needs. At last Charles could live
like a king and he revelled in it. He was able to set up a real court for the
300 or so men and women who now congregated on the island. Daily he
received the homage of the local gentry and permitted favoured subjects to
watch him dining in public. A French visitor who beheld this spectacle
was impressed at the sight of a table crammed with delicacies, court
cupboards heavily adorned with plate and a corps of kneeling servants
proffering dish after dish. It was a return to the good old days.

But did this generous and devoted royal servant also make Charles the
gift of his daughter? Long accepted tradition names Marguerite Carteret as
the woman with whom the prince had his first real affair. She was loyal to
the Stuart cause and, like the rest of her family, charged with making the
stay of her father's guest as agreeable as possible. So, the prince, able at
last to relax and with time on his hands, may have enjoyed the favours of
the twenty-year-old Miss Carteret. Like all myths the story of their liaison

exists to explain something – in this case the development of Charles' sexual appetite. The notorious womaniser must have started on his libidinous career some time, so who was the first woman he slept with? Christabella Wyndham? Marguerite Carteret? The story has a certain romantic appeal – the young couple enjoying a brief interlude of happiness away from the horrors of war and enjoying themselves in the balmy sunshine of a Jersey spring.

Unfortunately, the evidence for it is as meagre as that for Charles' fling in Bridgwater. In 1668 a certain James de la Cloche became a novitiate of the Jesuit order in Rome and offered credentials in which he presented himself as the son of Charles and Marguerite (the surname is that which Marguerite took on her marriage in 1656). The young man died the following year and no one took any notice of his claim for two centuries. Then the historian, Lord Acton, declared his belief in the genuineness of some recently rediscovered documents. Other scholars denounced them as fakes manufactured by an anonymous adventurer trading on Charles II's reputation for his own advantage. Since the king, who never balked at acknowledging his bastards, did not publicly recognise de la Cloche, it seems unlikely that there was any truth in the story.

There is no contemporary support for this liaison. Indeed, circumstantial evidence points in the opposite direction. George Carteret was a man of upright character who is unlikely to have been indifferent to his daughter's honour, even if it had been compromised by a royal personage. In later years Pepys was very struck with the strait-laced behaviour of both Carteret and his son, Philip. The father spoke most indignantly of the scandalous lives of many at court, declaring that if he discovered his own son to be a debauchee he would instantly put a stop to his imminent marriage to Lady Jemima Montague. When the wedding did take place it was a very proper affair accompanied by none of the customary bawdy humour: 'the modesty and gravity of this business was so decent that it was to me ten times more delightful than if it had been twenty times more merry and jovial',[44] Pepys declared. The upright Hyde also greatly approved of Carteret when the two men became acquainted in 1646. All his anxieties about Charles getting into bad company or behaving in an unseemly fashion appear to have evaporated the moment his party landed in the Channel Isles, and he was strongly in favour of the prince remaining in Jersey.

This now became a bitter bone of contention between the Hyde faction and the Francophile councillors clustered round the queen. Henrietta Maria sent embassy after embassy across from the mainland and bombarded both her husband and her son with urgent entreaties for Charles to join her in Paris. Her only concern was for the restoration of her family's position and power. She pressed the king to agree to anything that would lead to his restoration and assured him and his supporters of French aid in holding on to his crown. But, should anything happen to her husband, then everything would depend upon the Prince of Wales and she was determined to bring Charles within her Francophile ambit. Of course she was not open about this. She covered her real motivation with protestations of a mother's concern for the safety of her favourite son. Jersey, she insisted, was not a secure haven while parliament's ships patrolled the Channel.

Hyde was equally determined to prevent Charles taking a step which, he protested, would destroy his credibility in England. He told the king's council, 'I will not be hurried by any command whatsoever into an action that I think will prove so pernicious to the king, queen, prince and realm as this unnecessary going of the prince into France.'[45] As to the promised help from Henrietta Maria's friends, it had not materialised so far and if they did now provide troops to aid the recovery of royal power, Hyde was appalled at the prospect of Prince Charles returning at the head of a French army. It would 'never reconcile those hearts and affections to the king and his posterity, without which he hath no hope of reigning'.[46] What Hyde feared above all things was the prince's conversion to Catholicism, for of one political fact there could be no doubt: the people of England and Scotland would not countenance a Catholic monarch. Hyde knew, as did the king, that Charles did not share their passionate commitment to the Church of England; indeed, that the boy's religion was, as yet, only skin deep. He also knew that Henrietta Maria would stop at nothing to bring her own children safely back into the Roman fold. Therefore it was of the utmost importance to keep Charles out of his mother's clutches.

For a while the council's advice prevailed. On 11 May Charles instructed that the queen's emissaries were to return a courteous but firm answer:

> You shall inform her majesty that we have, with all duty and sub-
> mission, considered her letters to us concerning our speedy repair into
> the kingdom of France; the which direction we conceive to be grounded
> upon her majesty's apprehension of danger to our person by any
> residence here; the contrary whereof we believe her majesty will be no
> sooner advertised of, than she will hold us excused for not giving that
> present obedience which we desire always to yield to the least
> intimation of her majesty . . .'[47]

Henrietta Maria was not to be so easily fobbed off. The urgent entreaties continued. There were also no less determined efforts to inveigle the prince into Ireland. One 'loyal' captain even proposed kidnapping him if he seemed disinclined to go willingly.

The war of words came to a head on 21–22 June. A lavish entourage of seventy or eighty courtiers had arrived from Paris, accompanying the queen's representatives who were, for several hours, locked in heated debate with the prince's councillors. At one point the meeting degenerated into a slanging match and Charles suspended it overnight to allow everyone to cool off. As well as the formal arguments presented in debate, the queen's delegates worked on Charles in private, offering who knows what blandishments. A psychological moment had arrived. A moment of choice. Would he follow that intuitive, pleasure-seeking side of his nature inherited from his mother or the devotion to stern principle his father had tried to inculcate into him, most recently via Hyde and his episcopal attendants? Charles was torn – until the Francophile party produced a trump card. They presented messages from the king instructing him to join Henrietta Maria. Hyde was convinced that this *coup de main* was a fraud but either the Prince of Wales accepted it at face value or he surrendered to the sugared entreaties of the queen's friends. In changing his mind he gave way to the importunity of his mother – still the most powerful woman in his life. Edward Hyde and some of his colleagues resigned – perhaps as a last-ditch effort to make the prince reconsider.

Before his departure on 25 June, Charles left instructions that a prize ship recently captured and valued at £8,000 should be sold and the money divided between Hyde and one of his colleagues. It was the kind of gesture which was to become typical. Viewed from one perspective it was gracious and generous. Looked at from another angle, it was a shamefaced response inspired by guilt. To reject the advice of his loyal councillors, whom he knew to be true to the Crown, came close to being an act of betrayal and he felt the need to buy off his conscience. The most important personality development of Charles' troubled mid-teen years was the acquisition of a sixth sense for people he could trust, whose loyalty was more or less sincere. But to recognise devoted, disinterested service was not always to repay it in the same coin.

The prince who emerged from this first phase of the Civil Wars was sixteen, an adult by contemporary standards. His education and training in kingship had been a mess and, in any formal sense, non-existent for the last four years. What he had experienced was involvement in the lives of a wide variety of ordinary people. The fragile glamour of the royal court was now a distant memory, though one he may well have hankered after, but to it he could add something his father had never known – an understanding of the hopes, fears and concerns of the Crown's subjects. One fact he will speedily have grasped about all sorts and conditions of men was that few gave him their allegiance, their wealth, their bodies out of love and without expecting rich proof of princely gratitude. There were not many men or women for whom loyalty was its own reward. Generals squabbled over their privileges; soldiers wanted booty; townsmen and villagers begged for the return of peace. And they all looked to Charles to supply their demands. Even his old nurse, who welcomed him with such exuberant displays of affection, was calculating the advantages she and her family could secure in return for supporting the future king and was ingratiating herself with him in case the present occupant of the throne should, one way or another, be obliged to vacate it. It is scarcely surprising that Charles was developing that shrewdness which is second cousin to wisdom.

Reaching an understanding of himself and other people against the background of war was hard work, and where was he to look for emotional support? Since the dispersal of his family, the affection Charles had found consisted in the camaraderie of the camp, the companionship of a few friends he had known since childhood, and relationships with men and women he encountered on his travels. Probably some of those relationships were of a casual, sexual nature. If so, they have no significance. No female fellow fugitive shared his hardships or provided the comfort and support which might have helped to sustain him. No member of the opposite sex held a special place in his life.

But neither was he a sybaritic libertine, pursuing women as objects of pleasure. Writers of sensationalist popular history have often tried to identify Charles' earliest 'conquests', taking it as axiomatic that the middle-aged debauchee must, of necessity, be prefigured in the adolescent and that the prince was already a sexual athlete before he reached full manhood. This is to misunderstand not only Charles' emotional development but also the social and moral revolution which overwhelmed English womankind during the Civil Wars and their aftermath. If the prince was eager to escape from his father's puritanical restraints it was not in order to live the life of a wild Lothario. If he enjoyed the company of unprincipled friends of whom his father did not approve that does not signify that he had abandoned the guidelines set out for him by the Earl of Newcastle concerning the courtesy expected of well-bred gentlemen, especially towards women. Charles cut a handsome, noble and tragic figure among royalist ladies; as one remarked, 'what loyal eye could look upon so glorious a prince, thus eclipsed, and not pay him the homage of tears?'[48] But if the young royal fugitive melted hearts there is no indication that he behaved anything less than honourably towards those whose hospitality or generosity he was obliged to accept.

> You maidens that desire to love
> And would good husbands choose,
> To him that you do vow to love
> By no means do refuse.
> For God that hears all secret oaths
> Will dreadful vengeance take
> On such that of a wilful vow
> Do slender reckoning make.[49]

Thus ran the moral of a doleful popular ballad about a 'wanton' who had the effrontery to promise herself to one man and then change her mind and marry another. It encapsulates most of the prevailing politically correct attitudes towards sexual relationships before the middle years of the century. Women were subservient to men. Marriage was inviolable. Wives were to address their husbands respectfully in public and not employ Christian names or terms of endearment such as 'sweeting', 'love', 'duck', or 'pigsnie'.[50] (Hence Hyde's abhorrence of Christabella Wyndham's vulgar familiarity towards Prince Charles.) While husbands' errant behaviour might be tolerated, it was accepted that their spouses must be at all times chaste and faithful. It was not only Puritans who argued that sexual intercourse was for procreation and should not be casually indulged in even within marriage. Of course, not everyone lived up to these ideals. As we have seen, Charles I and Henrietta Maria presented themselves as the perfect couple in order to raise the moral tone of court life. Preachers regularly cried out against adultery and prophesied divine wrath on a nation slipping into moral anarchy. Yet, strict standards were widely acknowledged, especially in aristocratic and gentry society, where family honour and the fear of property rights confused by illegitimacy under-pinned them. All this was about to change. War shook loose social relationships and conventions. Puritan rule, by using the law to enforce morality, provoked a backlash. The next two decades witnessed an upheaval of attitudes and values similar to that which occurred in western society in the 1960s and 1970s. The mores of Charles II and his court had as much to do with this underlying shift in popular attitudes as with the decadence of the king.

The young man who left English territory in June 1646 was as yet uncorrupted. He was stepping into an uncertain future. He was leaving behind the mentors of his youth. He was entering a social world very different to that of England. And he was about to rejoin the powerful woman who was desperate to re-establish a dominant influence in his life.

CHAPTER 3

A Nation Which Hath Brought All These Miseries Upon Us

For the next eight years, the years of his early manhood, Charles was much under the influence of four women, his mother, his sister (Mary, Princess of Orange), his aunt (Anne, Queen Regent of France) and his first 'significant other' (Lucy Walter), all of whom behaved towards him with mingled possessiveness and indulgence. During those years, as during his adolescence, he could exercise little independent judgement and nor could he develop the skills necessary for effective rule. He no longer presided over his own court. He was a wandering, impoverished prince or king in exile, regarded with scorn or pity among the royal houses of Europe but also with a degree of calculated amity as a possible future ally, should his fortunes change. It was the uncertainty of his position and the pre-occupation of other monarchs with events nearer home that disinclined them to come to the aid of Charles and his increasingly frantic mother.

As for the prince, his arrival in Paris was a severe anticlimax. The excitements and dangers of the last four years were behind him but ahead stretched an indeterminate period of grey boredom. There were two possible ways of overcoming the tedium: he could throw himself into those pleasures that lay to hand or he could re-enter the conflict across the Channel and attempt something effective on his father's behalf. What he, in fact, did was to hover between these two courses.

He could scarcely have arrived in France at a more unfortunate time. The years 1647–52 saw the government of that country faced with a combination of problems amounting to the worst crisis in its recent history. The great Richelieu and the pliant Louis XIII had died within months of each other, leaving the country to be governed in the name of the infant Louis XIV by his mother, Anne of Austria, and her chief minister, Cardinal Mazarin. The devastating Thirty Years War was staggering to its exhausted conclusion, but that did not permit the populace much respite. They were burdened with massive taxation and their aristocratic leaders were now free to challenge the government. Mazarin misjudged the mood of the country. He was determined to continue the policies of his predecessor to make the king absolute within France and the

49

dominant figure in the councils of Europe. But the parliament of Paris set its face against the former and the Spanish Habsburgs withstood the latter.

National indignation focused on the two 'foreigners' who ruled France and who were, in the popular mind, despised and considered guilty of every vice from adultery to peculation and card-sharping. The disaffected elements looked abroad and saw rebellion, not only in Britain, but in Portugal, Naples and Catalonia. If elsewhere reform could be enforced from below, why could it not in France? The result of this thinking was the two 'Frondes' (1648–52) in which nobles and parliamentary delegates joined with the Paris mob to shake the monarchy to its foundations.

Turbulence was, however, hidden beyond the horizon when Charles arrived at his mother's residence, Saint Germain, in the high summer of 1647. To Henrietta Maria, her son was still the thirteen-year-old she had last seen in 1644, an obedient boy who would dutifully play the role she had devised for him in her ongoing dynastic drama. She made him no allowance out of the meagre grant she received from her French relatives and, as a penniless stranger in her world, he had no alternative but to be guided by her and her favourites. The main themes of Henrietta Maria's policy were very clear in her own mind. Everything depended on re-invigorating the auld alliance, the traditional strategy by which France and Scotland had, over and again, collaborated to inhibit England from pursuing policies which might be inimical to either. The queen's scenario involved her husband seeking the safety of his northern kingdom, making whatever religious concessions were necessary to the fanatical Presbyterians (what could some obscure points of church order matter since they and the Anglicans were both heretical sects?) and using Scotland as a base for the reconquest of England. Meanwhile, the heir to the throne would make a suitable marriage to some wealthy princess which would ensure diplomatic support among the fraternity of continental royals and, more urgently, funds with which to pay for mercenary troops, who would assist the Stuarts in exacting revenge upon their presumptuous subjects.

The young lady selected as Charles' bride was Henrietta Maria's niece, Anne-Marie Louise de Montpensier, the eighteen-year-old daughter of the duc d'Orléans, and the mistress in her own right of one of the greatest fortunes in Europe. The possibility of an alliance with the Grande Mademoiselle, as she was known, was never a reality anywhere except in the frenzied imagination of the English queen. Anne-Marie was a vain, calculating woman who had her sights fixed upon far larger fish than the very unamusing, immature exile. But, even if she had allowed herself to succumb to Charles' charm, Mazarin would have vetoed any scheme which involved this rich prize being bestowed upon a husband who was of little use in his political machinations. Pushed into a courtship with this overpoweringly beautiful and self-assured young woman, Charles was completely out of his depth. Their first encounter was moderately disastrous. While Mademoiselle eyed him candidly and found him 'passably agreeable', his mother launched into a long eulogy of her son's many excellent qualities. As for Charles, he could only stand in uncomprehending silence, since he knew not a word of French. During the performance of an Italian comedy at the Palais Royale some weeks later the awkward young Englishman made an attempt at romance. While Anne-Marie surveyed the proceedings from a raised throne, Charles prostrated himself at her feet, doubtless attempting to express through looks and sighs the devotion to which he was incapable of giving voice. The princess was accustomed to much more eloquent flattery, as her own memoirs testify:

> No-one was more magnificently dressed than I that day, and I did not fail to find many people to tell me of my splendour and to talk about my beautiful figure, my graceful bearing, the whiteness of my skin and the sheen of my blond hair. These, they said, adorned me more than all the riches which glittered upon me.

Poor Charles was manifestly out of his league and Mademoiselle felt only pity for him. Her preoccupation was with the possibility of marriage to the emperor and the magnificence of the position she would then enjoy.

> the Queen of England noticed that I looked at her son somewhat disdainfully. When she learned the cause of it she reproached me and said that my head was full of nothing but the emperor. I defended myself as well as I could but my face disguised my sentiments so poorly that one had only to look at me to discover them.[51]

Charles had no great enthusiasm for the proposed match and acknowledged more readily than his mother that it was a non-starter, but he would have been less than human not to feel the snub. It contributed to his growing sense of being smothered by his mother and forced into embarrassing situations and undesirable policies.

As well as plotting his future, she was trying to make up for his lost education. The prince was allotted a routine of lessons, devotions and exercise. He was still under the tutelage of Dr Earle and now the philosopher-mathematician, Thomas Hobbes, joined his entourage. Charles was as attracted to his new mentor as he had been earlier to Newcastle. Hobbes was witty and intellectually daring, a man who delighted to challenge existing taboos. He was currently working on his great book, *Leviathan*, which later scandalised the upholders of traditional Christian values. The concept of man as 'a little lower than the angels' was one he rejected totally. Human beings were animals, driven solely by passions and appetites. It followed that such abstracts as 'right' and 'wrong' had no objective reality. Such categories were only defined by the individual as he pursued what he adjudged to be best for himself and by the sovereign who alone made the rules by which society was to be ordered. Hobbes boldly asserted his belief in absolute monarchy:

> [The monarch's] power cannot without his consent be transferred to another. He cannot forfeit it. He cannot be accused by any of his subjects of injury. He cannot be punished by them. He is judge of what is necessary for peace and judge of doctrines.[52]

Hobbes was employed to instruct the prince in mathematics and we cannot know to what extent he passed on his own political and ethical principles but it is important to understand the philosophical nutrients which were being added to Charles' ideological soil.

For a century royal authority in France had had to compete with the power claims of aristocrats, parliaments, Catholic dignitaries and Huguenot leaders, while at the same time preserving the integrity of the state and asserting its influence internationally. It had been bolstered by such absolutist theories as Hobbes now expressed. In practical terms there was little difference between this intellectual prop to the autocracy of the king and James I's assertion of the semi-divine power of the Crown:

> Kings are justly called gods . . . they make and unmake their subjects; they have power of raising and casting down; of life and death; judges over all their subjects and in all causes and yet accountable to none but God only. They have power to exalt low things and abase high things and make of their subjects like men at the chess.[53]

Charles I had attempted to live out this high doctrine, with disastrous results. Even Hyde, who yielded to no one in his devotion to the king, rejected the assertion that government of any kind had legitimacy apart from the consent of the people. The origin of sovereignty was the central issue contested by constitutional theorists in the seventeenth century.

It is unlikely that dry-as-dust debating points held much attraction for Prince Charles. Unlike his father, he had never been devoted to his books and had never acquired the mental discipline to apply himself to subjects which did not capture his imagination. He was by no means a dullard; his inquisitive mind eagerly applied itself to things scientific and mechanical. But his only recorded statement on political principle was 'that he thought a king who might be checked, or have his ministers called to account by a parliament was but a king in name'.[54] What Charles cannot have failed to appreciate was the difference in *style* between his mother and father over the exercise of sovereignty. The king was earnest about living up to his high calling. Even on the scaffold he would claim that his misfortunes were the result of striving to maintain that firm government which alone could guarantee the rights and freedoms of his subjects. This was why he could not yield on the central points of episcopacy and control of the army. For the pragmatists of the French court power was the only reality. The queen regent and her entourage were, in most respects, above the law and also above moral restraint. They might say or do anything to maintain their authority. Mazarin simply could not understand why the King of England would not make empty promises in order to outwit his rebellious subjects. Brought up to the code of political realism/cynicism, Henrietta Maria was constantly frustrated by her husband's devotion to principle, and the prince's French friends ridiculed Charles I's fastidiousness.

Catholicism, absolutism, the hedonism and atheism with which Hobbes was later charged introduced into Charles' thinking elements which were clean contrary to much that his English guardians had brought him up to believe. Edward Hyde, assessing the situation from his island sanctuary, was almost in despair. In the autumn of 1646, he wrote to Francis Cottington, the aged statesman-diplomat:

> Oh my Lord, it breaks my heart to see that the hopes of the king and the recovery of the kingdom must be carried on and depend upon the counsels and principles of a nation which hath brought all these miseries upon us, and I fear hath not a less fatal projection at this time upon the honour and interest of the king than they have hitherto had.[55]

There was more to this than English Francophobia. Hyde believed that French and Catholic influences, stemming from the queen's household, had done more than anything else to alienate the Stuart dynasty's subjects. Bourbon ambassadors had muddied the diplomatic waters. The queen's favourites had encouraged the royal family to be distanced from their people behind a veil of absolutist mystique. Richelieu had successfully kept England out of involvement in the continent, not so that she could enjoy the benefits of peace, but as part of his policy of isolating the Habsburgs and breaking their power. But the clash of cultures went deeper. Englishmen looked across the Channel and saw an arrogant, over-weening France which, having laid waste vast areas of neighbouring territory, now assumed a dominance in Christendom affairs which was more than political.

> The French, having no fear of Germany, which was prostrate and never likely to be strong, took pleasure in regarding themselves as the guardian angels and tutelary guides of a . . . much retarded people. They noted with pride the spread of French literature, French acting and French fashions among the awkward and submissive Teutons and

regarded it as a wise dispensation of Providence that France was now able to resume . . . the civilising mission of Charlemagne.[56]

And it was not only over her eastern borders that France looked with patronising gaze. Many in England sensed this proprietorial attitude and regarded their nearest neighbour as an alien and dangerous nation – heretical, morally decadent, effete, reactionary and also a formidable military power, seeking insidiously to infiltrate the life of the Stuart state.

From Hyde's vantage point in Jersey things looked black indeed. Dismal tidings reached him by almost every ship from both sides of the Channel. From May 1646 to the following February the king was the guest of the Scottish army, besieged by both his hosts and his wife to give way on the religious issue. Henrietta Maria's letters became steadily more hysterical until she threatened to wash her hands of her husband and retire to a nunnery if he did not act on the excellent advice he was receiving from France. Charles I's refusal to yield on what he considered a fundamental point of principle had Hyde's full support. Eventually the Scots despaired of reaching an agreement and handed the king over to parliament and, in June 1647, he fell into the hands of the army.

Meanwhile, the prince was reported to be falling increasingly under the influence of his mother's friends. Chief among them was Henry, Baron Jermyn, a *politique* who enjoyed 'freedom from personal scruples and political principles'.[57] This handsome man, accomplished in little but the arts of the courtier, had charmed the queen in the early days of the reign and been her constant companion ever since, becoming her master of the horse and secretary. Jermyn was no stranger to scandal and but for Henrietta Maria's intercession would have been dismissed from the court on at least one occasion. The king disapproved of this shallow creature but Henrietta Maria was indulgent of his peccadilloes and indiscretions and, as so often when husband and wife disagreed, it was her will that prevailed. She and Jermyn understood each other perfectly: they were soulmates in a way that Henrietta Maria and Charles never were and inevitably rumoured to be lovers. Hyde was not surprised to learn that this favourite of the queen was lavishing flattery on Charles, pointing out that, whereas his council had treated him like a mere schoolboy, now his 'real' friends would show him the honour and deference due to his position. Sober influences were, as far as possible, kept away from the prince who was diverted by all the entertainments the court and capital had to offer.

Charles was, in fact, under numerous pressures. His mother's ambition, his own sense of family responsibility, the robust moral earnestness of his tutors, the glamour of Europe's fashion capital, the unabashed hedonism of the queen regent's court, the easygoing French Catholicism which was tolerant of human frailty and the fun-loving irresponsibility of his own little group of close friends all competed for the soul of the footloose young man. Thus, while on the surface Charles seemed to be enjoying his escape from the seriousness of Hyde and the impossible expectations of his father's subjects, these years in Paris and Saint-Germain-en-Laye were years of underlying uncertainty, stress and unhappiness. Freed from responsibilities, he was also freed from the possibility of fulfilment.

This unsatisfactory situation came to an end in the summer of 1648 with the sudden chance for positive action. Briefly royalist fortunes seemed to take a turn for the better. The opposition was fragmenting. Parliament and New Model Army mistrusted each other and factions had appeared within the military ranks. The king, though now a secure prisoner in Carisbrooke Castle, was in secret correspondence with activists at home and abroad and succeeded in inspiring that series of military manoeuvres known as the Second Civil War. The Duke of Hamilton led a Scottish army across the border and there were risings in Kent, Essex, the North of England and in Wales. At the end of May disaffection spread from the east coast ports to part of the navy stationed in the Downs. The mutinous seamen put their officers ashore and sailed their ships to Holland. Charles insisted that, amidst all this activity, there was work for him to do. But what and where? The queen, as eager as ever for the Scottish alliance, wanted to send her son to take over the generalship of Hamilton's army but she was balked in this by Mazarin. The cardinal was happy to hold the royal heir as one of the cards in his game of European diplomacy but had no intention of placing serious money on that card's winning abilities. Charles was permitted to go as far as Calais to wait on events but had no authorisation to leave French territory. What added to his humiliation was that he also lacked the funds necessary to make a suitably impressive appearance among his father's subjects.

Not until the beginning of July, when Jermyn had raised a loan and William of Orange had added his entreaties to those of Henrietta Maria, was Charles able to leave French territory and make for the port of Helvoetsluys. In doing so he became involved in more political complications. The younger sister with whom he was now reunited was no longer the child she had been when they parted six and a half years before. Mary was now a self-assured sixteen-year-old and a sovereign's consort. Her husband, William II, was stadtholder of six of the seven United Provinces, and captain-general of the republic's forces. He had just presided over the final stages of his country's eighty-two-year struggle for freedom from Spain but this by no means exhausted the ambition of this young ruler, who planned to make himself king in all but name and, with French aid, to expel the Spaniards from the southern Netherlands. His democratically inclined opponents complained bitterly of William's autocratic behaviour. Angry pamphleteers charged him with seeking to fill all offices with his own yes-men and to drag the country into war, not only with Spain, but also with England, 'in order to please the frivolous Frenchies, to whom he had wholly lost his heart'.[58]

The Princess of Orange had much of her mother about her. She was proud, intolerant, disliked her husband's people and refused to learn their language. She was also intensely loyal to her family and was determined that the resources of the Dutch state should be employed to enable her father to regain his throne. William shared this commitment to interventionism. Unfortunately, he was not backed in this by the States-General, the government of the United Provinces. Their Calvinist and republican sensibilities inclined them to support, if they supported anybody, the English parliamentarians. Thus William had to resort to his own purse when he raised a small force of men and ships to place at his father-in-law's disposal. Such political realities were pushed into the background when the stadtholder and his wife eagerly made the short journey from the Hague to greet their kinsman. It was a joyful meeting for the siblings and it was heartening for Charles to know that he was supported by royals of his own generation.

He needed this reassurance because the divided counsels which had plagued him since his departure from Oxford were still sabotaging his desire to achieve something positive on his father's behalf. In fact, the squabbling in his entourage was now worse than ever. The success of any naval operation depended on the support of crews, 'the greatest officer among them being not above the quality of a boatswain'.[59] Their priorities were pay and prize money, followed closely by the choice of their leaders. Having mutinied once, they were not above doing so again if they disapproved of their captains or the tactics they were called upon to implement. Therefore, the prince's advisers and lieutenants who wanted to influence policy played the popularity game, seeking the support of the main deck men.

Then there was the problem of brother James. The fifteen-year-old Duke of York had escaped England disguised as a girl and had joined his sister at the Hague. Being on the spot first, he had nominated himself admiral of the fleet, had been welcomed by the sailors and supported by his own court favourites. This was the immediate cause of Charles' rushing to Helvoetsluys. There he remonstrated angrily with his brother in private and sent him back to the Hague, while at the same time commending himself to the seamen. This is the first real evidence we have of that common touch Charles had developed as a result of his mingling with all sorts and conditions of men. The fleet received him with great enthusiasm and cheered him to the echo when he went aboard the flagship. Afterwards he joined his family at the Hague, where Mary gave a lavish banquet in his honour.

Now there arose the question of who was to be given practical command of the fleet. There were half a dozen high-ranking royalists competing for this honour. Some had defected from the parliamentary ranks, some were newly arrived from England and some, like Jermyn and Prince Rupert, were the queen's men. That issue could not be resolved without creating fresh resentments which destabilised the prince's council of war. These divisions completely threw away the enormous strategic advantage the defection of the fleet had handed to the Stuart cause. While Fairfax and Cromwell regained the military advantage ashore, the prince's advisers squabbled over tactics. Should the fleet sail northwards in order to link up with the invading Scots, or position itself in the Thames estuary to strengthen the revolt in the Home Counties, or make for the Isle of Wight to rescue the king, or sweep the Channel taking merchant prizes and thus providing funds for the war effort? Small wonder that the prince sent for Hyde to resume the leading place in his council. But long before Sir Edward (who came with mixed feelings, being a poor sailor) could reach his side the failure to achieve a consistent line of policy had deprived Charles of the opportunity to make a real difference. This was the backdrop, painted in the vivid colours of excited anticipation and the drab hues of frustrated hope, to Charles' first real love affair. For it was in Holland that he met Lucy Walter.

Lucy, a beautiful young woman about the same age as Charles, was one of life's victims. She was far from unique in this regard: many of her sex were destroyed morally, physically and mentally by the turbulence of the age. Deprived of fathers or husbands, their family fortunes obliterated by the war, they had only their wits and their charms to keep them from penury and starvation. Lucy came from respectable Welsh squirearchy stock though her parents, William and Elizabeth Walter, moved to London in the late 1630s. They set up house in fashionable Covent Garden, the most expensive quarter of the capital where Inigo Jones was employed in laying out England's first Italian-style piazza. It is reasonable to suppose that they were attracted to high society and hoped to gain access to the court, the fount of all patronage, for their neighbours included many who were intimates of the royal couple, such as Sir Kenelm Digby and Sir John Winter, the queen's secretary.

Their attempt to establish themselves in the *haut monde* may have been something of a desperate gamble – and one which did not pay off. There were strains in the marriage which, to judge by their severity, must have built up over many years, and within a short time William and Elizabeth had separated. Bitter mutual recriminations led to court proceedings. Elizabeth accused her husband of leaving her and their children destitute. William counter-claimed that he had never received his bride's marriage settlement and that she had been unfaithful to him. The family now split up, Mr Walter retiring to his Welsh estate, Mrs Walter moving in with her mother and sister, Mrs Gosfright, husband of a Dutch merchant, in the well-to-do suburb which was gradually engulfing the village of St Giles in the Fields (in the area of the present intersection of Tottenham Court Road and New Oxford Street); the children were lodged with their grandfather, probably at his house near Exeter.

So far this is an all too familiar story of a relationship disintegrating under the pressure of financial and sexual problems. It might have occurred at almost any time in the last millennium. It was, however, exacerbated by the war. If William had pinned his hopes on making influential aristocratic connections these will have been dashed by the court's preoccupation with the growing crisis and its eventual move to Oxford. Once hostilities had broken out, London became a society disrupted by street gangs, neighbourly mistrust and general anxiety. Moral and social norms held less sway and, since the future was unsure, there was a growing tendency to live for the moment. This was precisely the time that Lucy reached the age when normally the family would be making arrangements for her marriage, but with no money to dower her and the majority of young men fighting on one side or the other there was little prospect of finding a husband. The girl's movements during these years are unknown. Perhaps we should imagine her bounced back and forth like a tennis ball between her parents and various of her relatives. Legends tell of visits to Wales or Devon coinciding with the arrival of the Prince of Wales in one or other of those locations but such attempts to place the lovers together at an early date have no substance.

The few facts that we can rely on are that by her mid-teens Lucy Walter had developed into a beautiful and spirited girl, that she had returned to London, which she found much more congenial than the boorish rural environment of Devon or Wales, and that she or her mother had sought the 'protection' of some of the wealthy young bloods who were strutting the City streets. Foremost among them was Algernon Sidney, a younger son of the Earl of Leicester. Sidney was brave, dashing, ardent, a parliament man through and through, and he came to London in July 1644 to be treated for wounds received at the battle of Marston Moor. A year later he was still not fit enough to resume active service and he was still in London in the summer of 1646, when he assumed his seat in parliament as MP for Cardiff. Some time during these months he took Lucy under his wing.

In the seventeenth century it was impossible to disentangle fundamental sexual associations from master–servant or patron–client relationships. The very fabric of society was composed of large households and extensive clientage networks. The supremacy of the upper classes depended on the support of men, women and children tied to them by economic necessity and personal ambition. The lower orders just as fundamentally needed the employment and protection their superiors offered. This was particularly true of women, who had few other employment opportunities, and even more so of unmarried women who lacked the support of their families. They had virtually no legal rights and their bodies belonged to their masters as much as their services. Whatever favours they could demand depended on their charms and the force of their personality.

Lucy had both in abundance. All contemporaries who described her, even those who were outraged by her easy virtue, acknowledged that she was a rare beauty. The diarist John Evelyn offered the most succinct appraisal when he described Lucy as 'brown, beautiful, bold but insipid', meaning by the last word that she was unsophisticated. In modern parlance she might be called a 'dumb brunette'. Lucy's was a very basic, 'animal' kind of loveliness, as we can see with stunning clarity from a portrait miniature attributed to Nicholas Dixon, and her outward form clothed a spirit that had in no measure been crushed by her earlier experiences. If anything, the estrangement of her parents and the financial straits she had endured for so long had bred in her a fiery independence and a determination to use whatever advantages nature had bestowed on her to better her condition.

She evidently made an enormous impact on Algernon Sidney, for he is said to have paid the considerable sum of £50 for her (presumably to the girl's mother). This must have been some time towards the end of 1646, because in the following January Sidney was despatched to Ireland on military duty and, according to the only contemporary source, he had not at that time received from Lucy what he had primarily paid for. As soon as her protector had departed, the latest round in the long legal contest between William and Elizabeth Walter was fought. In the House of Lords Lucy's father won custody of his children. This eventuality seems to have been discussed between the girl and her protector, for, rather than return to her hated father, Lucy immediately ran away, changing her name to 'Mrs Barlow' (after one of her maternal relatives). She took ship for Holland and the family home of her uncle, Mr Gosfright. But she also carried letters of recommendation from Algernon to his younger brother. Robert Sidney, as convinced a republican as his sibling, had taken military service in the United Netherlands and was now colonel of the English regiment there. By the spring of 1647, Lucy had become his mistress and his prestige must have been considerably enhanced by his being able to flaunt around the streets and salons of the Hague this fresh, lovely creature as his latest status symbol.

Charles met Lucy as soon as he arrived in Holland – and fell head over heels in love with her. She had that kind of obvious, up-front sexuality that today would be exploited by girly magazines. A French observer wrote later that from the moment of their meeting Charles 'was so charmed and ravished and enamoured that in the misfortunes which ran through the first years of his reign he knew no other sweetness or joy than to love her and be loved by her', and she goes on to point out how proud the young prince was to have made such a stunning conquest to parade around the court of Orange.[60] This was for him a grand passion and, as such, it defies attempts at analysis. However, we may suggest that the prince was ripe for his first love. The imminence of real action and the escape from his mother put him into a state of rare excitement and optimism. He may well have relished the challenge of winning the mistress of one of his father's enemies. How he managed to achieve this we can only conjecture. Was his sister instrumental in warning off Robert Sidney? Perhaps. However it happened, Charles and Lucy were together for only a few days before he sailed off with his fleet. That in itself may have added urgency to the prince's courtship. That it was completely successful is evidenced by the fact that, before he and his ships disappeared over the western horizon on 17 July, Lucy was pregnant. This was to set the pattern for the couple's romance. Charles was absent for about half of their three-year relationship.

In September the prince returned from his ineffectual naval expedition. Nothing had been gained by a campaign that had promised so much. The various land engagements had all ended disastrously for the royalist cause and, what was most damaging to Charles and his hopes, trust between the king and the radical leaders of the army had completely broken down. For Cromwell and his colleagues the prisoner in Carisbrooke who had provoked a second round of military conflict and now kept parliamentary commissioners tied up in labyrinthine negotiations was a 'man of blood' who must be brought to account for his crimes against his people.

There was a bitter-sweetness about Charles' exile throughout the autumn and winter of 1648–9. He alarmed his host and hostess by succumbing to smallpox but made a complete recovery and was able to enjoy family life for the first time since the flight from London. He was lodged in the stadtholder's palace where he had the company not only of his sister and brother but also of his aunt and a clutch of cousins. Elizabeth of Bohemia knew all about the hand-to-mouth existence of dispossessed royals. For almost thirty years, since her husband's deposition by the emperor, this sister of Charles I and her large family had been mendicants around the courts of Europe, eventually being granted asylum by the hospitable House of Orange. Now Elizabeth, who had learned to bear cheerfully her griefs and misfortunes, was at the Hague for Christmas, together with her son, Prince Rupert and three of her daughters. The youngest, Sophia, was Charles' exact contemporary. She was lively and witty and Charles found her very attractive. There was some talk of marriage, particularly encouraged by the ex-queen's devoted servant and virtual financial mainstay, the Earl of Craven, but it came to nothing. Politically there was no advantage to be gained from the union of two Stuart paupers and, in any case, Charles was still under the spell of the vivacious Lucy.* He might flirt with his cousin but his passion for his mistress was of an altogether different kind and was enhanced by the fact that she was about to introduce him to the new experience of fatherhood. Christmas 1648, then, with its succession of feasts, dances, plays and hunting expeditions, was a time of gaiety in which members of the Stuart family circle were able to revive at least something of the good old days.

---

*Sophia twice missed out on the British Crown. In 1701 she was proclaimed the heir of Queen Anne but died two months before the queen.

But there could be no avoiding the shadow which overhung the festivities. The latest news from England was that the king was to be put on trial for treason against his people. Charles now acted with unprecedented energy. For the first time he assumed command of his own destiny and his father's cause. Freed from his mother's domination, with Hyde back at his side and enjoying his brother-in-law's warm support, Charles presided over his own council and energetically addressed all the important matters that had to be discussed. He made personal but fruitless appeals for support to the States-General and to Mazarin. He raised money to pay the wages of his sailors and put fresh heart into them with a personal address. He sent passionate entreaties to the leaders of the army and parliament begging for his father's release. As the news became increasingly grim, he took it upon himself to reject the king's explicit instructions that no concessions should be made to save his life which would weaken the monarchy or prevent his heir eventually enjoying fully his undoubted rights. The prince provided his enemies with a sheet of parchment, blank except for his seal and signature upon which the victors were invited to write whatever terms they wished and he offered his own person as surety for the fulfilment of any obligation to the country's new rulers. It was a desperate, impulsive, politically ill-advised gesture but it was the action of a dutiful son who was only just coming to terms with the hideous possibility of what might actually happen to his father.

On 4 February, William of Orange was sailing his yacht when he was hailed by an incoming fishing boat with the sensational news that the King of England had been executed in public like a common felon. The Dutch prince hurried ashore to break the appalling tidings to his wife. Mary was devastated, both because of her own loss and because of the sad responsibility of conveying the information to her brothers. Unable to face Charles herself, she entrusted the task to Dr Stephen Goffe, his chaplain. The clergyman went to Charles' chamber, made obeisance and began his doleful message with the words, 'Your Majesty . . .'

It is worth making a slight digression at this point to indicate how the seventeenth-century crisis could cruelly split families. Stephen Goffe was an ardent royalist who had served the king as a secret agent during his captivity and who later converted to Rome. His brother, William Goffe, was an equally enthusiastic parliament man. He commanded a regiment in the New Model Army and was one of the judges who signed the warrant for the king's execution. After the Restoration he fled to America and lived the rest of his life as a member of one of the Puritan communities. One wonders how Stephen may later have reacted to the irony that his brother was in part responsible for the grim tidings that he was charged with conveying to the dead sovereign's son.

Hyde recalled Charles' reaction in a few words: 'the barbarous stroke so surprised him that he was in all the confusion imaginable and all about him were almost bereft of their understanding'.[61] It is the kind of conventional comment we would expect from a dedicated royal servant. There can be no doubt that Charles, no less than the other family members in exile, experienced a profound shock. Yet what is intriguing is the paucity of contemporary evidence about Charles' reaction. Court gossips had virtually nothing to say about his private grief or his public expression of that grief. The reason is obvious: there was little to report. Beyond the formalities of mourning Charles made no great show of filial devotion. It was as though he had closed a door both quietly and firmly on the past. In that past he had not seen eye to eye with his father nor made any attempt to model himself on him. Since his departure from Oxford he had listened to a great deal of criticism about the king's conduct of the war – from his mother, from Prince Rupert, from royalist generals and from the rank and file in the shires. It would be difficult for him not to come to the conclusion that his father was, in large measure, the author of his own misfortunes. And if his own, then, by extension, the misfortunes of his family. As long as the king lived his son did all in his power to rescue him and his cause. But once the king was dead, then survival and living for the present became the only realities. He was released from the need to respond to, or at least respect, parental admonitions to piety, principle, moral behaviour and keeping good faith with all men.

Thus, after he had recovered from the initial impact, Charles spent little time brooding over fond memories of his father or nursing thoughts of revenge against his 'murderers'. Within months the Duke of Buckingham was admitted to the position of royal favourite and the new king's more staid advisers were appalled at the scornful mimicry of Charles I that he was allowed to display quite openly. At the Restoration it was assumed and expected by many that the 'royal martyr's' remains would be brought from their unmarked grave at Windsor and ceremonially enshrined in Henry VII's Chapel at Westminster. Charles did, indeed, bow to royalist sentiment by promising to honour his father's bones in this way but he did nothing and the idea was allowed quietly to drop. As to exacting vengeance on all those responsible for the late king's death, Charles displayed little taste for it. Some of the regicides and a handful of others most closely associated with the tragedy of 1649 suffered the rigours of the law but there was no witch-hunt. Reconciliation was Charles' watchword.

But this apparent coolness towards his father's memory was not a unique phenomenon. Rather it was symptomatic of a dramatic character change. Richard Ollard describes it thus:

In the years 1649–51 most of the tenderness perceived by early students of the King's character hardened. Spontaneity and warmth of heart were replaced by an indifferent agreeableness that sought only the reflection of itself. The King contracted into a colder, cannier figure though his manner remained deceptively open.[62]

The suddenness of Charles' accession signposted another – and the sharpest – turning point in his moral and psychological development. Untrained, lacking familiarity with the processes of government, driven from his own country and for long the recipient of furiously competing counsels, now, at the abrupt fall of an axe, this eighteen-year-old young man was king. That meant that he was alone. No longer was he one among a number of agents fighting the forces of anarchy and fanaticism. If his new position was to have any reality he had to put emotional distance between himself and his servants. He had to establish his own style of kingship and it would be very different to the style associated with his father or the one urged by his mother. Charles knew that he had to assert his authority, to throw off all restraints and to make clear to those around him that he was now his own man. And all this despite the humiliating reality that he was a penniless refugee, wearing worn-out shoes and living off the charity of relatives and devoted fellow exiles. All this was a burden the pretend king lacked the maturity to carry and inexorably it forced out most of his finer feelings.

On 9 April Charles' first son was born. He came into the world at Rotterdam in the house of Lucy's Uncle Gosfright, was christened James and bore his mother's assumed surname of Barlow (the first of many names he would bear during his troubled life). Charles was delighted and from the very beginning was extremely fond of the boy. The Duke of Monmouth, as he later became, was one of the few people who received from Charles genuine affection that was not the product of self-interest or lust. The boy was left with a nurse and Lucy returned to the arms of her grateful lover. The significance of recent events cannot have been lost on her. Her bedfellow was now a king and her son, potentially at least, was heir to his throne. Did she try to exploit her position? Did she require marriage or was she content with whatever perks might accrue from being Charles' mistress?

Thirty years later these questions were being posed in all seriousness and the answers were fraught with constitutional significance. At that time the king had a childless marriage and the Duke of Monmouth was being championed as an impeccably Protestant successor in contrast with Charles' Catholic brother. Several stories were current of a clandestine marriage between the king and Lucy Walter. Witnesses 'remembered' details of the secret nuptials and documentary 'proofs' were set forth in support of Monmouth's claim. Conspiracy theories have abounded ever since, relating to the destruction of evidence and the silencing of informants. All the versions of the supposed ceremony cannot be true and none may be.

The account which seems to have most substance and which was certainly the longest-running rumour concerns a certain 'black box'. It is founded upon the assertion that Charles and Lucy were joined in wedlock by Dr John Cosin, chaplain to the Protestant members of Henrietta Maria's court some time in 1648 or 1649. This staunch Laudian Anglican and royalist is supposed to have retained the wedding certificate for fear of its falling into the wrong hands, Lucy's reputation being such that it might have proved an embarrassment to her husband in his claim to the throne. Subsequently, Cosin attended Lucy on her deathbed and heard her last confession, which, so the story has it, included intimate details of her relationship with Charles. After the Restoration Cosin was appointed Prince-Bishop of Durham, in which office he died in 1672. He had consigned all the sensitive documents to what became known as *the* black box and willed it to his son-in-law, Sir Gilbert Gerard. He, in turn, passed it to the Duke of Monmouth's descendants, the Dukes of Buccleuch. Unaccountably, the container disappeared among the family muniments until the 1870s. Then, Walter Francis, the fifth duke, rediscovered it and examined its contents. Buccleuch was a privy councillor and very close to Queen Victoria. The existence of a document purporting to give him and his heirs a prior claim to the British Crown appalled him and he did what he believed any loyal subject ought to do: he threw the marriage certificate into the fire. Thus the core version of the story (variants exist which differ in detail).

It is one of those intriguing tales, all the more fascinating for its implications, but does it have any contemporary support? The major obstacle to credibility was provided by Charles himself. In 1679 he made no fewer than three public declarations to the effect that he had never had any wife other than Queen Catherine. That would be enough to settle the matter were it not for the fact that Charles, never a shining example of transparent honesty, was at the time determined to secure the succession for his brother. The fact that he had to go to such extraordinary lengths to scotch the rumour indicates how widespread it was. Among those prepared to challenge the official version of events were Mr and Mrs Gosfright, Dr Cosin's steward and Edward Prodgers, a groom of the bedchamber, all of whom claimed to know that a secret ceremony had taken place. And if we go further back, to the time of the supposed contract, we can find at least circumstantial evidence. Marchamont Nedham, editor of the parliamentary weekly newsbook, *Mercurius Politicus*, informed his readers that Lucy was parading herself at the Hague as the king's mistress or wife. At the opposite end of the political spectrum, the Stuart family, Charles' inamorata was openly received by both Mary and Henrietta Maria, which might not have been the case if they had regarded her as a mere strumpet. However, it is also true that Charles' mother had by no means abated her matchmaking activities and was still casting around for a suitable princess for her son. Meanwhile, the mother of the 'bride' insisted that her daughter was married to the king but we might conclude that she would, wouldn't she?

What seems most clearly to give the lie to any formal contract between the lovers is their subsequent behaviour. Neither regarded their sexual relationship as exclusive. Furthermore, when Lucy was desperately trying to regain Charles' affection she did not insist on her rights as his wife. The most obvious understanding of the situation is that Lucy Walter regarded herself and was regarded as a courtesan, a word coming increasingly into fashion and one which, according to a contemporary cleric, was 'the most honest synonym that is given to a whore [and which] had his original from the court of Rome'.[63]

The possibility that the Hanoverians and their successors might be usurpers of the throne from the true Stuart bloodline is no more than a historical curiosity. What is significant is what Charles II's first love affair tells us about his character. He had turned his back on his father's moral earnestness and commitment to chastity and the sacredness of marriage and accepted the easygoing Catholic ethics of the French court. This was precisely what Hyde, knowing his charge's weaknesses, had feared. However, it was the king's Protestant sister as well as his Catholic mother who fully accepted Lucy as his unofficial consort.

Not that Charles much cared whether they approved or disapproved. He was intent on establishing his independence. To that end he despatched Hyde on a mission to Madrid and sent other senior advisers to various European courts to canvass support. By the summer of 1649 he had outstayed his welcome in the United Provinces. His sister and brother-in-law wanted him to stay but the States-General found his presence an increasing embarrassment. They were anxious to regularise their relationship with the new regime in England and when an envoy from London was assassinated by royalist agents the time had come to request the king's departure. With as much dignity as he could muster, Charles, accompanied by Lucy, made his way through the Spanish Netherlands into France, being honourably received and lavishly entertained by the Habsburg officials who met him along the route. At Saint-Germain he was reunited with his mother, who had suffered much since their last meeting. Not only had she been devastated by her husband's death, but she had experienced great privations at the height of the Fronde. The French king and his court had fled Paris and Henrietta Maria had been reduced to considerable poverty. At one stage she had had to rely on the charity of the leaders of the insurrection who had taken pity on her and provided wood for her fire and food for her table. Her spirit, however, was far from extinguished and she tried to take control of her son's policy making.

This Charles now warmly resisted, as Hyde, not, one imagines, without some relish, noted:

He made no apologies to her; nor any professions of resigning himself up to her advice. On the contrary, upon some expostulations, he had told her plainly that he would always perform his duty towards her with great affection and exactness, but that in his business he would obey his own reason and judgement, and did as good as desire her not to trouble herself in his affairs: and finding her passions strong, he frequently retired with some abruptness, and seemed not to desire to be so much in her company as she expected . . .[64]

But Charles' wavering resolution was no match for his mother's stubbornness. His insistence that he would follow entirely his own counsels was more than a little ingenuous. If he dispensed with older advisers whose recommendations he found boring it was to replace them with younger companions and men more to his taste. A colleague reported to Hyde lamenting the quality of the king's intimate circle: 'Sir John Berkeley hath no greater proportion of religion than a creature of Lord Jermyn's is obliged to have . . . Mr Long will serve all turns and says honour and conscience are bugbears.'[65] Sir Robert Long was a member of Henrietta Maria's entourage who had recently transferred to the king's service as a member of his privy council. He was in charge of Charles' finances, a position which he turned to his advantage, and was later dismissed. (As so often with disgraced servants of Charles II, he was eventually restored to favour.) We have already noted Buckingham's reappearance in the new king's suite.

Another familiar face that showed itself as soon as the mantle of monarchy settled on his old master's shoulders was Thomas Elliott. He had come to the Hague with his wife (the daughter of Edmund and Christabella Wyndham) and rapidly resumed his influence over Charles.

He was never from the person of the king and always whispering in his ear . . . and when he had a mind that the king should think well or ill of any man, he told him that he was much beloved by or very odious to all his party in England.[66]

Elliott poisoned Charles' mind against some of his older and wiser councillors and tried to insinuate his father-in-law into the office of secretary of state. The king would have appointed the grasping Sir Edmund Wyndham had not the venerable councillor Francis Cottington used humour to expose the unwisdom of such a move. He suggested that Charles should also elevate one of his falconers to the post of royal chaplain. The man was a very honest fellow, Cottington pointed out. 'That does not qualify him to hold an ecclesiastical office,' the king objected. 'No more does it qualify Wyndham for the responsibilities of secretary,' Cottington replied. Everyone laughed and no more was heard of Sir Edmund's candidature.

A name that was to be closely associated with the court of Charles II for the next thirty years now enters the story. Henry, Lord Wilmot (later first Earl of Rochester) was a turbulent, brave man of fixed opinions and resolute action. Hyde called him 'a man of a haughty and ambitious nature, of a pleasant wit and an ill understanding,'[67] a biased judgement arising from the fact that Wilmot was one of the more vociferous army leaders who consistently opposed the old king's civilian advisers. He was one of the more effective royalist generals and responsible for some of his side's few outstanding victories. Though utterly loyal, he had always been critical of Charles I's policies and had been among those who advocated rallying the royalists around the Prince of Wales, as the best means of pulling the rug from beneath the parliamentary rebels. As an officer who 'worked hard and played hard' Wilmot was popular with his men, and for much the same reason the new king liked him. He lost no time in attaching himself to Charles II's entourage in 1649, becoming a gentleman of the bedchamber and one of the king's closest intimates.

Yet it was not just a handful of hangers-on covering their own inadequacies with cynical mockery who set the tone of the youthful king's entourage. They constituted but the sparkling summit of a human mountain of displaced and footloose soldiers, penniless adventurers and social riff-raff who clustered round the king wherever he happened to be. These were men and women who for one reason or another could not or would not return to their native land: royalist officers with a price on their heads; sons estranged from their fathers; landless gentlemen whose estates had been sequestered; wild and irreligious spirits who had no taste for submitting to the rule of the saints; female camp followers who, either by inclination or necessity, had become the playthings of the rootless soldiery; and the motley of social misfits who, in any age, cannot accommodate themselves to the prevailing mores. This multitude may – perhaps surprisingly – be compared to that other contemporary exodus, the steady stream of men and women making their way to the New World. Both groups had shaken off the dust from their feet against the prevailing culture. Both looked to a better future when the sacrifices they had made would receive divine or royal reward. Both took 'Freedom' as their standard.

Freedom for many of Charles' adherents meant absence of moral and social restraint. They were attracted to the person of a young king whose face was set against the sombre Puritan regime being established in England. They regarded as glamorous a lifestyle of swagger, panache and pleasure seeking. It would have been difficult for Charles not to have allowed himself to become the icon worshipped by this liberated 'band of brothers', and Charles rarely applied himself to what was difficult.

However, there was still a kingdom to be re-won and that for the next two years did take up the greater part of his attention. As usual, there were conflicting ideas put forward as to how to go about this. No aid was forthcoming from the continent and parliament controlled the Channel.

That narrowed the options to three: work patiently to build up opposition within England; invade from Ireland; invade from Scotland. Neither the king nor his 'death-or-glory' young companions were interested in the political alternative and the situation in Ireland slipped from the grasp of Charles' supporters. Therefore negotiations had to be opened with those Scottish Presbyterians who had proved so unreliable to the king's father. But, while supping with the devil, Charles was also in league with the angels – in this instance a small multi-national force assembled by the headstrong Montrose, which landed in Sutherland in an attempt to seize the initiative in favour of a monarchical regime unencumbered by sectarian control. This double-dealing might have had the appearance of clever politics but the scheme collapsed completely when Montrose's little army was completely routed and the marquis brought to Edinburgh for public execution. The Covenanters were thenceforth masters of the situation and yet another brave man had been sacrificed on the altar of Stuart incompetence.

Charles' little court had, meanwhile, been meandering to and fro. Leaving France, where it was no more welcome than in the Low Countries, it resorted once more to Jersey, the last vestige of royalist territory. Then, early in 1650, the king was back again in Breda for his talks with the Scottish negotiators. Everywhere the king went he was accompanied by Lucy Walter. But in what capacity – apart from the obvious one? Was she, in any real sense, a helpmeet, someone who supported him as he faced up to the pressures and frustrations of his hand-to-mouth existence? Did she have any political identity? Most of Charles' life had been lived in close proximity to influential royal consorts who, either from the wings or from centre stage, had helped to shape the course of events. Henrietta Maria had discussed national affairs with her husband and steeled him to stand firm against all opposition in the 1630s. She had influenced the appointment of royal officers and increasingly sought to dominate policy. Princess Mary was much more than a cipher in the government of the Netherlands. At only a slight remove were those powerful women, Marie de Medici and Anne of Austria, the latter even now fighting a spirited, and eventually successful, battle against the leaders of the Fronde. Such were the patterns of royal lovers with which Charles was familiar. He was always attracted to strong-minded women and several of his later companions used their positions to exert political influence.

Spirited, adventurous and vivacious as Lucy was, she did not come into this category. She lacked the education, training, background and, probably, the intelligence to interest herself in the mysteries of her lover's attempts to turn king *de jure* into king *de facto*. Even if Lucy had any pretensions to be a Messalina, she lacked the opportunity. Ivy can only suck life from a flourishing tree and the tree of English monarchy was at this time a very insecure sapling. There was little she could expect to gain in terms of wealth, power and social status. She was not perceived as a gatekeeper, providing or denying access to the king, so she did not attract supporters who wanted to keep her in place for their own ends. As for Charles, his experience with his mother and his observation of how the behaviour of Anne and Mazarin seemed to be propelling France towards that same chaos into which the British kingdoms had fallen can only have warned him against the pretensions of *femmes formidables*. In 1649–50 the future for the young lovers was uncertain and the present unstable – but exciting. They lived for the moment in the midst of an itinerant court of adventurers who flouted convention and behaved as flamboyantly as their circumstances allowed, in very conscious contradistinction to the 'hypocritical dullards' who held sway across the Channel.

Sexual licence was an inevitable part of their liberated code and Charles subscribed to it. Though no Adonis, the king was a *king* and could have the pick of court beauties. If his inability to reward sexual favours generously was a drawback, it was, in part, compensated for by his pitiable state. Many a tender heart was touched by his misfortunes. We do not know how many brief affairs he had in these months but one of them resulted in his second bastard. During his brief visit to Paris he made the acquaintance of Elizabeth Boyle, wife of Viscount Shannon. This lady, one of Henrietta Maria's attendants, was some eight years older than the king and a member of the Killigrew family, whose court connections went back several generations. Her stepfather, Sir Thomas Stafford, was Henrietta Maria's gentleman usher and of her mother it was said, 'she was a cunning old woman who had been herself too much and was too long versed in amours'.[68] It seems to have been a case of like mother, like daughter. Betty Killigrew was yet another of the strong-minded women who so much appealed to Charles. Having gained a place at the Orange court, in 1647 she declined to return to the obscurity of her husband's Irish estate, preferring the gaiety and sexual freedom of a European capital. She perhaps owed to her brother her introduction or re-introduction to Charles, for it was about the same time that Thomas Killigrew joined the Prince of Wales' court in exile. This much-travelled, ardently royalist rakehell had been a page to Charles I and emerged during the 1630s as one of London's leading writers of bawdy plays. One of them, *The Parson's Wedding* ('a comedy whose coarseness is not redeemed by any notable wit or humour' – *Oxford Companion to English Literature*), was performed repeatedly between 1637 and the closing of the theatres. Charles enjoyed Killigrew's ribald conversation and the tales of his many sexual conquests. In 1651 he sent the dramatist as his representative to the doge's court at Venice, but within a year he was obliged to recall his agent amidst clamorous complaints of grotesque debaucheries. Killigrew was to reappear as one of the leading masters of the Restoration theatre. Meanwhile, his sister had removed to Paris where, in 1650, she gave birth to a baby girl, opportunistically christened Charlotte Jemima Henrietta Maria.

The king's philandering implied no loss of affection for Lucy or their son. 'Mrs Barlow' was still Charles' first great passion; she enjoyed his continued attention and, as Hyde observed, 'lived for some years in the king's sight'. In the early summer of 1650 the king was preparing for his imminent departure for Scotland. Lucy could not accompany him and there was no question of his abandoning her. He obtained a place for her at his mother's court and, apparently, provided her with a protector in the shape of one of his close companions, Theobald, Viscount Taaffe, a colourful member of Charles' free-living band of brothers. Taaffe was an ebullient Anglo-Irish peer who had fought with the Catholic rebels against their parliamentary masters but whose loyalty had been called in question. He came to Charles by way of Henrietta Maria, and Charles, as ever weighing personality more heavily than character, made him, in the words of one observer, his 'great chamberlain, valet de chambre, clerk of the kitchen, cup bearer and all'.

His loved ones thus provided for, King Charles II set forth on what he would always speak of thereafter as his great adventure.

CHAPTER 4

The Great Adventure

In later life Charles II became something of a bore on the subject of his military campaign of 1650–51 and his subsequent escape from England. Whenever he had the chance he regaled company with anecdotes about the dreadful behaviour of his Scottish hosts, the reasons for his lost battles and his hairsbreadth deliverances from enemy patrols. The fact that he had been able to cock a snook at the regime that had put a price on his head enabled him to look back on his kingdom's rejection of him as some kind of victory. The reality was that he tried his hand at political negotiation and military leadership and, not entirely because of his own shortcomings, he failed.

What was important for his own development – and therefore the development of British monarchy – was that he once again came into close contact with ordinary men and women to whom he owed his safety and, probably, his life. Unlike any monarch before him, Charles possessed the common touch. The only possible exception was Elizabeth, who also came to the throne after a period of personal insecurity and suffering during which she had come to appreciate the loyalty of servants who aided her with little prospect of reward. But her much publicised love for her people was, in some measure, a carefully developed political ploy. She understood the needs of the commonalty and was careful to identify with them in her public utterances. But such moving set pieces were definitely *de haut en bas*. She developed, or allowed her councillors to develop, around her the Gloriana aura. The concept of being at one with her people – married to them – and at the same time an object of distant adoration was unique and never to be repeated. Charles absorbed the common idiom into himself and was happy in the company of those without money or power. He seldom stood on ceremony and had no desire to make his court a rarefied domain set somewhere between earth and heaven, after the pattern of his father's. If there was any political calculation behind all this it was that he believed his people would warm to him if they felt he was one of them. Elizabeth never allowed familiarity to breed contempt. The same could not be said of Charles.

The terms offered by the Scots to Charles at Breda were clear, uncompromising and humiliating: he would be recognised as King of Scotland if he accepted Presbyterian church order, rejected the aid of Irish Catholics and all political and religious moderates and signed the Covenant to this effect. The extremists, led by Archibald Campbell, Marquis of Argyll, wanted to glue the Crown firmly to their own cause, against other Scottish factions, against England and against all non-Calvinist Europe. In return they were prepared to make no substantial concessions, not even pledging their assistance in helping Charles recover his English throne. Argyll hoped to enhance his personal position and bind the king even more tightly to his cause by marrying his own daughter to Charles.

The more staid royal councillors advised strongly against this total capitulation. Even Henrietta Maria realised that her son was contemplating too high a price for his return to real power. But for Charles and the young bloods who, for reasons of principle and personal advancement, were eager for the king's restoration this was the only game in town. The choice lay between accepting the role of puppet king at the hands of a Scottish aristocratic faction or continuing a shadow existence living on the charity of foreign princes and wealthy royalist exiles. The one ace that Charles had in his very poor hand was that, however reluctant Argyll and his friends might be to go to war with the neighbouring Protestant state, recognising the Stuart claim would lead inevitably to conflict.

The king may have thought that much of what he had signed up to was, if not mere formality, at least something from whose rigours time and opportunism would deliver him. His hosts were quick to disabuse him of any such hope. The sombre Presbyterian clergy and their allies were determined that Charles should live up to the solemn promises he had made. They intended that he should be a beacon of righteousness, a leader converted from his earlier licentious ways to blaze forth as a shining protector of the true faith. It was an attitude the king's father would have understood even if he rejected the theology behind it. The Covenanters were fully aware of the mammoth task before them and so, from the moment in mid-June that Charles arrived in Scotland, they undertook his education and reformation. They debarred all his frivolous companions except Buckingham (a strange concession) from waiting upon him and carefully monitored his activities.

> They placed other servants of all conditions about the king but principally relied upon their clergy, who were in such a continual attendance about him that he was never free from their importunities, under pretence of instructing him in religion: and so they obliged him to their constant hours of their long prayers and made him observe the Sundays with more rigour than the Jews accustomed to do; and reprehended him very sharply if he smiled on those days and if his looks

and gestures did not please them, whilst all their prayers and sermons, at which he was compelled to be present, were libels and bitter invectives against all the actions of his father, the idolatry of his mother and his own malignity.[69]

To all outward appearances Charles had the trappings of kingship. He was well attended. He dined in state. He was provided with good horses for travelling and hunting. 'The king's condition seemed wonderfully advanced and his being possessed of a kingdom without a rival, in which there was no appearance of an enemy, looked like an earnest for the recovery of the other two.'[70] The inner reality was that Charles not only presided over a court devoid of gaiety but that he also lacked any political power. The parliament in Edinburgh took all the important decisions and did not even trouble to inform him of their agenda. He was, to all intents and purposes, a prisoner. The result was to cast him into an uncharacteristic melancholy. He was permitted no gambling and no dancing. He was obliged to be agreeable to his hosts and also diplomatically to stall over the issue of his possible marriage to Lady Anne Campbell. But what he found hardest to bear, as he afterwards affirmed, was the absence of female company. Months of enforced celibacy imposed an enormous strain on a red-blooded male in his sexual prime who had but recently enjoyed the ministrations of a delectable mistress and been developing his own venereal techniques in the company of emotionally immature roistering companions who regarded wenching as normal behaviour, in a society which was free and easy. No wonder that, in October 1650, he made an abortive attempt to escape from his gilded confinement at Perth. He managed to put a mere forty miles between himself and his 'hosts' before being tracked down in a wretched hovel. The effort was spirited but it only reinforced the unwelcome fact that no subjects were ready to rush to his aid in defiance of the Covenanter leaders.

The real angel of his deliverance was his family's arch-enemy, Oliver Cromwell. Fresh from the subjugation of Ireland, the general had been sent north at the end of the summer to face the new threat. Of all his campaigns this was the one he embarked upon most unwillingly. He loathed the thought of fighting fellow Protestant zealots and tried all the arts of diplomacy and persuasion to avoid a bloody outcome. His plea to the bigoted kirk leaders has become his most oft-quoted statement: 'I beseech you in the bowels of Christ, think it possible you may be mistaken.'[71] But such detached self-analysis was beyond the Covenanter leaders and their obduracy paved the way for what many claim to be Cromwell's greatest tactical victory. Exhausted by long marches over a wasted country, his force had fallen back on Dunbar where they were confronted by an army twice the size of their own. David Leslie, the Scottish commander, had expected the English to fight a defensive action while trying to get as many of their men as possible away by ship but, before dawn on 3 September, Cromwell had launched a surprise frontal attack on the besiegers. The Scots were routed and 10,000 were taken prisoner.

In the ensuing atmosphere of confusion and mutual recrimination the unity of Charles' hosts disintegrated and he was, for the first time, able to take his place as one of the leading players in the game. He set himself to prise Argyll, royalists and religious moderates away from the extremist kirk party and form an army under his own leadership which would cross the border and advance on London, being swelled as it went by bands of his English supporters. He would be further assisted by troops sent over by his brother-in-law. Such was the plan. It was flawed from the start. On 6 November 1650, the twenty-four-year-old William of Orange died of smallpox. His widow was immediately engulfed in acrimonious debate with the States-General about the regency of her infant son. No help would be forthcoming from that quarter. Recruitment in the Highlands went quite well, but while Charles could find many clansmen ready to support the establishment of a strong Scottish monarchy, discovering any who were prepared to invade England was another matter altogether. Argyll's support was based on self-interest. Charles managed to string him along by sending an emissary to Paris to consult with his mother over the proposed marriage but when the marquis realised that nothing was likely to come of this and that the king only wanted his backing for a campaign in England he withdrew his support.

As Charles went about during the first half of 1651 to assemble a motley army and put heart in them he seemed to be in his element. He had broken out of the prison house of Calvinist righteousness. He had turned his back upon canting pietists and was back in the world of men of action. He rode before his troops on a fine horse, wearing a buff jerkin proudly displaying the Garter insignia as his father had done. In several places the local populace turned out to cheer him enthusiastically. It was true that Cromwell held Edinburgh and the surrounding Lowlands but he was still reluctant to resort to a pitched battle and, in any case, had been seriously ill throughout much of the winter. The king had the encouragement of being joined by a few detachments of English royalists and news reached him of landowners south of the border who were ready to support him. There was much to encourage him but he was sufficiently canny by now not to be carried away by brave displays of loyalty. About the Scots he wrote, 'the truth is, they seek themselves and their own interests too much to be a solid aid, or to be totally relied upon'.[72] The royal host did not swell as much as he had hoped. Nor was he universally popular. While brave and adventurous spirits rallied to his standard, inspired by pipe and drum and by his regal person, the more religious citizenry could not bring themselves to give wholehearted support to a man whose morals were not above reproach and who was known to consort with Catholics. There was more than one alarming report of plots to hand the king over to his enemies. Charles might conclude, as a result of his experiences of the sober kirkmen, that 'Presbyterianism is not for gentlemen', but the earnest Calvinists just as openly believed that Charles Stuart was no Christian king.

It was partly due to divisions among the king's generals that his army made no definite move before midsummer. This allowed a recovered Cromwell to grasp the initiative. At the beginning of July he crossed the Firth of Forth, came between the contingents commanded by Charles and Leslie and moved on Perth, where Charles had his headquarters. The king rode out of the town the day before Cromwell entered it and joined up with his general. Leslie, a veteran of the Civil Wars who had earlier served under the great Gustavus Adolphus, now counselled facing the English in battle on ground of the king's choosing. Charles ignored this advice. He saw, or thought he saw, a now-or-never opportunity to strike into England. He would head southwards, outrun Cromwell and link up with his expected English reinforcements. Mournfully, David Leslie yielded to the king's orders.

As soon as the army crossed the Esk, Charles was in a Catch-22 situation. Without the Presbyterian Scots, the invasion would not have been possible. With them, it could not succeed. When they were some days into the march, Charles came alongside his commander, asking why, riding at the head of such an impressive body of men, he looked so glum. Leslie replied in the king's ear that 'he well knew that [the] army, how well soever it looked, would not fight'.[73] It was true enough: with every mile away from their homeland the Scots became more restless. The detachments of eager English royalists did not materialise. The noblemen and gentlemen of the northern shires resented Charles' taking of the Covenant and had no intention of placing themselves under the command of a Scottish general. The king's army was harried repeatedly by parliamentary forces and had to abandon the plan of a direct march on London. As if all this were not bad enough, Charles' officers were afflicted by that disease which seemed to infect all royalist military endeavours: bitter rivalry. At one stage Buckingham pointed out to the king that the English captains resented taking orders from Leslie and that, therefore, Charles should appoint Buckingham himself to replace the Scottish general. To his credit, Charles did not give in to his favourite's demand. At first he tried to shrug off the suggestion but when the duke pressed him further Charles told him straight that he was too young and inexperienced for such a responsibility. Buckingham sulked for days.

In two weeks of rapid marches the royal army made its way down the western side of the country, arriving, weary and dispirited, in Worcester on 22 August 1651. It was a good place to recoup and to take up a defensive stance. It had been the royalist headquarters in the West from

1642 to 1646 and had capitulated only after a two-month siege. Yet the defenders must have understood before many days had passed that their position was desperate. Attempts at recruitment had produced disappointing results and Charles' garrison numbered no more than 13–14,000 men. In a few brief skirmishes around the country bands of royalists had been easily routed and Cromwell had the leisure to assemble a besieging force of 30,000 with which to invest the city. However unpopular republican government might be with many Englishmen, few were sufficiently motivated to take up arms against it. They had had their fill of civil war and desired only that their menfolk would now be free to stay at home, tend their fields and shops and care for their families.

The main government assault came on 3 September, the anniversary of the battle of Dunbar. A two-pronged attack from the south-west and south-east in the late afternoon forced the front-line royal forces back within the walls but there was no immediate, unspirited capitulation. Watching from the cathedral tower and seeing that Cromwell had weakened his own force to go to the aid of Colonel Charles Fleetwood, forcing his way across the Teme, the king ordered an attack on the main government lines. But this successful manoeuvre only delayed the inevitable. Even as enemy troops fought their way up to the city gates in the gathering gloom of evening, Charles refused to concede. Contemporary accounts acknowledge his personal courage and commitment:

> Certainly a braver prince never lived, having in the day of the fight hazarded his person much more than any officer of his army, riding from regiment to regiment, and leading them on upon service with all the encouragements (calling every officer by his name) which the example and exhortation of a magnanimous general could afford.[74]

Only when all the exits from the city except St Martin's Gate were in enemy hands did the king make his escape.

Throughout the next forty-two days he was on the run. The details of Charles' adventures during those days rapidly became the stuff of legend. What Hyde referred to as a 'miraculous deliverance in which there might be seen so many visible impressions of the immediate hand of God' was first blazoned in broadsheets and popular ballads. These fanciful accounts more than made up in dramatic incident what they lacked in accuracy. After the Restoration a Catholic lawyer, Thomas Blount, wrote an account but it was rejected by the king and subsequently disavowed by its author. Charles preferred to record his own version and dictated it to Samuel Pepys. This narrative remained in manuscript for over a century. The king, having left for posterity an accurate account of the events of 1651, did not sanction its publication. While he was prepared to bore the pants off his courtiers with his anecdotes, he declined to give them wider circulation. In the same way he abandoned earlier plans to establish an exclusive Order of the Royal Oak for those who had played a part in his deliverance. Gratitude and self-advertisement, it seems, gave way to prudence. The restored king deliberately discouraged displays of triumphalism which might have bestowed on party feeling an unwelcome longevity. This, however, did not prevent some of the people who had aided the king in his wanderings from going into print with their own stories. Hyde, who was usually so careful about his sources and had access to the king and other leading players in the drama of the great escape, notoriously got this part of his narrative very muddled. Eventually, it was left to Sir Walter Scott and the romanticists and antiquarians of the nineteenth century to create the fully rounded myth of a monarch, 'brought in contact, man to man, with the humblest of his subjects, in situations calculated to draw forth the good qualities, and show the undisguised feelings of both parties', and one who 'bears his part manfully amid the dangers and perplexities occasioned by his sojourn, and even sets the example of decision and presence of mind to his preservers'.[75]

The romance of Charles II's post-Worcester meanderings lay in their later recollection and recounting rather than their on-the-spot reality. Within the space of a few months the king had exchanged the humiliation of a supplicant, itinerant princeling for the joyless conditions imposed by religious bigots, followed by the sense of failure attendant upon an inglorious military campaign. Now, to fill the cup of his woes, he was obliged to skulk about England, with a £1,000 price on his head, fearing daily betrayal and totally dependent on subjects who risked their life for him and whom he was in no position to reward. Living on humble fare, dressed as a servant, sleeping in verminous beds and putting other people's lives at risk were not experiences he enjoyed.

With a handful of companions, Charles rode through the night into Shropshire where, the party having split up, he found temporary refuge with members of the Penderel family. These well-to-do Catholic yeomen rented a house at Boscobel which had been built by a recusant ancestor and contained several priest-holes. For four days the weary fugitive was concealed here, either curling his long limbs into the cramped secret compartments in the house or perched among the soaking foliage of the celebrated Boscobel oak. Here, he exchanged his own clothes for a woodsman's garb and had his hair cropped.

Despite all these precautions, it is unlikely that he could have long avoided capture by relying on his own wits and the native cunning of his humble hosts. He was a royal personage and had never been without advisers and attendants to oversee the details of his daily existence. He needed someone to plan an escape route and to put that plan into operation. The man who fulfilled this role was Henry Wilmot. He remained in the vicinity, seeking out safe lodgings for the king and trying to discover a means of conveying him to the coast where he might find a ship to carry him to the continent. But not for the proud Wilmot the discomforts of hiding-holes or the indignity of coarse artisan's clothes. He stayed with friends or put up at comfortable inns. He refused to wear a disguise and he was often to be seen riding with his falcon on his wrist. But he was active among his contacts in the area and it was he who arranged the longest leg of the king's escape route.

Somehow Charles had to be conveyed down the Severn to a point where he could be smuggled aboard a ship, but the river and bridges were closely watched so the journey would have to be made by road, past enemy garrisons and checkpoints. Wilmot confided his problem to a dedicated royalist, Colonel John Lane, who lived at Bentley Hall, near Wolverhampton. He had staying with him his unmarried sister, Jane, and she was in possession of a permit to travel to Abbot's Leigh, near Bristol, to visit her pregnant friend, Mrs Norton. Wilmot devised a plan which would cost him dear: the sacrifice of his own dignity. He would accompany Jane in the guise of her servant in order to find a captain prepared to undertake the risky business. In the event, Wilmot's *amour propre* was protected. A sudden crisis enforced a change of plan. Government hounds were on the king's scent and it would be unsafe for him to remain several days in the area waiting on Wilmot's negotiations. Thus, it was Charles who arrived under cover of darkness at Bentley Hall to be transformed into William Jackson, the Lanes' retainer. Before dawn he was supplied with appropriate raiment and given a crash course in how to comport himself as a servant. Then, he helped his 'mistress' on to her horse before himself mounting the saddle in front of her and setting off on the long journey to safety. The plan was as clever as it was bold. No one would expect a woman to expose herself to such danger nor the king to humiliate himself by dancing attendance on a woman.

The following week brought many alarums and excursions. Near Stratford the travellers encountered a troop of horse, and two of Jane's companions fearfully turned aside. But the lady and her man rode on as calmly as they could and attracted no attention. On an occasion when they were staying at the house of some friends of Jane, Charles was sitting with the servants in the kitchen. The cook asked him to wind the roasting jack, a request which flummoxed him completely. All he could think of to cover his ignorance was to claim that his poor family rarely enjoyed the luxury of meat and that when they did they never used a jack to turn the spit. When they arrived at Abbot's Leigh, one of the Norton servants recognised Charles because he had once been employed in the royal court. He had to be taken into the secret. In order to avoid further discovery William Jackson took to his bed, ostensibly suffering from a fever. But the most unpleasant shock was the one brought by Henry Wilmot, who had travelled by another route and spied out the situation at Bristol dock. He reported that the port was closely watched and that there was no chance of obtaining a berth for Charles, whatever disguise he might put on. It seemed that the journey had been in vain.

The plan was now to convey the king to some smaller haven on the south coast. For this new stage of the expedition more trustworthy friends would have to be found. Fortunately, there lived at Trent, near Sherborne, a member of a family that had served the Stuarts ardently in peace and war. Colonel Francis Wyndham was the brother of Sir Edmund Wyndham and Charles had complete faith in his loyalty. So it was decided that William Jackson and his mistress should ride to Trent to pay their respects. But now a sad – and inconvenient – occurrence threatened to throw a spanner in the works. Mrs Norton, that same night, suffered a miscarriage. How could Jane Lane possibly leave her seriously ill friend, who now needed her more than ever? But how could her servant make a sudden and unexplained departure without her? With government troops patrolling the area and spies everywhere, each day the king spent at Abbot's Leigh increased his danger. There had to be another drastic change of plan.

It seems to have been Charles himself who suggested a solution. Jane was to be seen to receive a message that her father was gravely ill and that she was needed urgently at home. She and her servant would then make an abrupt departure, apparently for the North but in reality for Trent. The proposal seems callous and self-interested. It is only partly excused by the knowledge that natal complications were extremely frequent in the seventeenth century. Among the higher orders of society 75 per cent of first marriages which came to an end within ten years did so because of the death of the wife, and most of those deaths were connected with childbirth. Everyone at Abbot's Leigh seems to have agreed that the king's safety was more important than the nursing of Mrs Norton back to health. Thus, on 16 September, Jane and her servant set out for Trent and arrived there the next day. Having been prepared by Wilmot for their surprise guest, the Wyndhams welcomed him and pledged themselves to his safety. And Jane made her way back to Bentley.

But her association with the king was by no means at an end. Within weeks it was the turn of Jane and her brother to adopt disguises and flee for their very lives. Rumours were running round the countryside about the king making his escape as a lady's manservant and Colonel Lane thought it prudent to get his sister away to safety before snooping government agents arrived to interrogate her. Had the Lanes been unmasked, they would have faced charges of high treason, with their appalling attendant penalty. Dressed as peasants the two of them walked all the way to the coast, were conveyed to the Isle of Wight and, in early December, obtained passage across the Channel from Yarmouth. They sent word to Paris of their arrival and immediately set out for the queen mother's court. Charles and Henrietta Maria hastened from the city to meet the Lanes on the road and to greet them with that warmth that was no more than their due. Jane and her brother thus swelled the ranks of dispossessed royalists who had given up everything for the cause they believed in and expected some recompense at the hands of the Stuart exiles. After a while John Lane thought it would be safe to return home where he was needed by his aged father. Unfortunately, he misjudged the persistence of England's new rulers. In 1655 the family at Bentley Hall were interrogated and both men were thrown into prison, though for how long we do not know. Thousands of men had risked their lives for the king and many had died on the field of battle or in captivity but few women had placed themselves in the same category by aiding the escape of the government's arch-enemy and thus provoking the wrath of the new regime. Charles recognised his obligation to the woman he called his 'life' and, as far as was in his power, he honoured it. Jane was fêted at the French court and then escorted to the Hague, where she entered the service of Princess Mary.

There, to all intents and purposes, the story of Charles Stuart and Jane Lane is generally considered to end. There exist only a few scraps of later correspondence and evidence of the king's generous remembrance of his rescuer and her family after the Restoration and chroniclers have been happy to take at face value the simple account of a loyal subject risking life and fortune for a king who, as soon as he was able, gratefully rewarded her. But is that all there was to it? Knowledge of Charles' character and the motivations of other individuals who clustered round him suggest that there may have been more to this relationship. There are also a couple of other facts which sit uneasily with the received version of events.

It would be fascinating to know what passed between Jane and her 'man' in those long, anxious hours on the road from Bentley to Trent. They faced a common danger and were in close physical proximity, Jane actually clinging to her companion as she rode behind him. Charles, who felt keenly his fifteen-month deprivation of female company, found himself in an emotionally charged situation with a spirited young woman who was obviously devoted to him. Jane, for her part, was alone with her king and actively involved in saving his life. What hopes, dreams, fantasies that might have awakened in her, especially if the two at some point became lovers. Leaving this possibility aside for the moment, we need to look more closely at the master/servant relationship and its implications in the mid-seventeenth century. Charles had to consent to being 'bossed about' by his 'mistress'. Whenever strangers were around Jane would have spoken to him curtly, given him orders and, possibly, let him feel the sharp edge of her tongue when he got things wrong. And Charles enjoyed the masquerade. He had always been surrounded by strong-minded women and he adored them. Submission to dominant females was a fixture of his psyche, to the increasing despair of his advisers over the years.

It was something that ran counter to the divine order of things for men to be under the power of women. The word 'mistress' has many nuances but at its root is the idea of a woman who exercises rule, control, influence or guidance. It was by provoking sexual desire that young beauties most obviously exerted power over their admirers – a sovereignty that contemporary poets both celebrated and resented.

> In losing me, proud nymph, you lose
> The humblest slave your beauty knows;
> In losing you, I but throw down
> A cruel tyrant from her throne.

So wrote Sir Charles Sedley when he had been given the brush-off, and other rhymesters, as we shall see, could be much more bitter about the lovers who held them in thrall. But, in common parlance 'mistress' more normally implied control of a household or business establishment. Women could also be a dominant influence in the lives of their menfolk by means of family connections or strength of personality or intellect. The presence of powerful women made most men nervous and it was particularly worrying when female companions appeared to be influencing kings. We shall see what vicious satires and libels were written about Charles' mistresses in later years. After the Restoration the account of the king's escape disguised as a woman's body servant was suppressed. The same nervousness about acknowledging female power over the king surfaced in early ballads about Charles' escape. In the song 'The Last News from France' quoted at the beginning of this section of the book, the 'heroine' who aided Charles' escape is not Jane Lane but a royalist gentleman in drag. Many supporters of the Stuart cause would probably not have relished the idea that the words 'the king himself did wait on me' related to a real woman.

But did the relationship between Charles and Jane go beyond that of an amusing and arousing role reversal and did it reach the point at which Jane might feel she had a special place in the king's affection and a strong hold over him? A tantalising sentence in the journal of a brilliant young scholar who spent the winter of 1651–2 in Paris suggests that we might need to examine the relationship more closely. John Finch was the twenty-five-year-old son of Lord Finch, one of the most hated of royal justices, who had fled into exile as early as 1640. John, a graduate from both English universities, was on his way to Padua to study medicine and stayed for several months, presumably with his father, who was high in favour with Henrietta Maria. On 4 March he recorded, 'Mrs Lane came to Paris and is called the King's mistress.'[76] Finch may have been noting mere gossip, based on nothing more than the warmth of the reception Jane always received from the Stuarts. On the other hand, he did have entrée to the court and knew what was being discussed by those closest to the king. What the medical student's eleven words underline is the intimate nature of the relationship between Charles and Jane. Perhaps he also had the evidence of his own eyes. It is not difficult to read the body language of couples in love.

Then there is the evidence of the correspondence. That Charles wrote to Jane at all is an indication of his affection, for he was always a reluctant correspondent. Yet, throughout the years of exile he was frequently in touch with her. They met whenever Jane attended his sister on visits to the king's court and in the intervals they maintained written contact. In November 1652 he excused his earlier lack of response to her letters:

> I have hitherto deferred writing to you in hope to be able to send you somewhat else besides a letter and I believe it troubles me more that I cannot yet do it than it does you . . . [when my fortunes improve] you shall be sure to receive a share, for it is impossible I can ever forget the great debt I owe you, which I hope I shall live to pay in a degree that is worthy of me. In the meantime I am sure all who love me will be very kind to you, else I shall never think them so to your most affectionate friend.*
>
> Charles R[77]

Mistress Lane did at other times complain of neglect but Charles was swift to reassure her:

> I did not think it necessary I should ever have begun a letter to you in chiding, but you give me so just cause by telling me you fear you are wearing out of my memory, that I cannot choose but tell you I take it very unkindly that after the obligations I have to you 'tis possible for you to suspect I can ever be so wanting to myself as not to remember them on all occasion to your advantage. Which I assure you I shall, and hope before it be long I shall have it in power to give you those testimonies of my kindness to you which I desire.

Jane had passed on the distressing news that her aged father and her brother, who had returned to England, had been arrested and thrown into prison. Charles sympathised and added, 'I am the more sorry for it since it hath hindered you from coming along with my sister [to Cologne], that I might have assured you myself how truly I am, your most affectionate friend, Charles R.'[78]

Between the lines of another letter we read something even more surprising which has never been picked up by historians and biographers:

---

* 'Friend' was a word he often used for ladies who were certainly more than that.

Charles and Jane discussed important political matters and she offered him confidential advice on affairs which his ministers and attendants would have considered to be none of women's business. We know this because she became indignant when it appeared that the king had betrayed her trust, something he was at pains to deny:

> . . . for that which Mr Boswell is pleased to tell you concerning your giving me good counsel in a letter and my making it public in my bed chamber, is not the first lie that he has made, nor will be the last, for I am certain there was never anything spoken in the bed chamber in my hearing to any such purpose, nor, I am confident, when I was not there . . . Your cousin will let you know that I have given orders for my picture for you and if in this or in anything else I can show the sense I have of that I owe you, pray let me know it and it shall be done by
>
> Your most assured and constant friend,
> Charles R.[79]

This relationship had become so close that Jane felt at liberty to discuss matters of moment with the king. This is precisely the kind of contact that Charles' councillors complained of with regard to royal mistresses and it would seem that Boswell and other close attendants of the king found it risible or even objectionable that Jane should offer her sovereign 'good counsel'.

Now we come to the king's treatment of the Lanes after 1660. Charles was true to his word in rewarding Jane and her brother but the extent of his bounty was remarkable. Like others who had aided the king's escape, Jane was awarded by parliament a standard payment of £1,000 to buy herself a commemorative jewel. But Charles added to this out of his personal income a pension of £1,000 p.a. which was enough for her to set herself up in considerable style. He also gave her a gold watch with the request that it be passed down the female side of the family as a permanent reminder of Jane's services. Other *ad hoc* payments were made over the years and Jane also received further mementoes which were long cherished by her descendants. This was the way Charles habitually behaved towards lovers and ex-lovers, for whom he felt a particular kind of obligation. Jane's rewards bear no comparison to the profusion lavished on established post-Restoration mistresses but they are on a par with the gifts the king made to other women who had shared his bed.

John Lane also benefited hugely from a grateful king. He received £500 a year, £1,000 marriage portions for each of his daughters and a later grant of £2,000. Even more remarkably, when he died, the government paid for a funeral monument to be erected in St Peter's church, Wolverhampton. But this relatively humble country gentleman was also offered another singular mark of royal favour, and one usually associated with the families of royal mistresses. Charles proposed to raise John Lane to the peerage. John declined the honour and we are left asking ourselves 'Why?' It may have been a becoming modesty or Lane may have felt that he lacked the means to sustain such a position in society. But was there more to it? Did he think that acceptance would be an open acknowledgement of his sister's shame?

We have one more piece of evidence to consider and it is the most intriguing of all. After the Restoration Jane commissioned a portrait of herself. In it she was depicted as holding the royal crown with a veil over it. The symbolism is obvious: it depicts her as hiding the king from his enemies. But, in the picture's top left-hand corner she had painted a scroll with a Latin legend upon it – and its meaning is far from obvious to the casual observer. The words are *sic sic iuvat ire sub umbra* and they are an almost precise quotation from Virgil's *Aeneid*. In translation they read, 'thus, thus it pleases me to go into the shadows'.

Is this the humble affirmation of a loyal servant who, having played her part in the king's preservation, was thereafter content to retire into obscurity? Her correspondence with Charles during the 1650s suggests otherwise. Then it was Jane who took initiatives to keep the relationship alive. Knowing Charles well enough to realise that out of sight could well mean out of mind, she obviously feared that, once he had made provision for her in his sister's household, he might forget her. She was determined not to let that happen. After what they had shared, she was not going to let Charles avoid his obligations. But what *had* they shared?

Here we have to seek Virgil's help. The words Jane chose to quote from the *Aeneid* come at the dramatic climax of the story of Dido and Aeneas. The Trojan hero arrives in Carthage where Queen Dido falls passionately in love with him. She begs him to stay and share her throne but he secretly makes plans to sail away. She discovers his perfidy and, failing to dissuade him, stabs herself and has her body placed on a funeral pyre. Her final words express her own resignation but also her curse upon her inconstant lover. As she twice plunges the knife into her breast she exclaims, 'Thus, thus it pleases me to go into the shadows [of death]. Let the cruel Trojan's eyes drink in these flames from over the ocean and let him take with him the ill omen of my death.'

It is inconceivable that Jane did not know the context of the words she quoted and that, knowing it, it did not have meaning for her. Dido's dying words are the complaint of a woman who has fallen in love with a wandering prince and been betrayed by him. Aeneas, like Charles, travelled on in search of a crown. When Charles found his crown he quickly married and busied himself with another mistress. He did not summon Jane to court. He merely paid her off handsomely. Did she expect more? Did she believe she deserved more? The behaviour of Jane and her brother suggests that their pride at having been of service to the Stuart cause was richly mingled with resentment.

Jane's after-story reveals a woman who, like the king's resident mistresses, loved luxury and took a pride in living up to her income (hence her occasional need of royal subsidies). She married Sir Clement Fisher, a Warwickshire neighbour who had also been involved in the king's escape. By him she had no children and made a point of leaving no fortune when she died in 1689. She is reputed to have told her friends that 'her hands should be her executors'. It was an attitude Charles would have approved of.

Now we resume the story of the king's escape from the point of his arrival at Trent. It was written by Francis Wyndham soon after the Restoration and presented to the king. He secreted it for twenty years and only permitted Anne Wyndham, the colonel's widow, to publish it in 1681. It is not difficult to see why Charles suppressed the offering in the early days of the reign when the country was by no means united in rejoicing at his return. Wyndham did not mince his words:

> ... the Almighty so closely covered the king with the wing of his protection, and so clouded the understanding of his cruel enemies, that the most piercing eye of malice could not see, nor the most barbarously bloody hand offer violence to his sacred person; God smiting his pursuers (as once he did the Sodomites) with blindness, who with as much eagerness sought to sacrifice the Lord's anointed to their fury, as the other did to prostitute the angels to their lusts.[80]

The author was at pains to pay back the Bible-bashing Puritans in their own coin and those who considered themselves the chosen instruments of God's wrath against the lascivious and heretical Stuarts would not have appreciated being likened to the unnatural inhabitants of the cities of the plain who were punished for their lusts. Charles, on the other hand, had a country to run and peace to establish throughout the land. The last thing he needed was inflammatory narratives that harked back to the past and kept alive old divisions.

But there was another reason for the compilation of this tract. We would expect that the Wyndham narrative would present the family in the best possible light but in a throwaway sentence the author reveals another motive: 'The reproaches and scandals by which some envious persons have sought to diminish and vilify the faithful services which the colonel, out of the integrity of his soul, performed unto his majesty shall not be mentioned.'[81] The Restoration court was a crowded arena of thrusting, trampling, elbowing royalist clans desperately competing for places close to the king. Everyone wanted to prove that they had served the Stuarts valiantly in battle or during the years of exile and that their neighbours' claims were spurious. Wyndham's tract has to be seen against this background of bickering. The fact that emerges clearly from it once the obscuring heroics have been cleared away is that the Wyndhams failed in their efforts to smuggle Charles out of the country.

The masquerading which was a marked feature of the king's journey through the shires took on a more elaborate nature at Trent. Wyndham rode to Charmouth, near Lyme Regis, under the assumed name of Captain Norris to seek out some coastal vessel whose owner would take a group of passengers across the Channel. The party was supposed to consist of an eloping couple and their attendants. Wilmot was to be the ardent lover, Wyndham's kinswoman, Juliana Coningsby, his trembling bride and Charles the groom in charge of their horses. A loyal shipman called Limbry was located and admitted to the secret. He agreed to assist the king and it was arranged that the party should wait at the Queen's Arms until summoned to go aboard during the night. The escapees were comfortably lodged and they waited. Hours passed and their anxiety rose. When day broke with no sign of Limbry the king and his guardians sped away to Bridport. What had gone wrong? According to Limbry (or according to Wyndham) the mariner's wife, suspicious that her husband had been hired by fleeing royalists, was petrified of his bringing down the government's wrath upon them and so locked him in his bedroom. It reads like a very slender excuse and the truth may have been that, on mature reflection, Limbry himself had decided not to risk his own life in order to save the king's. That, of course, would not have served the propaganda purpose of the tract, which wished to create a picture of a nation of devoted royal supporters of all classes ready to stand together against the republican tyranny.

The next incident presents the king in the guise of a seventeenth-century Scarlet Pimpernel. Still posing as a groom, he was in the stable yard of the George Inn at Bridport when a group of soldiers came in. Charles calmly entered into their conversation and cunningly extracted from them the government plans for the invasion of the Channel Islands. The king and Wilmot next went by a roundabout route back to Trent, but not before they had spent another anxiety-ridden night sharing the hospitality of a small village inn with a troop of billeted cavalrymen.

Charles remained for another fortnight as guest of Francis and Anne Wyndham while Wilmot spied out alternative routes to safety. This part of the narrative is fleshed out with anecdotes of the perturbations and sufferings of various members of the family as bands of soldiers, acting on the advice of spies and informers, scoured the countryside. Sir Hugh Wyndham (whose loyalty had been called in question at Barnstaple) was represented as having suffered the indignity of a thorough search of his house at Pilsdon, near Bridport: 'They took the old baronet, his lady, daughters and whole family, and set a guard upon them in the hall, whilst they examine every corner, not sparing either trunk or box. Then taking a particular view of their prisoners, they seize a lovely young lady, saying she was the king disguised in woman's apparel', and took great pleasure in putting their theory to the test.[82]

Charles was anxious to be on the move but enquiries through the royalist grapevine produced only the mournful assessment that there was little chance of reaching any of the Dorset or Hampshire havens undetected. The king's restlessness grew by the day, so when a Colonel Phelips of Salisbury reported that he might be able to arrange a passage from some point further along the coast, he grabbed the opportunity to move on. Anne Wyndham informs us that her husband begged to be allowed to accompany his royal master but that Charles very firmly refused the offer on the grounds that 'it was no way necessary and might prove inconvenient'. On 6 October he took a warm farewell of the Trent family but one gets the distinct impression that he was not all that sorry to be leaving them. Accompanied by Wilmot and a succession of local gentlemen who knew the country, he travelled eastwards along the line of the present A303, having exchanged his menial's attire for clothes befitting a gentleman of modest means. Skirting Salisbury, he came by byways to Brighton on the 14th. His latest guardian had arranged with a merchant to transport out of the country a group of young bloods who were in trouble for duelling. In the small hours of Wednesday, 15 October 1651 the king went aboard a brig in Shoreham harbour. The following day he landed at Fécamp. The name of his ship was the *Surprise*. In 1660 he gave permission for it to be rechristened the *Royal Escape*.

The five children of Charles I, 1637, by Van Dyck.
Left to right: Princess Mary, James, Duke of York, Charles, Prince of Wales,
Princess Elizabeth and Princess Anne.

Henrietta Maria appearing in a court masque: detail from a painting by Gerrit van Honthurst.

When Maria de Medici came to stay in England she was so unpopular that a popular lampoon represented the king and queen yielding to her the symbols of power.
(P. de la Serre, *Histoire de l'Entrée de la Reyne Mère*, 1639)

Charles II *c*.1651.
Miniature by David des Granges.
Versions of this portrait were rare
and bestowed upon loyal subjects
by the exiled King.

*He was 'swarthy, with fine black eyes
and a wide ugly mouth... His head was
noble, his hair black, his complexion brown,
his person passably agreable.'*
Madame de Montpensier

Jane Lane who helped Charles escape in 1651, had this portrait painted after the Restoration. The quotation from Virgil is enigmatic in the extreme.

Charles, dressed as a servant, escaping with Jane Lane. (Painted by Isaac Fuller, 1660s)

The ship in which Charles left England in 1651, afterwards renamed *The Royal Escape*.
Painting by William van de Velde the Elder.

Charles and Mary of Orange dancing at The Hague, by Hieronymus Janssens.

Chalk drawing of Charles II by Samuel Cooper, *c.*1660

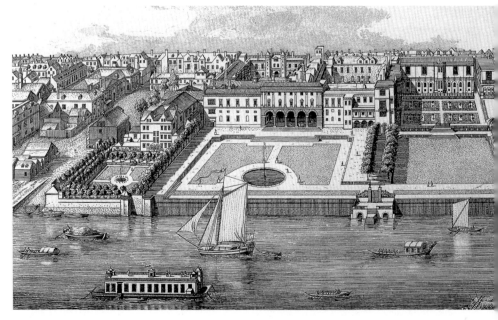

Somerset House, residence of Henrietta Maria and, later, Catherine of Braganza.
(L. Knyff, *Britannia Illustrata*)

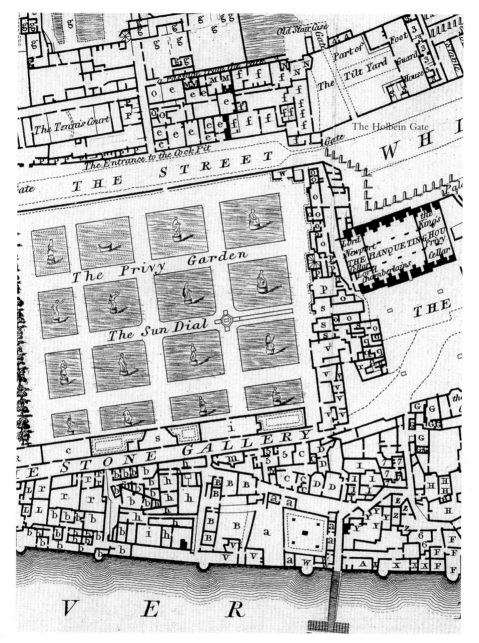

A plan of the Palace of Whitehall, 1680.
According to Samuel Pepys, *'the King sups at least four or five times every week with my Lady Castlemaine and most often stays till the morning with her and goes home through the privy garden all alone privately and so that the very sentries take notice of it and speak of it.'* Lady Castlemaine's lodgings were around the Holbein Gate and the King's quarters fronted the river.

Tin-glazed earthenware dish
with a portrait of Charles II
with Catherine of Braganza, *c*.1662

An orange-seller – the occupation
from which Nell Gwyn rose to be
an actress and the King's mistress.

PART TWO

KINGSHIP – NEW STYLE

. . . Beyond sea he began,
Where such riot he ran
That all the world there did leave him;
And now he's come o'er,
Much worse than before.
Oh, what fools you were to receive him . . .

He spends all his days
In running to plays,
When in his shop he should be poreing [sic];
And wastes all his nights
In his constant delights
Of revelling, drinking and whoring . . .

Anon, 'Of his Majesty's being made free of the City'[1]

CHAPTER 5

His Present Deplorable Condition

The prelude to Charles' next eight and a half years was succinctly written by Hyde:

> Though this wonderful deliverance and preservation of the person of the king was an argument of general joy and comfort to all his good subjects, and a new seed of hope for future blessings, yet his present condition was very deplorable.[2]

The political situation in those countries to which he looked for succour had deteriorated sharply in his absence. In the Netherlands the States-General had celebrated the death of William of Orange by striking a medal whose legend ran, 'The last hour of the prince is the beginning of freedom'. They refused to allow his posthumously born son to inherit his offices. The stadtholdership was left vacant and the posts of admiral and captain-general abolished. They refused to allow Mary to exercise guardianship of the boy, establishing instead a council of which she was only one member. The Princess of Orange, or, as she insisted on being called, the Princess Royal of England, thus became the latest of the Stuarts to be deprived of political power. But she had too much of her mother in her to allow herself to become a cipher. She continued to fight for what she considered her son's inalienable rights and she became more determined than ever to give all the assistance in her power to her benighted family. Mary deliberately cultivated all things French at her own court and lost no opportunity to let the Dutch leaders know that she held them and their countrymen in contempt as uncivilised boors. This was, to say the least, a somewhat sweeping condemnation to make of 'Golden Age' Holland. Riding through the streets of the Hague the princess can hardly have been unaware that the city was undergoing an architectural rebirth, or that it was famed for its printers, silversmiths and potters. It was the capital of a nation which boasted geniuses in every branch of human endeavour and which rivalled the states of Italy in devotion to painting. A foreign visitor to the land of Rembrandt, Hals, Terborch, Teniers, van Goyen, de Hooch and Ruisdael commented on the democratisation of art: 'All in general . . .

adorn their houses . . . with costly pieces; butchers and bakers . . . black-smiths and cobblers, etc., will have some pictures or other'.[3]

Mary's consuming interest was the wellbeing of her Stuart relatives. Though her relationship with her mother went through some stormy passages she was devoted to her and she was prepared to spend and be spent in the service of her exiled siblings. This had repercussions on the political life of the Netherlands. The States-General wanted to normalise relations with the *de facto* government of England. Part of the price exacted for fraternalism between the two Protestant states was that the Dutch republic should not provide a refuge for the sons of the traitor Charles Stuart. This made for very difficult negotiations between London and the Hague, a city which pursued an open door policy to the persecuted of all nations. Mary's contribution to the process of international under-standing was to parade every day past the English ambassador's residence with her entire suite and her brother James at her side. She was encouraged in her haughty demeanour by her aunt, Elizabeth of Bohemia, an embittered old woman who constantly lamented her poverty and managed to fall out with almost all her many children.

France was in chaos. The Second Fronde had erupted in 1650 and was much more devastating than the first. It was led by Louis, Prince de Condé, one of the most talented generals of the Thirty Years War, and other powerful magnates who, by raising their tenantry, spread revolt and misery in several parts of the country. Once discontent with centralised government had been manifested there was no controlling its expression. Provincial agents were murdered, churches pillaged, mobs swarmed through city streets, soldiers ravaged the countryside. In terms of sheer spontaneous, unorganised devastation it was worse than anything that had occurred in England during a decade of civil war. France was marked, in the words of one historian , by 'gangsterdom above, anarchy below and humiliation without'.[4]

In February 1651 the Frondeurs had forced the hated Mazarin into exile and, in July of the following year, Condé took possession of Paris. This event had direct implications for Charles in that it demonstrated yet again that he was nothing more than a sideshow in the fairground of European politics. Henrietta Maria had revived her plan to marry her son off to Mademoiselle de Montpensier. Charles was no longer the tongue-tied youth of five years before and now welcomed with cold calculation a scheme which would whisk him out of the poverty trap. As for the lady in question, she was still in want of a prestigious husband, and Charles was a king, if only in name. It seemed that, this time, there might really be an outside chance of pulling off a matrimonial coup. Then, La Grande Mademoiselle decided to become a player in the political game. She threw in her lot with Condé and was actually to be seen in soldier's garb, manning the barricades. This made her the enemy of the queen regent, upon whose meagre bounty the Stuarts were dependent.

That formidable matriarch, Anne of Austria, now proved herself a mistress of Machiavellian political calculation. She patronised division among the Frondeurs by the simple expedient of bribing some of the leaders to turn against Condé. Her agents fomented disaffection among the Parisian bourgeoisie, who now turned their resentment away from Mazarin, who had fled the capital, and directed it against the swaggering princelings and their indisciplined followers, who looted shops and disrupted trade with the provinces. What the Frondes demonstrated was that the diverse parties, united in their position to absolute monarchy, could not sustain their cohesion. 'Divide and rule', the age-old technique employed by determined and politically acute dictators, was still the most effective means of dealing with rebellion. In October 1652, it was Condé's turn to retreat from a capital whose citizenry had turned against him. The thirteen-year-old Louis XIV and his mother were cheered as they returned to their palace and, weeks later, Mazarin joined them. By the autumn of 1653 royal troops had mopped up the last pockets of resistance and 'The Great Condé' had fled to Spain with a price on his head. Seven years later the French king showed how much he had learned from his tutor, Mazarin. He stripped the arrogant and headstrong prince of any possibility of remaining a potential opposition figurehead by the simple expedient of forgiving him. Condé was embraced by his sovereign and given an honoured place at court – where the king could keep an eye on him.

The conduct of French politics in the 1650s provided Charles with an object lesson. The cardinal and his royal charge set about laying the foundation of a centralised and powerful state. They did so in a calmly calculated way which made no concessions to sentiment, ethics, principle or religious allegiance. In foreign affairs they did not hesitate to sponsor rebellions in the territories of their enemies nor to make a defensive/ offensive alliance with Cromwell's England, one of the terms of which was the expulsion of the Stuarts from their French sanctuary. However, Louis' government did not hurry to fulfil this treaty obligation and for the moment the Stuart court had a home. Charles welcomed the triumph of his French cousin in 1653. The restoration of the royal court brought him and his mother once more into the centre of Parisian social life. The round of balls and banquets was resumed, the Stuarts being obliged to borrow wherever they could money to spend on court clothes so as not to be embarrassed in the sight of French high society. It was all very gay but Charles quickly learned that any sense of security was an illusion.

Meanwhile, he had his own political affairs to set in order. Once more this involved strenuous efforts to keep his domineering mother at arm's length. His first task was to set up his own council. He sent for Hyde, who was at Antwerp, but Henrietta Maria could not prevent her old animosity from coming to the surface. She despatched her messenger with instructions, as from the king, to order all royal servants not to come to

Paris since Charles was undecided how long to stay there. Hyde was not taken in by this ruse and reached his master's court in time to celebrate Christmas. The queen dowager was obliged to give way with as good a grace as possible but she made plain her animosity towards the man she considered her most influential opponent. She refused to receive Hyde and snubbed him whenever they met by chance. Encountering him at a court masque, she asked loudly of those around her, 'Who is that fat man?' Nor did she lessen her efforts to minimise his influence. She tried to neutralise him by placing more of her own men on the council. Charles accepted Jermyn, her creature, because he was an invaluable intermediary with the French court but he put his foot down when she pressed him to add the name of Jermyn's kinsman, Sir John Berkeley, to the list of advisers. Berkeley, a devoted but not notably effective intriguer, was, according to Burnet, 'a very weak man and corrupt, without shame or decency' and an example of the phenomenon of 'with how little true judgement courts distribute favours and honours'. Sir Edmund Wyndham thought him 'the greatest vapourer* in the world' and Pepys later discovered him to be 'the most hot, fiery man in discourse, without any cause, that ever I saw'.[5] He was certainly incandescent at having his advancement balked and swore eternal enmity to Hyde.

The atmosphere in the impoverished and increasingly disillusioned household of the exiled king was poisonous, as the tortuous biography of Sir Robert Long well illustrates. This able Stuart servant was appointed secretary to the prince's council in 1644 and occupied that position almost continuously throughout the difficult years that followed. He enjoyed the patronage of Henrietta Maria and was considered as belonging to her faction. However, there seems to have been a falling-out between the secretary and his friends and, in 1652, the queen dowager's agents tried to prise him out of office. They backed a spurious accusation by a certain Colonel Wogan that Long was a traitor who had earlier been in secret correspondence with the parliamentary general, Henry Ireton, and, specifically, that he had betrayed Great Torrington into the hands of the enemy. Long was summarily dismissed. In his anger he suspected (or was informed) that Hyde was behind the conspiracy. Now the Louvre party (as Henrietta Maria's faction was called) realised that they could use the ex-secretary's resentment. They concocted a story that it was, in fact, Edward Hyde who was in the pay of the hated republicans. A serving woman, they affirmed, would give evidence of a clandestine meeting between Hyde and Cromwell. Long was uncertain how this story would be received by the king and waited over a year before passing it on to Charles via an intermediary, who was sworn not to reveal his source. Charles, however, insisted on getting to the bottom of the affair, which quickly evaporated in

* Vapourer: a bragging, grandiloquent and fantastical talker' – OED.

the glare of accurate scrutiny, though not before Long had petulantly passed on a complaint made by Hyde of how difficult it was to get the king to attend to business. Hyde was exonerated and Long remained for the time being in limbo.

The struggle for influence with the king was unremitting and the efforts to displace his most trusted advisers produced some bizarre alliances. While the Louvre party wanted Charles to look towards Catholics at home and Catholic princes abroad as his surest hope, a group of Presbyterian Scots in Paris were equally adamant that their fellow countrymen still constituted the most effective potential force for helping Charles regain his throne. The two religious factions had nothing in common, save their hatred of Hyde and the other councillors who continually impressed upon the king that any deviation from the theological and liturgical settlement represented by the Church of England would be fatal to his chances of restoration. Charles knew very well that they were right. He had had enough experience of ordinary English men and women to realise that they would never return to the Roman fold or embrace the religious fervour of the Scots. The party enthusiasts, however, were blind to these realities. They combined to agree a common policy: they would present petitions to the king asking for the dismissal of Hyde. This improbable scheme only failed when a member of the whispering gallery that was the Stuart court sneaked details of it to the king. Charles thought it a huge joke and 'made himself very merry with the design, and spake of it sometimes at dinner when the queen was present, and asked pleasantly when the two petitions would be brought'.[6] These petty intrigues were among the few things which did give him genuine amusement in these grey days when past, present and future coalesced in a blur of meaninglessness. Like a boy watching the antics of insects in a jar, he liked to consider himself above the jealousies and animosities of his companions. Shortly after the petitions fiasco he restored Long to his office – after extracting from him an apology to Hyde. It was, Charles discovered, always more pleasurable and less stressful to be forgiving, agreeable and easygoing.

But the malice was real and manifested on a daily basis. In council meetings Hyde and Ormonde were opposed almost as a matter of course by Jermyn and Wilmot. Moreover, the queen dowager's supporters constantly humiliated their opponents. While Hyde and Ormonde were on exceedingly short commons, living in cheap accommodation and obliged to walk the streets of the capital, Jermyn kept an ostentatiously lavish table and went everywhere in a carriage put at his disposal by his French backers. Henrietta Maria was pursuing an active proselytising policy among prominent exiles, her main agent being Stephen Goffe, the Anglican priest who had brought Charles the news of his father's death. Converted to Catholicism in 1651, he was now an ideal lieutenant in the queen dowager's religious campaign. In her designs she made the best possible use of her French family. She continued her quest for suitable brides for both of her sons and she could always rely on the emotional support of Anne of Austria. The French queen also knew what it was to have to hold her own in a man's world and could sympathise when Henrietta Maria complained of Englishmen who tried to come between her and her firstborn.

When Hyde commented on his master's lack of enthusiasm for business he was not being pernickety. Charles grew daily more despondent about his ability to make any impression on the course of events. The attempt to regain his throne by military means had been a fiasco. Nothing had come of various schemes to make a financially advantageous marriage. Even a plan to recover the Scottish royal regalia had to be abandoned. The treasure was held in one of the last royalist coastal strongholds. In the spring of 1652, Princess Mary fitted out a ship and put it at her brother's disposal for a quick raid. In the event, there was nothing quick about it. Arguments and changes of plan delayed the expedition long enough for news of it to reach London and for Commonwealth troops to be deployed. A brief sortie into European statesmanship had, similarly, ended in humiliation. In the summer of 1652 Queen Anne's government found a job for him. The Duke of Lorraine was an adventurer with a private army available to the highest bidder. Currently he was supporting Condé, and Anne wanted to bribe him into changing sides. Charles was sent as a negotiator whose royal status would, it was hoped, impress the duke. It did not. Lorraine asked the king to arrange for Lord Jermyn to come instead because he carried more weight in the French court. By the time Charles got back to Paris it had fallen to Condé. The prince offered him another snub by packing him off ignominiously to Saint-Germain, from where he could only watch while the royal general, Henri, vicomte de Turenne, regained control of the capital.

What made matters worse for Charles was that his brother, James, was serving, and serving rather effectively, in Turenne's army. While the king had been absent in Scotland and England, the Duke of York had conceived a strong passion for a military career and been encouraged in this by some of his advisers. Henrietta Maria was not enthusiastic to see her son put his life at risk and no decision could be made while Charles was, himself, fighting across the water. Should any misfortune befall him, all Stuart hopes would be concentrated on the heir apparent. So James had to chafe at the bit until his brother's safe return. Early in 1652 Charles summoned the duke and their mother to a council meeting to discuss James' possible enlistment. As they all sat round the table the king called for comments. There was silence and a distinct lack of eye contact. No one was privy to Charles' thoughts and feelings on the matter and no one was ready to commit himself in what was essentially a family issue. The relations between both brothers and their domineering mother were uneasy and

Charles was finding the headstrong and stubborn James something of a handful. The king, himself, was undecided. There would be a definite financial advantage in allowing the duke to earn his own living but letting him disport himself on the field of honour would carry a double risk. One was that he might get himself killed and thus weaken the Stuart hold upon their throne. The other was that he might cover himself in glory and so outshine his brother and sovereign. Charles may well also have asked himself why he should permit James to escape the claustrophobia and penury of Paris which he was doomed to endure once more. In the end it was the financial argument that carried the day, supported by the urgings of the Louvre party that the king would find his brother's military skills valuable in any future attempt to regain the throne. Thus, in April, James went off to join Turenne. He rapidly showed himself to be, if not a brilliant, certainly a brave and dedicated soldier of above average skill in battlefield tactics. He had discovered his *métier* and loved it. Charles had not and did not.

The repeated blows to Charles' self-respect could not fail to influence his character. Here he was in Paris, an unwelcome guest, living on hand-outs from his mother's family, from sacrificial donations which came to him from fellow exiles who had hitched their stars to his cumbrous wagon and from the offerings of well-wishers at home which were collected by agents who risked their own lives to support a monarch who spent his income trying vainly to keep up with the continental royal Joneses. As month gave way to hopeless month the trickle of funds dwindled. More and more royalist families were coming to terms with reality and making their peace with the new regime in London. It was a matter of sheer survival. Their estates had been confiscated. They lived as long as they could on whatever liquid capital they had managed to escape with. As that dried up they were obliged to return, make grovelling submission and compound for their property. They were doing no more than their political superiors. Mazarin, the Dutch States-General and other European rulers had accepted the English *fait accompli* and were doing business with the republican government in London. There was an element of resigned pragmatism in James' choice of a military career. It grew progressively harder for Charles to sustain self-belief and commitment to the right-eousness of his cause. The burden of expectation placed upon him by his family and the little coterie of devoted followers who expected him to defend his birthright to the last drop of Stuart blood as long as there remained any hope of a reversal of fortune was oppressive. To stay sane was to live for the day and not to brood on the morrow.

One possible source of substantial income for the court in exile was piracy. Royalist privateers were commissioned to scour the nearer seas for English merchant vessels to plunder. The leading maritime scavenger in Stuart service was Prince Rupert, who, from the autumn of 1650 to the spring of 1653 prowled the Atlantic and Mediterranean and captured several prizes. Unfortunately, he also lost many of his own vessels and had to deploy most of his loot in keeping the rest of his fleet in seaworthy condition. News of Rupert's safe return to France filled Charles and his entourage with joy and eager expectation. The king sent his own coach to meet his cousin and greeted him warmly on his arrival at court. However, the atmosphere cooled when Rupert made his report on the subject of the profits of the voyage. There were none.

> ... what treasure had been gotten together (which he confessed had amounted to great value) had been all lost in the ship in which he himself was, that sprung a plank in the Indies, when his highness was miraculously preserved and in the boat carried to another ship . . . [and] with all the men and all that had been gotten sunk in the sea . . . much of their other purchase had been likewise cast away in the ship in which his brother [Prince Maurice] perished . . . so that all that was brought into Nantes would scarce pay off the seamen and discharge some debts at Toulon . . .[7]

When Rupert was pressed for detailed accounts he flew into a rage, claimed that the king and his councillors were all against him and that his arduous service was poorly repaid. He left the court in high dudgeon and Charles was more than content to let him go. The king, forced by circumstance into unheroic idleness, found the company of men of action disagreeable, especially when they were as unmanageable as Rupert, whom he privately described as 'mad'.

Someone else with whom the king parted company at about the same time was Thomas Hobbes. The witty ex-tutor published *Leviathan* in 1651 and, on Charles' return to Paris, the author presented him with a beautiful copy on vellum. The result was not what he had hoped. His majesty,

> being afterward informed by some of his priests that the book did not only contain many principles of atheism and gross impiety . . . but also such as were prejudicial to the Church and reflected dangerously upon the majesty of sovereign princes . . . when Mr Hobbes came to make a tender of his services to him in person, he was rejected and word brought to him by the Marquis of Ormonde that the king would not admit him . . . by which means Mr Hobbes declines in credit with his friends there of the royal stamp . . .[8]

Hobbes hastily returned to England and made his peace with the republic. It is extremely unlikely that Charles read the treatise and formed his own judgement but he was influenced by people from all parties in the royal entourage. This is not surprising. Hobbes was too independent and original a thinker not to be a challenge to men with blinkered vision on matters of monarchical or ecclesiastical authority. Though he believed in strong government, the philosopher had no romantic attachment to the Stuart cause and was not prepared to dissemble in order to win favours. There has seldom been room for honest and outspoken men in the courts of kings and there certainly was none in that of Charles II in exile. When Charles came into his own he once more extended royal favour to Hobbes – a characteristic, patronising gesture, based not upon any attempt to understand the man's observations about human relationships, but simply to enjoy his stimulating company. 'Here is the bear, come to be baited,' he would say to his companions as the aged philosopher approached.

When Sir Robert Long 'blabbed' about Hyde's complaining that the king neglected business and sought diversion in pleasure, he spoke no more than the truth. The king's longest-serving councillor had always experienced a degree of frustration with his master's lack of enthusiasm for desk work but the problem grew worse after Worcester. In June 1653 he confided to his colleague, Sir Edward Nicholas,

> When anything is to be done by the king's own hand we must some-times be content to wait, he being brought very unwillingly to the work, which vexes me exceedingly . . . if I did not serve the king for God's sake, I would not stay here a day longer . . .[9]

What particularly annoyed Hyde was that the king was no empty-headed voluptuary, incapable of attending to state affairs. On the contrary: 'he hath more judgement and understanding by many degrees than many who pretend it and that is the only thing that breaks my heart, that he makes no more use of it'.[10] Charles' disinclination to the more tedious aspects of kingship was born of his earlier lack of training and his current depression. Everything was going wrong for him and the future looked bleak. There was little incentive for an active young man to bury himself in reports and policy discussions which seemed irrelevant to the destiny of his country and his dynasty. And he *was* a young man, with all that that implied, as Hyde openly, if ruefully, acknowledged:

> . . . there are and always will be some actions of appetite and affection committed which cannot be separated nor banished from the age of twenty-one and which we must all labour by good counsel to prevent and divert . . . kings are of the same mould and composition as other men and must have the same time to be made perfect . . .[11]

Mademoiselle de Montpensier was more curt in her memoirs. Remarking that Charles inclined to his French rather than to his English genetic inheritance, she explained, 'car les Bourbons sont gens fort appliqués aux bagatelles et peu aux solides'.[12]

Both these observations are discreet and tell us nothing about how Charles actually was filling his days. It would be tempting, as many historians have done, to go along with the high Victorian S.R. Gardiner's sweeping analysis that Charles' mood on his return from England was such that he consoled himself 'in low debauchery for the kingdoms he had lost',[13] but that verdict oversimplifies the king's reaction to his fate. Cromwellian spies delighted to send home salacious reports about the king's circle and to note that 'fornication, drunkenness and adultery are not considered sins' in the Stuart court.[14] But even among these hostile, prudish witnesses there were those who acknowledged that the king distanced himself to some degree from the carousings of his companions. Charles was fully aware that his behaviour was under daily scrutiny by his enemies and he was far too streetwise to provide them with gratuitous ammunition they could use to further jeopardise his prospects of a return to England. It amused him to have witty and raffish companions who cared little for convention but he did not allow them to set the tone for his own behaviour. Hobbes was not the only person to be swiftly removed from his presence for fear of contagion with ideas or actions that might defile the royal image. The entertainments an impoverished, peregrinatory prince could afford to indulge, according to Commonwealth newsbooks, were no more scandalous than 'hunting, dancing, balls and masking' and other sources tell us that Charles also enjoyed gambling, billiards, swimming and brisk walks. His sins were those prompted by ennui, despair and laziness rather than unrestrained hedonism and he always exercised refinement and discretion.

This certainly applied to his sexual liaisons. John Evelyn commented sourly to Samuel Pepys in 1667 that Lady Byron, whom Charles bedded in 1652, was 'the king's seventeenth whore abroad',[15] but it is an assertion that cannot be taken at face value. Who kept such an exact tally? If there were that many royal mistresses how is it that only the names of four (five if we include Jane Lane) are known? And if the king's bed was seldom empty why were there not more resulting Stuart bastards (Charles was never reticent about acknowledging his offspring)? The conclusion that must be drawn is that, at this stage of his life, the exiled King of England was no more promiscuous than other contemporary rulers, including his relatives, the King of France and the Prince of Orange. He certainly was not much of a catch for women who looked for a sound return on the investment of their physical charms. (Courtesans were nothing if not calculating.)

But there was always the delectable Lucy. Theirs was an intense relationship, as passionate in its beginning as it was coldly rancorous in its ending. We do not stray beyond the bounds of historical accuracy if we imagine Charles, during his womanless days in Scotland, his campaigning months before Worcester and the fugitive weeks that followed, longing to be reunited with his bold, brown mistress and their son. On his return to Paris he was in for a surprise. It is possible but perhaps unlikely that news of Lucy's infidelity would have reached him while he was involved in the military struggle for his kingdom. When they met the evidence was irrefutable: Lucy had a baby daughter. The father, or so it has usually been believed, was Lord Taaffe, the very man entrusted with oversight of the young woman's wellbeing. This casual alliance was taken as further evidence by those opposed to the king's relationship with Lucy that she was no more than a common strumpet.

Most historians who have attempted to untangle the Lucy Walter mystery have been concerned either to endorse this verdict or to whiten Lucy's reputation. Feeling a way through the tortuous maze of accusation, counter-accusation and conspiracy is a task verging on the impossible. Lucy Walter's story has all the drama and convolutions of romantic fiction, and truth might be as well served by a novelist as by a historian. Two facts are beyond doubt: Lucy did have a daughter, christened Mary, and Charles was not the father. Whether or not Taaffe indulged his desires with Lucy, he betrayed the trust that his king had, seemingly, imposed upon him. But that is not how seventeenth-century social morality would have judged the matter. In sexual misdemeanours 75 per cent of the blame was always attributed to the woman. It need not therefore surprise us that Taaffe did not forfeit his master's favour and that relations between Charles and Lucy suffered a blow from which they did not recover. This was certainly unfair by any objective standard. 'Mrs Barlow's' lover had gone off to the wars. During the sixteen months of their separation rumours concerning Charles' fate were rife on the continent and one very strong story told of his death in battle. This cannot fail to have devastated Lucy. She and her son were faced with destitution in a foreign land. She could not look to the Stuart family for succour. On Charles' presumed death all their hopes were focused on his heir, James. Lucy and her offspring no longer had any place in the scheme of things. They might even be regarded as a potential threat to the tranquil transition of the Crown from Charles to his brother. Lucy was desperately in need of a new protector and had only one way of attracting one.

It goes without saying that, while Charles considered himself free to engage in a variety of amours, he expected Lucy to keep herself for him. However, there was no immediate estrangement. Hyde recorded, with infuriating vagueness, that Lucy 'lived afterwards for some years in France in the king's sight'.[16] From his exceedingly slender means Charles made provision for her and the boy. He managed to find £400 a year. In 1655, a much increased pension of 5,000 livres was authorised by royal warrant. This figure, so vastly in excess of anything the king or his ministers could lay their hands on, was never paid. It was offered as hush money after the relationship had disintegrated to the point at which Lucy was threatening to make a nuisance of herself.

But the magic had gone out of the affair long before matters came to that pass. It may be that Lucy was making unrealistic demands, attempting to cling to her privileged position as her lover's ardour cooled. She began to be an embarrassment to those who had previously looked kindly upon her for the king's sake. The time arrived when Henrietta Maria asked Hyde's help in having removed from her court a woman whose behaviour had become insufferable and it seems almost certain that this was Lucy Walter, driven by insecurity to assert her 'rights' with increasing desperation as her position grew steadily more untenable.

Other women, with less justification though no less determination, looked for financial support to the impoverished king. One such was Eleanor, Lady Byron. She was the young second wife of the much older John, first Baron Byron, one of the staunchest adherents to the Stuart cause. John was a soldier by profession, who had learned his craft in the Low Countries and had served his king with courage and dedication on most of the major Civil War battlefields. Only when hope of military success was abandoned had he escaped to Paris to place his services at the disposal of his late master's queen. Subsequently he was appointed superintendent of the Duke of York's household and did all in his power to stir a longing for military valour in James and to secure for him a place in the French army. Byron was one of the seven leading royalists specifically exempted from any possibility of pardon by the parliament in London. He was a man of the camp and not of the court, uncomfortable with the fripperies of Parisian life and the claustrophobic intrigues of the royal council. Both his marriages were childless and it may be that his wives saw little of him in more senses than one. Whatever attraction there was between Charles and Eleanor, it would have been unthinkable for the king to have cuckolded a man who had spent himself and his fortune to the uttermost in the royal cause. It was not until after Byron's death in August 1652 that he and the widow became lovers.

We know nothing of their relationship apart from the scathing reminiscences of Evelyn and Pepys. According to them the 'whore' tried to squeeze money from the impoverished monarch during his exile and successfully extorted a promise of £4,000 worth of plate after the Restoration (though, 'thanks be to God, she died before she had it').[17] There must be another side to the story alluded to by these censorious gossips. Eleanor was one more female victim of her menfolk's wars. Married to an absentee husband, she had been conveyed abroad, probably with little or no say in the matter, and been obliged to share his uncomfortable exile. There could be no question of returning to England. The Byron estates had been sequestered and her own family were deeply embroiled in royalist intrigue. Her brother, Charles, Viscount Kilmorey, died in prison a few years later after a failed uprising. As to the family of her first husband, the Warburtons, she could look for no succour there, for they were high in favour with the new regime. Therefore, it was only reasonable for her to seek support from the king for whom she had sacrificed home, comfort, social standing and the prospect of a peaceful and respected life.

The shadowy women who were part of Charles' life in Fronde-torn Paris and the subsequent disturbed years form a distinct category. The king's sexual relationships during his wanderings were quite different from those he indulged after his return to the throne. He and his mistresses were living in a house of cards, grabbing what pleasures and comforts were available to them in the knowledge that they probably had nothing better to look forward to. They were comrades in misfortune, sharing a precarious lifestyle to which the constraints of conventional morality, while demanding the employment of discretion, may have seemed irrelevant. What they all needed was comfort in the midst of misfortune. Daily entertainments took their minds off their predicament. Nightly trysts encouraged the women to hope that their lover would look after their interests and boosted Charles' fragile self-confidence.

Charles' close relationship with Lucy Walter seems to have petered out by the end of 1653, for the next sighting we have of her is the following year in Brussels, where she had found a new protector. Trouble was just around the corner for her and the king but, meanwhile, Charles had his hands full sorting out dissension among his female relatives. Henrietta Maria was still trying to control the lives of her children and they still resented it. She took every opportunity to drive a wedge between them and Sir Edward Hyde. In 1652 there arose a complaint that she was using Princess Mary's closest confidante, Lady Stanhope, to thwart the policies of the king's ministers. This lady, whose second husband, John Kirkhoven, Lord of Heenvliet, was the superintendent of Mary's household, had been at the princess's side ever since her arrival in the Low Countries. She enjoyed her mistress's complete trust and after the death of William the two women were inseparable. Because Lady Stanhope had always been a favourite of the queen dowager, Hyde, genuinely fearing her influence at the Orange court which was so vital to the king's interests, urged Charles to remonstrate with his sister. The reply of high-spirited Mary might have been predicted. She flew into a rage, informing her brother that she would choose her own attendants and would thank him not to interfere.

The unpleasantness passed like a summer storm. Not so another three-sided conflict a couple of years later. Once again mother and daughter fell out over Edward Hyde. Mary provided the harassed minister and his wife with a house at Breda and also offered their daughter, Anne, a position as one of her ladies-in-waiting. Henrietta Maria was furious at this display of affection for a family she considered as her sworn enemies. She insisted that Anne be dismissed. Once again Mary dug her heels in. Even when Hyde, via Lady Stanhope, tactfully suggested that it might be as well in the interests of family harmony to accede to the matriarch's wishes, the princess would not give way. Anne stayed and became one of the liveliest members of the Orange court. She even won the approval of the hard-to-please Queen of Bohemia. More significantly, within a few years, she had captivated the Duke of York. The couple's marriage, in 1660, was to have dire consequences for all concerned.

But what most lethally poisoned relationships within the royal family was Henrietta Maria's behaviour towards her youngest son. Having largely failed to dominate Charles and James, she was determined to keep the teenage Henry, Duke of Gloucester, tied to her apron strings and to her Bourbon interests. More specifically, she considered it her duty to engineer his conversion to Catholicism. In February 1653, 'Harry Stuart', as he was referred to by the government, was allowed to leave his confinement in Carisbrooke Castle and be reunited with his family. He arrived at the Hague to be smothered by the affection of his sister, his aunt and his female cousins. Mary wanted to keep him in the United Netherlands, the States-General were prepared to turn a blind eye to his residence and Charles happily gave his consent. Henrietta Maria, however, demanded that her son be sent on to Paris. The other members of the family were not happy about this but Charles felt that he could not refuse a reunion between Henry and his mother. He sanctioned a visit to Paris which, he stipulated, should be of no more than a few months' duration. He also made it clear that the Duke of Gloucester was to be placed under no duress in matters of religion. The queen dowager accepted these conditions – with no intention whatsoever of abiding by them.

Nothing untoward could happen while Charles remained in Paris but, in the following summer, he was virtually forced out. Cromwell commanded Europe's best navy, recently triumphant over the Dutch, and was a major player in international affairs, courted by both France and Spain. The triumph of Protestant republicanism across *La Manche* was a *fait accompli* and most observers in Paris, including, even, Henrietta Maria, regarded the restoration of the Stuarts as a pipe dream. The continued presence of the sponging Charles II could now only be an encumbrance to Mazarin's foreign policy. He offered the impoverished king a considerable financial bribe to leave the country within ten days. The council had for some time been exploring the possibility of alternative residences. Despite Mary's urgings, the government of the United Netherlands would have none of her brother. Charles could not openly appeal to Spain, France's enemy. What he did was send mendicants to all the other princely courts which might lend him some support. He was quite unscrupulous in his approaches: he appealed to Lutheran and Calvinist monarchs on the basis of their shared Protestantism while to Catholic rulers he promised toleration for their co-religionists.

His most successful emissary was Wilmot, recently elevated to the peerage at his own request as Earl of Rochester. He made a favourable impression on the emperor and several of the German princes. They voted him a grant of £45,000 at the imperial diet at Ratisbon and the Elector of Cologne offered the Stuart court asylum in his territory. Thus it was that, with a lighter heart and an embellished entourage, Charles set out from Paris in July 1654. He looked upon the immediate weeks ahead as something of a holiday. Mary was to join him and together they would take in the sights and be sumptuously entertained by fellow royals.

The weeks of late summer and early autumn were a relaxed interlude in the king's harassed and unsatisfactory life. He and Mary met up at Spa and moved in a leisurely progress to Aachen and Cologne. Everywhere there were sights to be seen and new friends to be made. The Stuart siblings were lodged palatially and welcomed by local worthies who tried to outdo each other with banquets and balls and hunting expeditions. But the idyll did not last. Charles could not totally escape anxiety about the situation back in France. He had left precise instructions with James to keep an eye on their mother, in whose word he had very little trust:

> I have told you what the queen hath promised me concerning my brother Harry in point of religion, and I have given him charge to inform you if any attempt shall be made upon him to the contrary; in which case you will take the best care you can to prevent his being wrought upon, since you cannot but know how much you and I are concerned in it.[18]

Those last words are a give-away. They tell us what lay at the root of Charles' fears. He was not concerned about his brother's religion *per se*. It was his own *raison d'être* that was at stake. To wink at Henry's conversion would be to admit that he no longer believed in the cause of a restored Stuart monarchy. Once that message circulated throughout Britain and Europe the trickle of funds from royalists at home and well-wishers abroad would dry up. He would become plain Charles Stuart, a man of little talent, no training and no fortune.

His anxieties were only too well founded. As soon as he was out of the way Henrietta Maria began her mischief. She sent the boy off to join his brother James in Turenne's camp. On his return the fourteen-year-old, who had a generous share of Stuart arrogance and stubbornness, was not disposed to settle to his studies. This was all the excuse his grandmother needed to discharge the tutor appointed by the king and to establish in his place one of her priests, who whisked the boy off to a Jesuit seminary. James, as he had been ordered, rushed to Paris and he was far from being the only one to address urgent letters to Charles.

Sir, no minute must be lost for prevention and no middle way will do it. Certain it is the queen did lately tell the Duke of Gloucester that the return to England was laid out of her thoughts and all wise men's and that there was no way left him to rise but his book and the Church.[19]

The news arrived in Cologne soon after Mary had returned home and it shattered Charles' newfound sense of wellbeing. The normally imperturbable king was roused to a great fury. Hyde reported he had never seen his master so impassioned. He despatched a flurry of letters, which was, in itself, unusual, urging everyone who had any influence in Paris to intervene. To his mother he wrote in a tone which just managed to be respectful:

I must confess that this news does trouble me so much that I cannot say all that I could at another time . . . I must conclude that if your Majesty does continue to proceed in the change of my brother's religion, I cannot expect your Majesty does either believe or wish my return into England . . . if your Majesty has the least kindness for me I beg you not to press him further in it . . . remember the last words of my dead father (whose memory I doubt not will work upon you) which were to charge him upon his blessing never to change his religion . . .[20]

Charles informed Jermyn that if his ministers in Paris did not use all their endeavours to thwart the queen dowager's plans he would have nothing more to do with them and he sent Ormonde to escort Henry to the safety of his sister's court at the Hague. Relations between Charles' entourage and the Louvre party plummeted to their lowest level.

Charles won this particular battle and Henrietta Maria was obliged to yield. She did so with an exceedingly bad grace. When Henry came to take his leave of her she ranted at him, refused her blessing and screamed that he was no longer her son. One might have supposed that this episode would have caused a final breach between Charles and his mother but within a couple of years family harmony had been restored. Mary acted as an intermediary. She and Charles made another royal tour in the late summer of 1655, visiting Aix, Frankfurt and Cologne. Mary picked up the bill for most of their incidental expenses, as she had done the previous year. A few months later the princess travelled to Paris for a long stay with her mother after which she was able to express to Charles the hope that there would henceforth be a good understanding among them all in spite of 'hot heads'. Charles was more than ready for such a reconciliation. He treated the queen dowager with affectionate respect while taking no notice of her wishes on all matters political.

This reveals to us something of how his character was developing under the pressures of his exile. His way of dealing with unpleasantness was simply to sidestep it whenever possible. Just as he dealt with poverty by not paying his bills and with unpalatable policy decisions by procrastination, so he refused to allow his equanimity to be ruffled by personal conflict. Over and again he restored to his good graces servants who had in one way or another betrayed his trust. For the most part he held aloof from the squabbles of rival ministers and factions. When mistresses and companions plagued him for favours he made promises that his slender means made it impossible for him to keep.

Had this been a calculated attitude, a demonstration of royal *mysterium*, designed to indicate that a gracious king was above the sordid emotions and prosaic reactions of ordinary mortals, it would have impressed more people. Without doubt there were those who were so dazzled by the aura that they were genuinely blinded to the man within it. For those who knew him better, however, Charles' consorting with companions of low rank and lower morals somewhat tarnished the sacred image. Insofar as the king consciously developed an easygoing personality he had two very good reasons for doing so. His very survival depended upon his being agreeable to men and women of all estates – to princes who admitted him to the royal 'club', to ministers and attendants who supported his lifestyle and political pretensions for very meagre reward, to agents who maintained vital contact with activists in Britain, to humble royalists who had helped him escape or shared his exile or simply clung to an inherited conviction that 'the breath of worldly men cannot depose the deputy elected by the Lord'. The other reason was his father's commitment to that very doctrine. The signpost that had pointed Charles I along the inevitable road to the scaffold had been his commitment to the concept of semi-divine kingship. He had told the crowd on that frosty January afternoon that 'a subject and a sovereign are clear different things' and that he stood before them as a 'martyr of the people'. Not only did his son shy away from such fatal inflexibility, he did not hold the principles which underlay it. Whatever ideas he did have about his inherited role totally lacked the theological underpinning that had sustained his father through the years of warfare, tortuous negotiation and imprisonment.

Charles' open, friendly and forgiving nature was the despair of his ministers. Not only did the king damage his own image by surrounding himself with worthless companions, he also made it easy for Cromwell's industrious spymaster, John Thurloe, to keep himself well informed of the king's plans. In January 1655, a well-set-up young man bearing the scars of active service in the royalist cause arrived at Cologne. His name was Henry Manning, a relative and attendant of the Marquis of Worcester, a ferocious Catholic, who had served Charles I in Ireland, suffered the sequestration of his estates, lived in exile until shortage of funds obliged him to return home, and had until recently been a prisoner in the Tower. Manning's father had been killed at the battle of Cheriton in 1644 and the young man had, himself, been wounded in the same engagement. He arrived with letters of commendation to Dr Earle, the king's faithful tutor and companion, from friends of impeccable trustworthiness, and declared that he wished to place himself and the funds he had been able to salvage at his sovereign's disposal. He brought with him, or so he claimed, information about secret royalist plans being hatched at the very highest levels in England. Manning was so plausible that the Earl of Rochester fell for his story hook, line and sinker and introduced him to the king. Hyde was dubious but Charles was won over by Wilmot's persuasion and the young man's charm.

Posing as a vital intermediary with English agents, Manning tried to make himself privy to the court's plans regarding the encouragement of disaffected elements in Britain. He then passed the information on to Thurloe. However, Hyde was using his own intelligence network to check on Master Manning. This led to the spy's correspondence being intercepted at Antwerp and his treachery exposed. Manning was arrested, interrogated and tried by a private court. On 15 December 1655, he was taken to a wood just outside Cologne and shot.

Seventeen months of political idleness had been forced on Charles because the republican government in London was strong, royalist opposition was disorganised and ineffective, and the international situation offered no circumstance of which the king might take advantage. There was nothing he could do, except, in Hyde's words, 'sit still and expect God's own time'.[21] But now, at last, in the closing weeks of 1655, a sudden window of opportunity opened. Cromwell, having made peace with the Dutch, re-invigorated that popular, anti-Spanish sentiment that had lingered ever since the days of Elizabeth. Asserting that Spain's maritime activities were a threat to England's commercial interests and a means of spreading Catholicism around the globe, he began an onslaught on Spanish transatlantic shipping and established a new Caribbean stronghold by capturing the island of Jamaica. Mazarin was not slow to cash in on the changed situation. He offered Cromwell a new treaty, one of the terms of which was to be the continued exclusion of Charles and his brothers from French territory.

If the Stuarts were an embarrassment to France, they had now become a potential asset to Spain, or so some of Philip IV's ministers believed. It would do no harm, they reasoned, to support, at modest cost, English royalists whose activities might distract the Lord Protector's government from the war effort. They gave little thought to the possibility of Charles actually regaining his throne, but if he were to do so, with Spanish help, then he would have a profound debt to repay to his Most Catholic Majesty. Peace with England would be restored and the threat to Spain's vital colonial supply lines halted.

A new understanding between the exiles and the world's leading colonial power which, from Madrid, looked like nothing more than a possibility worth exploring was much more attractive from Charles' point of view. He and his advisers worked enthusiastically to make it a reality. That meant negotiating with the Archduke Don Juan-José, Governor of the Spanish Netherlands and Philip's bastard son by an actress. Charles sent a succession of emissaries to Brussels to prepare the ground for substantive talks but Don Juan-José was not convinced that an impoverished, dispossessed, playboy king whose supporters were notoriously disorganised could serve any useful purpose in the scheme of Spanish statecraft, nor was he prepared to take any initiative without specific instructions from Madrid. Charles and his council were desperate to gain the effective backing of a major power. Therefore, everything that could be done to impress their desired allies had to be done. Among other things, that meant revisiting the Lucy Walter problem.

The erstwhile mistress was becoming more and more of an encumbrance and it was not entirely her fault. She and her children could not live on promises of royal handouts that materialised at best sporadically. From time to time she travelled to the royal court, wherever it might happen to be, seeking further aid from the father of her son, only to have Charles fob her off with trifles or with yet more promises. She had become an irritant and the king's response was always to get rid of her as quickly and easily as possible. When, in 1655, he made out a warrant for the payment of a pension, he stipulated that the instalments were to be paid in Antwerp – far away from where he was living. By any standards this was shabby, cowardly treatment. Rather than tell Lucy that their relationship was at an end, he strung her along with expressions of affection and petty gifts. She had no alternative but to find other men to whom she could sell herself. Since everyone knew of her relationship with the king this could only cause tongues to wag. Such gossip was harmful to Charles and an annoyance to royal ministers who were trying to create the impression that he was a serious-minded monarch worthy of restoring to his father's throne. They were especially alarmed when, in Brussels, capital of the Spanish Netherlands, Lucy began an affair with the king's personal representative, Sir Henry De Vic. Salacious rumour was not the only problem. Lucy was a magnet for Cromwellian spies. She knew intimate details about the life of Charles and his companions that could be used to his discredit and the more desperate she became, the more likely she was to sell her secrets.

By the beginning of 1656, when Charles was trying to impress the representatives of Philip IV, Lucy was at the Hague, living with Thomas Howard, a member of the Princess of Orange's entourage. But this brother of the Duke of Suffolk had other employment; he was in the pay of John Thurloe, head of Cromwell's intelligence service. Mary had by now turned against her brother's ex-lover. Having made her peace with Henrietta

Maria, she was once again under the Stuart matriarch's sway and both women regarded Lucy as an encumbrance to the king. From his sister Charles learned that Mrs Barlow was living a life of open depravity and bringing discredit on all who were associated with her. Presuming upon her royal connections, and encouraged by affectionate letters sent to her by Charles, via Taaffe, she was dragging the king's name through the Dutch mud. How much of this was truth and how much vicious gossip is impossible to say but if Lucy had become wildly promiscuous it is likely to have been more from necessity than lust. Charles and members of his circle could not make the same claim. And if this bold creature relied on emotional blackmail to back her continual demands for money, she certainly had more claim than most on the king's generosity. Anyway, as Hyde was constantly urging, this was a critical time in which projecting a good image was more than ever vital for the Stuart cause. Enquiries had to be made into Lucy's conduct.

The man Charles used as his eyes and ears was one of the most trusted servants of the royal family, Daniel O'Neill. This soldier-courtier had proved his loyalty on the battlefield and his usefulness in several private intrigues. Hyde described him as 'a great observer and discerner of men's natures and humours . . . very dextrous in compliance where he found it useful'.[22] In modern parlance we might call O'Neill 'streetwise'. He was a frequent go-between for Mary and her brother and the obvious choice to investigate Lucy's behaviour. O'Neill's reports did not make pleasant reading. He pointed out as bluntly as he considered seemly that his master's weak attitude of giving in to Lucy's demands simply encouraged her. She would only mend her ways if she was 'necessitated', i.e. starved into submission.

But what ways was she supposed to mend? O'Neill's vivid picture of Mrs Barlow's lifestyle presents an alarming image of a woman driven by circumstance or character defect close to the brink of insanity. He writes of bribery, prostitution, abortion, murder and blackmail and he warns the king, 'I am much troubled to see the prejudice her being here does your Majesty; for every idle action of hers brings your Majesty upon the stage.' O'Neill recounted that only by paying off Lucy's maid had he managed to avoid the latest appalling incidents becoming the talk of the town:

> I had the opportunity to save her from public scandal . . . Her maid, whom she would have killed by thrusting a bodkin into her ear as she was asleep, would have accused her of . . . miscarrying of two children by physic and of the infamous manner of her living with Mr Howard but I have prevented the mischief, partly with threats, but more with 100 guilders I am to give her maid. Her last miscarriage was since Mr Howard went . . . Though I have saved her for this time, it's not likely she'll escape when I am gone; for only the consideration of your

Majesty has held Monsieur Heenvliet and Monsieur Niertwick not to have her banished from this town and country for an infamous person and by sound of drum.[23]

O'Neill urged the king to take a tough line with this unruly wanton. He should make any further aid conditional upon Lucy mending her ways and upon conceding custody of her six-year-old son to some responsible guardian.

This was expecting too much of Charles. He would not add to Lucy's distress if some less confrontational way could be found of dealing with the problem. His more immediate concerns were bringing the Spanish to commit themselves to a treaty and finding lodgings for his court. In March he travelled incognito to Brussels and sought permission to establish residence there. This alarmed Don Juan-José. Having the English king and his household in the capital would make far too definite a diplomatic statement. After weeks of awkward negotiation, Charles agreed to establish his headquarters at Bruges. Some time during this period of toing and froing he seems to have paid a flying visit to Lucy and, according to her maid, spent a day and a night with her. It may have been then that Charles put forward an easy compromise that would appeal to Lucy, that would remove her from the Hague and that would get her out of his hair. Funds were found to despatch her and the children back to England. Thither they went at the beginning of June. They were supposed to be travelling anonymously but since Thomas Howard was a member of the party there was no possibility of their remaining unrecognised. Cromwell's men soon had Lucy whisked into the Tower for interrogation.

There was little she could tell them of any political significance but she did have propaganda value for the republican regime. Details of her life and liaisons were widely published and the lesson hammered home that it was on such creatures as this that Charles Stuart chose to spend the money sacrificially provided by misguided English well-wishers. Having made as much salacious capital as possible from the story, the government cleverly crowned the achievement by sending Mrs Barlow and her offspring back to the Low Countries so that she could continue to be an embarrassment to the Stuart family.

The policy worked. Lucy elected to make her home in Brussels which, from Charles' point of view, was the most inconvenient location possible. The twisted threads of her emotional life, tangled as they were with those of Stuart politics, continued to attract attention and were more than a mere irritant to Charles and his advisers. Hyde, who never referred to the king's mistresses by name, must have been alluding to Lucy when he reported to Ormonde in the summer of 1657, 'There is much talk here of a certain lady who is at Brussels and, I assure you, very shrewd discourses of it, which will quickly get into England. I pray you let her go to some other place.'[24]

The scandal he was referring to concerned Lucy's falling out with Thomas Howard. Their affair having ended acrimoniously, she sent a friend or relative after her ex-lover with a knife. There was a brawl in the streets of the capital in which Howard was injured but the unseemly brouhaha did not end there. Shortly afterwards Howard instigated legal proceedings, not for personal injury, but theft. He charged Lucy with appropriating certain papers which were important to him and could prove harmful if they fell into the wrong hands. Bearing in mind Howard's shady life, it is not difficult to guess at the contents of these documents. Blackmail can scarcely have been a novel inspiration to the discarded woman but she certainly now turned to it. She possessed the means to obtain money by force from unfaithful lovers when appeals to their better nature failed. Later she used this tactic on the king and she may already have been letting it be known that she would stop at nothing in her desperation.

There can be little doubt that, had he been in a position to do so, Charles would have taken the line of least resistance and met her demands. That was no longer possible. He was financially worse off than ever before. He had pawned everything pawnable. The wages of his household officers were eighteen months in arrears. The Spanish subsidy, when it was paid, was quite inadequate to meet his needs. His situation was painfully brought home to him every time he sat to meals at the royal table: he and his companions had to slake their appetites with just one course. The leading citizens of Bruges were hospitable to the new celebrity in their midst and laid on banquets and other entertainments but there was a limit to their generosity and as the flow of invitations dwindled to a trickle Charles became bored with the life of what he referred to as this 'dead' provincial town whose people were too ready to complain at the outrageous antics of his more boisterous followers.

Reports of Charles' behaviour at this time present a double image. He was active in numerous ways to make the Spanish alliance work in his favour. Rather than sit in idleness while others were taking up arms, he volunteered to serve in the Spanish army (a request which was declined). He despatched representatives to Brussels and Madrid requesting – at times demanding – the provision of funds and men for the invasion of England. He sent other emissaries across the Channel to activate his scattered bands of supporters. He was prepared to discuss terms with anyone who might support what must have seemed his last chance of making a bid for a return to power. Messages were sent to groups opposed to the Cromwellian regime, as diverse as Scottish Presbyterians and ultra-republican Levellers. The king even backed a scheme to assassinate the Lord Protector. None of these initiatives came to anything. As well as the old problem of lack of cohesion among royalists in Britain, Charles was bedevilled by the half-heartedness of the Spanish. Whereas he wanted money and materiel up front for his invasion attempt, they expected him to set the military campaign in motion before they would commit any resources. The only thing the king did achieve was the assembly of a royal army. Recruits from home arrived to swell the ranks of fellow countrymen who had hitherto served as mercenaries in France and, by the middle of 1657, 2,500 men had gathered to the Stuart standard and were fighting for Spain on the southern border of the Netherlands.

Yet the inspiring image of an industrious, majestic, intellectually astute leader was not the one recognised by many of those close to the king. He was petulant. A fresh round of quarrels broke out within the royal family. James, who resented being ordered to give up his command under Turenne and enlist with the forces of France's enemy, stormed out of Bruges after one heated argument with his brother, and even Mary, who spent all her time travelling between Breda and Charles' court to minister to her siblings' needs, was again alienated for a few months. Hyde's admonitions did not cease. He was appalled at his master's refusal to stick to clear principles: instead he would promise anything to anyone to gain some perceived advantage. The minister was now receiving frequent letters expressing the growing disillusionment people felt with Oliver Cromwell. 'This audacious hypocrite,' one such correspondent inveighed,

> has, by the unsearchable wisdom of his deep-laid counsels, lighted such a candle into the dark dungeon of his soul that there is none so blind who does not plainly read treachery, tyranny, perfidiousness, dissimulation, atheism, hypocrisy and all manner of villainy written in large characters on his heart.[25]

Never had there been a better opportunity for the king to project himself as an attractive alternative. 'The eyes of all men are upon you,' Hyde urged. He pointed out that most people had no idea what kind of an adult the boy prince had grown into over the last decade. 'It is that which men are most solicitous and inquisitive to understand, and upon the manifestation whereof most of your good or ill fortune will be founded.'[26] To his intense frustration, Hyde realised that Charles II presented to the world an image that bore very little relationship to that of his sainted father. He found himself having to agree with Ormonde who opined that Charles' desire to quit Bruges had little to do with his proclaimed desire to be nearer the centre of the action and much to do with his pursuit of pleasure. The king would need sterling qualities, the earl suggested, to unite all his friends and confound all his enemies,

> but I fear his immoderate delight in empty, effeminate and vulgar conversation is become an irresistible part of his nature and will never suffer him to animate his own designs and others' actions with that spirit which is requisite for his quality and much more to his fortune.[27]

'Effeminate' is the key word and Ormonde was not alone in applying it to the king. We need to understand its implications because in the seventeenth century the term had different nuances than it has today. No one ever accused Charles II of speech and mannerisms verging on the homosexual. On the contrary, outraged Puritans dubbed him a lusty womaniser and the label has stuck. What Ormonde was objecting to was certainly not prissy affectation but neither was it libidinousness. The minister was a man of the world who would certainly not have been shocked by the king's bedroom antics. When Ormonde mentioned effeminacy he meant, quite literally, *unmanliness*, and in his mind it was a quality that made a king unfit to rule. Fundamental to his thinking and to the thinking of all educated Christendom for a thousand years and more was the divine ordering of human society. Women had been created physically, intellectually, emotionally (and some would say spiritually) inferior to men. This appeared to be a glaringly self-evident truism which scarcely needed proving. Nevertheless, philosophers had demonstrated the logic behind the assumption. Thus, the contemporary Dutch thinker, Baruch Spinoza:

> Surely among so many different nations some would be found where both sexes ruled on equal terms, and others where the men were ruled by the women . . . But since this has nowhere happened, I am fully entitled to assert that women have not the same right as men by nature, but are necessarily inferior to them.[28]

Equally obviously, all men were not equal. Some were born to rule and some to be ruled. It followed then that kings stood at the apex of society. James I had admonished his son ever to give thanks to his Maker, 'first for that he made you a man and next for that he made you a little god to sit on his throne'. Therefore, for a monarch to indulge excessively in female company and to display those traits associated with women was doubly scandalous. Kit Marlowe's Tamburlaine had observed sneeringly,

> How unseemly is it for my sex,
> My discipline of arms and chivalry,
> My nature and the terror of my name,
> To harbour thoughts effeminate and faint![29]

In a man's world a king should be the most manly of men.

When it came to his relationship with women this meant that he should use them for his purposes. The opposite sex had very few legal rights. Princesses were given in marriage to cement international treaties. Queens had the primary function of bringing royal sons into the world. Heiresses were bought and sold in the interests of building up or maintaining territorial holdings. Since these conventions left little room for affection, men resorted to a variety of irregular liaisons to meet their physical and emotional needs or, simply, to express their male dominance. That was the hard reality of seventeenth-century life. If adultery and fornication were denounced by Christian preachers, as they were, and if the principles of monogamy and restraint were, in theory, accepted throughout society, as they were, and if the demands of the Ten Commandments were prominently displayed in every British church, as they were, this was not out of respect for women or consideration of their feelings. Proscription rested upon divine fiat and the practical consideration that loose sexual morals led to the appearance of bastards whose claims frequently frustrated the smooth working of inheritance laws. Kings and princes of the blood were not exempt from the precepts of the Bible but neither were they oblivious to the basic assumptions about the relative status of men and women. Whether they maintained private harems or, like Charles I, upheld the sanctity of marriage, they accepted that men, and especially monarchs, should exercise control over their womenfolk.

It was Charles II's departure from this norm that earned the censure of Ormonde and Hyde. His 'unseemly' behaviour consisted in surrounding himself with attractive women and putting himself under obligation to them. By 'effeminate conversation' the writer meant that Charles spent his time playing love games when he should have been attending to more serious affairs. He and his companions danced and played cards and sang the latest songs and flirted and gossiped about one another's amours.

We can obtain a flavour of this lighthearted, women-dominated world from the letters exchanged between the king and Theobald Taaffe, which are couched in terms of self-conscious naughtiness, use code names for the principal characters and hint at romantic indiscretions. Charles entrusts his collaborator with a secret note for 'Terese' with the strict instruction that it is for her eyes only.[30] He urges Taaffe to enlist the aid of a female co-conspirator in his latest pursuit: 'encourage her in the doing of me all good offices and assure her in the end *qu'elle ne repentira pas de l'amitié qu'elle m'a temoignes en cette affaire là*'.[31] The same correspondence reveals that Thomas Howard, the erstwhile spy and reprobate, came to be accepted among the king's intimates. Charles stated that he had written to Taaffe's friend Tom Howard and only regretted that he could not aid him with money. This alarmed even Hyde who, by now, was very familiar with his master's bewildering choice of unsuitable companions. 'I cannot believe it possible,' he told Ormonde, 'that the king, who hath evidence more than enough would say any such thing to please Lord Taaffe.'[32] Even when he was involved in March 1660 with negotiating his triumphant return to England he was casting roving eyes around: 'Pray send this enclosed *à la petite souris*. There is here a very pretty *souris* but the devil on't is the dame is so jealous that it must be a very good mouser that can take it.'[33]

Charles was in his element in this kind of society. It was what he had been used to intermittently since his earliest days in his mother's chambers at Whitehall. The continental courts where he had spent most of his time since 1646 had been governed by female rulers. He could relax in the company of women and courtiers who amused him with witty conversation and scurrilous tales. Retreating from the failures, disappointments and frustrations of the political arena, he could have his self-confidence boosted by the ladies who fawned upon him, laughed at his jokes, listened to his stories and assured him in the privacy of the bedchamber that he was a wonderful lover. From the point of view of his senior advisers, all that would have been tolerable in moderation. If the king had adopted the habit of clapping his hands to dismiss the royal playmates when there was serious work to be attended to his hard-pressed ministers would have been happy to allow him his diversions. But permitting his women to have first call upon his time, his emotional resources and even his slender purse meant that he was handing them power over the King of England. He was displaying feminine weakness. That was what his worried minders objected to.

Despite what has just been suggested, there is no evidence that Charles was massively promiscuous at this stage. Much of his confidential talk and letters were sheer bravado. He knew well that his sexual athleticism was enormously exaggerated by scurrilous or envious tittle-tattle and he acknowledged the truth of Hyde's admonitions that this could only harm his cause. As he pointed out to Taaffe, there were not enough hours in the day for him to have achieved the number of assignations attributed to him. He did not litter Bruges with royal bastards and he did seem to prefer fairly longstanding relationships. One such was with Catherine Pegge, the daughter of yet another loyal royalist in exile, Thomas Pegge of Yeldersley, Derbyshire. He sired two children by her – Charles Fitzcharles, commonly known as 'Don Carlos', and Catherine. The boy was later ennobled as the Earl of Plymouth but of the girl nothing is known and the likelihood is that she died in infancy. Charles enjoyed playing the father with his new family but when he tired of the role Catherine was wise enough to accept the fact. After the Restoration, Charles provided for her and her kin, and, although she never occupied an important position at court, she did have her own house in Pall Mall. In 1668 she married a much older man, Sir Edward Greene. The very absence of any more details about Catherine Pegge suggests that she knew how to accept the subservient role which was the lot of her sex. Perhaps there were others of whom we know nothing for precisely the same reason. But Charles' indulgence encouraged other mistresses to adopt a very different attitude.

Lucy Walter clearly came into this category. Because he had long been captivated by her and had yielded to her demands over and again Charles was in large measure responsible for the scandalous situation which had developed by the late 1650s. He had protested his love for her, long after his ardour had cooled. He had strung her along with tokens of affection and made her extravagant promises he was unable to fulfil. Whose fault was it that now she was threatening to publish his letters to her as the only way of extracting money from the king and keeping her and her children from penury? Of course, she had to be stopped. Charles' advisers pressed him repeatedly to deal firmly with the wayward woman before the damage she was doing to his reputation became irreparable. Charles, character-istically, declined to act personally. He went off to the front line in the autumn of 1657 and obtained permission from the archduke to be present at the defence of Mardyke. This was no token viewing of the carnage from a safe distance; while he was riding forth to examine the outworks with Ormonde the marquis had his horse shot from under him. Meanwhile, the other 'campaign' – against Lucy – he assigned to George Digby, Earl of Bristol. Digby, after a frenzied and controversial career as soldier and diplomat, had fetched up in the French army, fallen out with Mazarin and recently appeared in Bruges. He was exactly the kind of handsome, well-educated, witty and entertaining man that the king liked. Hyde tells us that Digby was

> of great eloquence and becomingness in his discourse . . . and of so universal a knowledge that he never wanted subject for a discourse. He was equal to a very good part in the greatest affair, but the unfittest man alive to conduct it, having an ambition and vanity superior to all his other parts and a confidence peculiar to himself which sometimes intoxicated and transported and exposed him.[34]

Charles soon admitted Digby to the royal council. But almost as soon he discharged him, for the earl debarred himself by announcing his con-version to Roman Catholicism. However, Bristol still had his uses and the king sent him to the archduke's camp where he rapidly ingratiated himself with Don Juan-José. (Among Digby's gifts he numbered fluency in Spanish.) To Charles this smooth-talking adventurer seemed to be the ideal person to persuade Mrs Barlow to see reason. But Digby was to demonstrate the accuracy of Hyde's assessment of him.

The first plan was ill-conceived and ludicrously bungled. The object was to get Lucy into prison so that she would have to agree to whatever conditions Charles imposed to regain her freedom. The executant chosen for this malevolent charade was Bristol's secretary, Colonel Arthur Slingsby, who, for his compliance, extracted a baronetcy from the king. Slingsby was newly married and had a house in Brussels. On 1 December Charles personally validated Slingsby's mission in a letter of introduction to Taaffe: 'This bearer, Sir A Slingsby, returns as plenipotentiary in the matter of the child. If you can contribute anything to it by your good counsel, I pray do it.'[35] Slingsby befriended Lucy and persuaded her to take lodgings with him. After a few weeks he confronted her one night with an unpaid bill for bed and board and tried to have her removed to the local jail. If he had supposed that the 'beautiful, brown and bold' woman would go quietly, he vastly underestimated her. She set up such a hollering that all the neighbours threw open their shutters or ventured out on to the darkened street to see what all the commotion was about. All that could be seen in the confusion was that a defenceless lady and her infant children were being attacked by a bunch of foreign ruffians. One of those whose nocturnal peace was disturbed was Don Alonso de Cardenas, the ex-Spanish ambassador to England. He took it upon himself to restore order. Lucy he sent to the safe haven of another house, and the prison cell that should have received her became the temporary lodging of the officer who had tried to arrest her.

The next day Cardenas lost no time in complaining to the king and he also instructed his secretary, Egidio Mottet, to pursue the matter with Ormonde. Mottet did not mince his words.

> My Lord, I am so much ashamed of the proceeding of Monsieur Slingsby and all his family against Madame Barlow and her child that I am loath to relate the particulars thereof to your excellency . . . My Lord Ambassador hath written to the king about it being forced thereunto by the clamour of the people, who found this action most barbarous, abominable and most unnatural. The worst of all is that Sir Arthur doth report and say to all that the king hath given him order for it. But out of my obligation and respect to the king, I do endeavour to disabuse all of it . . .[36]

Tactfully worded replies were soon on their way back to Brussels. In his response to the secretary, Ormonde thanked him for his care and expressed his master's regret for the fracas. To clarify the situation he pointed out that the king had indeed issued instructions to Slingsby, 'in a quiet and silent way, if it could be, to get the child out of the mother's hands, with purposes of advantage to them both, but he never understood it should be attempted with the noise and scandal that hath happened'. But now followed thinly veiled threats in the king's name. Ormonde asks for help in detaching young James from his mother. This, he represented, would be,

> a great charity to the child and in the conclusion to the mother, if she shall now at length retire herself to such a way of living as may redeem in some measure the reproach her past ways have brought upon her. If she consents not to this she will add to all her former follies a most unnatural one in reference to her child, who by her obstinacy will be exposed to all the misery and reproach that will attend her when neither

of them is any further cared for or owned by his majesty; but that, on the contrary he will take any good office done to her as an injury to him and as a supporting of her in mad disobedience to his pleasure.

The letter concluded with a reiteration of what, Ormonde insisted, was the king's determination in the event of Lucy continuing obdurate: 'he will free himself the best way he may from any further trouble or scandal and leave her to her fortune'.[37]

These harsh words represented a gloss on Charles' actual sentiments. If he could have bought Lucy off, there can be little doubt that he would have done so, but he did not have the means to buy her silence. Therefore, she became the victim of the king's impecuniousness, her own obstinacy in refusing to be parted from her son, and that change in the political climate which made it imperative for Charles not to lose face internationally. The king simply gave his ministers *carte blanche* to do whatever was necessary while he looked the other way. Now the full force of the Stuart establishment could be unleashed upon the wretched ex-mistress. Ormonde and Bristol brought pressure to bear upon Don Juan-José, whose attitude towards the English had changed because he now needed their help in the military conflict. He, in turn, instructed Cardenas to abandon his protection of Lucy. Her belongings were searched and any damaging documents removed. She did not give up her son without a fight. She insisted that she would only grant custody to someone she trusted. Eventually, little James was taken from her by a trick. Asked to produce a paper that had some bearing on her relationship with the king, she went to a trunk to find it. While her back was turned the boy was hurried out of the house. Some time during the next few months he was taken to Paris, where his grandmother took charge of his upbringing.

In the following autumn two deaths occurred which altered the course of Charles Stuart's life. On 3 September 1658, the anniversary of the battles of Dunbar and Worcester, Oliver Cromwell breathed his last. A few weeks later, on a date which has gone unrecorded, Lucy Walter alias Barlow died in Paris where she had gone, presumably, to be near her son. It was typical of the Stuart attitude towards Monmouth's mother that James II should record in his memoirs that Lucy had succumbed to a 'disease incident to her profession'. Charles' treatment of the woman he had once loved was ultimately callous. Yet he cannot be accused of simply casting her aside when he had lost interest in her. If he allowed her to impose on him over and again it was because he felt some responsibility for her and her situation. Where he failed was in his insensitivity. Emotionally stunted himself, he simply could not understand how she felt – about him and about their son. Had Lucy entered his life at a later stage when he was secure on his throne, he would have paid her off handsomely and thought that that discharged his duty towards her. It was his inability to do that and her inability to live modestly and quietly away from the 'bright lights' which had dazzled her that caused her tragic downfall. Lucy Walter was of a type with the likes of Marilyn Monroe, an unsophisticated child who could not cope with life inside the walls of Camelot – or outside them.

CHAPTER 6

Return from Babylon

In October 1659 the wily Cardinal Mazarin made an uncharacteristic miscalculation. Charles Stuart asked him for the hand in marriage of his youngest niece, Hortense Mancini, and the French minister refused. As well as his own distinctly cool feelings towards the king who had lived for years on French subsidies, then sent his own troops into the field against France, he had good reason for not attaching his family to the royal house of England. Even a year after Cromwell's death the smart money was not on a return to hereditary monarchy. The passing of the Lord Protector, who, whatever his reputation at home, had enjoyed more international prestige than any of his predecessors in living memory, had left unresolved a host of political and constitutional issues and all the concerned parties – parliament, army, Presbyterians, radicals, republicans, royalists – were down in the arena belabouring each other with their varied ideological weapons. The situation ought to have played right into Charles' hands. Was this not the moment that Hyde had been waiting for; the opportunity for which he had long counselled his master to hold himself in patient readiness? The answer brought back by Ormonde after a secret sortie into England was 'No'. There was no consensus for the return of Charles I's son. Indeed, if any opinion poll could have been taken in 1659 it would probably have revealed a majority decision not to tolerate any single head of state but to entrust power to some kind of representative assembly. As for those who did support the king's return, they were as disunited and ineffective as ever. On the continent Spain had proved a broken reed as far as the Stuart cause was concerned. In fine, nothing seemed to have changed.

Had Mazarin taken a gamble, the future of Charles II, the House of Stuart, and the British nations would have been profoundly different. Hortense Mancini was a woman who would have proved herself a strong, intelligent consort, more than a match for her husband, his squabbling ministers and the other women who vied for his favours. Hortense was as lively as she was beautiful. She was much given to practical jokes, such as presenting her governess with a box of sweetmeats beneath whose coloured wrappings was concealed a colony of mice. The 'Mazarinettes', as she and her two sisters were called, turned many heads in the Louvre, where they were brought up. Charles knew them from quite early on in his exile but there is no record of him taking especial interest in them until now. But, in 1659, he was approaching his thirtieth birthday, which meant that by the standards of the day he was middle-aged – and still unwed. Earlier attempts to secure a useful political alliance or an even more useful fortune by marriage had come to nothing. Added to that, he was very choosy. He rejected all German princesses out of hand because they were 'all so foggy' (i.e. physically bloated or mentally flabby – perhaps both). If he preferred the Latin temperament he certainly observed it in Hortense Mancini; there was nothing 'foggy' about her. She had blossomed into a bright-eyed, vivacious fourteen-year-old, union with whom offered the prospect of a huge dowry, alliance with France, the likelihood of healthy offspring and considerable pleasure in the begetting of them. It was to the misfortune of both parties that, in the closing weeks of 1659, a matrimonial arrangement had no political attraction for France.

Charles and his ministers had nothing to bring to the bargaining table. Militarily, their alliance with Spain had been a disaster. The only major battle in which royalist troops shared had taken place in June 1658. It was fought on the coast near Dunkirk and has gone down in history as the battle of the Dunes. The Duke of York fought under Don Juan-José with five British regiments against his old commander, Turenne, whose superior force of 28,000 men included six regiments sent over by Cromwell. It was the swansong of the New Model Army and they made a spectacular exit from the annals of military history, leading the pike charge that dislodged the enemy musketeers from their commanding position among the sandhills with fearsome losses.* The engagement was remarkable for a number of reasons. In that British royalists faced British republicans, it might be called the last confrontation of the Civil Wars. On the other hand, there was an irony about Cromwell's men fighting alongside papist troops. The battle also marked an intriguing centenary. By the terms of their treaty, Mazarin handed over the port of Dunkirk to Cromwell – exactly one hundred years after Catholic Mary had abandoned the English foothold of Calais.

As the victorious Anglo-French army swept onward, Charles fled from Brussels into the neighbouring United Netherlands, despite the proscription of the States-General. But there was more to the move than the search for a temporary haven. The fact that England now bestrode the Channel made it more than ever impossible for the king's Spanish allies to convey an invasion force across the water, even if they were seriously to consider it. However, the Dutch boasted an effective navy. Perhaps the nation that had recently been humiliated by its sister republic might like to

---

* Although the bulk of the English force was composed of volunteers, they were drawn for the most part from the regular army.

take revenge by coming to his aid. Not only was this plan a clutching at straws, it also risked another family rift. By making overtures to the States-General Charles' emissaries were going behind the back of Princess Mary, who had made sacrifice after sacrifice to help her brother.

But the attempt to cement relations with the Dutch nation was, for Charles, more than a dry, diplomatic exercise. He fancied himself to be in love again. His new passion was not the volcanic eruption of emotion that had afflicted him when he set eyes on Lucy Walter and which was resistant to the cold deluges of reason. Charles had known his new 'friend' (as he archly referred to her in correspondence with Lord Taaffe) for some years. She was Henrietta Catherine, one of the daughters of the Dowager Princess Amelia of Orange and, therefore, his sister-in-law. Henrietta had grown into the sort of woman Charles found irresistible – pretty, vivacious and strong-willed. The fact that, at twenty, she was still unmarried was not because she was unattractive but because she stubbornly refused to give herself to any suitor she did not like, something which aggravated her mother beyond measure. During the winter of 1657–8, at the very time that his minions were extricating him from his relationship with Lucy, the king took to slipping across the border to pay court to Henrietta. These visits had to be kept secret, not only because Charles was forbidden entry to Dutch territory but because they threatened yet another row with his sister and his mother. Mary was still at daggers drawn with her mother-in-law and Henrietta Maria, determined to secure a Catholic bride for her son, would be highly displeased at his forging an alliance with the Protestant House of Orange.

When he could not call in person, Charles employed the rakehell Theobald Taaffe as intermediary. The coy letters he wrote to his go-between indicate the progress of this wooing, in which he assumes the pseudonym of 'Don Loran' and Henrietta becomes his 'friend' or the 'infanta'. The affair got off to a promising start.

> Don Loran went yesterday to see his friend when he was very well satisfied and finds that absence has wrought no ill effects. There passed many kind expressions between them and I think I know him so well that I may say he loves her if it were possible every day more than other and truly I find he has reason, for I cannot choose but say she is the worthiest to be loved of the sex. I should do her wrong if I should undertake at this time to say that which I ought. It would require more time and quires of paper than I have.

The writer added a frustratingly enigmatic note which suggests that a member of the dowager princess's household was in on this delicious amorous intrigue: 'There was another that did not forget her friend. I had not time to say much to her but the few words that passed were pithy.'[38]

By midsummer it was not just the weather that was hotting up. Charles' attentions had provoked a storm. Henrietta and her mother were engaged in a battle royal and Taaffe's emissary, seeking to play the peacemaker, had received a buffeting for his pains:

> my friend has been most horribly ill used and so has yours, too, even to some hunches [sharp blows with the knee] in the bum . . . in relation to the infanta and me . . . [the man's report] what between laughing and crying . . . set us both so laughing that we had like to have burst.

Charles had every hope that the estrangement of mother and daughter might prove to his advantage and lead to the prospect of assignations far from the matriarch's gaze:

> I have kept them from separating till the old woman goes into the country . . . My friend does intend to hire a house here and live by herself . . . and not receive visits from any whatsoever (that is to say men) but she promises that there shall be means found that Don Loran shall see her privately sometimes and ordinarily in third places.

There was, however, another cloud in Charles' summer sky. He had had to tax the 'infanta' about letters exchanged with a rival suitor. Henrietta had managed to set his mind at rest on this matter but it would seem that the king was not the only adept when it came to love games.[39] The princess was well aware of Charles' reputation with the ladies and there can be no doubt that her mother would have eagerly passed on any new gossip. If he was serious about this wooing, the king would have to tread warily.

He persisted with gifts, tokens and messages of devotion delivered by the smooth-tongued Taaffe over the ensuing weeks. Then came the bombshell news of Cromwell's death. Charles felt the moment was propitious to approach Henrietta's ogre of a mother. She would hardly be able to resist the prospect of seeing her daughter wearing a queen consort's crown. He penned a formal declaration of his intentions:

> I beseech you to let me know whether your daughter, the Princess Henriette, be so far engaged that you cannot receive a proposition from me concerning her; and if she be not, that you would think of a way how, with all possible secrecy, I may convey my mind in that particular to you.[40]

Princess Amelia's response was favourable and the courtship continued its course into 1659. But it became steadily more obvious to everyone except the ardent lover that both the lady and her mother were stringing him along. It did not take the princess dowager long to reach the conclusion about Charles' prospects that was held by almost everyone else: the Lord Protector's death had changed nothing; the Stuart pretender was doomed, like the wandering Jew, to pass to and fro across the earth, crownless, restless and hopeless. She gave her backing to a rival suitor, probably John George of Anhalt-Dessau, and looked upon him with increasing favour. When the king wrote to Taffe in optimistic vein on 19 February he was deceiving himself:

> I find that Don Loran is not jealous of the new gallant the infanta has got, being most confident of her justice to him and that the new assurances she gives him are real . . .

He persuaded himself that he could hold on to Henrietta's affection until she came of age and was free to marry without parental consent. The machinations of the girl's mother did not worry him. The effects of his own reputation did:

> . . . any who think that Don Loran will have any intrigue with Mlle du Pont are very much mistaken, for he never thought her handsome, and though he did, he is now so taken up that I am sure his heart cannot be anywhere but where it is and [he] will deprive himself of any satisfaction of the *nephretique** way rather than give the least jealousy to her he loves more than himself. [41]

Despite his protestations, the situation in Amelia's palace at Turnhout was not favourable. At the beginning of March Taaffe reported that Henrietta was angry with Charles. The king was convinced that her mother had redoubled her efforts to turn the girl against him and furiously responded that Amelia was bitterly resentful of not getting her own way. 'I see now how an old strumpet takes it not to be f——,' he responded indecorously. He consoled himself with Taaffe's assurance that this was no more than a lovers' tiff and with Henrietta's written promises of affection:

> I find Don Loran very well pleased with the assurances you give him of his friend's firmness to him and the rather because he finds the same confirmed by the kind expression she makes in her letters, which I am confident she would not do if they were not real. [42]

Those last words betray the wishful thinking of a desperate lover. But the affair was over and the following year Henrietta married her German prince. Thus Charles had to swallow yet another humiliation and one which was particularly hard to digest because it reflected on his manhood

---

* An odd use of the word, presumably indicating a determination to refrain from urinating.

and because he had been genuinely fond of the young woman who now eluded him.

To add insult to injury, the English ambassador complained to the Dutch government about Charles' presence in the country and he was obliged to scuttle back across the border. From euphoria, he now descended into depression. The situation in England and Scotland was extremely confused – Hyde complained that no two reports reaching his desk told the same story – but the overall trend was extremely discouraging. It was very difficult for the king and his advisers to know how to respond to the chameleon variations of fortune but, even when allowance had been made for slow communication, distortion of facts and the termite behaviour of English agents, we are forced to conclude that there was no consistent thread of policy in Charles' behaviour. He made no committed effort to be proactive, but swung back and forth between decisiveness and lethargy. He laid down no negotiating principles, outlined no strategy, observed no loyalty. He raised no standard to which supporters might rally. Even when he had set himself upon a course of action he easily allowed lethargy or some amusing distraction to dig beneath the walls of his resolve.

In the summer of 1659, after months of ducking and weaving, Charles had definitely decided to head for Fuenterrabia, on the Franco-Spanish border. Talks were due to start there between the two great powers aimed at putting an end to three and a half decades of intermittent warfare and the English king resolved to attend the banquet to gather any crumbs of comfort that might fall from the great men's table. But the journey presented a problem: it would involve Charles and his suite riding from one end of France to the other and he was definitely *persona non grata* with the government. At first, he contemplated slinking through the country in disguise, as he had through England during the months of his great adventure. But he decided – or, perhaps was persuaded by his sober advisers – that this was impracticable. He would therefore have to travel openly and with permission. The only thing to do was to swallow his pride and write to his mama, asking her to intercede for him with the cardinal so that he could obtain a pass. Henrietta Maria did what she could but no one would ever have regarded her as a smooth-tongued diplomat and as soon as she broached the matter with Mazarin he became apoplectic. Charles was obliged to drop the idea – for the time being.

He now decided on a completely different course of action. Word from England spoke of a successful rising in Cheshire and he resolved to take ship for north-west England to place himself at its head. He had ridden as far as Saint-Malo, *en route* for Brest, where he expected to find a vessel, when he decided to wait there for Ormonde to catch up with him before proceeding on his way. The delay saved him from possible disaster. In the nick of time fresh messengers arrived with the news that this rebellion, like all the others that had preceded it, had been successfully suppressed. What to do now? There was, it seemed, only one answer to that question. The Fuenterrabia expedition was on again and it would be conducted incognito.

In mid-August the small royal party set off from the Brittany coast, travelling through France by back roads to avoid any encounter that might be reported back to Paris. The Earl of Rochester, partner of Charles' earlier adventure, had died of camp fever the previous year while serving in the little royal army and Charles now chose as his companions the convivial Digby and O'Neill, with Ormonde on hand to attend to any serious business. Even following a circuitous route, the riders should have been able to reach their destination within a couple of weeks. Yet the king did not enter Fuenterrabia until 18 October. Part of the delay arose from unforeseen mishaps but the principal cause must be located in Charles' character. What was supposed to be a diplomatic mission took on the air of an extended vacation. Hyde sourly commented that the tourists were 'so well pleased with the varieties in the journey that they not enough remembered the end [i.e. 'object'] of it'.[43] The king's 'autumn break' was a welcome escape from the depressing business of trying to make sense of his life. He had left behind repeated disappointments, solemn ministers and bickering relatives. Before him lay the humiliation of going cap in hand to the rulers of France and Spain. Charles simply made the interval last as long as possible.

There is an element of farce about the toings and froings of these lazy but occasionally frenzied days. The travellers resolved to take ship from La Rochelle but changed their minds and rode south-eastwards towards Toulouse. Discovering that the French court was lodged there, they veered away. Ormonde, meanwhile, had been despatched to soften up Mazarin and to report back. Then the travellers heard an incorrect rumour that the Franco-Spanish treaty had already been signed and settled, whereupon Charles bestirred himself to rush to Madrid in a belated attempt to present his case. As a result Ormonde missed the rendezvous and more days passed before Charles discovered the true state of affairs: that royal lawyers were still arguing over the small print of the Franco-Spanish agreement at Fuenterrabia (the Treaty of the Pyrenees was not finally signed until 7 November). He wheeled around and headed back to the border.

The English king was courteously received by his Spanish hosts but his request for an interview with Mazarin was brusquely brushed aside. The cardinal's personal animosity towards Charles was not softened by a bad attack of gout but he had sound policy reasons for cold-shouldering the king. His main reason for being at Fuenterrabia was to secure for France a peace, to be cemented by a marriage between Louis XIV and Philip IV's daughter, Maria Theresa, that would enable the government to consolidate the territorial gains of the war and concentrate on centralising the administration of a conglomeration of regional identities that was, as yet, far from being a French nation. Beyond that, he genuinely desired harmony among the

Catholic states of Europe so that the work of counter-reformation – restoring heretic lands to papal allegiance – might be resumed. He was convinced that the Stuart cause was lost and, even had it been otherwise, he would not contemplate risking French blood and gold on a restoration bid unless Charles, for his part, would convert to the true faith.

While her son had been meandering his way to the conference centre, Henrietta Maria had been pursuing her own, behind-the-scenes diplomacy. Her aspirations were the same as Mazarin's. She, too, wished to see Catholicism restored in the British nations and a Stuart monarch working in close harmony with his Bourbon cousin. The only difference between dowager queen and minister was that while she held to her rekindled hope with visionary intensity, he regarded it as no more than a pipe dream. It was Charles' mother who raised the possibility of a marriage between her son and Hortense Mancini. The idea may well have been sparked off by the amorous longings of her royal nephew. The twenty-year-old Louis had conceived a fiery passion for Maria Mancini, another of the cardinal's nieces. Mazarin had been quick to nip this romance in the bud. He would not countenance a marriage between the young people; love matches did not for one moment enter into his scheme of things and he had no intention of allowing them to upset his international diplomacy. But might he not see the value of allying his own family with the House of Stuart? Henrietta Maria, desperate to find a suitable bride for her son, who had suffered serious rebuffs in the royal marriage market, argued that a wedding between Charles and Hortense – to which both principals were agreeable – would fit in well with the grand design of French policy. A Catholic bride who was thoroughly Gallican in upbringing would tie Charles to French interests and her fortune would help him to recover his throne. She despatched the trusted Lord Jermyn from Paris to present this proposition to Hortense's uncle.

There is no indication that Mazarin gave the suggestion any serious consideration whatsoever. Apart from being his own blood relation, Hortense was one of those destined to inherit a substantial portion of that immense fortune he had acquired during his years in power and the head of the family had no intention of squandering it on the impoverished English wastrel. It must be said that Charles did not improve his own chances by including in his negotiating team George Digby, a man the cardinal heartily detested. Mazarin was intensely protective of the girl and her prospects and had become very accustomed to saying 'no' when approached by hopeful suitors. Over the years, he received many applications for the hand of his niece, who was, of course, one of the greatest catches in France. Hortense, for her part, having reached the age when marriage was the most exciting prospect on her horizon, was eager to be paired off with a suitable man. But Uncle Jules had never found anyone good enough for her. A few months later, when Charles' prospects had changed so completely and so unexpectedly, it was the cardinal who indicated his willingness to open negotiations but by then the king was no longer prepared to consider any prospective bride with a long purse and passably agreeable features. The royal houses of Europe had added his name to the list of highly eligible prospective husbands.

As for Hortense, she had to wait impatiently until her uncle was on his deathbed. Then she was given to a middle-aged member of the lesser French nobility who had pursued her for years – something of a come-down for a woman who might have been a queen. On their marriage, in February 1661, her husband, Charles de la Porte de Meilleraye, was granted the title of Duc Mazarin and, since the great cardinal died days later, he entered straight away on his wife's monumental inheritance. The couple's many properties included the sumptuous Palais Mazarin in Paris, furnished with the finest works of art from many of the great masters of the past two centuries. This wealth the duke and duchess systematically set about squandering. But if Hortense looked forward to a gay life of parties and conspicuous consumption, she was soon to be disappointed.

Her husband was determined to tame his wild bride. He began by ensuring that she was kept pregnant for as much of the time as possible. In the intervening periods, he forbade her the company of other men, received no guests and, in an effort to prevent secret assignations, forbade Hortense to go out. It soon became lamentably clear that this was not merely evidence of intense jealousy; Duc Mazarin was the victim of obsessive mania. He took to raising the household in the middle of the night and searching, candle in hand, for concealed lovers. None were ever found but that does not mean that none existed nor that Hortense did not energetically apply herself to escaping from her incarceration whenever opportunity arose and seeking solace elsewhere. Raised on the moral standards of the French court, she probably gave her husband genuine cause for suspicion. Hers was certainly not the kind of temperament to sit back and meekly endure such tyrannical behaviour. She took to stealing out of the house when the duke was absent, thus ensuring that when any of her deceptions were discovered, the resultant tightening of domestic security became even more insupportable.

However, observing his wife through a green haze was not the only manifestation of Duc Mazarin's obsessive-compulsive neurosis. He saw moral contamination all around him, especially in court circles, and denounced the libertinism of Parisian high society with all the fervour of a Puritan preacher. Believing himself to be sent on a divine reform mission, he feared no mortal opponent and was oblivious to ridicule. He denounced Louis XIV to his face, challenging him to put away his mistress. His was the total commitment to an ideal that excludes all considerations of common sense or rational evaluation. Everything was black or white, good or evil, sacred or profane. Unsurprisingly, no one took him seriously but within his own domain he had the power to set his servants tasks that were at best ludicrous and at worst frightening. Because in the duke's mind handling cows' udders had inescapable sexual connotations, milkmaids were forbidden to do their work and men were appointed to take over, the offending areas of bovine anatomy discreetly veiled from their gaze. To prevent any of his pretty female staff succumbing to the libidinous advances of their male colleagues he ordered their looks to be marred by having their front teeth extracted. Villainous though such behaviour appears to modern readers, it was de la Porte's vandalism that may most appal posterity. He went systematically through his magnificent collection of paintings and sculptures and 'purified' them, by cutting out, smearing over and lopping off all the 'naughty bits'. The loss to the world of art is incalculable.

The duke's lunacy only served to intensify the duchess's eccentricity. When de la Porte whisked his wife off to Bordeaux to remove her from the temptations of the capital, she responded by beginning an affair with another woman. Their husbands had the lesbian pair immured in a convent for the good of their souls. It certainly was not for the good of the devout nuns, whose lives were made miserable by their wilful guests. Ink in the holy water; rat hunts round the cloister; an escape bid up the convent chimney – such were the escapades which convinced the mother superior that the attempt to reform these imps of Satan was a total failure. By this time it was obvious to all that the marriage was a farce. Hortense secured a separation. More adventures lay ahead but what surprised her friends was that the unpredictable duchess now developed a keen interest in culture and turned her fertile mind to intellectual pursuits. Her home at Chambéry in the distant Haute-Savoie became a Mecca for writers, artists and philosophers. Had Hortense been given to Charles in marriage she would have been one of the most remarkable English consorts in history. She did not become Queen Hortense – but neither did she disappear permanently from Charles' life.

Charles left Fuenterrabia with enough Spanish gold to pay his outstanding debts and a pass allowing him to travel through France on his return journey to Brussels. It was not much to show for all his journeyings but it was welcome. It made it possible for him to visit his mother for the first time in over five years. They met at Saint-Colombe, just outside Paris, because the king was still not welcome at court. Hyde later recalled that during his two-week stay under the parental roof, 'a good understanding was made upon all former mistakes',[44] but, in fact, any reconciliation had little depth and the relationship remained brittle.

The fissures that snaked their way across the surface of Stuart family relations had widened and deepened in recent years. The problems of exile had caused increasingly severe strains which each of its members had had to cope with in his or her individual way. Henrietta Maria and her children were all desperate to preserve their solidarity but they also had their own interests to look after and the two often failed to go together. The queen dowager had lost her battle for control over Charles but that did not stop her interfering in his affairs and impressing upon him pro-French, pro-Catholic policies. On one occasion her arrogant interventionism drew from Ormonde a magnificent spontaneous response. She grumbled that if the king had taken her advice he would by now be back in England. Ormonde replied, 'If your Majesty's husband had *not* taken your advice the king would never have left England.' Charles' refusal to be guided by her deepened her resolve to retain the affectionate obedience of her other children. She and Mary had been reconciled and James turned to her when he wanted to assert his independence from his older brother.

The Duke of York had never reconciled himself to being obliged to take up arms against Turenne and his old comrades and he resented the high-handedness with which his brother treated him. Although he remained loyal to the idea of placing his sibling back on the throne, he realistically considered that his own future lay in a military career. Charles and James were often not on speaking terms and at any time a small incident could flare up into a major row. In 1657 the king insisted that his brother dismiss from his entourage Sir John Berkeley and his nephew, Charles, members of the Louvre party and bitter enemies of Hyde. Charles thought (or was persuaded) that it was inappropriate that such rabidly pro-French elements should remain close to the duke now that he had changed sides. Hyde and his allies played upon this mistrust to convince the king that the Berkeleys were in secret communication with the enemy. James refused point-blank to abandon his friends. He stalked out of his brother's presence and rushed off to Breda to be comforted by Mary. He stood his ground and it was Charles who had to back down because he needed the military aid that James and his regiments could provide. As a goodwill gesture he raised Sir John to the peerage as Baron Berkeley of Stratton.

Given that Charles lacked the support of his family for his change of allegiance in the Franco-Spanish conflict, it is perhaps not surprising that he failed to take James into his confidence before embarking on his meandering journey to Fuenterrabia. In the event this secrecy resulted in more frustration and annoyance for the soldier-duke. James received an offer of massive assistance from Turenne for an invasion of England. He was, of course, extremely anxious to accept this unprecedented aid but Charles' agreement would be necessary – and Charles was nowhere to be found. For days James was in a whirlwind of activity, making military preparations, sending messages to the French general, trying to locate his brother. The propitious moment passed. The circumstances which had favoured an expedition disappeared. James' hope for glory evaporated. And all, or so the duke may have thought, because his brother did not trust him with his plans. As long as there was some prospect of a triumphant return to England the duke managed to tolerate a position he found increasingly humiliating and frustrating. By the beginning of 1660 there was no room left for optimism and James had decided that he must make a life for himself, as far as possible from his brother. 'The Duke of York had a great family [ie 'entourage'], impatient to be where they might enjoy plenty and where they might be absent from the king.'[45] It was, therefore, with great joy and relief that he received, in March, an invitation from Philip IV to take up the post of Lord Admiral of Spain. He hastened to accept. There was nothing to keep him in Brussels; certainly not the prospect of continuing to dance attendance upon a cardboard king.

When James was angry with his brother he could count on the support of his sister. The close relationship which Charles and Mary had enjoyed during their happy days of holidaymaking together became a thing of the past. By the spring of 1659 the princess had broken off relations and was telling any who cared to listen that she wanted nothing more to do with her ingrate of a brother. Trouble had flared up at the same time as Charles' rift with James and for the same reason. Hyde, Ormonde and Nicholas threw all their weight behind the Spanish alliance and took every opportunity to turn the king against any advisers who were suspected of having French sympathies. Mary found this volte-face no easier to accept than James, particularly when the demands of policy thrust themselves into her own household. One of her ladies of the bedchamber was Anna Lindsay, Countess of Balcarres, wife of a Scottish nobleman who had forfeited everything in the royalist cause and was, as a result, living on the princess's bounty. Charles, who had recommended the couple to Mary's service, now became convinced that the Lindsays were exercising a pro-French influence and demanded their dismissal. Mary, understandably furious, refused. Charles was adamant and wrote very tartly to his sister:

> I do not desire that you should prosecute all persons I am displeased with, but certainly I may expect from the kindness we have always had together, that those who are justly in my disfavour and who I have told you are so should not be the better for it . . . I shall for the present only name my Lord Balcarres, who I cannot choose but take notice of, that you have used him much better since I have been unsatisfied with him than ever you did before. Judge whether I have not reason to be troubled when everybody must take notice of this to both our prejudices.[46]

Mary coldly refused to oblige and, once again, Charles gave way with a bad grace.

There was no opportunity for time to heal this wound for, within months, Charles displayed what seemed to be total indifference to his sister's feelings. Mary received a visit from Lord Jermyn's nephew, Henry, and was very taken with the young man. Their friendship was exaggerated and salacious rumours reached Bruges. Charles flew into an indignant frenzy. What on earth was Mary thinking of? he wanted to know. Had she fallen beside her senses in throwing away her reputation and creating problems for him with his Spanish friends? He ordered her to despatch Henry Jermyn to Bruges for interrogation. She complied – but not without a stinging letter of complaint:

> Now that you see how exactly you are obeyed, I hope you will give me leave to desire you to consider what consequences your severity will bring upon me. To justify any of my actions to you in this occasion were, I think, to do as much wrong to both my brothers as my own innocency, since they have been witnesses to what some persons' insolency has declared to represent unto you as faults.[47]

She insisted that unless her friend were returned to Bruges people would believe the evil rumours or, at least, would assume that Charles believed them. But for Charles to comply with this request would be to admit that he had been wrong in the first place. Impasse. This time the roles of James and Mary were reversed; it was he who interceded for her and persuaded the king grudgingly to allow Jermyn to return to Breda. This did not stop the rumours. Half a century later it was still widely believed that Mary and Harry Jermyn had been secretly married, a suspicion which received some support from the great favour William of Orange (Mary's son) showed to Jermyn when he came to the throne.[48]

But this contretemps had not been resolved before Mary discovered to her intense chagrin that Charles was paying court to the daughter of the accursed Dowager Princess Amelia. It is not difficult to imagine her feelings. This was how her brother repaid the thousands of pounds with which she had succoured him throughout his exile! This was how the hypocrite who had presumed to lecture her on family loyalty behaved when it suited him! Some of those close to the family tried to engineer a reconciliation. The siblings gathered at Antwerp to sort out their differences and the old Marquis of Newcastle, Charles' onetime tutor, was there to act as peacemaker. But this time the wounds were too open to be salved with smiles and gentle apologies. Mary returned angrily to Breda and James and Henry went with her. There the Duke of York entered on an affair with Anne Hyde and it is a measure of his estrangement from Charles that he contracted a secret engagement to marry the girl, without bothering to obtain the king's permission. The genuine affection and the unity brought about by shared suffering had been worn away by the drip, drip, drip of their hopeless situation.

And utterly hopeless it now seemed.

> [The king] had not been long at Brussels before he discerned the same melancholy and despair in the countenances of most men which he had

left there and, though there had some changes happened in England which might reasonably encourage men to look for greater, men had been so often disappointed in those expectations that it was a reproach to think that any good could come from thence.

The best the king could look for seemed to be a permission to remain in Flanders, with a narrow designation for his bread . . . nor could that be depended upon, for there were secret approaches from both England and Spain towards peace . . .[49]

The situation in England was confused. Richard Cromwell, his father's designated heir, had rapidly lost the confidence of the political class and retired into private life but none of the contending parties could agree on who should replace him or under what constitution the country should be governed. Only one thing seemed clear from Hyde's viewpoint:

there was not one man who bore a part in these changes and giddy revolutions who had the least purpose or thought to contribute towards the king's restoration or who wished well to his interest; they who did so being so totally depressed and dispirited that they were only at gaze what light might break out of this darkness . . . and therefore it is no wonder that there was . . . dejection of spirit upon his majesty and those about him . . .[50]

The king was accustomed to turning to women when he was in need of comfort and at no time was his need greater than now. In these months he embarked on two very different relationships which were to be long-lasting and have profound effects upon him and his reign. At his mother's home he renewed his acquaintance with his youngest sister, Henrietta. It might be truer to say that he met her for the first time, for the captivating fifteen-year-old who demurely greeted him now bore little resemblance to the precocious child he had scarcely noticed five years before. Henrietta, or 'Minette' as he soon nicknamed her, was no great beauty. A birth defect had left her with one shoulder higher than the other and she enjoyed indifferent health, but this diminutive, porcelain-complexioned, cornflower-eyed adolescent had about her such an aura that, for most people, to know her was to love her. Since her escape from England at the age of two, she had been brought up at the court in Paris and had grown into a thoroughly French princess, lively without being frivolous, gregarious without being coquettish, able to throw herself into the varied amusements on offer yet not a slave to the self-indulgence which is oblivious to the feelings of others. According to one *habitué* of the court, she had 'a sovereign degree of beauty. All the recognised graces and charms were apparent in her person, her behaviour and her character and never has there been a princess so capable of being loved by women and worshipped by men.'[51] Even when we have made appropriate allowance for the obligatory flattery that was the due of royal personages, we have to recognise, because many others testified to it, that Minette in her teens was a sweet-natured and open-hearted young woman. Henrietta was the only one of her children whom the queen dowager was able to mould and she made a thorough job of it. The princess became as passionate as her mother about tying England to France and to papal allegiance. Henrietta Maria would have liked to see her daughter wedded to Louis XIV but the French king and Mazarin had other plans.

This was the young lady who, in December 1659, greeted her brother with a show of unaffected warmth. The attraction was mutual, immediate and total. The difference in their ages lent Charles a parental aspect. Henrietta's eldest brother was the nearest thing she ever had to a father, for she had never known Charles I. And she evoked in him protective, proprietorial feelings. They spent delightful hours in each other's company and as soon as Charles went on his way they began an intimate correspondence that was to continue intermittently right up to Henrietta's death. In the gloom and despondency of Brussels the king looked forward eagerly to his sister's chatty letters and he replied in a vein that was part parental and part amatory:

> I will never give up the friendship that I have for you and you give me so many marks of yours that we shall never have any quarrel but as to which of us shall love the other most, but in this I will never yield to you . . . We talk of you every day and wish a thousand times in the day to be with you . . . Let me know, I pray you, how you pass your time, for if you have been some time at Chaillot [Henrietta made periodic visits to a convent there and demonstrated her humility by waiting on the nuns] in this inclement weather you will have found it somewhat tedious . . . I beg of you, do not treat me with so much ceremony in according me so many 'Majesties', for I do not wish there to be anything else between us two but friendship.[52]

When he wrote that letter in February 1660, Charles was about to embark or had already embarked on a relationship with a very different kind of woman. At nineteen, Barbara Palmer was an accomplished courtesan. With her long, auburn hair, flashing blue eyes, voluptuous figure and unrestrained behaviour she was acknowledged by many as the finest-looking woman of the age. Pepys, who strongly disapproved of her, acknowledged in the privacy of his diary that he could never enough admire her beauty and that he phantasised about her in his dreams. He also recorded that the lady possessed 'all the tricks of Aretino'.[53] Probably what the diarist had in mind was the erotic or pornographic plays and dialogues which poured from the pen of the notorious Renaissance writer but Aretino also earned the nickname of the 'scourge of princes' for his vile but penetrating satires on the rich and famous of his day. Barbara Palmer too had the power to break reputations, as she was to demonstrate throughout her reign as Charles II's *maîtresse en titre*.

Born Barbara Villiers, she was the daughter of William Viscount Grandison, and a first cousin once removed of Charles' evil genius, the Duke of Buckingham. Like Lucy Walter, she was a victim of Civil War London. Her father died fighting for the king at the siege of Bristol when she was still a babe in arms and she was brought up by her mother's family until she acquired a stepfather (another Villiers) five years later. However, there was a marked distinction of status between the Walters and the Villierses. As a member of the cormorant family who profited handsomely from the first duke's connection with the House of Stuart, little Barbara had entrée to the proud, introverted world of the leading royalist sympathisers. After the triumph of the republicans that was a very dubious privilege. Reminiscences of the golden days buttered no parsnips and, though Barbara's new parent gloried in the title of Earl of Anglesey and possessed a house in fashionable King Street, St James's, he lacked the wealth to support the style he had enjoyed before the war when he had inherited several lucrative positions under the Crown. The child, therefore, grew up, if not in poverty, certainly in restricted circumstances, in the shadow of what had been the royal court and very much aware of the lifestyle of which she had been deprived by the rebellion.

Barbara hankered passionately after wealth and luxury as only someone can who believes that those things are her due. Her stepfather was an ineffectual peer whose main concern was to keep out of trouble, and the growing girl, raised on stories of her splendid relatives, probably had little respect for him. She gravitated to men who had more vigour and panache and, with the onset of puberty, discovered that she had the equipment to attract such gallants. So she followed the same career path as Lucy Walter, but with considerably more success. She may even have known something of the fortunes of the older woman, who had ended up in the arms of the distant king. By the age of fifteen Barbara Villiers was a member of the oldest profession. Her principal client was Philip Stanhope, Earl of Chesterfield.

This royalist nobleman had spent most of his life abroad, much of it in the Stuart courts in Paris and Breda. He was too young to have served in the Civil War (he was born in 1633) but he was involved, after his return in 1656, in various intrigues against Cromwell and spent a couple of short spells in the Tower. However, the government, rather than punish a man of Chesterfield's wealth and position, attempted to win him over. In his memoirs he actually claimed that he had been offered the hand of one of the Protector's daughters, though, as Cromwell vetted very closely the moral and political qualifications of potential suitors, we should perhaps not take this particular boast too seriously. It is, however, certain that a marriage was arranged with Mary, daughter of the parliamentary general, Lord Fairfax. The banns had actually been called three times before plans were abandoned. Soon afterwards, Mary became the wife of the Duke of Buckingham and this raises the question of whether some arrangement had been reached between the two potential grooms. Stanhope had close links with the Villierses at home and abroad and was careful to ingratiate himself with those close to the king.

It has been customary for biographers of Barbara to characterise her first known sexual partner as a thoroughgoing rake but this does him little justice. In the late 1650s Chesterfield was a young man in London who entertained a profound contempt for the pious regime being imposed on the country, was possessed of a considerable fortune and boundless energy and had no positive outlet for either. It was not surprising, therefore, that he spent much of his time drinking, gambling, brawling and recklessly involving himself in 'affairs of honour'. He took part in three duels, in one of which he killed his opponent. He was clearly a man with a short temper and prone to picking quarrels. (This may have communicated itself to his staff. Pepys records that 'in King Street, there being a great stop of coaches, there was a falling out between a drayman and my Lord Chesterfield's coachman, and one of his footmen killed' – an early example of road rage.[54]) However, there is no evidence that he was a spectacular womaniser. He contracted an early marriage to Anne Percy, daughter of the Earl of Northumberland, and was devoted to her but she died within two years and her grieving widower consoled himself in further travel. Later, as a member of the English queen's household, he disapproved of the lecherous behaviour of Charles' companions and on one occasion removed his second wife (the Earl of Ormonde's daughter) from court to protect her from the attentions of the Duke of York.

The correspondence which Chesterfield rather ungallantly kept and left among his papers suggests that it was the unrestrained Barbara who made the running in their relationship and her allusions to sexual practices bear out Pepys' reference to the 'skills of Aretino':

My friend [Lady Anne Hamilton] and I are just now in bed together and contriving how to have your company this afternoon. If you deserve this favour you will come and seek us at Ludgate Hill, about three o'clock at Butler's shop, where we will expect you but, lest we should give you too much satisfaction at once, we will say no more. *Expect the rest when you see, Yours etc., etc.!*[55]

The teenage Barbara Villiers was an oversexed little madam, who had rapidly abandoned whatever feminine modesty she may once have possessed and who had already come to realise the power she could wield over men. The common verdict, noted down by Pepys, that she was 'a little lecherous girl when she was young' was fully warranted.

In 1659 she was married off to Roger Palmer, a Buckinghamshire gentleman of a scholarly disposition. Her mother may well have hoped that a husband would tame the wild, wanton creature her daughter had grown into and that he would keep her away from the temptations of the capital. But Barbara was now eighteen and fast set in her ways. She continued to see Stanhope whenever she could get away from her boring husband and regarded him as her only means of escape from a humdrum rural life. 'Since I saw you I have been at home,' she wrote within weeks of her wedding, 'as I find the Mounseer [Palmer] in a very ill humour. He says he is resolved never to bring me to town again and that nobody shall see me when I am in the country . . . Send me word presently what you would advise me to do, for I am ready and willing to go all over the world with you and I will obey your commands that am whilst I live, Yours.'[56] Chesterfield had no desire to complicate his life by running off with another man's wife and Barbara fell into a panic at the thought that his ardour might be cooling. She wrote a desperate letter telling her lover that she was at death's door and imploring him to come to her. Whether he responded the records fail to show. This was how matters stood at the end of 1659. Thereafter events moved rapidly. Unfortunately, they also left little written evidence behind them.

In January 1660, Lord Chesterfield fled to the Low Countries. He had just killed an unfortunate Mr Woolly in a duel and was hastening to the royal court for a pardon. He may have felt that he could expect the king's favour because of rumours which crossed the Channel about events in the king's ill-disciplined household. His young gallants, having nothing better to do than drink, gamble and quarrel, were getting out of hand. Brawls and duels became commonplace and Charles was eventually obliged to threaten instant banishment to anyone who disturbed the peace with their unruly behaviour. To show that he meant business, he decided to make an example of Lord Taaffe, who had recently killed Sir William Keith in a duel over a tennis wager. Unfortunately, he spoiled the effectiveness of his own decree by sending privately to Taaffe to assure him of his continued favour. He urged the Irishman to keep his message secret but Taaffe could not resist showing his master's letter to all and sundry and boasting of his continued good standing with the king. Clearly, if you were Charles II's friend you could literally get away with murder. So Chesterfield discovered when Charles welcomed him graciously and readily forgave his felony.

The king was, perhaps, in a better mood than he had been for months, for Chesterfield's arrival coincided with that of intoxicating news which was as startling as it was welcome. Up until now the received wisdom about the state of affairs in England was, as an agent of Nicholas reported,

Though the republican party will not be prevalent with the nobility and gentry of England, yet the generality of people and especially the cities are so infatuated from abroad with that kind of government that nothing but justice will correct these malignant humours.[57]

Now, intelligence gleaned by Ormonde suggested that 'the general disposition of the people . . . promises great advantages to the king. Four parts of five of the whole people, besides the nobility and gentry, being devoted to him.'[58] Richard Cromwell's rule had survived the death of his father by little more than seven months and British politics had returned to that state of confusion from which the strong arm of the Protector had rescued it. Just as, after 1918, the horrors of the recent conflict lay like unburied corpses across the fields of the common mind, so the citizens of these islands dreaded, above all else, a drift back into what they desperately hoped had been a civil war to end all civil wars. As the cross-currents of conflicting interests – army, parliament, Presbyterians, Scots, religious radicals – began once more to foam and clash, the rock of hereditary monarchy seemed to many fearful observers the only feature of permanence and stability in the political seascape.

Yet hopes had been too often raised and dashed for the court in Brussels to embrace total euphoria. Reports from England were eagerly awaited and thoroughly scrutinised. Some spoke of encouraging developments, others indicated that parliament had successfully brought a troubled situation under control. It was the arrival, one dark February night, of a weary, travel-stained messenger called Bayley which marked the most decisive turning point. As Hyde, Ormonde and the king listened he explained how parliament had fallen out with their saviour, General Monck. George Monck, one of the most successful military leaders in government employ throughout the years of the Commonwealth and Protectorate, was an uncomplicated soldier who was loyal to his political masters and resisted any temptation to dabble in state affairs. Cromwell, who thought Monck an 'honest general' and a 'simple-hearted man', offered him a seat in the House of Lords, but he declined the honour, preferring to serve his country by commanding fighting men on land and at sea. Appointed commander-in-chief during the recent confusion, Monck had brought to heel dissident elements in the army, marched to London and negated an incipient rebellion by the City. He was now the pivotal figure in the nation and the parliamentary leaders assumed that they had him in their pocket. This was a miscalculation. The general, angered by the arrogance of the politicians and knowing that they did not have widespread support in the country, ordered the assembly's dissolution and the holding of new elections. Monck knew that one result would be the return of many royalist members and that there would be widespread support for an invitation to Charles Stuart.

Now the king met daily with his council in a mood of mounting optimism to send messages to Monck and other activists, to consider the terms they would accept for a restoration and to respond to the diplomatic overtures from continental governments who suddenly expressed their warm support for the Stuart cause and their desire for the closest possible fraternal ties. Hyde, who had always advised his master that all that was necessary was to wait for the people of the British kingdoms to come to their senses, could scarcely believe that the blessed moment had arrived. He devoutly observed that this was the Lord's work and 'marvellous in our eyes'.

It is doubtful whether Barbara Palmer echoed this pious expression of gratitude to the Almighty but she certainly had cause to do so. It was during these heady, busy, jubilant days that she came within the king's gaze. The encounter was to change dramatically both their lives and the future of their country. It would be fascinating to know when and how this pregnant meeting took place but it remains one of those historical voids we can only fill with conjecture. Charles will have heard of Chesterfield's voluptuous vixen from the earl himself and perhaps also from Buckingham, and their Rabelaisian stories would not have failed to whet his appetite. Within weeks the king had an opportunity to judge for himself Barbara's looks and demeanour. The Palmers were among the throng of English royalists who rushed across the Channel, tumbling over themselves to express their loyalty and hoping thereby to ingratiate themselves with the returning king. Roger pressed upon his sovereign a gift of £1,000 and promised his support in the House of Commons, to which he had just been elected. Then he had to dash back to take up his seat. Did he, as legend has always insisted, leave his wife behind with her relatives and court friends?

Whether or not this is how things happened, Barbara had been presented with an opportunity exceeding her wildest dreams but not her capacity for exploiting the situation. She had been handed a perfect excuse for following her lover to the continent but, to her surprise, she had gained something immeasurably more promising than being restored to Chesterfield's caresses. She had attracted the admiration of the king himself. Now, Stanhope, whom she had vowed to follow to the ends of the earth, was quickly forgotten. Months later the earl wittily wrote to beg his ex-mistress's portrait. He would value it, he assured her, as a permanent and *unchanging* likeness. Chesterfield, of course, had no reason to complain of being rejected. He must have known what was expected of him when he boasted to the king of Barbara's charms.

If Mrs Palmer was with the court throughout the next few frenzied weeks she would have met many of the men and women who were to be at the centre of the nation's life over the years to come, men and women who were to be her fast friends or dedicated enemies (in several cases, both). At the beginning of April 1660 Charles took horse at dead of night with a small entourage and made a dash for Breda. Prudence dictated a removal from

Brussels, for Spain was still technically at war with England. At Mary's palace he was reunited with his siblings and all animosities were forgotten in the atmosphere of mutual congratulation that the family's cause, which had seemed so irrevocably lost, was about to triumph. The princess laid on lavish celebrations and the small town tried to cope with the flood of well-wishers, supporters, foreign emissaries and adventurers who arrived seeking food and accommodation. Charles could not give himself up entirely to receiving gifts, congratulations and loyal addresses; he had work to do. Politically, this was his finest hour. The situation was delicate. Varied competing interests at home and abroad had to be carefully weighed. Individuals, groups and governments had to be reassured about the attitudes a restored monarchy would adopt. Charles was well qualified to deal with the hopes and anxieties that were expressed to him: he was a past master at being all things to all men. Thus, after his abrupt departure from the Netherlands, he made a point of cultivating the Spanish ambassador and promising that one of his first acts would be the negotiating of a peace treaty between their two countries. His celebrated Declaration of Breda told everyone in England, Scotland and Ireland what they wanted to hear:

> we do grant a free and general pardon . . . to all our subjects, of what degree or quality soever, who within forty days after the publishing hereof shall lay hold upon our grace and favour . . . and return to the loyalty and obedience of good subjects . . . and . . . we do declare a liberty to tender consciences, and that no man shall be disquieted or called in question for differences of opinion in matters of religion which do not disturb the peace of the kingdom . . . we are likewise willing that all . . . differences [relating to property disputes] shall be determined in parliament . . . we will be ready to consent to any Act or Acts of parliament . . . for the full satisfaction of all arrears due to the officers and soldiers of the army under the command of General Monck.[59]

To the Speaker of the new House of Commons Charles gave a solemn assurance that there would be no further attempts to rule without parliament:

> We do assure you upon our royal word that none of our predecessors have had a greater esteem of parliaments than we have . . . we do believe them to be so vital a part of the constitution of the kingdom and so necessary for the government of it that we well know that neither prince nor people can be in any tolerable degree happy without them; and therefore you may be confident that we shall always look upon their counsels as the best we can receive and shall be as tender of their privileges and as careful to preserve and protect them as of that which is most near to ourself and most necessary for our own preservation.[60]

When those words were read out to the assembled members it may well have seemed to those present that all that they had been striving for had been accomplished and that the abuses parliament had suffered at the hands of Charles I and Cromwell were things of the past. That, at least, is what they wanted to believe.

One day in mid-May Charles called Mary gleefully into his chamber to show her something. There stood a small chest full to the brim with coin – £4,000 worth. It was the first instalment of a £50,000 parliamentary grant agreed by the Commons. If ever there was a moment that could be called in every sense of the word 'golden' this was it. It signified that the years of penny-pinching and humiliating penury were over. Henceforth, if the king played his cards right, he could live in a style that was truly kingly. The panache and exuberant self-indulgence of Louis XIV's court, which he had only been able to gaze upon as a poor relative, he would be able to emulate. And he would also be able to yield to his own generous nature by rewarding faithful service. May 1660 was, truly, a *mensis mirabilis*, ever to be savoured in memory.

> God put an end in one month . . . to a rebellion that had raged nearly twenty years and been carried on with all the horrid circumstances of parricide, murder and devastation that fire and sword, in the hands of the wickedest men in the world, could be ministers of . . . Yet did the merciful hand of God in one month bind up all these wounds and even made the scars as undiscernable as in respect of their deepness was possible.[61]

It was on the 1st of this momentous month that parliament proclaimed Charles II as king. On the 14th the court left Breda and made their way in a procession of gaily decked yachts up the coast to Delft. On the 15th they were met by representatives of the once-surly States-General, who now could not have laid on a more lavish welcome. Seventy-three coaches made the short journey to the Hague along roads lined with soldiers. On the 16th Charles received the homage of several emissaries from England, Scotland and Ireland. On the 21st, days of celebration ended with a magnificent banquet given by the Dutch government at which dishes were presented on a service of gold plate which was afterwards given to the king. During the festivities Charles enjoyed the distinct pleasure of being offered by the Dowager Princess Amelia the hand of her remaining unmarried daughter – and politely declining the honour. On the 23rd he rode to the harbour of Scheveningen to the cheers of 100,000 people and went on board the *Naseby*, now symbolically renamed the *Royal Charles*. On the morning of the 25th the king's flotilla came to anchor off Dover. On the 29th Charles II entered his capital amid scenes that John Evelyn vividly recorded:

This day came in his majesty Charles II to London after a sad and long exile and calamitous suffering both of the king and church, being 17 years. This was also his birthday and with a triumph of above 20,000 horse and foot, brandishing their swords and shouting with inexpressible joy, the ways strewn with flowers, the bells ringing, the streets hung with tapestry, fountains running with wine, the mayor, aldermen and all the companies in their liveries, chains of gold, banners, lords and nobles, cloth of silver, gold and velvet everybody clad in, the windows and balconies all set with ladies, trumpets, music and myriads of people flocking the streets and was as far as Rochester, so as they were seven hours in passing the City, even from two in the afternoon till nine at night. I stood in the Strand and beheld it and blessed God . . . for such a restoration was never seen in the mention of any history, ancient or modern, since the return of the Babylonian captivity . . .[62]

At Whitehall more feasting followed and interminable speeches by notables eager for prominence in welcoming their sovereign. It was late when Charles finally tumbled into bed. According to legend, he relaxed (if that is the appropriate word) in the arms of Barbara Palmer.

CHAPTER 7

Forgiveness and Revenge

> She was a woman of great beauty but most enormously vicious and ravenous; foolish but imperious, very uneasy to the king and always carrying on intrigues with other men, while yet she pretended she was jealous of him. His passion for her and her strange behaviour towards him did so disorder him that often he was not master of himself nor capable of minding business, which, in so critical a time, required great application . . .[63]

That was Bishop Burnet's verdict on Barbara Villiers. We might expect a churchman to take a dim view of a woman of notorious moral laxity but his opinion was so widely shared that we cannot attribute it to mere prudery. The new woman in the king's life was loathed, feared and envied by many men and women about the court, including those who relied on her patronage. The better read among them compared her to Jane Shore, the mistress of Edward IV, who wielded enormous political influence and was accused of controlling the king by witchcraft. Her critics fondly hoped that Barbara would share Jane's falsely reputed fate of dying poor and abandoned, her body flung on a dunghill. The two royal paramours were outstanding examples of a type of sexual predator not altogether un-common, though it was left to the twentieth century to coin the word which most succinctly describes it: 'vamp'.

By her unrestrained appetite, her physical vigour and the variety of her blandishments she kept the king enslaved for more than a decade and, when her talent to amuse failed to gain her those rewards she desired, she fell back on temper tantrums and palace intrigues. She accumulated a fortune in cash, property and jewels, as well as noble titles for herself and the five children whose paternity Charles acknowledged. As the years passed she presumed more and more upon her position until, as with Lucy Walter, she became an embarrassment which had to be disposed of. It was Barbara, and not the queen, who dominated the distaff side of the royal court and who garishly coloured the public image of the king. And it is Charles' relationship with this appalling woman which has done much to damage his reputation with historians. It is, therefore, important for us to chart as precisely as we can the rise and fall of this turbulent affair.

The first and unavoidable fact to record is Barbara's obvious beauty. Fashions change and few of the many portraits of her would probably set the blood of twenty-first-century males racing but in the 1660s she became *the* icon of feminine perfection, the Mona Lisa, Jersey Lily, Marilyn Monroe or Madonna of her day, to be lusted after by all men and copied by all ladies of the *haut monde*. Sir Peter Lely, the king's principal painter, was enraptured by her and gave it as his professional opinion that her 'sweetness and exquisite beauty are beyond the compass of art' – though, in saying that, he was saying something that she and her royal lover wanted to hear. Lely made several studies of Barbara between 1662 and 1668 and these became the templates for the Restoration concept of sophisticated womanhood. The face that gazes at us from these depictions has full lips and heavy-lidded, almost sleepy eyes; the sitter's poses are languid and her silks and pearls lustrous. These images were intended to be blatantly voluptuous without being obviously sexy. It is not at all surprising that Barbara Villiers was a popular pin-up of the day. Engravings after these portraits sold well. Pepys recorded that, in December 1666, he bought three copies as soon as they were available at the print shop, 'which indeed is, as to the head, I think, a very fine picture and like her'.[64]

Yet, if we want to see the face with which Charles was enraptured, perhaps we should look at a miniature of *c*.1662 by Samuel Cooper. Here, the twenty-two-year-old looks younger. Her hair hangs loose and natural and there is no artificial pose to set the mood of the piece. Yet the frank frontal gaze, the partly closed lids and the suggestion of sardonic humour about the lips reveal the essence of the woman. It emphatically supports our understanding of what Charles sought in the opposite sex. He liked women who were strong, bold, uninhibited. His long-lasting amours were with women who made the running. He was no seducer. In all his human relationships he was rarely proactive. He had little need to be. Just as politicians vied with each other for the privilege of handling state business, so potential mistresses beat a path to his bedchamber. The indolence of which his ministers complained allowed both them and their rivals to exercise a considerable degree of power. It also ensured that, once Charles was secure on his throne, his court would become a cockpit in which men and women fought for mastery and the perks that went with it. Barbara Villiers grasped this simple truth at a very early stage and became one of the principal contenders in the ring.

So great and notorious was her influence that it is easy to see why it was generally assumed that she had been at the king's side from the very first night of the reign. The hard evidence we have suggests that Charles was slightly more circumspect, at least for the first few weeks. He knew well how important it was to make a good impression – and if he ever forgot it, Hyde was on hand to remind him. The image of the old king was still vivid in people's memories and they looked to his son to revive a concept of monarchy that had about it an appropriate mystique. Popular songs generated by his return piously assumed that Charles II would fit the mould of semi-divine kingship:

> He is God's anointed sure,
> Who still doth guide him,
> In all his ways most pure,
> Though some deride him.
> Then let us give God praise,
> That doth defend him,
> And sing with heart and voice,
> Angels attend him . . .

'Though some deride him' – the line indicates the sombre thread of caution woven into the glowing tapestry of national rejoicing. The stories of goings-on in the exiled court were common currency, deliberately spread and frequently exaggerated by the king's enemies. Rejoicing was by no means as unbridled and universal as Evelyn suggested.

Samuel Pepys, an avid watcher of the comings and goings of the great and famous, was not aware of Barbara's presence until 13 July. On that summer's night he was working late at the King Street house of his boss, Lord Sandwich, lieutenant-admiral of the fleet, when the sounds of revelry next door disturbed him. He and his colleagues were intrigued to know who the merrymakers were in the house belonging to Mr Palmer, so 'Here at the old door that did go into his lodgings, my lord, I and W Howe did stand listening a great while to the music'. They discovered that the king and his brothers were there 'with Madame Palmer, a pretty woman that they have a fancy to, to make her husband a cuckold'.[65] Pepys was almost certainly behind the times but if this is so it demonstrates the effectiveness of the secrecy surrounding Charles and Barbara's assignations. The only people who seem to have been in the know at this early stage were members of Barbara's family who, of course, had the very best of reasons for wishing to further the liaison. Her uncles, Viscount Grandison and Colonel Edward Villiers, and her aunt, the Countess of Suffolk, were the couple's main confidants.

By the autumn the secret was out and no attempt was being made to keep it. Barbara was, by now, obviously pregnant and although the father of her first daughter (born in February 1661) was almost certainly her husband (the child was christened Anne Palmer), there was sufficient doubt for tongues to be set wagging. It may be that Barbara told the king that the little girl was his in order to increase her hold over him, though it was several years before Charles actually acknowledged her as his own.

He had need of a mistress to distract him for, once again, he was having to cope with problems caused by his own female relatives. His mother and sisters were, of course, eager to come over to England to share the triumph of their House but the seemingly simple business of arranging their travel created family problems. Charles could not invite one without inviting them all. Yet, he was only too well aware that his mother was still highly unpopular with many of the common people and some of their superiors. There was also the little matter of persuading Hyde to receive his enemy with at least an outward show of cordiality. For her part, the queen dowager was not sure that this was the most apt time to make the trip. The exact nature of the reunion was, therefore, a matter for delicate consideration. What Charles did not need was his mother creating fresh difficulties in her habitual, imperious manner. But this is exactly what she did. She had recently succeeded in negotiating a marriage between Minette and Louis XIV's brother, Philip, Duke of Anjou (soon to be created duc d'Orléans and Chartres), and she wished Mary to come to Paris to share in the rejoicing at her sister's good fortune. If Charles was impatient to receive the Princess of Orange, he would just have to wait; their mother would not take 'no' for an answer:

> I earnestly beg and invite you to come as soon as you can . . . I shall perhaps be able to go into England myself. If that happens, you will be ready for the journey. If I do not go, you can leave from here to join him, and even if he wishes, as I have heard, that you should go at once, my answer will be resolute to send him word that you wished to see me in passing, and to see your sister.[66]

This put Mary in a quandary. Once again she found herself in the role of a tennis ball in a game being played by her mother and brother. She expressed her frustration to Charles, impatiently demanding that he sort things out:

> I received a letter from the queen this last post, wherein she says by the next she will send for me into France. I have let her know your resolution of sending for me directly into England. Therefore, for God's sake, agree between you what I have to do, which I hope you will not consider an unreasonable desire, since I have made this same to the queen. And pray do not delay it, for I have a great impatience to be gone from hence, and yet, rather than displease either of you, I would suffer the greatest punishment of this world (that is to live all my life here), for I know what it is to displease both of you. God keep me from it again![67]

The parenthetical aside, 'that is to live all my life here', refers to the struggle that Mary was going through at this particular time and which further complicated arrangements for her journey to England. Her dearest wish was to return permanently to the country of her birth and to put behind her the years of bickering with the republican rulers of the Dutch states. But she also wanted to ensure her son's future and was trying to extract a promise from the States-General that, if she left young William in their care, they would allow him to inherit all his father's offices when he came of age. The burgesses at the Hague were understandably reluctant to sign such a blank cheque. Mary looked to her brother to exert his influence on her behalf. He did so but, in Mary's opinion, very half-heartedly. Thus, as their reunion drew nearer, she had yet another bone to pick with Charles. It was while all these messages were passing to and fro that a thunderbolt was hurled into the midst of family and national life.

Around eleven o'clock on the night of 3 September (an ominous date in Charles' life story, being the anniversary of his defeats at Dunbar and Worcester and also of the death of Oliver Cromwell) a tiny group of people met in a chamber at Worcester House in the Strand, the home of Sir Edward Hyde, now lord chancellor. The householder was not present and had he been he would have put a prompt end to the ceremony about to take place. The Duke of York had come with his chaplain, Dr Joseph Crowther, and his close friend, Thomas, Lord Ossory (Ormonde's son and heir), to be married to Anne Hyde. Anne was now heavily pregnant and determined to hold her lover to his promise. In view of James' reputation with the ladies, which was very little different from his brother's, it is surprising that he should have decided to do the honourable thing. When Pepys later discussed the affair with Lord Sandwich, the earl passed on the rumour that James had intended to cut and run but that the king had obliged him to marry Anne. Sandwich added his opinion that, 'he that do get a wench with child and marry her afterwards is as if a man should shit in his hat and then clap it on his head'. Pepys commented, 'I perceive my lord is grown a man very indifferent in all matters of religion and so makes nothing of these things.'[68] The diarist found it difficult to accustom himself to the fashionable new cynicism. The rumour was, in fact, wrong. However, because the embarrassing secret was well kept for several weeks, it was inevitable that speculation should have given rise to numerous stories.

The aftermath of the clandestine marriage was highly dramatic. A few days later James went to his brother and shamefacedly confessed that he had married without his king's permission and sought leave to acknowledge his wife openly. Charles called two of his councillors, Ormonde and the veteran Earl of Southampton, lord treasurer, into conference. There were important constitutional issues to consider, for, if the marriage was declared official, not only would a prince of the blood have married a commoner, thereby taking him out of the European royal marriage market, but Anne's child would be second in line to the throne. Significantly, these matters weighed less with the king than the immediate problem of the impact of this news on Sir Edward. In the first few months following Charles' return the restored monarchy was no more than a hugely popular idea. Now it had to be turned into a political and constitutional reality. That meant long hours of tedious paperwork, meetings to reconcile ideologically incompatible enemies and the hammering out of new relationships between Crown, Church and Parliament. Charles had neither the ability nor the inclination for this task. He needed Hyde, who was, in effect, his first minister. He could not allow the chancellor to be disgraced and forced out of office, or into exile. Ormonde and Southampton were, therefore, despatched to break the news to the man who had, *malgré lui*, become the king's relation by marriage.

The account of the following interviews Hyde had with his colleagues and the king was written years later by the chancellor. He may have exaggerated his reaction. Certainly, it seems extreme to modern minds. He raved at his daughter's excesses while being careful to make no complaint against the duke. He advocated that Anne should be immediately carted off to the Tower and incarcerated in the deepest, darkest dungeon, while parliament prepared an Act of Attainder which would result in her execution. There can be no doubt about Hyde's genuine sense of moral outrage. He had always been a stern critic of the lewd behaviour of the king's circle and now the defiling ooze of fashionable promiscuity had seeped across his own threshold. But he was also worried about his own position. It was quite clear that his court rivals would gleefully spread the slander that he had deliberately insinuated his daughter into the duke's bed in order to bolster his own prestige and power. Beyond Whitehall he had many enemies among those who were dissatisfied with the nature of the settlement that he was brokering and they would be happy to see him replaced by a minister more to their own taste. But his concerns were not entirely selfish; he, too, had a sense of the enormity of the political task as yet scarcely begun. Having played no small part in engineering the Restoration, and knowing that national life could still fall back into the anarchic confusion of contending parties, he did not want to see all his work wasted.

This crisis was resolved by the application of that talent which the king had mastered during the many crises of the preceding years: under-reaction. Having satisfied himself that, by the laws of Church and State, James and Anne were, indeed, husband and wife, he advised the outraged father that they must all make the best of a bad job; he certainly would not hear of Hyde's resignation. James – or possibly some friends on his behalf – made a last-ditch, ungallant attempt to wriggle out of his responsibilities, asserting that the lady had lain with several other men and could not prove that the duke was the father of her child. She had, then, tricked him into a promise of marriage, which could not be considered lawful. Charles was not taken in. He told his brother plainly, to his face, that he must 'drink as he brewed'. As far as Charles was concerned, that was the end of the matter. It could not be so for the chancellor. As he told his son, this marriage 'must be all their ruin sooner or later'.[69] The words were prophetic. The groom had married in haste; the father-in-law would repent at leisure.

Nor did the king's kindred share his serene resignation. His mother, sisters and other brother were furious at the disgrace they believed James had brought upon them all. If Henrietta Maria had been in two minds about coming to England, the latest news removed all doubt. Not only had her son married beneath him, he had married into the family of that creature, Hyde. Therefore, she 'sent the king word that she was on the way to England to prevent with her authority so great a stain and dishonour to the Crown'.[70] Mary was no less indignant. She made it known in advance of her arrival that she would never yield precedence to a woman who had been one of her own ladies-in-waiting. And Henry, Duke of Gloucester, remarked sneeringly that Anne 'smelt so strong of her father's green bag [i.e., his lowly status as a mere lawyer] that he could not get the better of himself whenever he had the misfortune to be in her presence' in order to show her any civility.[71] Suddenly the family reunion which they had all been eagerly awaiting looked like becoming a very fraught occasion.

It was at this moment that tragedy struck. Henry Stuart was spared the indignity of being polite to his sister-in-law. He fell victim to the smallpox that was virulent in London that summer. On 13 September he died, sincerely mourned by all who knew him. But especially so, according to Bishop Burnet, by the king, 'who was never in his whole life so much troubled as he was on that occasion. Those who would not believe he had much tenderness in his nature imputed this rather to his jealousy of the brother that survived, since he had now lost the only person that could balance him.'[72] The two events, occurring almost simultaneously, certainly did nothing to improve relations between the remaining brothers. They were very different. Where Charles was clever but lazy, James was industrious and dull-witted. James was also sincerely religious and high-principled and, as a result, experienced crises of conscience when his passions led him into sin. Charles, who famously asserted that God would not judge him harshly for enjoying a few little pleasures, was a stranger to inner turmoil. Buckingham tersely summed up the characters of the two men in an epigram as perceptive as it is typical of the cutting, irreverent witticisms of the Restoration court. 'The king', he said, 'could see things if he would and the duke would see things if he could.'[73]

Vengeance was one of the issues on which the royal brothers differed. While the Stuarts were experiencing their little, in camera difficulties, throughout the country at large the surviving regicides were being hunted down, tried and executed. Over several days in mid-October thirteen men who had been involved in the death of Charles I suffered, in public at Charing Cross, the gruesome punishment meted out to traitors. Seasoned royalists, like Evelyn, took grim pleasure in their fate:

> This day were executed those murderous traitors at Charing Cross, in sight of the place where they put to death their natural prince and in the presence of the king, his son, whom they also sought to kill, taken in the trap they laid for others . . . I saw not their execution, but met their quarters, mangled and cut and reeking as they were brought from the gallows in baskets on the hurdle. Oh, miraculous providence of God![74]

James also relished this judgement on the murderers of his sainted father. He looked to a reaffirmation of the unrestricted authority of semi-divine kingship. Charles was blinkered neither by doctrinaire political philosophy nor by the grief that can only be assuaged in blood-letting. He wanted to put the past behind him as rapidly as possible and not risk scratching unhealed sores. As Burnet explained, the king knew well the quicksilver nature of the mob, especially in London.

> . . . though the regicides were at that time odious beyond all expression and the trials and executions of the first that suffered were run to by vast crowds, and all people seemed pleased with the sight, yet the odiousness of the crime grew at last to be so much flattened by the frequent executions, and most of those who suffered dying with much firmness and show of piety, justifying all they had done, not without a seeming joy for their suffering on that account, that the king was advised not to proceed farther, at least not to have the scene so near the court as Charing Cross.[75]

But Charles needed little persuasion. When the rabble erected a gallows within sight of the palace and strung up an effigy of Cromwell, he ordered it to be taken down. The Act of Indemnity and Oblivion, to which he assented in August, had reduced by a half the number of his enemies originally marked by parliament for destruction. When the female members of the family arrived at Whitehall it was to a court in purple mourning and much subdued by recent events. Mary reached the capital on 25 September, having narrowly escaped shipwreck on a sandbank off the Kent coast, and then being triumphantly escorted by the king upriver in a procession of barges.

A month later, Charles set out with mixed feelings to greet his mother. Beneath the formal courtesies he was obliged to pay lay an irritation which he found difficult to suppress and for which he had ample reason. Try as he might, he could not stop her attempts to exercise control. She was still determined to tie England fast to the apron strings of Catholic France. Over the last few months she had worked assiduously to that end. To please her, Charles had given Jermyn the title Earl of St Albans and admitted him to the enlarged royal council. There the queen mother's agent was one among several voices and his influence was limited. Henrietta Maria was not satisfied with this concession. When the crucial negotiations with the English agents were mooted back in March, she and Mazarin had urged Charles to hold talks in Paris, rather than Breda, so that they could counter Hyde's influence. Unsuccessful in that, she intrigued directly with the French ambassador in London, Antoine de Bordeaux, instructing him to work with the enemies of Sir Edward. On Charles' return to England these machinations came to light and the king immediately sent Bordeaux packing.

Relations between the two countries were at their lowest ebb for many years and, ironically, it was the queen mother who was in large measure responsible for that. Mazarin was now eager that she should go to England and work for a complete *rapprochement*. But the cardinal could no more contain her dynastic and religious ambitions than could her son. She made it clear to all that she was now bound for England to 'marry one son and unmarry the other'. Henrietta Maria 'had the art of making herself believe anything she had a mind to'.[76] As far as her children were concerned, she saw herself as a marriage broker *par excellence* and her scheming knew no bounds. At different times she had tried to unite both her daughters with Louis XIV and she now had her own very definite ideas about potential brides for her two remaining sons. For Charles she had revived the Hortense Mancini proposal. As for James, the first imperative was to prise him loose from the Hyde girl.

Once again, she had, eventually, to admit defeat over both these objectives, but not until several unpleasant weeks had passed. Charles had already begun negotiations about his marriage, negotiations which remained firmly under wraps, and were very specifically kept hidden from his mother. As for James, his first legitimate son was born a few days before the queen mother's arrival and the duke, hoping for a blessing, hovered round her quarters in Whitehall. This was an almost Arctic zone. Henrietta Maria declined to acknowledge Anne or see her grandson. She would not receive Hyde and he staunchly refused to beg an audience. Finally, she threatened to return immediately to France if her wishes were not respected. It took all Charles' charm, laced with firmness, and a message from Mazarin to soften the queen mother's attitude. Jermyn was sent to act as intermediary between the two reluctant grandparents and was able to secure a grudging meeting. Meanwhile the cardinal stressed the importance of cordial relations between the two countries and hinted to Henrietta Maria that if she wished to be welcomed back to her nephew's court she must put an end to the friction in her own family. And to ensure his mother's compliance, Charles turned the financial screw. The queen dowager was entitled to the income from various properties in England which had not, of course, been paid since the outbreak of the Civil War. The king now told her what she would have to do to get the money released.

But once again it was grief that wrapped its cloak around the family and, at least partially, drew them together. The change of air had not agreed with Princess Mary and she seldom ventured out of her rooms at Whitehall. No one was unduly worried about her but, as she and her family prepared for the first Christmas they had all spent together for twenty years, she was obliged to take to her bed with a fever. Her doctors reluctantly agreed on the dread diagnosis of smallpox. On Christmas Eve she died.

Charles came to her bedside several times during her last days, although he had sent his mother and Henrietta to St James's Palace away from the contagion. Theirs had been a turbulent relationship. Perhaps, in essence it had been too close – the highs too high, the lows too low. Mary was a strong-minded woman with more than her share of Bourbon arrogance. She had identified herself unreservedly with her brother's cause. They had spent idyllic days together – sightseeing, dancing, being fêted by German princes. And they had argued – violently, bitterly, because Mary had resented Charles' presumption in standing guard over her morals. Joy and anger were alike the children of devotion. But was that commitment rather one-sided? No contemporary record describes the king as being devastated by his sister's death. He should have been. Without her support, financial and emotional, it is difficult to see how he could have survived the years of exile. But now he had no need of her and her passing would not leave a gaping hole in his life. Yet, perhaps, we judge him too harshly if we represent him as being governed by purely selfish considerations. He did keep Mary's picture on the wall of his bedchamber ever afterwards and he did take an interest, albeit a very patronising interest, in her son's well-being. Samuel Pepys was very preoccupied with alterations to his house in the closing weeks of 1660. In the midst of his domestic arrangements he recorded, baldly, 'This day the Princess Royal died at Whitehall.'[77] Despite the lack of evidence we must charitably assume that the event made more impact on the king.

Mary's funeral took place at Westminster Abbey on 29 December, James taking on the role of chief mourner. Three days later, his son was christened with the name of Charles and was given the title Duke of Cambridge. The king and his mother were among the godparents and Henrietta Maria put a brave face upon her defeat. We have a typically frank description of the queen dowager and her daughter from Pepys, who had been received by the royal visitors a few weeks before: 'The queen a very little, plain old woman, and nothing more in her presence in any respect nor garb than an ordinary woman ... The Princess Henrietta is very pretty but much below my expectation, and her dressing of herself with her hair frizzed short up to her ears, did make her seem so much the less to me.'[78] The sixteen-year-old princess was the most popular member of the family. She had a natural grace and was able to adapt herself to any kind of company. Her youth and her talent for saying the right thing at the right time endeared her to all she met. When parliament voted her a wedding gift of £10,000 it was a political gesture but none the less enthusiastic for that, and when the Speaker read out her thank-you letter to the Commons, in which she apologised for her poor command of the English language but declared that her heart was wholly English, the members warmed to her. However they might have felt about other members of the family, they accepted this young lady as a charming ambassador.

A week later the princess's servants were packing in preparation for her to accompany her mother back to France. Both ladies were thankful to be leaving and putting behind them a stay which had been tense and immeasurably sad. But their trials were not at an end. First of all, the ship taking them across the Channel ran into vile weather and was forced to put back into Portsmouth. Then, while Lord Sandwich and his crew were waiting there for the winter storms to abate, the princess fell ill. Coming as it did after the tragedies which had befallen her siblings, it was natural that her mother and her attendants should fear the worst. However, this time the malady proved to be not smallpox but measles. After a couple of weeks Henrietta was able to resume her journey and to prepare herself for what would turn out to be yet another disastrous Stuart marriage.

Henrietta may have protested her English heart to parliament and the charm of her personality may have persuaded people to believe her but the truth was very different. She was a thoroughly French princess, relieved and delighted to be returning to the only home she had ever known. She was a Bourbon, a Catholic and her mother's daughter (though unable to match Henrietta Maria's proselytising zeal). She enjoyed the luxury and diversions provided by the court of Louis XIV and was intoxicated by the prospect of becoming the king's sister-in-law. As the result of one elaborate ceremony she would be transformed from a mere pensioner of the Crown into the second lady of France, fawned upon by courtiers, and a major player in the game of courtly love. Louis, who had once derided his brother's wish to be married to 'the bones of the Holy Innocents' (a reference to Henrietta's thinness and piety), had been won over by her charms and found increasing pleasure in her shrewdness, intelligence and wit. Once over her illness, to Minette the future looked golden, indeed.

The only veil obscuring her gleaming fate was the character of her espoused. Philippe, duc d'Orléans, conventionally known as 'Monsieur', was, in Burnet's words, 'a poor-spirited and voluptuous prince; monstrous in his vices and effeminate in his luxury in more senses than one. He had not one good or great quality, but courage; so that he became both odious and contemptible.'[79] What the bishop could not bring himself to write down without mincing words was that Philippe was bisexual. It may be that his more outrageous behaviour did not develop until later years and only revealed itself, in 1661, in an eccentric love of cross-dressing, but as time passed his behaviour became more scandalous. Not only that, but when Henrietta, not surprisingly, sought the more pleasurable company of other men Orléans became passionately jealous, having his wife watched and, when possible, removed from the court. He openly claimed that his love for Minette had come to an end about two weeks after their wedding. As his affection for 'Madame' (Henrietta's official title) waned, that of his brother waxed. The inevitable rumours soon began to circulate. They were, almost certainly, without foundation. Minette was not Louis' mistress; she was something more important – his confidante, and therefore valuable to the scheming king in his relations with her brother.

Louis XIV, now twenty-two, was, like Charles, a vigorous womaniser but his attitude to the opposite sex was markedly different from that of his cousin. In later years he advised his son, 'the time allotted to a liaison should never prejudice our affairs, since our first object should always be the preservation of our glory and authority, which can only be achieved by steady toil . . . and – more difficult to practise – in giving our heart we must remain absolute master of our mind, separating the endearments of the lover from the resolution of the sovereign'.[80] In his early years, at least, Louis followed his own dictum. He was passionately attached to his *maîtresse en titre*, Louise de la Vallière, formerly one of Minette's maids of honour, but he kept a rigid barrier between the bedroom and the council chamber. This ability to compartmentalise his life was one of the many crucial differences between him and Charles, differences that shaped their relationship and, therefore, much of the history of Europe in the second half of the seventeenth century.

Louis had been well trained by Mazarin and, on the cardinal's death in 1661, surprised his advisers by informing them that, in future, he would personally oversee the internal and external affairs of his country. He had grandiose objectives and was clear in his mind about how to pursue them. His simplistic Catholicism had its own internal logic which assumed that kings ruled by divine right, that rebellion was sin, that preservation of true religion was part of the sovereign's responsibility and that Protestantism was diabolical heresy. His fertile brain could conceive and hold in suspension a variety of schemes, ready to be applied as occasion served. The lessons of the Frondes had been well learned and Mazarin handed on to his master a centralised government served by a bureaucracy that was efficient by the standards of the day and a nobility who had been brought to heel. The French king was rich and knew how to deploy his wealth to impress observers with the grandeur of the monarchy – conspicuous display rather than conspicuous consumption.

Charles lacked both his cousin's advantages and the strength of character to make the most of the advantages he did have. France's civil war had left the monarchy strengthened. In Britain internal strife had had no such resolution. Issues such as the balance of authority between king and parliament and between institutionalised Church and private conscience had still not been resolved. The Commons controlled most of the revenue and exerted the right to scrutinise the king's ministers. If Charles were to preserve as much freedom of action as possible he was obliged to be duplicitous, to scrape up money wherever he could, and to do deals with groups and individuals. All this made it difficult to devise and carry through strategies. But, in any case, Charles' mind did not work like that. His policy making lacked the rigidity provided by religion and political philosophy. He had no training in the art of kingship. He was reactive rather than proactive. He spent money for pleasure rather than for effect. He allowed emotion to cloud his judgement. And the very fluidity of his court and council meant that mistresses, favourites and attendants exercised political influence alongside ministers and parliamentarians.

Louis understood his cousin's situation and also his weaknesses and he exploited them to the full in all his relations with Charles and those close to him – men and women. One thing Louis did not understand was British Protestantism, or, at least, anti-Catholicism. A century which had witnessed persecution, Rome-inspired plots, proliferating sermons, extensive personal Bible reading, civil war and national unity in the face of aggression from continental neighbours had introduced new elements into the social DNA of the British peoples. They were by no means all Puritans but moral earnestness and an acceptance of behavioural patterns which had their origins in Holy Writ were the norm throughout most levels of society. Specifically, the freemen of these islands were not disposed to submit to the 'tyranny' of pope and priest. British travellers on the continent were amused and appalled by the uncritical way peasants and even the better-educated classes accepted the absurd superstitions promoted by the clergy.

The leaders of French society were no less dismissive and scornful of the religious life of the heretic islands. Louis and his bishops genuinely believed that a nation containing less than 2 per cent of Catholics could be brought back within the Roman fold by government fiat. In his own country he backed the repression of the Huguenot minority and, in 1684, would revoke the Edict of Nantes which had guaranteed them freedom of conscience. He assumed that the Reformation veneer could be as easily stripped off the carcass of British religion. If Henrietta Maria, after twenty years of residence in England, had failed to understand what made her husband's subjects 'tick', it is scarcely surprising that her nephew should draw the wrong conclusions. Both of them were deceived by the culture of the English royal court, where Catholicism, libertinism and cynicism were fashionable precisely because they set the élite apart from the pious 'cant' and boring moral restraints of the common herd. Two antipathetical cultures existed side by side and the dominant one in modish society had more in common with that beyond the Channel than with what was accepted throughout the land outside the walls of Whitehall Palace.

The way of life of the social élite was increasingly resented in the provinces, and certainly not only by Puritanical propagandists. John Dryden, the poet and playwright who was frequently condemned for the vulgarity and licence of his work, eventually reached the conclusion,

> But sure a banished court with lewdness fraught
> The seeds of open vice returning brought.

And the writer of the following sarcastic diatribe against the corrupting influence of the fashion leaders was a fervent Stuart supporter who suffered prison and loss of employment for his adherence to James II:

> A fine gentleman is a fine whoring, sweaty, smutty, atheistical man. These qualifications, it seems, complete the idea of honour. They are the top improvements of fortune and the distinguishing glories of birth and breeding! . . . The restraints of conscience and the pedantry of virtue are unbecoming a cavalier. Future securities and reaching beyond life are vulgar provisions . . . Here you have a man of breeding and figure that burlesques the Bible, swears and talks smut to ladies, speaks ill of his friend behind his back . . . fine only in the insignificancy of life, the abuse of religion and the scandals of conversation. These worshipful things . . . appear at the head of the fashion.[81]

In 1661, it was not only Henrietta who was making plans to enter the temple of Hymen. Marriage, or rather, the perks that accompanied marriage, was a topic now very much on Charles' mind. The time had come for him to take a wife and to produce a legitimate heir to the throne. As he looked around the royal courts of Europe, the prospect was very fair indeed. Gone were the days of barren wooing, when no reigning sovereign was prepared to offer his daughter to a pretend king. Now Charles found himself in a buyers' market. In the delicate continental power balance an alliance with England, which had recently shown itself to possess a formidable navy and a useful army, had distinct advantages. The governments of the leading nations were all eager to cement their friendship with the rehabilitated monarchy. On the cynical assumption that even Edward Hyde had his price, the new French ambassador was empowered to offer him a £10,000 pension to use his influence in the Gallican interest. Though there was nothing out of the ordinary about such an arrangement, the minister made much of his shocked refusal of the bribe. Other diplomats were not so crass but they, too, were instructed to court the men closest to the king, and to line their pockets as necessary. Burnet was convinced that Charles' heart was set on a Catholic bride. Doubtless, he still thought that German women were 'foggy' and that a Protestant upbringing was unlikely to produce the sort of fun-loving consort that he could live with. Romance or sex did not figure prominently in his calculations; he had Barbara to meet his needs in that department. But he did want a wife whose company he could enjoy and who would grace his court. However, there was one consideration that outweighed all others – money.

The choice lay between France, whose behaviour over recent years still rankled with Charles, Spain, his recent ally, and Portugal, the smallest and weakest of the European superpowers. This last had established a phenomenal, worldwide trading empire in the sixteenth century, seen its prosperity leached away between 1580 and 1640 as a result of the union of the crowns of Spain and Portugal, taken advantage of Spain's conflict with France to assert independence under the House of Braganza and, now that its neighbours had settled their differences, was feeling very vulnerable. Portugal desperately needed a prestigious ally and was prepared to pay for one – handsomely. The horse trading that went on between the English government and the representatives of the neighbouring powers during the early months of 1661 was fast and furious but Portuguese gold won the day. Charles was offered the hand of the Infanta Catherine, together with a dowry of £330,000, the biggest sum ever brought into England by a foreign bride, plus the fortified trading posts of Bombay and Tangier and valuable commercial concessions throughout the Portuguese empire. In return he pledged 10,000 troops to aid his ally in the war with Spain.

The match was furthered enthusiastically by Louis. Failing a French bride, a Portuguese one was the next best thing because she would encourage Charles' adherence to the anti-Spanish camp. In terms of direct family connection he already had Minette and he was determined to make the best possible use of her as an ambassador. The regular correspondence between the English king and his sister was a principal line of communication between the two monarchs. It also had the advantage of bypassing, not only the normal diplomatic channels, but also Henrietta Maria and her network. Both Charles and Louis considered her a liability.

On 22 April the citizens of London and visitors to the capital, all of whom had for so long been deprived of spectacular ceremonial, turned out for their king's coronation procession. They were not disappointed. Charles and his master of ceremonies were determined to grasp the opportunity to demonstrate the superiority of monarchical government and to stir up loyalist fervour. Charles came downriver to the Tower and from there made the traditional triumph through the crowded, decorated streets of the City. (He was the last sovereign to do so.) Samuel Pepys, of course, had a good vantage point and recorded the brave show of soldiers, finely caparisoned horses, gorgeously attired nobles and bishops, London livery companies and bands of musicians. He declared himself quite overwhelmed by the lavish display: 'So glorious was the show with gold and silver that we were not able to look at it, our eyes at last being so much overcome.'[82] The following day Charles was crowned in the abbey church, using the Crown Jewels, made at a cost of £31,000 to replace those broken up during the Commonwealth. As part of the celebrations he had already made several new peers, including Sir Edward Hyde, who now became Earl of Clarendon. No one now could despise the king's brother-in-law as a commoner.

The next time Charles ennobled one of his servants he deliberately did so in a clandestine way so that Hyde would not know of it in time to raise objections. While the court was at Newmarket for the autumn race meeting he ordered a patent to be drawn up for Roger Palmer to be made Earl of Castlemaine in the Irish peerage. This meant that the document did not have to pass under the Great Seal, held by Lord Clarendon. The terms of the grant made provision for the title to pass only to Palmer's heirs 'gotton on Barbara Palmer, his now wife'. This made it humiliatingly clear to the recipient that the grant was a reward for Barbara's services, rather than his own. The 'honour' outraged Palmer, who rarely used his new title. His wife revelled in it because it provided her with the rank that fitted her to be the king's regular companion and it also prepared the ground for Barbara to join the entourage of the new queen, the conventional way of providing a place at court for royal mistresses. The king's marriage contract had been signed in June and arrangements were in hand to bring Catherine of Braganza over in the spring of 1662.

The timing of Barbara's promotion is significant. She had just discovered herself to be pregnant again and this time it was clear who was the father of her child. The assignations in King Street and at other rendezvous arranged by her relatives and friends had become frequent and there was no longer any attempt to conceal them. Mrs Palmer was often seen in public with the king and observers were left in no doubt about his feelings for her. But the liaison was not popular with many people. She met with jealousy and contempt among several of the ladies and gentlemen of the court, while Clarendon and Southampton blocked her path to those perks she craved. The chancellor treated Barbara as a non-person and later records reveal that he was 'an implacable enemy to the power and interest she had with the king and had used all the endeavours he could to destroy it'.[83] He forbade his wife to call upon her and refused even to mention her name; he could only bring himself to refer to her as 'the lady'. The treasurer would not allow any of the funds at his disposal to pass into her hands, even when she presented him with a royal warrant. A position of stalemate existed. Charles made promises to his mistress but his officers of state would not put them into execution. Since the king refused to interfere with day-to-day administration or pick a quarrel with the men he relied on to see his regime securely established, the ambitious Mrs Palmer had to endure the frustration of her ambition. The acquiring of a title, especially since it involved going behind Clarendon's back, was thus a major coup for her.

However, winning a battle was very far from winning the war. As Barbara looked apprehensively into 1662, she knew that the situation was going to change in ways which could not be accurately forecast. Charles' new wife would soon be arriving and there was no telling what kind of a relationship they might establish. He had actually promised the chancellor that once he was a happily married man he would have no need of other women. If Charles actually developed a deep attachment to his new wife or if Queen Catherine and Clarendon formed a strong alliance there would be no room in the court for Barbara. Nor was it only the Hyde camp that she feared. The following summer would see considerable changes in the royal household. Henrietta Maria would be returning to take up permanent residence in England. She would be bringing with her the king's eldest son, James Crofts, who, by all accounts, was growing into an impressive youth. As Charles became the centre of a royal family, surrounded by his own kindred and children, legitimate and illegitimate, he might very well lose interest in a mistress who had served her purpose. Barbara was insecure as long as she had only her lover's assurances of eternal fidelity to rely on, for, like all who were close to Charles, she knew exactly how much faith to repose in his word. If she were not to become just another paid-off mistress she would have to tie herself to the royal ménage with knots that could not be easily unfastened and she only had a few months in which to do it.

Her main objective was a formal position in the household. This would give her her own quarters in the palace and easy access to the king. Equally importantly, it would put her in the best place to win favours (money and jewels, lucrative offices, property, positions of influence) for herself and her friends. As a key source of patronage, Lady Castlemaine would be able to bind to herself ministers, diplomats and courtiers in a symbiotic relationship. Only then would she be strong enough to defy the hated Clarendon. She extracted from the king a promise to appoint her as lady of the bedchamber to the queen. She also built up her own body of supporters.

The early months of 1662 saw the steady emergence of an anti-Clarendon alliance with which Barbara was closely associated. Its chief members were Lord Bristol, Sir Henry Bennet, Charles Berkeley and Lord St Albans, all members of the old Louvre party and all in close contact with the queen mother and the French court. Henry Jermyn, Earl of St Albans had, according to the rumour which still persisted, for many years been a secret lover of Henrietta Maria and the father of a daughter who had been quietly removed to the care of nuns. The story probably indicates no more than the very close relationship existing between Jermyn and the king's mother. Berkeley, regarded by Pepys as 'a most vicious person', was a born intriguer and confessed to the king that he had been behind the plot to blacken Anne Hyde's name the previous year. George Digby continued to pursue a highly individualistic approach to politics. He had strenuously opposed the Portuguese match and blamed Clarendon for bringing it about. Bennet, a flamboyant, genial, self-advertising man who ostentatiously wore a black patch across his nose to draw attention to a 'wound' he had received fighting for the king in the Civil War, returned cautiously some months after the Restoration, anxious about Edward Hyde's hostility. He soon worked his way back into royal favour and began to accumulate valuable offices. Early in 1662 he petitioned for the lucrative post of postmaster-general and persuaded Lady Castlemaine to speak for him. Clarendon blocked the appointment and secured the position for another applicant.

Thus, there built up in court and council a nascent warfare between the 'old guard' of Clarendon, Ormonde, Nicholas and Southampton and a younger 'smart set', which was, in part, a continuation of the earlier Louvre party. The latter had little political clout as long as the king left the conduct of affairs in the hands of his old and trusted ministers. Pepys noted, in July 1661, Charles' attitude towards his chancellor: 'though he loves him not in the way of a companion, as he do these young gallants that can answer him in his pleasures, yet he cannot be without him for his policy and service'.[84] But, in the second half of 1662, the political balance shifted dramatically. There were very clear reasons for this: Clarendon's unpopularity grew and some of his policies failed. Charles rapidly fell out with his new queen. In a head-to-head confrontation with Catherine, Lady Castlemaine emerged victorious. And Henrietta Maria took up residence in Somerset House, as determined as ever to involve herself in state affairs.

In late April 1662 Catherine of Braganza left her family, her father's court, all the friends of her youth and her native land and set out to fulfil her pre-ordained destiny as the queen of a distant, foggy, heretic country. She came full of apprehensions but proud and determined. She knew little of the man with whom she was going to live or of the customs of his people. Both would come as a shock to her but she had been trained to maintain her dignity and to insist on her rights. Since there could be no turning back, she knew that it was important for her to demand all the privileges due to her position and respect for her religion. The Portuguese princess arrived in Portsmouth on 13 May and immediately took to her bed with a feverish cold. Charles was eager to meet the woman to whom he had tied himself but was detained several days by business in London and did not greet his bride until the 20th. What he discovered must have been rather daunting. He noted instantly that Catherine was not wearing any of the English clothes he had provided for her (although it seems that it was the Duke of York who had persuaded her to don a traditional Portuguese farthingale). She was small and slender, sallow of complexion and with slightly protuberant teeth. 'Her face,' Charles reported to Clarendon with evident relief, 'was not so exact as to be called a beauty, though her eyes were excellent good, and there was nothing in her face that in the least degree can disgust one.'[85] Her luxuriant black hair was Catherine's crowning glory, though it was some time before she could be persuaded not to have it dressed in the complex Portuguese style. Communication was difficult because the infanta spoke neither English nor French (though she had begun to learn her husband's language). However, nothing could obscure her spirit. She came to her new land defiantly virtuous and defiantly Catholic. Throughout her twenty-three years she had seldom ventured outside her father's palace and had been protected from contamination by the real world. A portrait executed by Catherine's royal painter, Dirck Stoop, at this time is in sharp contrast to the voluptuous images created to depict Charles' court ladies. It presents a prim young woman in sumptuous but sober dress, unadorned by jewellery, her pose that of a bygone generation, her eyes engaging ours in frank innocence, her lips compressed in dignified aloofness. As one courtier observed, there was nothing about her that might incline the king to 'forget his inclination to the Countess of Castlemaine'.

When Samuel Pepys made the queen's acquaintance he rapidly concluded that she was even more bigoted than the queen mother. She was committed wholeheartedly to the strict morality of her upbringing, which exceeded that of many English Puritans. For example, she was repelled by the thought that a chaste woman might enter the bed in which a man had previously slept. She was determined to keep herself from any defiling influences and she had a troop of monks and matriarchs to stiffen her in her resolve. The first problem bride and groom had to face was the wedding. Charles wanted to be married according to the Anglican rite but Catherine would not countenance anything other than the sacrament of matrimony performed by a Roman priest. They compromised. A secret, Catholic ceremony took place in the queen's chamber and was followed by a service conducted by the Archbishop of Canterbury. Even this arrangement Catherine found hard to endure: 'the queen was bigoted to such a degree that she would not say the words of matrimony, nor bear the sight of the archbishop'.[86]

Then followed the wedding night. It was an anticlimax. Charles reported to Clarendon:

It was happy for the honour of the nation that I was not put to the consummation of the marriage last night, for I was so sleepy by having slept but two hours in my journey as I was afraid that matters would have gone very sleepily.[87]

But why was the bridegroom 'not put to the consummation of the marriage'? Writing to Minette a few days later, he laid the blame squarely on Catherine, and for the most obvious of reasons: she had come to her nuptial bed at the wrong time of the month, something that had, apparently, interfered with Henrietta's own wedding night: 'though I am not so furious as Monsieur was, but am content to let those pass over before I go to bed to my wife, yet I hope I shall entertain her at least better the first night than he did you'.[88] The reason Charles gave for his failure to perform may have been perfectly true. Equally, it may have been an excuse to cover his own disinclination to make love to the demure and inexperienced Catherine. One gets the impression from the account he gave Clarendon of a man that 'doth protest too much':

> she has as much agreeableness in her looks altogether as ever I saw and, if I have any skill in physiognomy, which I think I have, she must be as good a woman as ever was born. Her conversation, as much as I can perceive, is very good, for she has wit enough and a most agreeable voice. You would much wonder to see how well we are acquainted already. In a word, I think myself very happy but am confident our two humours will agree very well together.[89]

On the same day Charles wrote to his new mother-in-law in even more euphoric vein:

> . . . enjoying in this springtime the company of my dearest wife, I am the happiest man in the world and the most enamoured, seeing close at hand the loveliness of her person and her virtues, not only those your Majesty mentioned in your letter – simplicity, gentleness and prudence – but many others also . . . And I wish to say of my wife that I cannot sufficiently either look at her or talk to her. May the good God preserve her to me and grant your Majesty long years of life in which to be a comfort to us both.[90]

Two of Charles' dominant traits are evident in these letters. The first is his genuine affection for and understanding of the opposite sex. He went out of his way to make himself pleasant to the nervous virgin who was faced with giving herself to a man she did not know. The second was his inclination always to tell people what they wanted to hear. The Braganza government in Lisbon was desperate for the recognition and material support that the English alliance provided. Clarendon was equally anxious that the union should be a success; that it would help the king to settle down to respectable married life (such as his father had exemplified) and forsake favourites, pimps and mistresses. So, whatever his misgivings, Charles indicated to all the interested parties that all was well.

All was very far from well. Charles had made mutually contradictory promises to people who were determined to hold him to them. He now had two women in his life, both of whom were strong-minded and determined to have the leading place in his affections. Catherine had heard about the king's mistress and was utterly opposed to receiving her at court. Barbara, isolated in King Street, was a bundle of anxieties. The birth of her child was imminent and she was impatient for the ordeal to be over – and successful. For several weeks her condition had prevented her exercising her potent sexual witchcraft over the king. She needed to recover quickly from the birth and to be able to present Charles with a healthy baby who would give her an extra hold over him. Meanwhile, her husband lost no opportunity to express his righteous wrath, and her lover, upon whom all her hopes depended, was away courting his new wife. In fashionable circles all eyes were fixed upon the principal players and the cogs of the gossip machine were whirring in salacious anticipation: 'there are great endeavours to make you-know-who a lady of the bedchamber,' wrote one royal watcher, 'but it is hoped by many they will not take effect. A little time will show us a great deal – I will say no more for fear of burning my fingers.'[91] It was common knowledge that Charles had promised to be faithful to his queen and common suspicion that he would be unable to keep his word. The sensation-mongers were not to be disappointed.

The court moved to Hampton Court at the end of May and Charles flirted assiduously with his wife. He helped her to learn English and they were seen to laugh much over her mistakes. Husband and wife dined together, rode together and spent happy nights together. Catherine was allowed the ministrations of her priests and her ladies and found her new environment agreeable. She was, it seems, completely won over by the attentiveness of her husband and perfectly ready to love him – as was her duty and her inclination. For his part, Charles was eager to soften his wife up for the confrontation that must soon take place. Some two and a half weeks after their arrival a confidential messenger came to the king with the news that Barbara had been delivered of a boy whom she had immediately named after his father. Charles stole away from Hampton Court for a flying visit to mother and child.

Whether Roger Palmer was present at this affecting reunion is not recorded but he certainly knew of it and he was not slow to react. For a man who had been made the laughing stock of the town it was the last straw to have his wife and her lover meeting together in his house to gloat over the result of their illicit union. For respectability's sake the child would bear Palmer's name – a paper-thin subterfuge which deceived no one. But it did give the outraged cuckold an opportunity for revenge. He had recently been converted to Catholicism. It was therefore his right – indeed his duty – to have his child baptised into the true faith. Doing so would be an intolerable embarrassment to the king. The country had accepted his marriage to a Catholic princess but there was no question but that any heir must be brought up as a Protestant. If the king was prepared to allow his illegitimate offspring to become papists that would be sending out a very dangerous signal. Roger grabbed the boy and rushed him to a priest, who obligingly administered the sacrament.

What followed has all the tumultuous angst and overacted drama of a popular soap opera. A distraught Barbara sent word upriver to the king. He hurried back accompanied by Lady Suffolk, his mistress's aunt, and Aubrey de Vere, Earl of Oxford (perhaps the only one of Charles' confidants who could be quickly found). Together with the baby and his mother they formed an impromptu christening party which hastened to St Margaret's, Westminster for an undignified Anglican ceremony. The king returned to Hampton Court, knowing that news of the sensational event would soon be following him. He was being forced into action and could no longer indulge the luxury of waiting for a favourable opportunity to speak to the queen. The list of Catherine's household officers had not yet been completed. Charles now had it drawn up and presented to his wife for her approval. The first name on it was Lady Castlemaine's. Angrily, Catherine struck it out. This first display of temper by his bride took Charles by surprise. It also obliged him to react.

Over the next few weeks the king's attitude hardened to the point that he behaved towards the queen and those who took her part with severity and even uncharacteristic cruelty. He had boxed himself into a corner and he had done so publicly. He could not yield without losing face and authority. The more he was accused by people he loved and respected – and probably by his own conscience – of being unkind and unreasonable, the more steadfastly he stuck to his guns. There were, of course, plenty of people around the court ready to encourage him to be firm, notably those who were in frequent contact with the queen mother. They urged him to take a leaf from the book of his maternal grandfather, Henry IV, who had regarded it as a point of honour that his close friends, male and female, should be welcomed by his wife. The exact course of events over the weeks of high summer is impossible to reconstruct but it is clear that Charles tried, by turns, every tactic he could employ. Unfortunately he was never at his best with men or women of principle. He adopted the cynic's assumption that everyone has his price and when he encountered a person who could not be cajoled, bribed or bullied his only alternatives were to give way or resort to force. He assured Catherine that his affair with Barbara was at an end. He told her that he had the right to decide who should and who should not be admitted to the royal household. He bargained with her: if she would accept Lady Castlemaine he would never interfere in her choice of companions thereafter. When all else failed, he gave way to threats; unless the queen complied with his wishes he would cease to visit her and he would send all her Portuguese attendants packing. Eventually he carried out that latter threat, leaving his wife stranded and comfortless in an environment where most of the people she encountered day by day were cold towards her because they were afraid to displease the king by appearing to succour her.

The dramatic high point of this confrontation occurred when Charles tried to introduce Barbara to the queen. He brought his mistress into his wife's crowded audience chamber. Catherine rose from her seat to acknowledge the king's presence and smiled at his companion. Only when Charles announced Lady Castlemaine's name did she realise who this attractive, well-dressed woman was. She fell back on to her chair. She burst into tears. Her nose began to bleed. Then she fainted away. Attendants carried her into an adjoining room to revive her and all eyes were on the king. Would he follow to minister to his wife in her distress, leaving Barbara to retire in confusion, or would he escort his mistress away with as much dignity as he could muster? It was a fulcrum moment. On Charles' very public decision depended the tone he would set for his court and the reputation he would have outside it. Typically, he took the easier option. Barbara's power was stronger than the new queen's and, as the king led her from the room, past bowing courtiers, Lady Castlemaine may well have experienced a *frisson* of triumph. She had won.

But Queen Catherine had still not offered her surrender. In fact, she continued her defiance and demanded to be allowed to return to Portugal if she could not have control of her own household. Such a snub would reverberate along the wires of international diplomacy and could, of course, not be even considered. The high-spirited woman must be made to submit. Charles turned to Clarendon, his Mr Fix-it, to carry out this distasteful task. He already knew the chancellor's opinion on the matter, for Clarendon had quite unequivocally told him that the French custom of parading royal mistresses before the court and loading them with honours was quite unacceptable in England. Since their return from abroad, Hyde had been unable to modify his attitude towards Charles. Throughout the long years of exile he had become accustomed to speaking his mind, more like a royal tutor than a politician. Now that his young charge was a mature king, in full possession of his throne, he continued to speak to him in pedagogic vein. Charles was beginning to find it tiresome.

This played into the hands of the chancellor's enemies. When the crisis at Hampton Court was simmering nicely Sir Henry Bennet presented a personal memorandum to the king in which he observed that 'the dissatisfaction towards the present government (though, God knows, very undeservedly) is become so universal that any small accident may put us into new troubles'.[92] The 'present government', of course, meant Clarendon, and Bennet was doing little more than stating the obvious when he wrote of widespread discontent. Considering the long agenda of issues left over from the political and constitutional crises of the last thirty years it could hardly be otherwise. The chancellor was caught between a king whose inclination was towards toleration, reconciliation and inclusivity and a royalist parliament eager for revenge on all those who had troubled Church and State.

Against Charles' wishes, Lords and Commons, having apparently learned nothing from the disastrous efforts of William Laud to fasten all British Christians into a liturgical straitjacket, had carried an iniquitous Act of Uniformity. As a result, over 1,800 Puritan, Presbyterian and Independent clergy were deprived of their livings on 24 August 1662, which, ominously enough, was St Bartholomew's Day. Thus, the vengeful bishops and their allies, by seeking to impose unity, sundered English Protestants into Anglican and Nonconformist communions. This was not what either Charles or thousands of his subjects had thought was meant by the 'liberty to tender consciences' guaranteed by the Declaration of Breda. If the hard-liners got their own way over religion they failed over issues of restitution and the punishment of rebels. As we have seen, very few men suffered execution for their part in the death of the old king and the government decided that it was quite impracticable to compensate royalists for every confiscation of property that had, allegedly, taken place since 1642. One other bone of contention that stuck in the throats of loyal Britons of every persuasion was Dunkirk. Charles and his ministers had decided that the upkeep of the port was not worth the expense entailed so they sold it back to the French. It was a sensible political decision and it added much needed gold to the Treasury but, inevitably, it was not very popular.

The role of scapegoat was built into the office of king's chief minister and Clarendon's enemies believed that they could persuade Charles to jettison the man as a means of deflecting blame from himself for the policies. The schemers and their allies among the young smart set at court kept up a constant sniping of ridicule against the chancellor, lampooning him as an old-fashioned, censorious, killjoy Malvolio figure. Lady Castlemaine had her own reasons for being a member of this group. Yet not even her access to the king enabled them to prise the old servant from his position of trust, as Clarendon told his friend Ormonde:

> I cannot tell you that I find, whatever other people discourse, my credit at all diminished with the king. He takes pains sometimes to persuade me the contrary . . . That which breaks my heart is that the same affections continue still, the same laziness and unconcernedness in business, and a proportionable abatement of reputation.[93]

Nothing more endangered that relationship with the king of which Clarendon boasted than the problems created by the mutual hostility of queen and mistress. Not even Minette's wryly expressed disapproval of his proceedings deflected Charles from his determination to have his own way with regard to Barbara's presence at court. Charles had given his sister a, doubtless carefully edited, version of events at Hampton Court.

Henrietta read between the lines and replied, on 22 July, in mocking tones:

> Alas! How can one possibly say such things? I, who know your innocence, marvel at it. But, jesting apart, I pray you tell me how the queen takes this. It is said here that she is grieved beyond measure, and, to speak frankly, I think it is with reason.[94]

Henrietta knew, by now, what it was to have a husband who behaved badly and she recognised the signs in her dear brother. Charles, however, was too firmly set upon his course to change it. Thus, Clarendon was sent to bring Catherine to heel.

The chancellor did not consent meekly to running this distasteful errand. He demanded and received from Charles an explanation for his conduct. The king was disarmingly frank – up to a point. He said that he enjoyed Lady Castlemaine's company and had no intention of being deprived of it. If he gave way to the queen the first time they had a disagreement he would become a laughing stock. That much Clarendon had no difficulty believing. What followed he may well have taken with a pinch of salt. Charles promised that, if Catherine would oblige him on this one point, he would be a model husband, living chastely with her and making no unreasonable demands. Lady Castlemaine, for her part, would be a devoted and faithful servant of the queen. Clarendon knew his master too well to take this at face value. He knew that Charles Stuart could never content himself with the close companionship of one woman and that he was fascinated by the variety of womankind. He knew that loyalty – to man or woman – meant little to him. However, the chancellor did his duty. He went to the queen and repeated her husband's lies. But Catherine held firm. After several tearful interviews Clarendon informed the king that he had failed in his mission and asked to be relieved of it. Charles accepted with a bad grace, sending after him a long note, warning him to keep his mouth shut about the affair and to restrain anyone else who might be inclined to gossip:

> I forgot when you were here last to desire you to give Broderick [Sir Alan Broderick, a client of Clarendon's and an ardent royalist parliamentarian] good counsel not to meddle any more with what concerns my Lady Castlemaine and to let him have a care how he is the author of any scandalous reports. For if I find him guilty of any such thing I will make him repent it to the last moment of his life.
>
> And now I am entered on this matter I think it very necessary to give you a little good counsel in it, lest you may think that by making a further stir in the business you may divert me from my resolution, which all the world shall never do.

And I wish I may be unhappy in this world and the world to come if I fail in the least degree of what I have resolved, which is of making my Lady Castlemaine of my wife's bedchamber, and whosoever I find use any endeavour to hinder this resolution of mine (except it be only to myself) I will be his enemy to the last moment of my life.

You know how true a friend I have been to you. If you will oblige me eternally, make this business as easy as you can, of what opinion soever you are. For I am resolved to go through with this matter, let what will come of it, which again I solemnly swear before Almighty God.

Therefore, if you desire to have the continuance of my friendship, meddle no more with this business, except it be to bear down all false, scandalous reports and to facilitate what I am sure my honour is so much concerned in.

And whosoever I find to be my Lady Castlemaine's enemy in this matter, I do promise upon my word to be his enemy as long as I live . . .[95]

What are we to make of this vehement determination in a king who, from force of habit, usually went for the easiest, less emotionally demanding option? It has become customary to explain it in terms of the hold Barbara Villiers had secured over his affections and we certainly cannot discount her sheer force of personality. Lady Castlemaine was totally focused on extracting all she could from her relationship with the king and made sure that she kept him on the hook. But Charles was not infatuated with his latest mistress. This relationship was no repetition of the grand passion he had experienced with Lucy. The fact that she remained vivid in his memory is evidenced by the great affection Charles had for their son, who was now brought to court. Certainly there was no question of the king being faithful to Barbara; his eyes were already wandering elsewhere. Nor did she grant him exclusive right to her favours. The Earl of Halifax, an incisive judge of character and a courtier who observed Charles closely over many years, concluded that he was incapable of 'true love':

his inclinations to love were the effects of health and a good constitution, with as little mixture of the seraphic part as ever man had . . . He had . . . a good stomach to his mistresses [rather] than any great passion for them . . . His patience for their frailties showed him no exact[ing] lover. It is a heresy according to a true lover's creed ever to forgive an infidelity or the appearance of it . . . In his latter times he had no love, but insensible engagements that made it harder than most might apprehend to untie them. The politics might have their part – a secret, a commission, a confidence in critical things – [which could raise] . . . difficulties in dismissing them. There may be no love all the while, perhaps the contrary. He was said to be as little constant as they were thought to be.

169

Halifax reflected that, since the mistresses were, 'in all respects craving creatures' and since the king was not in love with them, it was only his appetite for pleasure that addicted him to incessant female company.

> The definition of pleasure is what pleaseth and if that which grave men call a corrupted fancy shall administer any remedies for putting off mourning for the loss of youth, who shall blame it?[96]

Charles had become accustomed to being surrounded by beautiful and vivacious women. Their 'effeminate conversation' flattered his ego and encouraged him to hold on to a self-concept of youthful virility. Perhaps in the summer of 1662 he felt the need to put down a marker indicating that mere marriage was not going to put an end to his bachelor lifestyle (he would certainly not be alone among men of all times in finding the transition from single to wedded life difficult).

The king claimed in his letter to Clarendon that his honour was 'much concerned' in fulfilling his promise to Lady Castlemaine. It is obvious that he always felt an obligation to women who rendered him services, whether sexual or otherwise. His letters to Jane Lane and the sums of money he somehow found for Lucy Walter when he was hideously strapped for cash himself indicate this, and during his years of wandering he frequently lamented his inability to reward adequately those who made his exile bearable. Once he had been restored to his kingdom he became ludicrously lavish in showering gifts on those closest to him. The flip side of this genuine generosity was the cynicism which replaced love. 'He had,' according to Burnet, 'a very ill opinion of both men and women, and did not think that there was either sincerity or chastity in the world out of principle . . . He thought that nobody did serve him out of love, and so he was quits with the world and loved others as little as he thought they loved him.'[97] He believed that even many who had sacrificed so much for him while he was on his travels had been gambling on future prosperity and much of his new life consisted, as Halifax described, in being 'galled with importunities, pursued from one room to another with asking faces'.[98] Difficult, therefore, not to conclude that everyone had his/her price. And there was also the knowledge that judicious princely open-handedness was a political virtue. He had seen how Mazarin and Louis XIV distributed favours as a means of buying loyalty. Charles may have believed that he was honour bound to meet his commitment to Barbara. He had even told Clarendon that he felt responsible for ruining her reputation. However, we are dealing here with the king, in the words of the second Earl of Rochester, 'whose promise none relied on'. For Charles, vows and principles were infinite variables.

So we must seek other motives behind Charles' bulldog insistence on having Barbara Villiers as a fixture in his court. One is the need to assert

170

his authority. In the two years that he had been on the throne he had experienced growing opposition to his wishes on a number of issues. For the first time he knew what his father had had to endure from a recalcitrant parliament. Like Charles I and Louis XIV, 'he thought government was a much safer and easier thing where the authority was believed infallible and the faith and submission of the people was implicit'.[99] But a very different mood prevailed in the country after two decades of tumult and constitutional change. Even the Cavalier Parliament which swept away much of the legislation enacted since 1641 was careful to preserve those statutes which enhanced its own privileges and restricted the royal prerogative. It reinforced parliament's right to meet at least every three years, and not at the sovereign's pleasure. It declined to vote the king all the money he claimed he needed and even if he had not been so profligate with the supply he had received it is doubtful whether he could have made ends meet. The old prerogative courts were gone for good and all and the standing army was disbanded. As we have seen, Charles failed to have religious toleration built into the Restoration settlement, though he went on for many months trying to assert the right of the Crown to ameliorate the effects of the Act of Uniformity on Catholics and Nonconformists.

It was not just the legislature with which Charles found himself in conflict. Throughout the length and breadth of the three kingdoms a new malaise now affected thinking people; authority of every kind was questioned to a degree that it had never been before the Civil Wars. And criticism was raining down in a blitzkrieg of print. Since 1640 there had been a tenfold increase in the number of books and pamphlets coming from the presses. Charles was furious to find his policies, his court, his lifestyle being ridiculed and condemned. His ministers secured the passing of a Licensing Act imposing swingeing penalties on those convicted of 'endangering the peace of these kingdoms and raising a dissatisfaction to his most excellent majesty'. This was a victory, but only a minor one, because it failed to silence the underground presses and it also removed the power of censorship from the Crown to parliament. Facing all these challenges and having to give way on many of them, it is hardly surprising that Charles should have decided that in his own household, at least, he would be master.

And there he faced a conflict that was nowhere near as politically significant as differences of churchmanship or constitutional theory but which affronted him on a daily basis. It was a conflict of *styles*. The king and his circle of intimates set the tone of the court. Its liberal, easygoing, fun-loving character was best summed up in a word coined for it: 'sauntering'. The Duke of Buckingham, describing the character of the king, explained, 'A bewitching kind of pleasure called sauntering and talking without any constraint was the true sultana queen [i.e. favourite concubine] he exulted in.'[100] The words suggest to our ears almost the opposite of what it involved for Charles and his companions. The king took daily exercise in St James's Park or wherever the court was stationed but these perambulations were anything but leisurely. Halifax recalled that Charles walked very briskly, in order to shake off importunate suitors. Yet it was on these outings or in the privacy of his apartments after his post-dinner nap that sauntering occurred. The king's intimates gathered in an atmosphere of free and easy camaraderie to sit at the gaming tables, have the latest ballads sung to them and discuss anything that took their fancy.

The fare might include bawdy stories and delicious gossip. Courtiers and their servants, knowing how the king enjoyed scandal, scoured the backstreets and coffee houses for juicy tit-bits. The young Earl of Rochester posted one of his men dressed as a sentry and 'kept him all the winter long every night at the doors of such ladies as he believed in intrigues . . . this man saw who walked about and visited at forbidden hours'.[101]

> Like a cur who's taught to fetch he goes
> From place to place to bring back what he knows;
> Tells who's i' the park, what coaches turned about,
> Who were the sparks, and whom they followed out.[102]

The king's chamber was the finishing school of the Restoration wits – Dorset, Rochester, Buckingham, Sir Charles Sedley – who tried to outdo one another in clever verses, witty satires or gutter vulgarity. Sauntering admitted of no inhibitions and certainly no allowances for the tender ears of ladies.

> No ways to vice does this our age produce,
> But women, with less shame than men, do use.
> They'll play, they'll drink, talk filth'ly and profane.
> With more extravagance than any man.[103]

The king revelled in the company of clever and irreverent conversationalists, and those eager to continue in his favour strove mightily to keep him amused. Often this involved buffoonery targeted against the more sober members of the court. Buckingham was a clever mimic of Clarendon, and Charles roared with laughter when the duke cavorted pompously round the room preceded by confederates carrying a pair of bellows and a fire shovel, in burlesque of the chancellor who was often to be seen in a little procession with the mace and the Great Seal in its pouch borne solemnly before him. Nothing was sacred to these bright young things. They would ape popular preachers and thunder out eye-rolling sermons replete with *double entendres*, while their delighted friends giggled their inebriated 'amens'. But the king's laughter was not always unforced. Chatter really was 'without any constraint' and Charles, having decreed the motto *fay ce que voudras*, sometimes had to listen while he, himself, was satirised. Being able to take a joke helped to keep the free-thinking coterie together but it did little for the dignity of the Crown.

The activities of the king's inner circle were by no means confined to trivia, for Charles' lively and enquiring mind could embrace many topics. Politics might be discussed, or the building of new ships for the navy, or philosophy. Thomas Hobbes was readmitted to favour soon after the king's return. Then there were the several branches of science which intrigued Charles. In July 1662, while he was in the midst of his domestic crisis, Charles presented a charter to the Royal Society of London for the Improvement of Natural Knowledge. Its remit was as wide as its name suggested and Charles took a close interest in its work. He also carried out his own experiments. Pepys had a somewhat gruesome story from one of his court contacts concerning a foetus that was dropped by a lady who miscarried in the middle of a ball:

> the king had it in his closet a week after and did dissect it and, making great sport of it, said that in his opinion it must have been a month and three hours old . . .[104]

It is not difficult to imagine how the straitlaced Catherine of Braganza and her sombre guardians reacted to a style of court life that was shockingly amoral and quite alien to anything they had ever experienced.

Nor is it hard to conjecture Charles' reaction to their frowning dis-approval and their criticisms, whether stated or implied. There were few things he loathed more heartily than bigotry and pious cant. Religious zeal of whatever hue offended him because he could never understand people who had a deep commitment to principle. He carried uncomfortable memories of his brief sojourn among the Presbyterian Scots and one of the few occasions when he had displayed angry and determined resistance had been over his mother's attempts to convert the Duke of Gloucester. Now he was faced with the endeavours of a crew of unsmiling foreign Catholics to alter the character of his household. Their very appearance threw down a gauntlet. Exuberance and ostentation were the marks of English court dress. Charles may have inaugurated the fashion for full-bottomed, lice-harbouring wigs because his hair was thinning, but he was certainly determined to distinguish himself and his followers from the earnest, close-cropped rulers of the Protectorate. Much the same motivation lay behind the new mode for flamboyant clothes. Ribbons, bows, fine lace, ballooning silks and, above all, colour were now *de rigueur*. And that was just for the men! Court ladies spent fortunes on floral brocades, elaborate coiffures and bejewelled, immodestly low-cut dresses. What a visual contrast was struck by his wife's attendants. Her priests and monks shambled around Hampton Court in sombre browns and blacks, averting their eyes from the wanton, shameless braggadocio of the king's companions. Her ladies stubbornly espoused the quiet dignity of their native costume coupled with the outrageous farthingales which, as Charles joked, made royal transport difficult due to the problems of finding carriages large enough to accommodate the unwieldy garments.

These outward shows symbolised something deeper. Charles felt that his very way of life was being questioned and he would not stand for it. For years he had shrugged off the complaints of Hyde and Ormonde but they were men he respected; they were useful to him and he knew they had his best interests at heart. The same could not be said of his new queen's entourage. They were simply interfering, rosary-touting, narrow-minded fanatics and he was glad of the excuse to pack them off back to Portugal. His insistence on placing Lady Castlemaine close to the queen may well have been in order to introduce a little levity into her majesty's chambers. What, I believe, we can say is that Barbara was not promoted primarily because she was a voluptuous termagant whom the king could not refuse or because he felt honour bound to keep his word; she was a Trojan horse insinuated into the ladies' side of the court to introduce an element of debonair gaiety. Without some such move the royal household could well have become a place of rival camps divided by an iron curtain. As well as being intolerably uncomfortable for its denizens, this would have invited derision from observers, especially foreign diplomats, and would have provided ammunition for enemies of the regime who were always looking for things to ridicule.

The war of attrition was successful. Catherine capitulated, Barbara was installed in rooms at Hampton Court conveniently close to the king's and he rapidly forgot any vow he had made about forswearing her bed. Following the christening incident the Castlemaines had had a furious row which ended in Barbara storming out of the King Street house, taking with her every stick of furniture and every last knife and fork. The marriage was over and when George and Edward Villiers signed a bond in the sum of £10,000 for all Barbara's debts the separation was complete. It was probably the smooth-tongued Bennet who made the queen see the futility of continued opposition to her husband's will. She could either accommodate herself to the ways of the Stuart court or place herself in perpetual purdah. Once her priests were no longer on hand to stiffen her resolve and to encourage her to see herself as a religious martyr, Catherine accepted the lesser of two evils. She now seems to have gone overboard in her effusive show of friendship towards Lady Castlemaine.

Charles' immediate reaction to this change of heart was to display, not gratitude, but an indifference bordering on contempt. He liked women of spirit and habitually gave way to mistresses who boldly asserted their claims. But where there was no strong sexual interest he found feminine opposition annoying. He had displayed anger towards his mother and his elder sister when they challenged his wishes. He had cruelly turned his back on Lucy once passion had died. Now he went through a phase of being emotionally cold towards his wife. Barbara and their tiny son filled his thoughts and he felt a stronger obligation towards them. Courtiers, diplomats and hangers-on were not slow to read the runes. They clustered round Barbara as the leading woman of the court. These intimate relationships were, however, kept from the general populace. When, on 23 August, Charles brought his wife downriver to Whitehall it was, according to an enraptured John Evelyn, amidst scenes of unparalleled splendour.

I this day was spectator of the most magnificent triumph that certainly ever floated on the Thames considering the innumerable number of boats and vessels, dressed and adorned with all imaginable pomp, but above all the thrones, arches, pageants and other representations, stately barges of the lord mayor and companies with various inventions, music and peals of ordnance both from the vessels and shore going to meet and conduct the new queen . . . far exceeding, in my opinion, all the Venetian bucentaurs [the bucentaur was the doge's gilded barge] etc on the Ascension [Day] when they go to espouse the Adriatic. His majesty and the queen came in an antique-shaped open vessel, covered with a state or canopy of gold made in the form of a cupola supported with high Corinthian pillars, wreathed with flowers, festoons and garlands . . .[105]

Another and, perhaps, a more *au courant* witness described Catherine's state entrance to the capital as more like a Roman triumph in which she played the role of a captive princess.

Another of the king's women made a quieter but politically more important arrival at about the same time. On 20 July Charles and James set out across the Channel in vile weather to escort their mother to England. Henrietta Maria was eager to take up her position in her son's kingdom, an influential position which she regarded as similar to that exercised by Anne of Austria. Although Louis' mother's regency had officially ended when he assumed complete power in 1661, the woman who, with Mazarin, had defeated the Fronde and saved the monarchy continued to enjoy a prominent position and considerable respect. Despite being an extremely bad sailor, Henrietta Maria left Calais at the earliest possible moment and, on 28 July, she was ensconced, temporarily, at Richmond Palace. She was able to take up residence in her new home, Somerset House in the Strand, in time for her son's return to Whitehall.

On 8 September, Charles wrote to Minette with considerable diplomatic artistry about their mother's wellbeing:

The queen has told you, I hope, that she is not displeased with her being here. I am sure that I have done all that lies within my power to let her see the duty and kindness I have for her. The truth is, never children had so good a mother as we have, and you and I shall never have any dispute but only who loves her best, and in that I will never yield to you . . .[106]

Why the extravagant protestation if not to counter some grumbles by Henrietta Maria about the warmth of her reception? It was inevitable that the queen mother should be dissatisfied with her situation. She could not disabuse herself of the conviction that she was her son's natural guide but, whatever his personal feelings for her, he could only regard her as a political embarrassment. Charles I's widow was widely unpopular. To the Stuarts' enemies, she was the representative of a hated regime, while many royalists shared Clarendon's conviction that the queen mother had been responsible for much of her husband's misfortune. Charles was also anxious about how his mother would conduct herself. He knew how difficult it would be for her to keep a low profile.

He was right to be concerned. Henrietta Maria now became a focal point for the pro-French party and one means of close contact between the courts in London and Paris. She wasted no time in establishing herself in fashionable society and winning friends among its leaders. She devoted much time and thought to redecorating and furnishing her rooms at Somerset House, striving eagerly to recreate something of the splendour and high taste of the long-lost, happy days when she and her husband had set the fashion in London. Courtiers and upwardly mobile aspirants hastened to pay court and John Evelyn glowed with pleasure when 'her majesty the queen mother, with the Earl of St Albans and many great ladies and persons, was pleased to honour my poor villa with her presence and to accept of a collation, being exceedingly pleased and staying till very late in the evening'.[107] Three weeks later it was Samuel Pepys' turn to have the thrill of being admitted to the dowager queen's intimate circle:

Mr Pierce, the chirurgeon . . . took me into Somerset House and there carried me into the queen mother's presence chamber, where she was with our own queen sitting on her left hand (whom I did never see before), and, though she be not very charming, yet she hath a good, modest and innocent look, which is pleasing. Here I also saw Madam Castlemaine and, which pleased me most, Mr Crofts, the king's bastard, a most pretty spark of about fifteen years old, who, I do perceive, do hang much upon my Lady Castlemaine and is always with her . . .[108]

Barbara Villiers and Henrietta Maria – a formidable alliance and one that now took on a very political character. Samuel Pepys closed his diary for the year 1662 in a mood of melancholy reflection:

[The king is] following his pleasures more than with good advice he would do – at least, to be seen to all the world to do so. His dalliance with my Lady Castlemaine being public every day, to his great reproach, and his favouring of none at court so much as those that are the confidants of his pleasure, as Sir H. Bennet and Sir Charles Berkeley, which, good God, put it into his heart to mend before he makes himself too much despised by his people for it![109]

It was a prayer destined to go unanswered.

CHAPTER 8

'The Junto at Somerset House'

The queen mother's court is now the greatest of all.[110]

Thus Pepys recorded the political reality in February 1663. Now that the opposition to Clarendon and his colleagues had a respected figurehead and a place where its members could meet without hindrance it coalesced into an active faction. Ormonde called it, 'the junto at Somerset House' and its leading members were Henrietta Maria, Bennet, Berkeley, Bristol, St Albans, the French ambassador, Godfroi, comte d'Estrades and, sporadically, Lady Castlemaine. The Louvre party had simply relocated. The queen mother and Henry Jermyn, Lord St Albans, attempted to steer policy in a pro-French direction and maintained close contact with Paris. Their agents continually passed to and fro across the Channel and Henrietta, duchesse d'Orléans, was their main contact. Although her correspondence with Charles throughout the 1660s has been carefully collected and analysed it is important not to isolate it from the constant flow of family communication of which it formed a part and most of which has not survived. It was to her mother that Minette often wrote detailed letters about Anglo-French affairs. On 19 December 1664 she casually told her brother, 'I send the queen all the news from here, which I am sure she will give you.'[111] Two months later she urges him, in connection with the French negotiations with Holland, 'Do not fail to answer me concerning what the queen and my Lord Fitzharding [Charles Berkeley] will ask of you for they are only waiting for that.'[112]

The queen mother's clique was rendered more powerful by the king's lackadaisical attitude to everyday affairs. Charles was so easily distracted from the tedious business of ruling his country that Lady Castlemaine had only to send word that she wished to see him for him to leave the council table and wait upon her. There was nothing discussed between Charles and his senior advisers that did not reach the ears of the schemers at Somerset House. Their first objective was to increase the wealth and influence of themselves and their clients and to replace the 'old guard' of royal councillors. This would involve a pro-French foreign policy and the easing of restrictions against Roman Catholics at home. Henrietta Maria's religious zeal had not abated and she scored a notable success in 1663, when Barbara Villiers was received into the Catholic faith. It is difficult to imagine that anything other than calculation lay behind this conversion and Barbara was able to get much closer to the pious Queen Catherine thereafter. Bennet was generally believed to be a covert papist who concealed his allegiance because it would debar him from holding office. He lacked the arrogant bravado of Lord Bristol, who made no attempt to disguise his faith.

The routine of government seems to have been very loose. In addition to council meetings there were *ad hoc* gatherings at Somerset House, to which Clarendon was only occasionally summoned. In addition the king came every day to Lady Castlemaine's table attended by councillors and leading courtiers. Ambassadors vied with each other to be invited to these meals or to discover afterwards the subjects that had been discussed. These foreign representatives also paid private court to both Barbara and Henrietta Maria to gather information and to put their own gloss on international events in the hope that their opinions would reach Charles' ears. By keeping open all these lines of communication the king was able to be fully informed of events and to keep his own counsel. Outsiders (and often insiders) speculated about how decisions were actually made. The council took care of the dull day-to-day business and inaugurated policy but it only took a comment at the inner table, a suggestion from the queen mother or a word murmured in Charles' ear across the bedtime pillow to bring about shifts in the direction of policy.

Throughout the autumn and winter of 1662–3 Henrietta Maria's entourage was engaged in vigorous intrigue for government offices. St Albans made an unsuccessful bid for the treasurership and Bennet's importunity knew no bounds. As well as his attempt to secure the office of postmaster-general, he had applied to be sent as ambassador to the court of Louis XIV. Charles agreed, but the French king declined to accept the nominee. Now the favourite and his friends lifted their sights to focus on those offices held by the conciliar triumvirate of Clarendon, Ormonde and Nicholas. They all shared a sense of frustration that their ambitions were being blocked by those who controlled the mechanism for ratifying grants and releasing money but in Lady Castlemaine's case impatience was spiced up by sheer vindictive fury. She was now on the very brink of being deranged by power. While she usually had the subtlety to use flattery, sulks or sexual improvisation to obtain her own way with the king or others who could be useful to her, she sometimes gave in to bouts of temper which starkly revealed her passionate hatred for those who thwarted her, as when she shouted out that she longed to see Clarendon's head on a spike alongside those of the regicides. It was obvious to all those who frequented the squalidly cramped apartments of Westminster that Barbara was a lead player in what Lord Sandwich called the 'high game' of the Somerset House gang.

Their easiest prey was the seventy-year-old Sir Edward Nicholas. For almost two decades the queen mother had nursed a bitter hatred for the secretary of state 'for a service he did the old king against her mind and her favourites'.[113] Bristol also bore a grudge against Nicholas which dated from the tumultuous days of the Civil War, when the two men had been joint secretaries and had frequently given Charles I conflicting advice. Now the moment for revenge had come. Acting in concert, Henrietta Maria and Barbara persuaded the king to get rid of his old servant. Charles offered Nicholas £10,000 and a barony to resign the secretaryship. When Nicholas turned for advice to the chancellor, Clarendon was deeply distressed but realised that Sir Edward had been outmanoeuvred; the king was determined to please the Somerset House junto. All he could do was advise his old friend to stick out for a high price. Eventually, Nicholas retired with a golden handshake of £20,000. Bennet immediately took on the secretaryship, was soon afterwards created Baron Arlington and his position as keeper of the privy purse passed to Berkeley.

It was indicative of the changed style of government that Bennet turned the secretaryship into a more intimate, courtly role than an administrative one. He rarely addressed parliament or bothered much with the council, preferring to work in secret with the king. One of his first acts was to have a privy door made which gave him access to his master's chambers. Burnet best identified his core talent when he described Bennet as having 'the art of observing the king's temper and managing it beyond all the men of that time'.[114] He was the kind of opportunist politician who says, 'These are my principles but, if you don't like them, I have some others I can show you.' This flexibility, so much at variance with Clarendon's tunnel-visioned attitude to politics, perfectly fitted the king's inclination to work as covertly as possible, avoiding confrontation, declining to explain himself and not hesitating to go behind the backs of his ministers and parliaments. The 'most vicious' Berkeley, who, Burnet thought, was 'without any visible merit, unless it was the managing the king's amours',[115] was the closest of Charles' favourites and soon to be created Viscount Fitzharding and, later, Earl of Falmouth.

In the spring of 1663 the fall of the chancellor and his supporters was confidently expected. Lord Sandwich told the secretary to the admiralty that the old minister was 'irrecoverably lost' and when the diarist went to sit by the sickbed of Sir Thomas Crew he heard much the same: the king was ruled by Lady Castlemaine and those who frequented her apartments.

If any of the sober counsellors give him good advice and move him in anything that is to his good and honour, the other part, which are his counsellors of pleasure, take him when he is with my Lady Castlemaine and in a humour of delight and then persuade him that he ought not to hear or listen to the advice of those old dotards or counsellors that were heretofore his enemies, when, God knows, it is they that nowadays do most study his honour.[116]

However, a few weeks later, Lord Bristol, ever the loose cannon in the Somerset House artillery, ruined everything. He made wild allegations against the chancellor in parliament in an attempt to have him indicted for treason. All he succeeded in doing was casting aspersions on the king's government and rousing Charles to angry reprisals. The charges were quashed and their author forced into hiding and political obscurity.

The Somerset House faction continued to pile every possible humiliation on Clarendon. They monopolised the king to such an extent that the chancellor was obliged to wait in anterooms with ordinary supplicants when he desired an audience. They may well have hoped that their relentless pressure, coupled with his own indifferent health (Clarendon was often incapacitated for weeks at a time by gout), would persuade him to follow Nicholas into retirement. The chancellor certainly found life difficult, as he confided to his friends. 'Since your departure,' he wrote to Ormonde,

> I have had so unpleasant a life as that, for my own ease and content, I rather wish myself at Breda . . . Sir Henry Bennet and his friends have more credit, which I do not envy them, except for our poor master's sake, for he doth every day so weak and unskilful things as he will never have the reputation of a good minister . . .[117]

But Clarendon refused to submit to bullying. He took every opportunity, not only to influence the king in private, but publicly to return his enemies' fire. Speaking in parliament in February 1663, he vigorously attacked Henrietta Maria's chaplain, Stephen Goffe, who was still an energetic Catholic proselytiser. Clarendon survived, not because he was stronger than his opponents, but because Bristol's impetuosity forced the king to stand squarely, and publicly, behind his established ministers. But the backstairs intrigue continued. The queen mother and Lady Castlemaine both tried to persuade Charles to lift Bristol's banishment and the king did relent so far as to meet Digby in private but he refused to restore him openly to favour.

A similar struggle was taking place within the royal household. Although most courtiers saw clearly which way the wind was blowing and allied themselves with the reigning favourites, Queen Catherine had her supporters and, as long as there were places in her entourage to be filled (the list was not finally approved until June 1663), she exercised considerable power of patronage. Few were prepared to stand up for their mistress against the awesome combined power of the king's mother and his whore but one who was was Jane Gerard, wife of Lord Brandon. Jane was French and had been one of Henrietta Maria's ladies in Paris when she met Charles Gerard, a royalist soldier in exile. Now they were both firmly ensconced in the court, Charles as a gentleman of the bedchamber and Jane as one of Catherine's ladies-in-waiting. Appalled at the way the queen was being deliberately elbowed out of her husband's life, Lady Gerard resolved to do what lay in her power to strengthen the royal marriage.

In January the Gerards hosted a dinner party to which the king and queen were invited and Lady Castlemaine, very pointedly, was not. Before the company sat down to eat Charles realised the hidden agenda. He excused himself and went straight to Barbara's lodgings, where he spent the night. The humiliated hostess was so upset that a few days later she grasped the opportunity to pass on to the queen some of the worst gossip about the countess. There was a great deal to choose from. Only a few weeks before, Harry Jermyn had been banished from the court for dalliance and Charles Berkeley was confidently reported to be a frequent visitor to her bedchamber, and they were not the only men with whom Barbara amused herself. Charles was not ignorant of her infidelities (he could hardly fail to be in the swarming, busy anthill of Whitehall Palace and its adjacent park and streets) but, while it was one thing to know, it was quite another to be told. Told he was, probably by Catherine, and that annoyed him. He decided on a public punishment. At a court ball in February, he led Jane on to the floor and there confronted her with her offence, adding that she was forthwith dismissed from her position in the queen's household. This was a metaphorical slap in the face not only for Jane but also for her mistress. Once again Catherine was being dictated to by her husband on the subject of who might and who might not wait upon her.

Barbara Villiers was by now a fixture at court, having achieved that most sought after public mark of recognition – allocated lodgings at Whitehall. Early in 1663 she was assigned a suite of upper-storey rooms in and around Henry VIII's Holbein Gate, which spanned King Street, the main thoroughfare between Westminster and Charing Cross. Her apartments overlooked and provided access on the one side to St James's Park and on the other to the privy garden, beyond which lay the residential waterside block where the king and queen had their separate establishments. To appreciate the full significance of Barbara's lavish palace quarters it is important to understand the changes that were taking place in the royal household at this very time. Charles had returned determined to establish a magnificent residential/governmental centre *à la Louvre* in which all his extended family, officials, attendants and servants could be housed in suitable style. He planned a complete rebuilding of the century-old chaotic warren of structures in the style of Inigo Jones' Banqueting House. Economic reality soon poured cold water on these grand designs.

Not only was the new palace never built, but the staffing of the existing one was drastically cut. For example, the lord steward, one of the three great household officers, despite his protests, saw his personnel reduced from 350 to 147. This, however, did not create more space, because an extensive official and unofficial family clamoured for housing within the palace walls. Suitably lavish chambers had to be found for the Duke and Duchess of York, Prince Rupert, James Crofts (created Duke of Monmouth in February 1663) – *and* the Countess of Castlemaine. Thus, Barbara's move to Whitehall (which set a precedent for later mistresses) established her among the king's 'kindred'.

Her quarters, where she delighted to entertain the king, members of her faction and those whom she wished to impress in a style which rivalled that pertaining in the royal chambers, were luxurious – but, apparently, not luxurious enough for milady. In 1666–7, at a time when it might have been thought that all available capital and labour would have been directed towards rebuilding the city of London and providing for those rendered homeless by the Great Fire, the Office of Works undertook a complete refurbishment of Lady Castlemaine's rooms. She was provided with a carved and painted oratory, a panelled bathroom, a splendid bedchamber with an adjacent smaller chamber, presumably for her children, a library lined with seven-foot-high, glass-fronted bookcases, a grand staircase to the privy garden which provided an impressive entrance, and even an aviary.[118]

'Her principal business was to get an estate for herself and her children.' That fact, blatantly obvious to Clarendon, to everyone in the court and to most beyond the walls of Whitehall who listened to rumour, can scarcely have been lost on the king. He allowed Barbara to wheedle out of him anything it was in his power to give. He paid her gambling debts. She ordered jewellery and he picked up the tab. With Berkeley's aid she siphoned off money from the privy purse. Together the lovers devised plans to go behind Clarendon's back and obtain land grants in Ireland, several of which were made out to Barbara's relatives but were destined for her. On one occasion Charles handed over to his mistress all the New Year gifts that had been given him by his wealthier subjects. The manipulation of royal patronage was a lucrative source of income. When there were posts to be filled the advocacy of Lady Castlemaine and her friends worked wonders, and it was readily available – at a price. Barbara worked to accumulate every penny with the feverish assiduousness of a woman who had come from nothing and knew that her physical charms were not eternal. She was determined, not only to enrich herself, but to impress upon the world just how wealthy and powerful she was. It was important to her to be seen at balls and banquets more heavily bejewelled than any other woman present. Her carriage and her barge had to surpass in splendour those of her rivals. Whenever the king demurred at her importunity she fell back upon one of two techniques. Either she flew into a shrill rage or she flounced off to her uncle's house in Richmond, knowing that within hours Charles would follow, humbly begging her forgiveness.

The king undoubtedly knew what a vain, vengeful, grasping creature his mistress was, just as he knew that she was unpopular and that public ill-will towards her reflected on himself. It was not just the chancellor and his supporters or his wife's tiny band of sympathisers or prudish bishops or tut-tutting diarists who were offended by his relationship with his whore. In news-sheets, ballads and every organ which influenced public opinion Lady Castlemaine was identified as the great hate figure. An anonymous ballad, typical of many in the 1660s, catalogued the royal crew who were ruining the state:

> Good people, draw near
> If a ballad you'd hear,
> It will teach you the new way of thriving.
> Ne'er trouble your heads
> With your books and your beads:
> The world's ruled by cheating and swiving.
>
> Ne'er prattle nor prate
> Of the miscarriages of state,
> It will not avail you a button.
> He that sticks to the church
> Shall be left in the lurch,
> With never a tatter to put on.

The author then mocks the leaders of the government who are bleeding the nation for their own gain but his culminating and most biting ire is reserved for the royal mistress:

> Next comes Castlemaine,
> That prerogative quean;
> If I had such a bitch I would spay her.
> She swives like a stoat,
> Goes to't leg and foot,
> Level coil with a prince and a player.*[119]

When Barbara was with the court at Oxford in 1665 the king offered a £1,000 reward for information leading to the arrest of whoever pinned the following lines in Latin and English to the door of her lodging:

---

* 'level coil' = on equal terms. One of Barbara's lovers was Charles Hart, a leading player at the King's Theatre.

> Hanc Caesare pressam a fluctu defendit onus.
> The reason why she is not ducked?
> Because by Caesar she is fucked.†[120]

The previous autumn she had been accosted while walking across St James's Park at night by three masked men in court dress who shouted obscenities at her and chased her back to her quarters.

In this blazing hostility the question has to be asked: why did Charles persist for a decade or more in a relationship which was so obviously damaging his reputation? The first point that needs to be made in any attempt at an answer is that in the seventeenth century, just as in the twenty-first, salacious headlines oversimplified political realities. Today the sex lives of pop stars, cabinet ministers, presidents and members of the royal family are fervidly pried into because they sell newspapers. In the 1660s the equivalent scandals were just as tenaciously worried out by balladeers and Grub Street hacks for the same reason of profit.

> There's nothing done in all the world,
> From monarch to the mouse,
> But every day or night 'tis hurled
> Into the coffee house.[121]

And the most eagerly read stories concerned men and women in the public eye: theatre actors and actresses, courtiers, courtesans – and members of the royal family. But they do need to be read and evaluated with caution. Just as we would be unwise to regard the more sensational revelations of the tabloid press as more important than the day-to-day workings of local, national and international politics, which have a far greater impact on our lives, so we should be careful to keep a sense of proportion about the lurid exposés of misbehaviour in the Stuart court.

There were issues which loomed larger in the minds of the nation's leaders and of ordinary citizens. As early as 1662 there was a common proverb in circulation: 'The bishops get all, the courtiers spend all, the citizens pay for all, the king neglects all, and the devils take all.' The same ballad which inveighed against Lady Castlemaine, the 'prerogative quean', was just as insulting about Lord Clarendon:

> Old fatguts himself,
> With his tripes and his pelf,
> With a purse as full as his paunch is.[122]

The chancellor came under just as much popular condemnation as his enemy, the mistress, for pride, greed and peculation. Between 1664 and

† Ducking was the traditional punishment for shrews and prostitutes.

1667 he built, at a cost of £50,000, a large house (Evelyn called it a 'palace') on an extensive site given him by the king on the north side of Piccadilly. Inevitably this aroused angry comment, particularly after the ravages of the Great Fire. That is just one example of the conduct of national leaders that was pounced on by the writers of ballads, newspapers and pamphlets. These potentially damaging publications were read in the new coffee-houses which were springing up all over town. They were meeting places where a customer: 'His pipe being lighted begins for to prate, and wisely discourses the affairs of the state.'[123]

The government regarded these establishments as potentially seditious and actually tried to close them down in 1675, claiming that they were rallying points for 'disaffected persons' where 'divers false, malicious and scandalous reports are devised and spread abroad to the defamation of his majesty's government and to the disturbance and peace and quiet of the realm'.[124] Charles and his ministers were apprehensive about republican cliques, Nonconformists, parliamentary opponents and men critical of their wasteful and unsuccessful foreign policy. Such dissidents were more likely to combine into really dangerous opposition than people who were morally outraged by the king's bedroom antics. But it was not only political activists who followed government business. A scandalised French ambassador reported, 'In this country everybody thinks it his right to speak of the affairs of state, and the very boatmen want the mylords to talk to them about such topics while they row them to parliament.'[125]

Ordinary people had no business discoursing on 'the affairs of the state' – such was the fixed conviction of Charles and his ministers. And, in strictly constitutional terms, they were quite right. Parliament was the Crown's only partner in the making of policy and the king was doing his level best to exclude even them from effective decision making. He would never have been as provocative as his father in publicly proclaiming that 'a subject and a sovereign are clear different things' but he certainly considered himself above criticism. What was true of politics was also true of morality. While he could occasionally be stung into angry response to attacks on Barbara Villiers (as in the case of the Oxford lampoon), he, for the most part, considered it beneath his dignity to notice them. This attitude was shared by the whole court and we should not regard that as anything out of the ordinary. Every age and nation has its grandees and it is a common defect of such people to believe that the restraints acknowledged by the common herd do not apply to them. Just as the leaders of modern big business see nothing wrong in awarding themselves six-figure bonuses while shareholders suffer the vagaries of the market and employees have their wages pegged, so Charles II's cronies considered themselves free to flout the sexual ethics by which the bulk of the population at least tried to live and which provided one of the iron bands holding society together.

In the same barefaced way that Thatcherite economists attempted to sanctify greed, so some of the Stuart court wits went on to the offensive with their libertarian philosophy, extolling promiscuity in drama and verse:

> In pious times, e'er priestcraft did begin,
> Before polygamy was made a sin;
> When man, on many, multiplied his kind,
> 'Ere one to one was cursedly confined:
> When Nature prompted and no law denied
> Promiscuous use of concubine and bride;
> Then Israel's monarch, after heaven's own heart,
> His vigorous warmth did, variously, impart
> To wives and slaves: And, wide as his command,
> Scattered his Maker's image through the land.

Thus, Charles' poet laureate, John Dryden, in *Absalom and Achitophel*, portrayed the king's peccadilloes as positive virtues, deliberately parodying Milton's earnest religious verse and making a political connection between Charles' sexual potency and his sovereign power and authority. For those who sought a champion with harder philosophical muscle to defend their hedonism there was Thomas Hobbes, who argued away the very idea of subjective values. 'Good' and 'evil', he said, were purely relative terms. They 'signify our appetites and aversions which, in different tempers, customs and doctrines of men, are different . . . Nay, the same man, in divers times, differs from himself and, at one time, praises – that is, calls good – what another time he dispraises and calls evil.'[126] The king, at the centre of this fashionable élite pledged to the unrestrained pursuit of pleasure, was largely impervious to the barbs of Grub Street hacks and pious moralisers. Indeed, if criticism had any impact, it was in making him even more determined to stand by those – like Lord Clarendon and Lady Castlemaine – who were the targets of abuse. To do any less would give the impression that he was not master in his own kingdom.

However, sheer stubbornness cannot explain why he was for so long in thrall to Barbara Villiers. Nor can love. In this relationship there was no trace of that mutual respect which is the necessary foundation of love. Neither party was faithful to the other nor expected faithfulness. Faced with the near-impossibility of understanding the closeness of this relationship, most biographers have fallen back on such words as 'infatuation' or 'obsession'. One of Catherine's attendants suggested to her that Barbara had 'bewitched' her husband, meaning the term to be taken in its metaphorical sense. Catherine, whose English was still far from perfect, understood the explanation literally and set about praying earnestly for the release of Charles from the satanic coils embracing him.

She grasped at this interpretation as the only possible way of comprehending a relationship which was otherwise to her both distressing and intensely baffling. Most contemporaries and later commentators did not trouble their heads with fancies about spells and potions and acknowledged that Charles was, indeed, in the grip of a powerful sexual obsession.

There is no doubt that Barbara Villiers was a vigorous, sexy, feisty lady and an extremely accomplished high-class prostitute. She had a variety of wiles and techniques with which to please her clients and, according to all the canards written about her, an insatiable desire for her own sexual gratification. John Wilmot, second Earl of Rochester, the most unrestrained of the court wits, made frequent reference to her appetites in his verses. One poem satirised the prevailing fashion of court ladies to obtain satisfaction by using artificial penises and followed the now common convention of making lewd comments about several of the leading women about Whitehall. Barbara Villiers (by this time, Duchess of Cleveland) could not be left out.

> That pattern of virtue, her grace of Cl——land
> Has swallowed more p——s than the nation has land;
> But by rubbing and scrubbing so wide it does grow,
> It is fit for just nothing but Signor Dildoe.
>
> Our dainty, fine duchess having got a trick,
> To dote on a fool for the sake of his ———,
> The fops were undone, did their graces but know
> The discretion and vigour of Signor Dildoe.[127]

In common gossip Barbara was credited with every kind of sexual practice from seducing her own servants to lesbianism and even to removing the private parts from a mummified corpse which spilled from its tomb in St Paul's during the Great Fire – with her teeth! Even if some of these stories were the product of gossip and macabre imagination, they indicate that Barbara Villiers was widely believed to be capable of anything. It would be intriguing to know what Pepys meant when he described Lady Castlemaine as being accomplished in all those arts of Aretino which so captivated the king. Should we see her, perhaps, as some kind of seventeenth-century Miss Whiplash?

Here, I believe, we come closest to the heart of the secret. In a word it is 'domination'. However adventurous and novel Barbara's techniques were, even she ran out of ideas long before her relationship with the king dwindled. Yet, for years she entertained Charles several nights a week. The explanation lies in the fact that he was turned on by strong women. In his life Barbara was only the latest in a succession of domineering females:

Henrietta Maria, Christabella Wyndham, Lucy Walter, Jane Lane and probably other companions about whose personalities we know little. This was a time in which gender roles were changing radically, especially in the upper reaches of society. Staid observers were scandalised at the 'masculine' behaviour of court ladies, who drank, swore and exchanged bawdy jokes with their male counterparts. At the playhouse they found it difficult to come to terms with female roles actually being performed by women (a reform the king insisted upon in person). The new etiquette of the court, where the Hobbesian pursuit of pleasure governed all, implied that a greater freedom and even a degree of equality should be granted to women. Forgotten is the ethereal virtue of Charles I's court. Forgotten, too, the erotic lyricism of the Cavalier poets. Women are no longer the 'coy mistresses' to whom their devotees pledge unending adoration. Human relationships are now of the earth, earthy. In Dryden's poem *Marriage-à-la-Mode* it is the wife who insists,

> If I have pleasure for a friend,
> And farther love in store,
> What wrong has he whose joys did end,
> And who could give no more?
> 'Tis a madness that he
> should be jealous of me,
> Or that I should bar him of another:
> For all we can gain is to give ourselves pain,
> When neither can hinder the other.

Powerful socio-psychological forces were behind these role reversals and, as we shall see, they were profoundly disturbing. At this point it is sufficient to note that the acutest critics of the reign identified Charles' submission to his mistress as evidence of the greatest flaw in his character. The actor, playwright and poet, John Lacy, was a great favourite of the king's (Charles even ordered a portrait of Lacy to be painted) but they fell out over Lacy's unrestrained criticism of the court. Pepys recorded 'the king mighty angry' but conceded of one offending play, 'it was bitter indeed but very true and witty'.[128] Fear of royal disapproval did not prevent Lacy railing against the monarch in verse and pointing out to him the way mistresses should be used:

> Go read what Mahomet did, that was a thing
> Did well become the grandeur of a king,
> Who, whilst transported with his mistress' charms,
> And never pleased but in her lovely arms,
> Yet when his janissaries wished her dead,
> With his own hand cut off Irene's head.[129]

Better that Charles should play the oriental despot than that he should suffer the humiliation of being ruled by a mere woman. But that is precisely what Charles *did* suffer, and deliberately so. There was something in his psyche, and something only partially connected with sex, that needed the support, the control, the pain provided by a woman who dominated him. Whether or not this masochistic tendency had physical expression we cannot know but certain it is that, without it, we cannot explain the power that Barbara Villiers exercised over him. She would not have dared to be so importunate, to abuse him to his face – sometimes in front of other people – to force him to grovel on his knees for her forgiveness, if she had not understood that he had a need for these humiliations.

Having said all that, it is important to stress that there were clear limits to the influence Barbara was allowed to have. This was because, even from her, Charles maintained a degree of emotional detachment. Lord Halifax suggested that the king 'lived with his ministers as he did with his mistresses; he used them but he was not in love with them'. Because accessibility was part of the king's personal style and because he was ludicrously lavish in his generosity to his friends – and spectacularly so to Lady Castlemaine – it seemed to jealous courtiers and to the disapproving throng that he was as putty in the hands of those who ministered to his pleasures. This is an impression that Halifax was eager to dispel.

> He showed his judgement in this, that he cannot properly be said ever to have had a favourite, though some might look so at a distance. The present use he might have of them made him throw favours upon them which might lead the lookers-on into that mistake; but he tied himself no more to them than they did to him, which implied a sufficient liberty on either side.[130]

Charles Stuart was nobody's fool. As J. R. Jones has pointed out, his 'cynicism, opportunism and flexibility, his unsurpassed skill in dissimulation and in penetrating other men's thoughts and even intentions, gave him a clear margin of superiority over all ministers and politicians' and, we might add, mistresses.[131] The king was secretive, devious and an able exploiter of factions for his own ends – political 'virtues' that he had learned in his many years on the road. He had become incapable of emotional commitment. Mistresses and friends could get close to him physically and share in roisterous, relaxed pursuits but few caught any glimpses of the inner man. That is why it has always been difficult to assess the precise contribution Charles' bedfellows made to the framing of policy.

The voluptuous, undisciplined mercuriality that was Charles II's court did not permit the formation of two simple factions – old guard versus young Turks. It was riven by individual ambitions, rivalries, feuds, jealousies, alliances and love affairs. The relationship between Barbara and her cousin, the Duke of Buckingham, well illustrates the changeable nature of internal politics at Whitehall.

No contemporary had a good word to say for George Villiers. Many royalists blamed him for having made his peace with the Cromwellian regime, for having married General Fairfax's daughter, for being restored to his lands and for having established himself as the richest nobleman in England before the Restoration. They resented the way he had wormed his way back into Charles' favour, becoming a gentleman of the bedchamber and also gaining a seat on the council. Burnet unequivocally identified Villiers as the king's evil genius. The satirist Samuel Butler, though enjoying Buckingham's patronage, wrote of him that 'continual wine, women and music had debauched his understanding'. Pepys was astonished to learn that the duke enjoyed a certain popularity with some sections of the London populace: 'they must be very silly,' he wrote, 'that think he can do anything out of a good intention'.[132] But it was Dryden, who admittedly had had a falling-out with Buckingham, who delineated his character most spitefully in *Absalom and Achitophel*:

> A man so various that he seemed to be
> Not one, but all mankind's epitome.
> Stiff in opinions, always in the wrong;
> Was everything by starts and nothing long:
> But in the course of one revolving moon
> Was chemist, fiddler, statesman and buffoon;
> Then all for women, painting, rhyming, drinking,
> Besides ten thousand freaks that died in thinking . . .
> Railing and praising were his usual themes;
> And both (to show his judgement) in extremes:
> So over violent or over civil,
> That every man with him was god or devil.
> In squandering wealth was his peculiar art:
> Nothing went unrewarded but dessert . . .
> He laughed himself from court; then sought relief
> By forming parties, but could ne'er be chief.

Onlookers were appalled by Buckingham's turbulent behaviour – his scandalous love affairs, his frequent quarrels, some of which ended in duels or, at least, challenges, his persistent intrigues, his tendency to laugh at the king behind his back – and wondered that Charles could take such pleasure in his company. It was a court colleague who caught the essence of the man in lines which indicate why the monarch found Buckingham such an irresistible companion, despite his many follies:

Let him at business ne'er so earnest sit,
Show him but mirth, and bait that mirth with wit,
That shadow of a jest shall be enjoyed
Though he left all mankind to be destroyed.[133]

The words might have been written about Charles himself, and the king permitted Villiers a degree of familiarity he allowed to few others. The duke took full advantage of this and on several occasions overstepped the mark. For example, when Minette returned to France at the beginning of 1661, Buckingham not only accompanied her but began paying ardent court to her. This was a considerable embarrassment to Henrietta and an even greater irritation to her jealous fiancé, who complained to Charles and demanded the duke's immediate recall.

Buckingham had been one of Barbara's supporters in the early days of the reign and they were natural colleagues in the campaign against Clarendon. However, they fell out in 1663, probably over Barbara's receiving instruction in the Catholic faith. Buckingham, as a free-thinker, loathed the dogmas imposed by the hierarchies of both Rome and Canterbury, and his sympathies lay very much with the downtrodden Nonconformists. He may also have concluded that his cousin was getting too big for her expensive satin shoes. Whatever the reason for their estrangement, Buckingham decided that it was time that Barbara was replaced in the king's affections. This brings us to 'The Strange Affair of La Belle Stuart'.

On 4 January 1662, Henrietta, duchesse d'Orléans, sent a message to her brother:

I would not miss this opportunity of writing to you but by Madam Stuart who is taking her daughter to be one of the maids of the queen, your wife. Had it not been for this purpose I assure you I should have been very sorry to let her go from here, for she is the prettiest girl imaginable and the most fitted to adorn a court.[134]

Can Henrietta's introduction of little Frances Stuart really have been as ingenuous as it sounds? She understood Charles well enough to know that he would be intrigued to see for himself 'the prettiest girl imaginable' and that, if he liked what he saw, the matter would not end there. If Henrietta had a hidden agenda, the inspiration for it may have come from recent events in Paris. Only a few months before she had drawn the attention of Louis XIV to one of her own attendants, Louise de la Vallière, in order to dispel rumours of the king's attachment to herself, which were driving her husband to distraction. The plan had worked so well that Louise was now installed as *maîtresse en titre*. Henrietta may have reasoned that the same stratagem might work at Whitehall to lure Charles away from Lady

Castlemaine, whose character and ambition were already damaging her brother's reputation. Frances' mother was reputedly an extremely cunning woman and may very willingly have connived at a plan to dangle her daughter before the King of England's eyes.

Frances Teresa Stuart, still under fifteen at the time of Minette's letter, was, indeed, a striking young woman and very different in character and appearance from Charles' mistress in residence. She had spent virtually all her life in the household of Henrietta Maria, where her parents had taken refuge in 1649, and the queen mother felt fondly protective of her. On her transfer to the English court she made an immediate impact. There was about her a naïveté and a freshness which set her apart from the fashion set by Barbara. Within a year her portrait was being painted and eagerly sought after by connoisseurs of female beauty. The Duchess of York commissioned Sir Peter Lely to paint the likenesses of eleven 'Windsor Beauties' and that of Frances, in the role of 'Diana, huntress chaste and fair', was the most accomplished. The Grand Duke Cosimo III of Tuscany who was visiting England was among those who begged a miniature. And Pepys in his diary dethroned Barbara Villiers when he recorded, 'Mrs Stuart . . . with her sweet eye, little Roman nose and excellent [figure], is now the greatest beauty I ever saw, I think, in my life, and, if ever woman can, do exceed my Lady Castlemaine'. He went on to speculate on the impact her arrival at court was having: 'nor do I wonder if the king changes, which I verily believe is the reason of his coldness to my Lady Castlemaine'.[135] Whether or not this delicious bait was deliberately offered to Charles by a faction determined to use her for their own ends, once he had swallowed it such a faction did emerge eager to take full advantage of the king's latest obsession. Frances' principal mentor was the Duke of Buckingham.

He allied himself with Bennet in seeking to procure this latest beauty for the royal bed. Such pimping was commonplace. Halifax recorded that it was

> no small matter in a court and not unworthy the thoughts even of a party. A mistress, either dextrous in herself or well instructed by those that are so, may be very useful to her friends, not only in the immediate hours of her ministry, but by her influences and insinuations at other times. It was resolved generally by others whom he should have in his arms, as well as whom he should have in his councils. Of a man who was so capable of choosing, he chose as seldom as any man that ever lived.[136]

The schemers did their best to elbow Lady Castlemaine aside by monopolising the entertainment of the king and ensuring that their protégée was frequently in his company. Buckingham and his wife gave a dinner for the royal couple at Wallingford House, their town residence, in July 1663, from which Barbara was excluded. On this occasion she won, for Charles simply went on from the party to her quarters and spent the night there. Perhaps the sight of Frances' unavailable charms roused him to such a pitch of excitement that he had to find release in the place where he was most sure of being obliged.

For the main fact about La Belle Stuart, as everyone was calling her, and the only one that makes her story interesting, is that she was 'unavailable'. There was about Frances an unsophisticated, lighthearted girlishness that appealed to many of the jaded male palates about the court. She loved games and treated flirtation as just another amusement. But she always remained sufficiently in command of herself to know when to stop. She gained a reputation for virtue rare in the household of Charles II and this, of course, only excited her suitors the more. On one occasion the king drew the attention of the French ambassador to her maidenly modesty. Frances, he said, had confided to him a strange dream in which she had shared a bed with three envoys recently despatched from Paris. The naïve recounting of this nocturnal fantasy caused her to blush deeply, Charles observed approvingly. He, of course, was in a position to command more from her than the young bucks who tumbled over themselves to gain her attention. She permitted him greater liberties, and the easily shocked Pepys noted that the two of them were seen kissing in palace corridors quite openly. But that was as far as it went – even after Barbara joined in the game.

Lady Castlemaine was far too shrewd to try to undermine her young rival. She knew Charles well enough to realise that any displays of temper or backbiting would only rebound upon herself. So she treated the king's latest infatuation as a game and one in which she could join in wholeheartedly. She took the new girl under her wing, organising entertainments in her own rooms at which Charles could ogle and fondle Frances. Sometimes Barbara invited the *ingénue* to sleep with her, and Charles would visit in the small hours for three-in-a-bed antics, but even in these circumstances Frances kept her ankles firmly crossed. Early in 1663, a rumour reached Pepys that Lady Castlemaine had instigated the frolic of a mock wedding with herself as the groom and Frances the bride:

Married they were, with ring and all other ceremonies of church service and ribbands [the cuttings of ribbons from the bride's dress] and a sack posset in bed and flinging the stocking; but in the close it is said that my Lady Castlemaine . . . rose and the king came and took her place with pretty Mrs Stuart.[137]

Yet, all the talk around Whitehall was of La Belle Stuart's continued resistance. Sometimes Charles' impatience got the better of him, as when he told the irritatingly virginal Frances that he hoped the day would come when he would see her 'old and willing'.

Barbara also allowed herself to become agitated. Realising that her strategy had not worked, she suddenly turned against her young rival and forbade her her chambers. Charles' response was swift: if Frances did not come, neither would he. Lady Castlemaine resorted to her usual retaliation; she took herself off to Richmond. But this time she was not followed within hours by a supplicant king. It was her friend and collaborator, Charles Berkeley, who enabled her to save face. He took Frances down to Richmond and persuaded her to return to court. La Belle Stuart would have been dim indeed not to realise the potential power she now held in her hands and the question which now thrusts itself forward is whether she can have been as innocent as she seemed or whether she and her backers were playing for high stakes. Was she, in effect, assuming an Anne Boleyn role? The clever Tudor woman had held Henry VIII at bay for six years in the hope that he would divorce a wife who had failed to provide him with a male heir and marry her instead. The position, in 1663, was very similar. It was becoming painfully obvious to all concerned that Catherine was barren. It was imperative that the king, notoriously capable of siring bastards, should have a legitimate son, a requirement rendered the more urgent by the unpopularity of the current heir presumptive. James, Duke of York, was known to be more pro-Catholic than his brother and, even at this early stage, many of the king's subjects were appalled at the prospect of him inheriting the Crown. It will have occurred to several movers and shakers round the court that the simplest way of overcoming the succession crisis would be for Charles to divorce Catherine and marry a young, healthy woman to whom he was, manifestly, attracted. There would, of course, be diplomatic complications; the Portuguese would be furious. But Charles was not unduly bothered by what the Portuguese thought. The alliance had failed to deliver the advantages he had been led to expect. Bombay had not been handed over as promised. Tangier was already showing signs of becoming a maelstrom that would suck in inordinately more men and treasure than it was worth. English troops sent to the peninsula were complaining of being ill-treated and underpaid. Spain was taking reprisals against English ships. And, to cap all these inconveniences, a substantial part of that glowing dowry which had been Catherine's major asset had never been delivered. So, a change of wife was, theoretically at least, politically possible.

How did all this play with Frances? Was she, as many observers who judged from outward appearances thought, a frivolous, empty-headed creature, incapable of subtle designs, or had she decided quite clearly that she was not going to be satisfied with titles and jewels as payment for becoming another notch on the King of England's bedpost? It certainly beggars belief that a girl brought up in French and English palaces can have been reticent and inexperienced in matters sexual. Most of her colleagues in the queen's entourage had their delicious secrets to share as they giggled together in Whitehall's withdrawing rooms and, in a court atmosphere which was, according to Pepys, 'nothing almost but bawdry from top to bottom', their male counterparts were very explicit about what they wanted. Mistress Stuart may have been a fun-loving girl when she returned to England but her subsequent career showed her to be resourceful and intelligent. Pepys must surely have been right in his conviction that she was far from being an empty-headed, manipulated young woman. Referring to the failure of Buckingham and his confederates to achieve Charles' seduction for him, the diarist wrote, 'she proves a cunning slut and is advised at Somerset House by the queen mother and by her mother'.[138]

If we wish to know what this advice consisted of we should look carefully at the relations between the women closest to Charles, particularly during the autumn of 1663. Charles was tiring of Barbara Villiers. She would remain a fixture at court for several years and a continual drain on the royal purse, and, though her complete eclipse was often prophesied, this was more out of hope than from any informed knowledge of the king's feelings. She had become a habit whose dangers were obvious but whose hold was difficult to break. Charles needed, or thought he needed, a *maîtresse en titre* and no one else could fill that role. Had Frances succumbed to his importunity there can be little doubt that he would have grasped the nettle of dismissing Lady Castlemaine and replacing her with his new concubine. For the middle months of the year Barbara had once again been great with child and she was delivered of a son, christened Henry, in September. Charles, presumably for good reasons, refused to accept that he was the father and there was yet another row. Eventually, as always, Barbara won and Charles, thereafter, demonstrated great affection for the new baby but every crack in his relationship with Lady Castlemaine had the potential to widen into a chasm.

At the same time matters between the king and queen were improving. Catherine was trying really hard to be the sort of consort her husband wanted. Not only did she wink at his affairs, she learned his language, cast away her natural modesty to dress in the more revealing English style and adapted herself to court pastimes. Pepys observed that she began to be more 'brisk' and 'debonair' and to 'play like other ladies'. The French ambassador also reported that Catherine was entering into the spirit of things: 'There is a ball and a comedy every other day. The rest of the days are spent at play either at the queen's or at Lady Castlemaine's, where the company does not fail to be treated to a good supper.'[139] She was more demonstrative in her affection for Charles, riding out to meet him on the road on his return to court and there hugging him and assuming 'all the actions of a fond and pleasant lady'. The writer hoped that this might make the king 'like her the better and forsake his two mistresses'.[140]

The second of Pepys' aspirations was a non-starter but king and queen did draw closer together. Then, in October, there was a crisis: Catherine fell dangerously ill. Like an emotional magnifying glass, this had the effect of concentrating the king's affection. As his wife's condition rapidly deteriorated, he spent hours at her bedside. For some days he watched helplessly and with genuine concern as priests and doctors plied their bizarre remedies. Catherine's shaved head was covered with a nightcap reputed to possess miraculous powers. She had to endure the constant chanting of Latin prayers and her feet were festooned with the bleeding carcasses of slaughtered pigeons. When Charles could stand the mumbo-jumbo no longer, he drove everyone out, insisting that Catherine needed rest. With some of his wife's ladies, he watched over her and wept what observers believed to be genuine tears as she sank into a delirium and extreme unction was applied. The next few days made a deep and lasting impression on him. Catherine at times believed herself to be suffering the pangs of childbirth and to have presented Charles with the hoped-for son. She gazed upon the boy in her delusion and apologised that he was so ugly. Then, in more lucid moments, she told her husband that she knew she was dying and begged him to marry someone he would find more pleasing and who would, in very truth, bear him an heir. It was all extremely affecting and Charles would have been callous indeed not to have been moved. Just what his feelings were we can only guess but guilt must have had its place alongside pity and sadness. He could not return such devotion but that does not mean that he was not touched by it. When, according to the French ambassador, the king repaired, after his vigil, to Lady Castlemaine's rooms where he expected to find Frances Stuart, it did not indicate a callousness on his part. Whatever his emotional needs, Charles always sought their fulfilment in female company.

He was, of course, fully aware of the political implications of the queen's imminent death. Everyone was. As the French ambassador indicated, the king's 'remarriage is already discussed. Everyone chooses him a wife according to his own inclinations and there are some who do not look for her out of England.'[141] The Somerset House group had made their choice and matters seemed to be falling out better than they could have hoped. Little Frances had no political standing but, by the same token, she would bring with her no political baggage. Freed from a Portuguese alliance which had become an embarrassment, Charles would have no wish to tie himself in fresh diplomatic coils. He would be free to follow his own desires – and there was no doubt where they led.

But all schemes and speculations came to nothing. The crisis passed and Catherine lived. Her gradual recovery can be traced through the king's letters to his sister. On 2 November he wrote: 'My wife is now out of all danger, though very weak, and it was a very strange fever for she talked idly four or five days after the fever had left her, but now that is likewise past and [she] desires me to make her compliments to you and Monsieur, which she will do herself as soon as she gets strength.'[142] The greetings from Paris had been faithfully delivered by the comte de Cominges, for at this stage of her illness it was not only pain and the ministrations of her doctors that she had to endure. Etiquette demanded that, weak though she was, the ambassador be admitted to her chamber. Because her affliction had affected her hearing the message he brought had to be bellowed by Charles into her ear! Three weeks later the king reported, 'She mends very slowly and continues still so weak as she cannot yet stand upon her legs.'[143] Matters had improved considerably by 10 December: 'My wife is now so well as in a few days she will thank you herself for the concernment you had for her in her sickness. Yesterday we had a little ball in the privy chamber where she looked on . . . Pray send me some images to put in prayer books. They are for my wife . . . I assure you it will be a great present to her and she will look upon them often, for she is not only content to say the great office in the breviary every day, but likewise that of Our Lady, too, and this is besides going to chapel . . . ' Was it with a sense of irony that Charles then closed his letter with the words, 'I am just now going to see a new play, so I shall say no more but that I am entirely yours'?[144] By the following spring everything was back to normal – or, perhaps, not, for we can discern a greater degree of attentiveness even in Charles' sardonic description of his timetable: 'I have been all this afternoon playing the good husband, having been abroad with my wife, and 'tis now past twelve o'clock and I am very sleepy.'[145] Charles' attentiveness to Catherine throughout these worrying weeks calls into question the image sometimes presented of him as a neglectful, uncaring, even cruel husband. Too often attention has been focused on his monumental unfaithfulness without recognition of two aspects of his relationships with women: he was too detached to be capable of grand passion and too involved to be incapable of genuine sympathy.

The fact that Charles had almost lost his wife deepened his affection for her. Her recovery and her continued infertility prolonged the succession issue and there was still talk, from time to time, of a royal divorce and remarriage but it is doubtful whether the king ever, thereafter, took the possibility very seriously. He would have found it very hard to inflict humiliation and mental suffering upon the woman whose thoughts as she faced death were only for his continued happiness. And Catherine did everything possible to oblige him by bearing the desperately desired heir. She tried all the prayers and holy relics her priests prescribed and all the nostrums of her physicians. In the summer of 1662 she resorted to the waters of Tunbridge Wells which had a reputation for curing barrenness. That proving ineffective, the following year she took herself to the other ancient spa at Bath. She repeated these visits periodically thereafter. Everything that could have been done was done to get the queen pregnant. Not for one moment would Charles have faulted her genuine desire to give him a child or her efforts to carry that desire into effect.

This did not stop his vain pursuit of Frances Stuart, which continued year in and year out. In 1666 he flattered her by broadcasting her image widely abroad. To mark naval victories in the Dutch war he commissioned a gold medal, bearing his own likeness on one side and, on the reverse, a representation of Britannia. The woman chosen to personify the triumphant nation was Frances Stuart. The poet Edmund Waller drew from this a moral that Charles certainly had not intended when he compared Britannia's resistance to naval attack with Frances' staunch defence of her honour against the 'golden rain' of the king's bounty:

> Britannia there the fort in vain
> Had battered been with golden rain;
> Thunder itself had failed to pass;
> Virtue's a stronger guard than brass.[146]

It was about the same time that Charles approached the Archbishop of Canterbury to ask whether inability to produce children was, in the Church's eyes, valid grounds for divorce. However, he was only driven to this extremity by rumours that La Belle Stuart was about to be married (see below, pp. 210–12) and nothing more came of it. In 1672, when England's first copper coins were issued, Frances' Britannia once again was chosen to adorn the 'tails' side, and for over a century the woman Charles II never conquered chinked around in the nation's small change.

All these personal manoeuvrings had clear foreign policy implications. This was the one area of royal business in which Charles did take a close interest. It was accepted that relations with other European rulers formed an undisputed part of the royal prerogative, but this did not mean that council and parliament had no say in such matters, nor that the king's right to form alliances and wage war need take no account of the wishes and prejudices of his people. The English were, as usual, suspicious of their cross-Channel neighbours. The current focuses of their xenophobia were France and the United Netherlands; France because it was Catholic, militarily successful and, by long tradition, hostile to English interests; the Dutch Republic because it was a powerful commercial and colonial rival and because there was unfinished business left over from the war of 1652–4. Charles shared the mercantile community's dislike of the Dutch and responded with personal indignation to the clashes which were becoming more frequent between the convoys plying the Atlantic and Indian Ocean routes to distant trading posts and colonies.

Official attitudes towards France were not so straightforward. Charles was unsympathetic to the prevailing Francophobia. His objective was to remain on good terms with his cousin in Paris while not engaging in any overseas adventures that might prove costly. The queen mother's group worked closely with Louis' ambassadors. Those ambassadors were not always assiduous in furthering Anglo-French harmony. Intent on asserting the rights and dignity of their own masters and aware of the reserve that existed in some government circles, they tended to be prickly and provoke diplomatic situations. For example, when the comte de Cominges arrived late at a banquet given by the Lord Mayor of London and discovered that the host and his guests had already taken their seats at table, he returned home in a huff and sat down to write to Louis XIV complaining of this 'incivilité grossière et barbare'.

However, it was not only the agents who stood so stiffly on what they considered matters of national pride. Their masters could be just as sensitive. In the early 1660s a long-running dispute disturbed relations between the two kings over the courtesy to be shown to English ships in home waters. Charles insisted that the vessels of all other nations should dip their flags or topsails to ships of his navy. Louis demurred, assuring his brother monarch, 'I will be found ready to put mine own [state] in jeopardy rather than tarnish by any faint-heartedness the glory which I am seeking in all things as the principal aim of all my actions.'[147] Charles was equally adamant: 'I desire friendship with France but I will never buy it upon dishonourable terms and I thank God my condition is not so ill but that I can stand upon my own legs and believe that my friendship is as valuable to my neighbours as theirs is to me'.[148] But for all Charles' bravado, the fact was that he needed Louis more than Louis needed him. In the event of rebellion at home or war abroad he would find it very difficult to survive without the aid of Europe's richest and most powerful monarch. Whatever the prejudices of his fellow countrymen, Charles required the French king as an insurance policy. It was for this reason that he decided early on to make sure of Louis' friendship by opening a confidential 'hotline' to the Louvre which would avoid the inevitable distortions of the other channels. And the perfect courier was to hand: a person from whom he had hardly any secrets; a person much admired and respected by the French king. Henrietta, duchesse d'Orléans.

On 26 October 1662, Charles wrote one of his many letters to Minette but this one was different. It was formal in tone, lacked the sibling banter that usually marked their correspondence and it was written in French. There was a good reason for this: the letter was meant to be shown to King Louis.

> I consider nothing of greater value than the intimate friendship between the king my brother and myself and I assure you that the consideration has strongly influenced me . . . to forge a very close correspondence between us, in which I am strongly persuaded of your intervention. And if it please you to propose to him that we may communicate our thoughts to each other in our own hands by this private channel I shall be very glad, knowing how much this mutual confidence will contribute

towards maintaining our friendship. I have charged the bearer to acquaint you and the king my brother with the present state of my affairs and with the procedure I propose to adopt. He will assure you of all the respect I have for your person and of the desire I have that you should be the witness and pledge of the friendship between the king my brother and myself . . .[149]

For the rest of the decade Charles' sister played a central role in his secret diplomacy. The Somerset House junto had realised that Henrietta's changed status in Louis' court gave her an enhanced importance. The French king who had once been so dismissive of this 'bag of holy bones' remained utterly charmed by his sister-in-law. For his part, Charles was anxious to involve his sibling in the making of policy and not as a mere intermediary. 'I would not have this business pass through other hands,' Charles assured her, 'and I would be very willing to have your opinion and counsel how I should proceed in this matter.'[150] While, in the last analysis, Charles would always keep his own counsel, he relied heavily on his mother and sister in his relations with Cousin Louis.

It was not an easy position for Minette, because the interests of the two nations were not wholly compatible. Louis' eyes remained fixed on the isolation of Spain and ensuring her continued decline. He wanted to maintain peace between the other leading states to prevent any of them turning to Madrid for aid and to this end he had signed alliances with both the Dutch and the English. He was, therefore, far from pleased to see his two allies drifting inexorably towards war. Minette became the conduit for the grumbles of her brother and brother-in-law: the French ambassador was feeding lies to his master; the English ambassador 'must be given imperative orders' not to be so stiff and unaccommodating; the Dutch were bragging that they had the French king's friendship and must be silenced; Charles petulantly protested his constant commitment to Anglo-French amity and complained that 'it is not my fault if it do not succeed according to my inclination and desire'.[151] Charles blamed the belligerence of the Dutch and the eagerness of his own mercantile community for the outbreak of hostilities but his insistence that he desired nothing but peace was far from sincere. Parliament and the City were looking to him to repeat the naval triumphs of the Cromwellian regime and the bid to achieve some easy popularity could not be resisted. A French ambassador graphically confirmed this interpretation of events. 'The English,' he reported, 'are like their own mastiffs, which, as soon as they see other dogs throw themselves upon them and throttle them if they can – and then go back home and lie down and go to sleep.'[152]

However, it was essential that Charles should be as sure as possible of the intentions of his 'brother' of France. In letter after letter he urged Minette to find out exactly what Louis had in mind and to agree a new treaty of mutual defence that would deter Dutch aggression. In the event, the French king played a waiting game. When England entered the Second Dutch War (1665–7) she was alone but none the less self-confident for that. The conflict and its attendant calamities would savagely undermine national morale and the standing of the government. It all began well enough with the battle of Lowestoft, at which the enemy lost 5,000 men and twelve capital ships. Cynics claimed that the greatest element of the victory was the death of Charles Berkeley, newly created Earl of Falmouth, who was blown apart by roundshot while standing on the quarterdeck of the flagship next to the Duke of York, an event immortalised by Andrew Marvell:

> Such as his rise such was his fall, unpraised:
> A chance shot sooner took than chance him raised.
> His shattered head the fearless duke disdains
> And gave the last-first proof that he had brains.[153]

But while Berkeley's enemies exulted, Charles, it was reported, wept bitter tears.

The defeated Dutch had already, though inadvertently, launched their revenge. A fresh cargo of bubonic plague had been delivered to London in merchandise coming from the Levant via Holland towards the end of the previous year. Starting in May and continuing throughout a sultry summer, the epidemic claimed, week on week, more and more victims, until 70,000 out of a population approaching half a million had perished. This appalling visitation, seen by many as divine judgement on the sins of the nation's leaders, was described in the accounts of Pepys, Evelyn and other contemporaries and it takes little imagination to envisage the helplessness, despair and mental anguish of citizens cooped up in their overcrowded hovels with the dead and dying or, if they could, fleeing by road or river, often bearing the infection with them. Charles removed his court to Salisbury. At first all seemed well. The French ambassador reported that La Belle Stuart and her friends played bowls as though they had not a care in the world. But then, 'another man died this morning in the street, an unpleasant custom which begins to spread'.[154] The king hurriedly moved on to Oxford.

The cup of the nation's woes was not yet filled. Despite all that the king and his sister and England's politicians and sailors could do, fate had cruel tricks in store. Minette had urged her brother to come to a clandestine arrangement with Louis:

> In God's name . . . do not lose any time in obtaining the king's secret promise that he will not help the Dutch; for you understand that he cannot promise you this openly because of his engagements with them . . . But, as in this world appearances must be kept up . . . you ought, as I have already said, to content yourself with a secret agreement . . .[155]

Charles repeatedly assured her that that was precisely his desire and hinted that it was Louis who was holding back (as was, indeed, the case). Caught in the middle, Henrietta sometimes felt that Charles was not doing all he should to ease the progress of their underground diplomacy. When she accused him of not taking her fully into his confidence, he was stung to respond:

> . . . if you are not fully informed of all things, as you complain of in your letters, it is your own fault, for I have been a very exact correspondent and have constantly answered all your letters, and I have directed my Lord Holles [the ambassador] to give a full account of our dispute with Holland, if you will have the patience to hear it. I shall sum up all in telling you that I desire very much to have a strict friendship with France, but I expect to find my account in it, as 'tis as reasonable that they should find theirs.[156]

Clarendon noted that many people faced the year 1666 with anxious foreboding, because it was one 'long destined by all astrologers for the production of dismal changes and alterations throughout the world'.[157] It began ominously when Louis declared war on England. He claimed that he was in honour bound to meet his treaty obligations to the Dutch but his real interest was soon revealed in a series of raids in the West Indies, which the English navy, preoccupied in home waters, was powerless to prevent.

The French king, while delighted to make such opportunistic sallies, never intended to risk ships and men on behalf of his ally. He was playing a deliberate double game the objects of which were to keep the belligerents occupied with each other without seriously altering the military and naval balance in Europe, and to secure for himself the position of arbiter in the eventual negotiations for peace. He promised the Dutch naval aid but was deliberately slow in delivering it. However, the mere threat had a disastrous effect on the one major sea battle of 1666. At the end of May two massive fleets set out to confront each other off Ostend. However, the English received intelligence that French reinforcements were on their way, and Prince Rupert took twenty ships to go in search of them. In the ensuing four-day battle with the full force of the Dutch navy the depleted English force received a severe mauling. By the time Rupert returned from his fruitless quest for French ships a quarter of the English men-o'-war had been sunk or taken and the remainder were manned by depleted and exhausted crews. The result was a reversal of the battle of the previous year although the Dutch were, themselves, too battered to be able to follow up their advantage.

Then, just as in 1665, tragedy on land followed needless loss of life at sea. The Great Fire of London broke out on Sunday morning, 2

September. When, four days later, it was finally brought under control, 436 acres inside and outside the walls had been consumed, 13,200 homes and business premises had been reduced to mounds of hot, smouldering ash, and St Paul's Cathedral and eighty-nine parish churches, the symbols of civic and family continuity, had vanished. The impact of this series of disasters was devastating. The parliament which had clamoured for war now drew the purse strings tight and demanded peace. Charles approached Louis, and 'the king his brother' brokered a settlement. Magnanimously he offered to hand back England's West Indian possessions in return for the neutrality which would allow him to pursue his continental ambitions unimpeded. Talks with the Dutch began at Breda in March. As an economy move Charles ordered the bulk of his navy to be laid up at Chatham and the crews paid off. He thus paved the way for one of the worst defeats in British maritime history. The brilliant Dutch admiral Michiel de Ruyter was back in the North Sea and the no less brilliant chief minister Johan de Witt was delaying the peace talks to allow him time for a final strike at the enemy. In early June de Ruyter sailed his fleet into the Thames estuary and, unimpeded by English ships or any effective fire from the woefully inadequate shore batteries, harried the coast, worked his way into the Medway and sent fireships into the anchorage. Several men-o'-war were damaged, three were totally destroyed, and the flagship, the *Royal Charles*, was towed away, to the cheers of Dutch crews, by 'a sorry boat and six men' (as one bitter watcher from the shore recalled). Then the enemy withdrew, but only to patrol the river mouth for several weeks and keep the panic-stricken English guessing about their intentions.

London's citizens, who had survived the horrors of epidemic and inferno, were now terrified at the prospect of a new and wholly unfamiliar threat – rape and pillage at the hands of a triumphant foe. Samuel Pepys' reaction was typical of that of many of the better-off Londoners:

> I presently resolved of my father's and wife's going into the country, and, at two hours' warning, they did go by coach this day, with about £1,300 in gold in their night-bag. Pray God give them good passage and good care to hide it when they come home, but my heart is full of fear.[158]

All was panic and confusion. There was a run on the bankers. The value of gold soared as citizens rushed to turn silver and other valuables into more portable wealth. Horses and wagons were at a premium. Pepys was torn between his duties at the Navy Office and his concern for his own possessions:

> I sent for my cousin Sarah and her husband . . . and I did deliver to them my chest of writings about Brampton and my brother Tom's papers and

my journals, which I value much, and did send my two silver flagons to Kate Joyce's, that so, being scattered what I have, something might be saved. I have also made a girdle, by which, with some trouble, I do carry about me £300 in gold . . . that I may not be without something in case I should be surprised, for I think in any nation but ours people that appear . . . so faulty as we would have their throats cut.[159]

Pepys was terrified of mob rule and was anticipating that angry demonstrators looking for someone to blame for the present calamity would vent their fury on the administrators of the navy. He well judged the mood of the populace; as the risk of invasion subsided, fear gave way to anger. All the pent-up emotions of the last three years exploded in a cacophony of outrage against the government. There was no broad agreement about who was to blame. Disillusionment embraced everyone in authority. In tavern, coffee-shop, marketplace and wherever people discussed politics they railed against the king, the court, the ministers, the mistresses, parliament and the bishops. Pulpit orators inveighed against wickedness in high places, and self-appointed prophets wandered the streets naked, warning of the imminent *dies irae*. Those two sober citizens Mr Evelyn and Mr Pepys took a turn around Westminster Hall one April day,

> talking of the badness of the government, where nothing but wickedness and wicked men and women command the king: that it is not in his nature to gainsay anything that relates to his pleasures; that much of it arises from the sickliness [i.e. poor health] of our ministers of state, who cannot be about him as the idle companions are and, therefore, he gives way to the young rogues; and then from the negligence of the clergy, that a bishop shall never be seen about him, as the King of France hath always . . .

Evelyn regarded Charles as his cousin's inferior in every department of life.

> . . . the King of France hath his mistresses but laughs at the foolery of our king that makes his bastards princes and loses his revenue upon them and makes his mistresses his masters.[160]

Indeed, the contrast between the two monarchs could not have been more striking. Louis had grasped his opportunity to go on the rampage in the Spanish Netherlands. Conquering town after town throughout the summer, his spectacular advance had about it more of the air of a pageant than a military campaign. When Lille capitulated on 27 August Louis arrived with all his court, including his wife and two mistresses, and received the keys of the city at the hands of the chief magistrate while all the church bells tolled solemnly. He had certainly begun to live up to his own boast that he would 'show the whole earth that there is still a king in the world'.

Throughout these calamitous events England looked to its king for leadership and the common perception was that he failed lamentably to provide it.

> As Nero once with harp in hand surveyed
> His flaming Rome and as that burned he played.
> So our great prince, when the Dutch fleet arrived,
> Saw his ships burned and as they burned he swived.
> So kind was he in our extremist need,
> He would those flames extinguish with his seed.[161]

So an anonymous versifier lashed the king with angry satire. Such condemnation was not altogether justified. When Charles took his court away from the capital in 1665 he was doing no more than other monarchs had done for centuries (Henry VIII, for example, was positively hypochondriacal about possible infection and fled from one royal residence to another at the first sign of disease) and he was among the first to return to Whitehall at the end of the year. When the heart of the City went up in flames the royal brothers were soon in the thick of firefighting activities, wading in a conduit to fill buckets. In the immediate aftermath he took a lead in making emergency arrangements for the establishment of temporary markets and business premises and in commandeering buildings where citizens could store the possessions they had managed to salvage. In June 1667, when all London quaked in fear of the Dutch fleet advancing upriver and even of a French army being transported across the undefended Channel, Charles and James were up before dawn organising the sinking of ships in Barking Creek and elsewhere to impede the progress of enemy vessels. Charles was ambivalent about crises. No man more resolutely avoided conflict, at both personal and national levels, but when catastrophe confronted him he responded energetically and even enjoyed getting to grips with problems. The truth was, as Clarendon had long ago discovered, that Charles Stuart was lazy rather than incompetent.

However, in politics perception is all and, by this point in the reign, most observers had become convinced of two things: the king was sunk in depravity, and affairs of state were in the hands of favourites and mistresses. To discover how far this was true we shall have to review the in camera activities of the royal circle during the turbulent first decade of the reign. There was a considerable difference between what happened within palace walls and what the generality of people believed happened. One valuable source of information is to be found in diplomatic exchanges. It was part of a foreign ambassador's task to try to understand the way government worked and which personalities enjoyed the greatest influence, and this makes diplomatic reports more reliable than the scandalous stories spreading outwards from Whitehall and growing more sensational with each retelling. However, we do have to make allowance for national prejudice and that ignorance of the culture which could only be dispelled by long residence. In 1664, the comte de Cominges informed his master that Lady Castlemaine was worth cultivating because she and her cronies had a great deal of power behind the scenes. This, he indicated, was a national malaise: 'women . . . have such a hold over the minds of men in this country that it may be said the English are truly slaves to their wives and their mistresses through custom and through weakness'.[162] We may dismiss Cominges' xenophobic reasoning from the particular to the general but, in that he and his successors found it worthwhile to cultivate Barbara and to pay her for information, it is clear that she did know a great deal about government policy and used her position to sway political decisions.

Lady Castlemaine was mightily relieved by the queen's recovery in the closing weeks of 1663. She had everything to gain from the maintenance of the status quo and everything to lose if Catherine died and Charles offered marriage to Frances Stuart. Despite their occasional fierce quarrels (or, perhaps, because of them) Barbara and Charles had settled into a routine relationship. In the summer of 1665, another French envoy reported that Charles' passion had now cooled and that he derived more pleasure from their private dinner parties and his visits to their children, of whom he was very fond.[163] Berkeley's death at the battle of Lowestoft was an unpleasant blow but one from which she recovered quickly by urging Charles to appoint Baptist May to the vacant keepership of the privy purse. 'Bab' May was one of the wilder young blades about Whitehall who, according to Burnet, commended himself by 'serving the king in his vices'. Pepys described him more directly as a 'court pimp'. Now, thanks to Barbara, he bathed in the golden shower of royal favour. As well as his lucrative post he received land grants on Pall Mall Fields and King Street where he built houses for the booming market fed by courtiers and social aspirants who clamoured for property close to the palace. May showed his gratitude by keeping up the flow of cash from the privy purse into Barbara's coffers.

This happened at the same time that the mistress lost another valuable ally. The advent of plague convinced Henrietta Maria that the time had come to beat a temporary retreat to her homeland. The Somerset House junto had failed in its main objective, to keep England firmly tied to France. Louis' diplomats had made strenuous efforts during the early months of the Dutch war to bring the parties to the negotiating table. The queen mother and Lord St Albans had added their voices to those urging Charles not to force the French king to choose between his allies, but, not for the first time, Charles had rejected his mother's advice. Now, with the likelihood of England finding itself at war with France, the vicinity of London was not a safe place to be. Henrietta Maria's residence was an all too obvious target for the hostility of Francophobe mobs. At the end of June the queen mother left, planning to return only when it was safe to do so. It remained for an anonymous rhymer to assess, in brief, her English sojourn:

> The pious mother queen hearing her son
> Was thus enamoured with a buttered bun [a reference to
>   James' espousal to the pregnant Anne Hyde],
> And that the fleet was gone in pomp and state
> To fetch for Charles the floury Lisbon Kate,
> She chants Te Deum and he comes away
> To wish her hopeful issue timely joy.
> Her most uxorious mate she used of old;
> Why not with easy youngsters make as bold?
> From the French court she haughty topics [i.e. grandiose
>   ideas of absolute monarchy] brings,
> Deludes their pliant nature with vain things.
> Her mischiefbreeding breast did so prevail,
> The new got Flemish town was set to sale.
> For those and Jermyn's sins she founds a church [the
>   convent of the Visitation at Chaillot],
> So slips away and leaves us in the lurch.[164]

It is not entirely coincidental that Barbara's influence began noticeably to decline from this time. Without a figurehead and a pro-French policy around which to cohere, the Somerset House junto disintegrated. Personal rivalries asserted themselves, principally those between Clarendon, Buckingham, May and Bennet (recently created Earl of Arlington). The 'workings' of government became more fluid than ever. The council and its committees continued to regulate daily business but they had become the battleground of factions. Clarendon was progressively sidelined by Arlington, and the chancellor could later point out that between the summer of 1665 and the autumn of 1667 he had enjoyed less than half a dozen private audiences with the king and that any attempt to blame him as 'the sole manager of affairs' for the nation's calamities was absurd. The leaders in court and council manoeuvred around each other, daggers in hand, alert for opportunities to strike while at the same time watching their own backs. Lady Castlemaine, who needed allies, took care to be on good terms with the younger men with whom she was united in the desire to bring down the chancellor. This included making peace once more with her cousin, Buckingham.

But in the changed and highly tense atmosphere of these years it was difficult to pursue private agendas or even to be sure what those agendas were. The war disrupted the cosy pattern of informal and semi-formal meetings which had been part of the governmental process. Not only did the Somerset House gatherings cease, but Barbara was no longer able to enjoy mealtime tête-à-têtes with French and Spanish ambassadors. It also cut the hotline between Whitehall and the Louvre via Henrietta. The private correspondence had manifestly failed in its objective. Charles had convinced himself that 'the king my brother' would not take arms against him and the reality came as a profound shock. As matters went from bad to worse in 1666–7 the behaviour of all the lead players was highly coloured with irrationality. Humiliated at sea, confronted by an angry parliament unprepared to pour good money after bad into the war chest, recognising that his reputation in the country at large had reached its nadir, Charles veered between an insouciant, 'business as usual' attitude and bouts of bad-tempered stubbornness. He maintained his visits to the theatre and to Newmarket and persisted in his pursuit of La Belle Stuart. But he refused to yield ground when Louis suggested compromises that would bring about a rapid peace. He flew into sudden rages which took even his closest companions by surprise. On one occasion he turned on Barbara for some slighting remark she had made about the queen. Charles damned her for an 'insolent woman' and banished her from court for several days. Where the king led, the court followed. The atmosphere was electric. 'There are scarce any two that dare trust one another, but every man is jealous of his neighbour, and those in power practising to supplant one another. The king and court were never in the world so bad as they are now for gaming, whoring, swearing and drinking and the most abominable vices that ever there were in the world; so that all must come to nought,'[165] one of Pepys' informants told him and, though the diarist was ever ready to believe the worst, it is evident that the tensions of this nightmare period in the nation's life were wreaking psychological havoc at the centre. In the year from December 1666 to December 1667 they gave rise to a sequence of events that overturned the balance of forces at Whitehall and stripped Charles II of the last vestiges of honour.

The unstable Buckingham set the train in motion. He presented himself as the main opponent of the government in the House of Lords. His targets were Clarendon and Ormonde and he raged against policies they inaugurated or backed, totally unconcerned that, in so doing, he was opposing the king. He tried, with some success, to gain a popular following by his swagger and the splendour of his entourage, by his writing of popular, bawdy plays performed on the London stage and also by championing such underdogs as Nonconformists and unpaid sailors. In the closing weeks of 1666 he twice picked violent quarrels with parliamentary opponents which resulted in brief periods of incarceration. Charles was growing tired of the public antics of his court buffoon but he largely had himself to blame. His indulgence encouraged the wits to show off their talents without any restraint and the end result was that they had little respect for anyone, including their king. The Earl of Rochester, a new addition to the inner circle, would become the embodiment of irreverence. His cutting and vicious satires have survived because he was the most talented of the court poets but his verses are typical of the comment that many of Charles' companions were able to get away with:

> Restless, he rolls about from whore to whore,
> A merry monarch, scandalous and poor.

and:

> Here's Monmouth the witty,
> And Lauderdale the pretty,
> And Frazier, that learned physician;*
> But above all the rest,
> Here's the duke for a jest,
> And the king for a grand politician.[166]

Buckingham believed that he could never exhaust Charles' store of goodwill and, having stayed in town to witness the triumphant opening of his latest comedy, *The Chances* (in which Nell Gwynn drew great applause), he took himself off to the country without bothering with the courtesy of excusing himself from his royal household duties. This left his rivals in possession of the field.

Arlington gathered a miscellany of evidence against the duke, the most damning of which was that he had procured one Heydon, an astrologer, to cast the king's horoscope. This fell within the scope of the treason statute, which made it an offence to 'compass or imagine the monarch's death'. On 22 February the evidence was shown to Charles, who was genuinely appalled. He ordered Buckingham's arrest and stripped him of his court and council positions. Rochester was appointed to take his place as gentleman of the bedchamber. The duke went into hiding and did not emerge for four months.

Charles, meanwhile, was preoccupied with a different kind of rivalry. Frances Stuart had continued to be the recipient of the king's indecent advances and continued to resist them. It was clear that Charles was not going to divorce his wife and, indeed, Frances was sufficiently attached to her mistress not to be enthusiastic about supplanting her. By the spring of 1667 she was in a state of serious distress, possibly made worse by the

---

* Sir Alexander Frazier was one of the king's doctors and a firm adherent of Barbara Villiers. His principal asset appears to have been his skill as an abortionist.

disaster which had befallen one of the other young ladies about the court. Margaret, Lady Denham was, at eighteen, the same age as Frances and, to judge from her portrait, a very attractive woman. The previous year she had been married to the fifty-year-old surveyor of the king's works, Sir John Denham. He was a sick man and Margaret, like many another full-of-life bride, might have philosophically endured her lot in the hope that she would not have to do so for long. However, when the Duke of York paid his attentions to her, she willingly succumbed. This threw the cuckolded husband into a paroxysm of rage. Indeed, it seems to have turned his mind, for he stormed into the king's presence, declaring himself to be the Holy Spirit coming in vengeance. Days after this, Margaret fell suddenly ill and died. In her final agonies she claimed that her husband had poisoned her by means of a cup of chocolate but some gossips accused the Duchess of York of Lady Denham's murder. Whatever the truth of the matter, the tragedy and its moral implications profoundly shook the little world of Whitehall Palace. It even startled James into declaring that he would never again take a public mistress – though not into keeping this promise. Its impact on an impressionable young woman is not hard to imagine.

Frances could not stand the pressure any longer. John Evelyn told Pepys that she was ready to accept an honourable proposal from any man worth £1,500 a year who would rescue her from the king's clutches. Thus, when her distant kinsman, the Duke of Richmond, protested his love for her, Frances enthusiastically encouraged him. Richmond was a gentleman of the bedchamber and a courtier who had good reason to be grateful to his king. Since the Restoration he had received generous gifts of land and money. At last Barbara Villiers saw her opportunity. Nothing would infuriate Charles more than discovering that someone else had brought down the doe that he was so passionately hunting, especially when that someone was a man who should be tied to him by bands of gratitude. She conceived it to be her painful, loyal duty to open his eyes. Her accomplice was William Chiffinch, keeper of the king's closet or privy stairs. As Charles' general factotum, it was Chiffinch's job to know everything that went on in the palace. All Barbara had to do was bribe Chiffinch to let her know when Frances and her lover were together and the rest would follow easily. Thus it was that, late on a winter's night, she hastened the king through the Whitehall corridors to Mistress Stuart's room. There the couple were discovered, if not *in flagrante delicto*, certainly in a totally compromised situation. The king was angry and humiliated. La Castlemaine was triumphant. But Frances found the strength to stand up to her rejected lover, pointing out that Richmond could offer her the honourable estate of matrimony which Charles could not. The next day she implored Queen Catherine to intervene on her behalf and gradually the king was brought to give his grudging blessing to the couple's union – or so it seemed.

In reality, he was not prepared to resign his prey to another. No one had ever taken a woman away from him and he was not going to allow that record to be broken. He needed to unearth something discreditable about Richmond and he employed in the task, not one of his amoral cronies, who could have been relied on to manufacture what he could not discover, but the virtuous Clarendon, who would lend gravitas to proceedings which were essentially sordid. The chancellor was set to examine Richmond's financial status, the intention being that he would report that the young man could certainly not support a wife. But Clarendon, who profoundly disapproved of the king's amours, found that the proposed groom, though certainly not wealthy, was of sufficient standing to offer marriage to one of the queen's ladies. Charles was furious at being thwarted. He convinced himself that Clarendon had personal dynastic motives for opposing his sovereign's will: by blocking any possibility that the king might remarry he was securing the Crown for his own grandchildren. The reality was that Charles' pride had been severely dented and that he fancied himself deeply in love with Frances Stuart. Only that can explain why he continued to pursue her with uncharacteristic determination and vigour and why, in the aftermath of his defeat, he lashed out with vicious cruelty against the easiest target.

Charles' next ploy was to offer to elevate Frances to the position of *maîtresse en titre*. He would make her a duchess in her own right, thus raising her above the Countess of Castlemaine, and provide her with lands and income to support her dignity, ensuring that she would be far better off than poor Richmond could ever make her. Not only did Frances decline this magnanimous offer, she also returned all the jewellery the king had given her. Still he refused to take 'no' for an answer. It was at this juncture that he approached Archbishop Sheldon about the possibility of acquiring a divorce. If a marriage was not blessed by God with children and if both parties agreed to part, could the Church release them from their vows? Diplomatically, Sheldon asked for time to consider the matter. Presumably Charles told the object of his desire all that he was prepared to do for her; that he was now offering her, not a coronet, but a crown. Whatever the poor girl's ambitions may once have been, she was now terrified by the king's importunity. The more he pressed her, the more attractive a quiet provincial life with her own Charles Stuart, Duke of Richmond, seemed. One night at the end of March 1667, when driving wind and torrential rain kept all the denizens snugly indoors, she slipped out of her rooms at Whitehall and joined her lover at the Bear Inn by London Bridge. As soon as it was light the next morning, the couple crossed to the south bank, rode along the Dover road to the duke's estate at Cobham and were hurriedly married.

Frances had grown up quickly as a result of her experiences at court. Her later career showed her to be a level-headed and intelligent woman.

During her husband's long absences on diplomatic missions and after his death she administered the considerable family estates efficiently and, by prudence and thrift, added extensively to her own property. She overcame Charles' anger and was reinstated in society where she made a reputation for herself as a cultured patroness of writers and a knowledgeable collector of old master drawings.

On the morning after the couple's flight the sensational news was all round the court and Charles went to Frances' apartments to verify it for himself. In the doorway he met Lord Cornbury, Clarendon's son, who had gone to see Mistress Stuart on some quite unrelated business. In his fury, the king smelt conspiracy. 'Suspecting that Lord Cornbury was in the design [he] spoke to him as one in a rage, that forgot all decency, and for some time would not hear Lord Cornbury speak in his own defence.'[167] Only after several hours had passed had Charles cooled down sufficiently to allow the younger Hyde to explain himself. Whether or not he accepted Cornbury's protestations of innocence, he remained convinced that Clarendon, in cahoots with his lifelong friend, Gilbert Sheldon, had deliberately obstructed him. On the subject of Frances Stuart the king was beyond rational thought.

> False in thy glass all objects are,
> Some set too near, and some too far:
> Thou art the fire of endless night,
> The fire that burns and gives no light.
> All torments of the damned we find
> In only thee,
> O Jealousy!
> Thou tyrant, tyrant Jealousy,
> Thou tyrant of the mind!

(John Dryden, *Song of Jealousy*)

Deeper in his psyche than all the political calculation of the next few months lay the delusion of betrayal. It was this that motivated policy and which alone can fully explain the fateful decisions he made before the year's end.

The next significant event was the death, on 16 May, of the Lord Treasurer, the Earl of Southampton. Charles appointed a commission to look into the working of the department. The reforms they set in hand were probably long overdue but another member of the old guard had now gone, Clarendon was more exposed and Lady Castlemaine exulted that, at last, the stubborn cork had been withdrawn from the bottle of royal bounty. Buckingham surrendered himself two weeks after the 1666 Medway disaster. The timing was brilliant. The government, with which he now had no connection, was wallowing in the depths of unpopularity. A mob had descended on Clarendon's new house. They broke windows, hacked down trees, set up a gibbet before it and daubed on the gate: 'Three sights to be seen: Dunkirk, Tangier and a Barren Queen'. Throughout London, the people 'do cry out in the streets of their being bought and sold and . . . make nothing of talking treason in the streets openly, as that we are bought and sold and governed by papists and that we are betrayed by people about the king and shall be delivered up to the French and I know not what'.[168] They had identified Clarendon, Arlington and Co. as the villains and they were looking for a champion. They remembered that Buckingham had proclaimed himself the sailors' friend and opposed the administration in parliament and this was enough to make him their hero. The accused felon's journey to the Tower was no public humiliation, as his enemies had intended. He rode with his attendants and friends to the Sun tavern in Bishopsgate, where he appeared on a balcony to receive the plaudits of a large crowd of supporters who had gathered there. He sent word to the lieutenant of the Tower that he would be graciously pleased to wait upon him when he had dined. After a leisurely meal he sauntered the half-mile to his prison attended all the way by citizens who desperately needed something or someone to cheer.

On 8 July the prisoner was brought before the council for examination and then returned to the Tower awaiting the king's pleasure. Charles was in a dilemma. To leave Buckingham languishing in prison would be to make a martyr of him, and Charles' inclination was, anyway, always towards clemency. But to restore the miscreant would be to vindicate him over against the king's own ministers and to allow him to continue to make a nuisance of himself. At this point Lady Castlemaine gave the king the benefit of her wisdom. She saw things in very simplistic, selfish terms. The choice was between Buckingham and Clarendon. Both men were vulnerable. One would have to go. Would it be the people's darling or the obnoxious man who had for so long stood in her way, whom nobody loved and of whom it would soon be written,

> Pride, lust ambition and the people's hate,
> The kingdom's broker, ruin of the state,
> Dunkirk's sad loss, divider of the fleet,
> Tangier's compounder for a barren sheet:
> This shrub of gentry, married to the crown,
> His daughter to the heir, is tumbled down?[169]

Charles told her roundly not to meddle in things that did not concern her. She persisted; if he was set on having his most able servants thrown in prison while his kingdom was run by fools, he was as big a fool as they! The interview ended with Charles dismissing Barbara as a 'whore' and a 'jade'.

If Lady Castlemaine was now demonstrating a determination bordering on recklessness, it was in large measure because she had fallen to the desperate contagion that was in the air. She was panic-stricken by the recent collapse of the financial market which threatened to deprive her of whatever part of her fortune she had not frittered and gambled away. She had to cling to her position and make the most of it while she still exercised any power over the king. It was about this time that she suddenly began to be very hospitable to the French ambassador, offering him information for cash. That source, like all others, would dry up if she fell out of favour. Yet, recently she had put her own position in jeopardy by involving herself in either a renewed or an ongoing affair with Harry Jermyn and she was now pregnant with her sixth child. Charles was not pleased with his mistress's latest amorous adventure and made it clear that he would not acknowledge the baby as his. It was a crisis moment for the royal whore. If word spread that she and her brat had been cast aside she would be ruined in an instant. The role of royal mistress was a precarious one, as Charles' earlier lovers had discovered. But Barbara's natural psychology did not desert her. She had never been the kind of woman to wheedle and beg and she did not resort to that strategy now. Though blatantly in the wrong, and despite her disagreement with the king over Buckingham, she flew into one of her passions. 'Damn me, but you shall own it!' she shouted, and threatened that if he did not agree to have the child baptised in Whitehall chapel as a royal bastard, she would bring it to him and dash out its brains before his face.[170] Then she flounced out and retired to a friend's house, hoping that the old strategy would work. Days passed and there was no sign of Charles. Eventually, she sent word to him, to say that she would receive him if he cared to call. He came – and Barbara made him grovel.

The latest estrangement occurred against the background of a disastrous recalling of parliament. Unsure about the ratification of the peace treaty and, therefore, whether he would need more money to continue the war, Charles decided to summon the houses to meet on 25 July. Given the mood of the country this was a hazardous undertaking: 'everybody do nowadays reflect upon Oliver,' Pepys observed,

> and commend him, what brave things he did and made all the neighbour princes fear him; while here a prince, come in with all the love and prayers and good liking of his people, who have given greater signs of loyalty and willingness to serve him with their estates than ever was done by any people, hath lost all so soon, that it is a miracle what way a man could devise to lose so much in so little time.[171]

The king was understandably nervous. Matters deteriorated still further when among the wildly fluttering aviary of rumours appeared the suggestion that he was intent on overcoming all opposition by ruling with a standing army. Charles, it was said, had been urged to this by Lady Castlemaine and 'Bab' May. Alarming, vivid memories of 1642 haunted men's minds and, when the Commons assembled, one member delivered himself of a lengthy harangue on the theme of threats to the liberty of the subject. One after another, angry members stood to denounce the government and to demand the disbanding of the land forces which had been recruited for the nation's defence.

How well founded were the MPs' fears and suspicions? Had there arisen a serious conflict of interest between court and parliament similar to that which had pitched the British nations into civil war? Certainly the Crown had raised troops by somewhat dubious financial means to guard the coast against possible invasion. Certainly Charles and his closest advisers were highly frustrated by parliamentary opposition. At the same time, they were utterly inept at handling the assembly. Councillors used the Lords' chamber to play out their own rivalries, Clarendon treated the Commons with little less than contempt and none of the ministers had any skills in managing parliament. Meanwhile, around the palace unrestrained tongues were muttering about the king boldly asserting his mastery in the current crisis and bringing the rabble Commons to heel. It would not be at all surprising if Barbara Villiers was among the hawks. She had become very bold in airing her opinions on matters of state and her own security was very much in the balance during these crucial days. If the king failed to assert himself and allowed parliament to demand more concessions or exercise greater control over him, she, as the most bloated of the royal bloodsuckers, would find herself in serious trouble. Only recently, out of £400,000 allocated to the privy purse for war expenditure, Charles had used £30,000 to pay off her debts. This was not the kind of information she would want a parliamentary committee to insist on examining.

Charles, hovering between overawing his critics and appeasing them, ended up doing neither. As soon as he received confirmation that peace had been concluded, he grabbed at the opportunity to prorogue parliament, delaying only long enough to deliver himself of a homily about the members' unwarranted lack of trust in their sovereign. The representatives were sent back to their shires and boroughs after only four days, angry that they had put themselves to the trouble and expense of answering the royal summons without having any of their grievances addressed. Inevitably, fresh damaging rumours now ran round the City: the new king was treating parliament as cavalierly as the last one had done; Charles, like his father, was planning to rule without the assembly. On Sunday 28 July, the seventy-four-year-old Dr Robert Creighton, Dean of Wells, boldly upbraided king and court about the evils spreading out from the centre of the nation's life. He preached against adultery, 'over and over instancing how for that single sin in David, the whole nation was undone'. Somehow,

Charles II and Nell Gwyn by Edward Matthew Ward, 1854.
This painting, based on an incident from John Evelyn's diary shows the King pausing in his
morning walk to flirt with Nellie at her garden wall, while a disapproving Evelyn looks on.

Barbara Villiers, Countess of Castlemaine,
miniature by Samuel Cooper, *c.* 1660-1

Catherine of Braganza,
by Jacob Huysmans, *c.* 1664

Frances Theresa Stuart, later Duchess of
Richmond and Lennox in a riding habit, by
Samuel Cooper, *c.* 1663

Henrietta, Duchess of Orléans
by Sir Peter Lely, *c.*1662

Louise de Kerouaille, Duchess of Portsmouth
by Sir Peter Lely *c.* 1671–4

Hortense Mancini, Duchess of Mazarin,
by Jacob-Ferdinand Voet, *c.*1670

Mary Davis, by William Pawlet *c.* 1673

Lucy Walters, by Nicholas Dixon

Nell Gwyn, by Simon Verelst *c.* 1670

with a nice piece of declamatory legerdemain, he turned his discourse to the government's record of ineptitude, denouncing 'our negligence in having our castles without ammunition and powder when the Dutch came upon us and how we have no courage nowadays, but let our ships be taken out of harbour'.[172] (The aged cleric seems not to have suffered for this boldness, for three years later he was appointed Bishop of Bath and Wells. Perhaps, on this occasion, the king displayed his much-boasted talent of being able to sleep through sermons.)

It was obvious to Charles that he had to divert this flood tide of criticism away from the Crown. He had already thrown a sop to the Commons by releasing Buckingham, who once more preened himself in the House of Lords in all his resplendent finery. Within days the duke was restored to his offices and a self-interested truce was patched up between the people's hero and his old enemy, Lord Arlington. Now, all the major players were in place for the season's most cynical drama, 'The Lamentable Tragedy of Edward, Lord Clarendon'.

There was no inevitability about the events of autumn 1667. Charles could, at any time, have taken different decisions. Nor did he lack for sound advice. George Carteret, one-time lieutenant-governor of Jersey and now a councillor and treasurer of the navy, was among those who told the king that drastic reform of court and government was essential to any change of public attitude towards the administration. He pointed out that, whatever Charles and his close companions did in private, there must be 'at least a show of religion and sobriety'. This had, more than anything else, sustained Cromwell's regime and the reason was simple: the people expected their leaders to adhere to the prevailing morality. 'That is so fixed in the nature of the common Englishman that it will not out of him.'[173] Carteret's sense of the popular mood is confirmed by modern historical research, which presents a picture of a cultural revolution in swing throughout the seventeenth century. It was not a move towards greater libertarianism; quite the contrary. Illegitimate births were in decline and at the local level ecclesiastical and civil authorities worked together to enforce those laws and mores which held society together. 'A hardening attitude to bastardy; some decline in tolerance towards bridal pregnancy . . . tighter public control over marriage entry: these changes add up to a significant adjustment in popular marriage practices and attitudes to extra-marital sexuality, especially among the middling groups in society.'[174] Nor was this the result, as court wits liked to assert, of repressive Puritan preaching. Instead it stemmed from a variety of sociological developments to which evangelical Christianity gave legitimacy.

The life of the court in no way mirrored the life of the country; there was a deep-seated contrariety between them. Clarendon and Buckingham were more than personal rivals: they were the embodiments of wholly incompatible attitudes to life. Nothing less than that explains the destructive bitterness with which the two men confronted each other. As the summer of 1667 faded into autumn, rival camps struggled more frantically than ever for the mastery. 'While all should be labouring to settle the kingdom, they are at court all in factions, some for and others against my lord chancellor and another for and against another man.' Any who looked to Charles for clear direction were disappointed: 'the king adheres to no man, but this day delivers himself up to this and the next to that, to the ruin of himself and business'.[175]

On 9 August, Lady Clarendon, the support of her husband in good times and bad throughout more than thirty-five years, died. She was fortunate in being spared a share in the chancellor's utter degradation. It was a mere two weeks later that Charles sent his brother with the request that Clarendon voluntarily relinquish the seals of office. The king tried to make it appear that he was doing his old councillor a favour: parliament would be reconvening in October and they would be certain to demand Clarendon's impeachment for the mismanagement of the war. To prevent this Charles was giving him the option of retiring from public life and placing himself beyond the reach of his enemies. All this was only partly true. The new assembly would certainly be calling the government to account and all its members were fearful of the consequences. All, therefore, had a vested interest in setting up a scapegoat and the unpopular chancellor was the obvious candidate. There was nothing unusual about ministers of the Crown being thrown to the wolves to divert criticism; that hazard went with the territory. Nor can there be any doubt that Clarendon was in part to blame for his own downfall. He had never abandoned that schoolmaster–pupil relationship which Charles found increasingly irritating. In his policies he had failed to move with the times, seeking, as far as possible, to restore royal power in Church and State as it had been before the revolution. Illness combined with pressure of work had resulted in a lack of efficiency and Clarendon had not kept on top of government business. But for all his failings Edward Hyde had been the main architect of the Restoration and if he had accumulated too much power in his own hands, it was because the king had placed it there. He certainly deserved better than to be first abandoned by the king and then given over into the hands of his most hated enemy.

Clarendon asked for an audience with the king and this took place on 26 August. As well as protesting his complete loyalty, he warned Charles not to set a dangerous precedent. If he allowed enemies to displace ministers whom he trusted then there could be no stability in government. He urged the king to beware especially of Lady Castlemaine. That was the point at which Charles abruptly terminated the interview. As the dismissed minister crossed the privy garden around noon, word reached the royal mistress, who was still abed. She jumped up, called for her nightgown and ran into her aviary, where she stood, 'joying herself at the old man's going away'.[176] According to one witness, Hyde looked up and saw her. 'O, Madam, is it you?' he said. 'Pray remember that if you live you will grow old.' It was an excellent curtain line but an admonition that Barbara scarcely needed. Like Marilyn Monroe, she was fully aware that 'we all lose our charms in the end' and that insurance against that day was vital. In 1667, as in 1967, 'diamonds were a girl's best friend'. She was grasping her opportunities with both hands. She used her influence with the treasury commissioners to secure a £1,000 pension out of the profits of the post office. She obtained a warrant to 'borrow' some of the king's plate stored in the Tower and, when Clarendon was out of the way, she simply forgot to return it. Now that the old guard dogs had been removed Barbara found several new ways into the royal and national vaults. It is no wonder that most people believed that the decision to sack Clarendon had been taken in Lady Castlemaine's rooms.

As to that, nothing can be proved. The engineers of the minister's downfall were the king and Buckingham. Ironically, the only woman known to have played a central role in it was not Barbara Villiers, who had long schemed to bring about just such an event, but her rival, Frances Stuart, who had never shown an interest in politics. Clarendon refused to give his enemies the satisfaction of seeing him slink away. Charles had to send a minion to demand the seals from him and thereafter the ex-minister remained in his London house. His removal left a gaping hole in the administration and, to the absolute astonishment of most observers, the man who now filled it was the Duke of Buckingham. What few people knew was that the agent of this fateful reconciliation was Lady Castlemaine. She who had displeased the king by speaking up for the disgraced duke stuck to her guns and brought the two men together in her apartments. Once there Buckingham smooth-talked his way back into favour and subsequently achieved the leadership of government business by promising to deliver to the king all those political goodies that he craved – a pliant, well-managed Commons, religious toleration and generous grants of taxation. But none of these items headed Buckingham's personal agenda. He first pursued Clarendon with a lust for vengeance bordering on paranoia. Whether his cousin was behind this vendetta, as many suspected, cannot now be known but the campaign certainly has upon it the stamp of someone who had once promised to have Clarendon's head raised on a spike. Was vengeance her fee for having aided Buckingham's rehabilitation? And did this Delilah weave her spells on the king also? What is clear is that Charles, to his eternal shame, allowed himself to be manipulated.

By the time parliament met on 10 October, the duke had prepared articles of impeachment, charging Clarendon with misdemeanour. The punishment for this was banishment and, for the moment, that was all Charles was prepared to sanction. What he desired was to have the old man out of the way. But for Buckingham there could be no half-measures. He wanted Clarendon dead and he worked with manic determination to concoct more serious accusations. By intense and determined activity, Buckingham persuaded the king to accept and a reluctant Commons to agree on treason charges against Clarendon. But the upper house was not so pliant. Their lordships rejected a demand from the king for Clarendon's imprisonment. Suddenly Charles realised that they were not disposed to proceed against one of their own members for treason without very good and evident reason. Now the king was trapped. He could not afford to lose face and forfeit popularity by failing in this very high-profile enterprise. His response was a piece of manipulation worse than anything that had been attempted in his father's reign. He planned to prorogue parliament and then have the ex-minister tried by a special court of hand-picked peers. Whether this stratagem would have succeeded or stirred up more unrest will never be known because Charles never put it into practice. He simply used it as a threat to force Clarendon into exile. He strongly 'advised' the earl to flee the wrath to come and, when that failed to prise him out of the residence derisively known as 'Dunkirk House', he ordered the old man to seek refuge abroad. At the end of November Clarendon took coach for the coast and crossed to Calais. He who had succoured his master through long years of exile and seen him safely restored to his native land was destined never to see England again.

The reasons for Charles' ferocious persecution of the man who had served him faithfully for over twenty years were many and complex. He told Ormonde that his old friend's 'behaviour and humour was grown so insupportable to myself and to all the world also'[177] and there is no doubt that Clarendon's hectoring and censoriousness had worn down even Charles' igneous patience. There was an element of political awareness in the decision. Charles knew that parliament had to be handled with more skill than the chancellor could muster and he looked to Buckingham to be more accomplished in this field. Ruthless popularity seeking was another motive. Something dramatic had to be done to rescue the government's reputation from the depths to which it had sunk. And Charles was, as ever, all too easily influenced by his favourites who were possessed by an obsessive hatred. Then there was Clarendon's own obstinacy, which played right into his enemies' hands. If he had quietly withdrawn when the king first suggested it there would have been no need to wield the cumbersome weapon of impeachment. But the chancellor, mantled in his own shining virtue, refused to act in a way that would imply guilt and, to avoid being humiliated by Clarendon's vindication, the king had to agree to the stakes being raised.

But there was one intensely personal grievance which gnawed away at the king's vitals. The Frances Stuart affair had so deeply wounded him that eight months later he was still reacting to it. When Henrietta had heard about the elopement and her brother's angry response, she had written to intercede on behalf of the woman she had recommended to Charles' service. He replied at the end of August:

> I do assure you I am very much troubled that I cannot in everything give you that satisfaction I could wish, especially in this business of the Duchess of Richmond, wherein you may think me ill-natured. But if you consider how hard a thing 'tis to swallow an injury done by a person I had so much [here Charles wrote the word 'love' then crossed it out] tenderness for, you will in some degree excuse the resentment I use towards her. You know my good nature enough to believe that I could not be so severe if I had not great provocation, and I assure you her carriage towards me has been as bad as breach of friendship and faith can make it. Therefore, I hope you will pardon me if I cannot so soon forget an injury which went so near my heart.[178]

In November the stricken Clarendon wrote to his master protesting his abiding loyalty and dissociating himself from whatever misdemeanours his enemies were alleging against him. He declared himself perplexed to know precisely what offences he was supposed to have committed. Then, in an obvious allusion to the Richmond elopement, he continued,

> I am as innocent in that whole affair and gave no more advice or counsel or countenance in it than the child that is not born; which your Majesty seemed once to believe when I took notice to you of the report and when you considered how totally I was a stranger to the persons mentioned, to either of whom I never spake a word, or received message from either in my life. And this I protest to your Majesty is true, as I have hope in heaven.[179]

In the affairs of kings personal grievances weigh as heavily as matters of state and may have consequences out of all proportion to their apparent importance. Charles' rejection by La Belle Stuart is a dramatic example.

In the immediate aftermath of Clarendon's departure Charles wrote a detailed report of the whole business to the one person above all others whom he knew would receive the news with unalloyed joy. That person was his mother.

PART THREE

FICTION AND FACTION

See what the many-headed beast demands.
Cursed is that king whose honour's in their hands.
In senates, either they too slowly grant,
Or saucily refuse to aid my want,
And, when their thrift has ruined me in war,
They call their insolence my want of care.
Cursed be their leaders who that rage foment,
And veil with public good their discontent.
They keep the people's purses in their hands,
And hector kings to grant their wild demands,
But to each lure a court throws out descend
And prey on those they promised to defend.

John Dryden, *The Conquest of Granada, Part I*

CHAPTER 9

Debauching the Age

The new British film 'Nell Gwynn' with Miss Dorothy Gish in the title role is to be the first production at the opening of the New Plaza Theatre, close to Piccadilly Circus, on March 1 . . . A 'trade show' of 'Nell Gwynn' was recently given in New York, in the ballroom of the Ritz Carlton Hotel, and aroused so much interest that the performance was repeated.

Illustrated London News, 20 February 1926

None of King Charles' women has evoked more interest than the cheeky cockney girl who went from orange-seller to royal mistress. Nell Gwynn, unlike Charles' other bedfellows, enjoyed a measure of popularity in her own day and, if the steady stream of biographies, films and novels is a reliable guide, has seldom wanted for admirers since. Eleanor Gwynn was not the only actress the king lusted after but she was the only one to whom he remained deeply attached from 1667 to the end of his life. Burnet called her 'the indiscreetest and wildest creature that ever was in a court . . . and was such a constant diversion to the king that even a new mistress could not drive her away'.[1] Perhaps Charles saw something of Lucy in the slight, vivacious eighteen-year-old who performed with the King's Company under the leadership of his old friend Thomas Killigrew, and who embodied so much of the cynical, devil-may-care gaiety of the new-style drama.

Restoration theatre has come to be seen as a guide to the values and attitudes of English society in the last decades of the seventeenth century, and not wholly without reason. Nature always emulates art, as art does nature. Modern television soap opera consists of little more than permutated infidelities and violent confrontations within small groups of characters, whose numbers have to be augmented by new participants as the writers exhaust the potential for adultery and aggression among the existing dramatis personae. By exaggerating these tendencies as they already exist in contemporary society the producers and players accelerate change in that society. The audience and the screen are engaged in a bizarre kind of tennis match in which the velocity of the socio-ethical 'ball' increases with each stroke of the racket. Thus, for example, the

225

constant repetition of fictional verbal abuse and fisticuffs promotes the impression that uncontrolled behaviour is 'normal' with the result that, in the real world, emotional restraint more readily gives way to 'road rage', and people with disputes that could be sorted out over a friendly glass become the 'neighbours from hell'.

Popular entertainment has always played a part in the development of popular mores and the only difference between television and earlier forms of communication media is one of scale. So when Jeremy Collier observed, at the end of the seventeenth century, 'nothing has gone farther in debauching the age than the stage poets and playhouse,'[2] he was not being startlingly original nor stating anything that was not obvious to any objective commentator. Restoration theatre reflected the attitudes of a small section of fashionable, metropolitan society, magnified them and presented them as norms. 'When the greatest part of quality are debauched on the stage, 'tis a broad innuendo they are no better in the boxes.'[3] Inevitably, those who aspired to be regarded as among the 'quality' adopted the sophisticated values represented by the players. Sheridan observed, a century after the event, 'In Oliver Cromwell's time they were all precise, canting creatures. And no sooner did Charles II come than they turned gay rakes and libertines.' It was far too sweeping a generalisation to have total validity. The change in the moral climate was, in large measure, restricted to the court and the capital and those who had close contact with either. It did not take place overnight in May 1660 and there were several reasons for it. Any perception that the 'Merry Monarch' single-handedly delivered his dominions from the grey thraldom of an oppressive Puritan regime and inaugurated an era of relaxed *laissez-faire* ethics has to be consigned to the realm of myth. But change there certainly was, at least at the centre of national life, and a powerful engine for that change was the London stage, of which the most ardent patron was the king himself.

Charles gained his love of the stage from his mother. As early as the age of three he may have seen her performing at court in William Montague's *The Shepherd's Paradise* but she and her ladies had been enthusiastic participants in elaborate entertainments from her arrival in England as a young bride in 1625. Henrietta Maria's fascination with the magic of the fantasy world conjured up by the makers of masques and musical and dramatic diversions was something she brought with her from France. The Bourbon court had elevated baroque spectacle to a lavish pinnacle of effects and contrivances. No expense was spared to make indoor and outdoor presentations of plays, operas and pageants as visually stunning as possible. The stage became the focus for a deliberate fusion of classical, Christian and regal imagery, all designed to enhance the splendour of the monarch, and Louis XIV would, at Versailles, complete this fusion by making the daily ritual of the royal household a luxurious, unending, sumptuous drama.

The atmosphere in which Charles had grown up had been adorned with masques produced by Inigo Jones, William Davenant and a bevy of writers employed to create a heroic, Platonic image of the boy's parents and their household. They were pale imitations of the productions staged at the Louvre but they were none the less controversial for that. Charles I was deeply outraged when the Puritan propagandist, William Prynne, launched a vitriolic attack on the life of the court and especially its costly entertainments, which he castigated as morally outrageous and politically inadvised; Charles believed his chaste, idealistic music dramas were of a high moral tone. One of the practices which particularly outraged court critics was the fact that women appeared on the stage. It was the established English convention that all female roles in the public theatres were taken by members of a specialist coterie of boy actors. This restriction was ignored within the walls of the court, where ladies masqueraded as nymphs or shepherdesses, danced stately measures and delivered elegant, high-sounding verse. Thus, Davenant's *Salmacida Spolia*, the last masque performed before the Civil War (which the young Prince of Wales certainly saw and may have participated in), contained the spectacle of Henrietta Maria and her attendants descending on gilded clouds to bestow harmony and peace upon a land threatened with disruption by rude, turbulent spirits. It was all very precious and far removed from the harsh realities of life, as subsequent events all too clearly showed.

During his periods of exile in Paris Charles enjoyed the work of the highly accomplished writers, actors and actresses who performed for the delectation of Anne of Austria and her young son. The brilliant luminaries of the French stage were Racine and Corneille, whose neo-classical tragedies will have been, to Charles, reminiscent of the English court tradition, inasmuch as they had mythical or historical settings, employed verse dialogue, relied on elaborate scenic devices and glorified the virtues of honour, courage and chastity. But a very different, comedic, tradition existed alongside the elevated dramas of the neo-classicists, and the newly emerging master of this genre was Jean-Baptiste Poquelin, better known as Molière. His social satires were set very much in the contemporary world and he poked fun at all sorts and conditions of men and women. Despite enjoying the patronage of Henrietta's husband, the duc d'Orléans, the playwright's life was a constant struggle against church leaders and other authorities who did not appreciate seeing themselves lampooned and social conventions undermined. All French dramatists employed female players and regarded it as obvious that women's roles should be played by women. It was in the Parisian comedies that the type of the witty coquette, fully able to hold her own against men who sought to exploit her, came into fashion.

In 1660 the English monarchy was restored – but it was markedly different from its predecessor. The same was true of the English theatre. And the two institutions – monarchy and theatre – were closely bound up together. Charles set considerable store by royal patronage of the drama but what he had in mind was not a re-establishment of elaborate entertainments for the exclusive enjoyment of the court. The masque, with its esoteric style and didactic intent, was a thing of the past, associated in the king's mind with the closed, elevated environment of his father's failed experiment. What Charles wanted to do was revive the public theatre as a place where he and his friends could go and enjoy a new kind of dramatic entertainment together with his subjects. Stage plays had been banned by parliamentary edict in 1642 but, thanks to the veteran William Davenant, the drama was not totally defunct.

Davenant was a convinced royalist but an even more dedicated servant of the theatre. A man of fearsome aspect who had lost his nose in an early illness, he had fought for his king, subsequently fled to France, where he had enjoyed the patronage of Henrietta Maria and Henry Jermyn, been captured in the Channel while carrying messages for the queen, spent a couple of years in the Tower and come close to death. It seems to have been his obvious talent that saved him. Protected by powerful men of a literary bent, Davenant in the later 1650s obtained permission for a modest revival of private and public performances of stage pieces which combined dramatic and musical content, and which are recognised as the first operas in English. He hastened to commend himself and the thespian cause to the returning king and, as early as August 1660, Charles granted him a patent to erect a new playhouse and present public performances. A similar licence was granted to the king's friend in exile, Thomas Killigrew.

Killigrew, 'a brilliant conversationalist and a man little disturbed by moral scruples',[4] had spent many of the post-war years in various European capitals and, on at least one occasion, had been expelled for debauchery. One of his diversions during his wanderings was miscellaneous writing, some of it decidedly pornographic, such as the engaging narrative, 'The Possessing and Dispossessing of Several Nuns in the Nunnery at Tours in France'. The footloose courtier was one of those wits who seldom restrained his cleverness from leading him into irreverence. One story, related, perhaps by himself, told of a tour of the Louvre during which Louis XIV indicated a painting of the Crucifixion to the right and left of which hung portraits of Pope Innocent X and the king himself. Killigrew commented, 'Though I have often heard that our Saviour was hanged between two thieves, yet I never knew who they were till now.'[5] Charles welcomed him into his travelling entourage and Killigrew's outrageous behaviour lightened many of the gloomy days of exile, while his sister, Lady Shannon, performed a similar function during the nights. On their return to England Killigrew really cashed in on royal favour. He became groom of the bedchamber and, later, chamberlain to Catherine of

Braganza, while his wife was appointed first lady of the queen's privy chamber.

These two importunate adventurers, Davenant and Killigrew, well understood the hunger that existed for the reopening of the popular playhouses – and the potential profit to be made from giving the public what they wanted. They obtained a monopoly from the king and, over the ensuing months, set up two performing companies. Killigrew's troupe were the King's Men and Davenant's, patronised by James, the Duke's Men. But what were they to perform, and where? The latter question had been solved by 1663: after presenting their work in various temporary locations, Davenant opened a custom-built playhouse in fashionable Lincoln's Inn Fields and Killigrew welcomed patrons at the nearby Theatre Royal in what is now Drury Lane. Thus began London's theatreland. The choice of fare was not so straightforward. The two managers represented the old and the new, the native and the continental, in dramatic taste. They tested the market by offering a heroic number of pieces – between forty and sixty in a season – covering a wide variety of styles and subjects. There were revivals of Shakespeare, Jonson, Webster and all the leading Renaissance dramatists, translations from the French and new works by Davenant and Killigrew themselves, by a new breed of professional writers and by such courtier amateurs as Buckingham and Rochester. Theatregoers were offered bombastic, high-flown tragedy, light entertainment comprising music and dance, stunning 'spectaculars' relying on elaborate sets and *coups de théâtre*, and comedies of manners.

Certain novelties soon became popular and established themselves as expressive of the new, liberated style. The reason why playgoing became the height of fashion and a significant influence in the cultural and moral life of the capital is not difficult to see. Records from the lord chamberlain's office reveal what an immense fan Charles was. In the year from December 1666 to November 1667, for example, a list headed, 'His majesty hath had presented before him these following comedies and tragedies at court and at the Theatre Royal' comprises twenty-two items[6] and, in addition, the king attended performances given by the Duke's Men. Since royal parties were present in the audience on average two or three times a month it was inevitable that everyone who aspired to social eminence cultivated an interest in the drama. In the decade covered by his diary Pepys recorded over 200 visits to London theatres. There developed a theatrical coterie, almost a fashionable club and, inevitably, the court set the tone.

The role models portrayed in the satirical comedies were the young gallants and their easy-virtue women. To win approval playwrights invited their audiences to laugh with the hedonistic wits as they cuckolded husbands, swindled 'dullards' out of their fortunes, poked fun at middle-aged, middle-class virtues, exposed the 'hypocrisy' of the religious and ridiculed sexually unattractive men and women. Restoration comedy presented a world in which rewards and success went not to the virtuous, but to cynical, materialistic, self-aggrandising anti-heroes and anti-heroines who commended themselves only by carrying off their triumphs with wit and *élan*. As soon as the companies opened their doors to paying customers, Sir Henry Herbert, the master of the revels, tried to assert his authority as official censor and demanded that all plays be sent for his approval so that they might be 'reformed of profaneness and ribaldry'. Davenant and Killigrew resisted, knowing that they had the sympathetic support of the king. Herbert took the offenders to court and, as the law stood, he undoubtedly had right on his side. It mattered not. Pressure from Charles ensured Herbert's defeat, which effectively allowed playwrights, actors and managers to do whatever they wanted to pack bums on seats. And that meant, as it always does, appealing to the lowest common denominator of public taste. Many contemporaries shook their heads, reflecting, as Cole Porter reflected, 330 years later,

> In olden days a glimpse of stocking
> Was looked on as something shocking.
> Now, heaven knows,
> Anything goes.

As Paris was considered the centre of fashion, London now became synonymous with unbridled pleasure. It became the Mecca for the international jet set of the 1660s and 1670s. Everyone who had an establishment in town had to join in the round of party-giving. Those who wished to be noticed had to stay abreast of rapidly changing modes – face paint and patches, increasingly elaborate wigs, the precise measure of lace at cuff or neck. These years saw the Company of Barber Surgeons for the first time acknowledge the existence of women hairdressers. The demand for diversions was constant: the sophisticates of court and City became quickly bored if every hour of day and night was not provided with entertainment of some kind.

Foreign diplomats, if they were doing their job properly, had to join in the competition and were frequently obliged to excuse the expenditure of time and money spent staying 'in the swim'. The French ambassador gloatingly reported on a mishap which occurred when his Spanish counterpart gave a supper for Lady Castlemaine and a party of her friends. While the quality were feasting, their servants were also regaling themselves below stairs. When the time for departure arrived not one of the English coachmen was sober. Their host arranged for members of his own staff to be put at the disposal of the ladies and gentlemen. However, when they tried to mount to their positions in the vehicles the drunken servants thus displaced staggered forward to stop them. The resulting brawl was 'the greatest and most amusing disturbance imaginable'.[7] The abandonment of restraint was most flagrant and most obvious in relation to women and sexuality. On a frosty January afternoon in 1668 Samuel Pepys went to the Theatre Royal to see a performance of Fletcher's *The Wild Goose Chase*. The play did not please him but he was able to catch up on the latest stage gossip when the actress Elizabeth Knepp came and sat with him.

> . . . her talk pleased me a little, she telling me how Miss [Mary] Davis is for certain going away from the duke's house, the king being in love with her; and a house is taken for her and furnishing; and she hath a ring given her already worth £600; that the king did send several times for Nelly [Gwynn] and she was with him, but what he did she knows not. This was a good while ago, and she says that the king first spoiled Mrs [Elizabeth] Weaver, which is very mean, methinks, in a prince, and I am sorry for it, and can hope for no good to the state from having a prince so devoted to his pleasure.[8]

From the very beginning of the 'new' theatre, managers adopted the court practice of employing actresses to play female characters – and not only female characters. Within a few years the 'breeches roll' had become very popular with audiences and the sight of comediennes exposing their shapely legs clad only in silken hose and striding round the stage in imitation of lordly young bucks appealed, for different reasons, to different sections of the audience.

This innovation has to be seen as part of a deliberate attempt to close the gap between court and commons. Charles II was by temperament and upbringing very different from his father. The closed, esoteric world of the 1630s royal household gave way to the open, accessible style inaugurated by the Restoration, and the fusion of court drama and public drama was the most obvious expression of the new trend. All change has to overcome tradition-based prejudice and this was no exception. In 1629, when a mixed French theatrical troupe performed in London, they were hissed and 'pippin pelted' off the stage, and many worthy citizens were still scandalised at the appearance of women on the boards. It was the king himself who neatly turned moral outrage on its head in a patent of 1662, which declared

> for as much as many plays formerly acted do contain several profane, obscene and scurrilous passages, and the women's parts therein have been acted by men in the habit of women, at which some have taken offence, for the preventing of these abuses for the future, we do hereby strictly command and enjoin that from henceforth . . . that all the women's parts to be acted . . . for the time to come may be performed

by women, so long as their recreations, which by reason of the abuses aforesaid were scandalous and offensive, may by such reformation be esteemed, not only harmless delight, but useful and instructive representations of human life.[9]

It sounded very noble and may have stifled some criticism but the devotees of the stage knew that the change from boy actors to actresses had nothing to do with improving the morality of audiences. When Killigrew in 1664 put on his own play, *The Parson's Wedding*, with an all-female cast, a piece dismissed by one of Pepys' friends as 'a bawdy, loose play', he brashly explained to the audience the real advantage of the new arrangement:

> When boys played women's parts, you'd think the stage
> Was innocent in that tempting age.
> No: for your amorous fathers then, like you,
> Amongst those boys had playhouse misses, too.
> They set those bearded beauties on their laps,
> Men gave 'em kisses and the ladies claps.
> But they, poor hearts, could not supply our room,
> While we, in kindness to ourselves, and you,
> Can hold our women to our lodgings, too.[10]

Most actresses were prostitutes, either augmenting their wages (they were paid less than their male counterparts, irrespective of their audience appeal) or only remaining in the profession long enough to attract a wealthy protector. There was no attempt to conceal this attraction which brought many men to the theatre; quite the reverse. Before the fall of the final curtain in Thomas Shadwell's *The Libertine*, the following invitation was issued to the young bucks of court and capital:

> Item, you shall appear behind our scenes
> And there make love with the sweet chink of guineas,
> The unresisted eloquence of ninnies.
> Some of our women will be kind to you
> And promise free ingress and egress, too.[11]

And 'behind our scenes' the admiring men certainly did go. There was no restriction on visitors to the tiring house, where the actresses changed, and Pepys found himself on at least one occasion jostled by the 'many men [who] do hover about them as soon as they come off the stage'.

In all ages the public performances and private lives of the 'stars' hold equal fascination for fans and this was certainly true of those who ogled from the pit the ladies of the seventeenth-century stage. Writers and managers counted on the magnetic appeal of their actresses and this set the tone of the plays. 'The cynical focus on adultery, inconstancy and conflict in Restoration comedy can partly be attributed to the provocative use of the actress and society's view of her as whorish, fickle and sexually available.'[12] Action and dialogue in many of the new plays were quite explicit. Heroines were 'discovered', scantily clad, in their boudoirs or gasping upon a grassy bank as the bodice-ripped victims of recent violation. Even Shakespeare was not safe from the popularisers: Nahum Tate wrote a rape scene into *King Lear*. Thus, whether in the erotico-masochism of tragedy or the saucy bawdry of comedy, the actress was little more than a sex object. This was something upon which cynics and moralists agreed. Collier compared the women on stage with the whores who plied their trade, sometimes masked, in the pit:

Are these the tender things Mr Dryden says the ladies call on him for? I suppose he means the ladies that are too modest to show their faces in the pit. This entertainment can be fairly designed for none but such . . . It regales their lewdness, graces their character and keeps up their spirits for their vocation. Now to bring women under such misbehaviour is violence to their native modesty and a misrepresentation of their sex.[13]

The professional satirist and pamphleteer, Tom Brown, expressed the same truth more rumbustiously:

'Tis as hard a matter for a pretty woman to keep herself honest in a theatre as 'tis for an apothecary to keep his treacle from the flies in hot weather.[14]

Who were the members of this new, small profession? Certainly not women jealous of their reputation or social standing. Yet they had to be literate and intelligent as well as comely – a cut above the sisterhood of Dog and Bitch Yard, Lukener's Lane, Saffron Hill, Chiswell Street and other red light districts of the City. To win over audiences they needed precociousness and, more importantly, strength and stamina. As well as the emotional demands of acting, the work was physically and mentally draining. It was hard and the hours were long. Although the theatres usually closed in high summer, when the court was in progress and disease slithered around the fetid streets, for the rest of the year the companies worked six days a week, rehearsing in the mornings, performing in the afternoons and sometimes being called upon to make private appearances in the evenings. On top of this there were always new scripts to be learned. If actresses were to make the most of their celebrity status they had to be seductive and graceful but at the same time resilient and thick-skinned. Eager suitors could be generous, but also vicious if they thought themselves slighted. When Rebecca Marshall rejected the advances of a courtier, he employed a thug to waylay her as she went home and pelt her with excrement. Not every young wannabe dazzled by fame made it past Davenant's or Killigrew's auditions or survived if she did obtain a place in the company. It took a special breed of young woman to be a successful member of the King's or the Duke's players. But those who made the grade enjoyed the privileged status of royal servants and, more than that, were admitted to an élite society centred on the palace. Few of these 'King's Women', it seems, were dedicated to their profession. The stage was for them a showcase where they could display their charms to wealthy patrons who might whisk them away to a better life. This was completely understood by all and sundry. When Pepys learned that Frances Davenport had left the King's company, 'to be kept by somebody', he responded dismissively, 'which I am glad of, she being a very bad actor'.[15]

As to background, the actresses were a motley crew. Most of them came from – and many returned to – obscurity. Some, inevitably, were girls from good families who had lost everything in the royalist cause. Elizabeth Barry was the daughter of a barrister who had used up his capital raising a regiment for the king. She was 'adopted' by Mrs Davenant but later trained for the stage by the Earl of Rochester, who seems to have done a Professor Higgins job on her. A theatre historian recorded that she lacked dramatic talent and a musical ear until Wilmot, for a wager, transformed her into a 'star' within six months. Charlotte Butler was another whose family had come down in the world and were obliged to suffer the humiliation of putting their daughters to service or some other menial occupation. Girls like Mary or 'Moll' Davis were illegitimate offspring for whom, similarly, a living had to be found. In Moll's case the father was reputed to be Thomas Howard, Earl of Berkshire, although the tendency to aspire to noble lineage should make us wary of accepting the claim at face value. Then there were wives who went on the stage to support indolent or unemployed husbands. Elizabeth Knepp, who formed a strong attachment to Samuel Pepys (until Mrs Pepys made known her opinion about the relationship), came into this category. Samuel was captivated by her sweet voice and her 'excellent, mad-humoured' personality. The Knepps lived in drab lodgings and Pepys regarded the husband as an 'ill, melancholy, jealous-looking fellow' who probably beat his wife. As time passed, the stage produced its own daughters. Susanna Percival's father was a performer of supporting roles whose straitened circumstances led him into clipping coin, for which he was sentenced to be hanged (though reprieved while in the cart on the way to Tyburn). Susanna first followed the family tradition when she was fourteen and her life continued to be marked by that sensationalism often associated with stage people. Her first husband was assassinated. Her second, a fellow thespian with a reputation for wildness, fell foul of the Duke of St Albans (the son of Charles II and Nell

Gwynn), whom he branded a whoreson knave. Given the choice of apologising or being hounded from the stage, the actor went in front of the curtain at Drury Lane and told the audience that he had impugned the reputation of St Albans' mother, but added, 'It is true and I am sorry for it.' We are not told how his hearers received this attack on someone who had become a popular heroine and whose name was still revered.

Pepys, who was absolutely entranced by the ladies of the stage and was on close terms with several of them, would long enjoy delicious memories of the events he recorded on 23 January 1667:

> thence to the King's House and there saw *The Humorous Lieutenant*, a silly play I think, only . . . [Mrs] Knepp's singing did please us. Here, in a box above, we spied Mrs Pierce [wife of the Duke of York's surgeon] and, going out, they called us and so we stayed for them, and Knepp took us all in and brought to us Nelly, a most pretty woman, who acted the great part of Celia today very fine and did it pretty well. I kissed her and so did my wife, and a mighty pretty soul she is . . . Knepp made us stay in a box and see the dancing preparatory to tomorrow for *The Goblins* . . . and so away thence, pleased with this sight also and specially kissing of Nell.[16]

It was the closest he was to come to 'pretty, witty Nelly', whom he had admired for almost two years. Not until a century after her birth was a biography attempted of the most celebrated actress of the Restoration stage and few of the details about her origins can be relied upon. She was born, perhaps in Oxford, the second daughter of Thomas Gwynn, perhaps a captain in the king's army, on 2 February 1650. Her father appears not to have survived the war, for we find his widow later struggling to bring up her girls in Coal Yard Alley, behind Drury Lane. Though only a stone's throw from smart Covent Garden and Lincoln's Inn Fields, the street was as insalubrious as its name suggests, so that it is not fanciful to picture the girl leaving the slum cellar in which she lived to gaze on the finely dressed ladies and gentlemen passing by in their coaches and sedans.

Her mother and her sister, Rose, made a living as best they could in that murky world of tavern, theatre and whorehouse which formed the sub-culture of London's business and pleasure communities. Mrs Gwynn was a barmaid and a small-time madam; her elder daughter a prostitute and oyster seller. It was inevitable that Nell should follow the same career path as soon as she was sexually mature. The family was well placed to take advantage of the newly built Theatre Royal and, as soon as it opened, Nell gained employment there. She was hired by Mary Meggs, popularly known as 'Orange Moll', who had the fruit and sweetmeats concession in the playhouse. Moll doubtless saw the possibilities of the slight, gaminesque thirteen-year-old as a salesgirl and prostitute certain to appeal to men who 'liked 'em young'. So, day after day, Nell Gwynn stood in the pit selling fruit for patrons to eat or use as ammunition if they did not like the play, and occasionally accompanying one or other of them back to his lodgings. Having had no real childhood, she was pert, lively and well able to handle customers who tried to take liberties. She also dreamed, as did most starry-eyed young whores, of finding a wealthy gentleman who would lift her out of the squalor of the slums.

But Nell's first serious affairs were with actors. Charles Hart and John Lacy were both experienced performers and founder members of the King's Men. Lacy was a particularly gifted comedian and a great favourite with the king, who commissioned a portrait of him, which hangs to this day in the Garrick Club. Evelyn recorded one hilarious private entertainment given by Henrietta Maria: 'passing my evening at queen mother's court and at night saw acted *The Committee*, a ridiculous play of Sir R Howard's, where that mimic Lacy acted the Irish footman to admiration – a very Satyrus or Roscius'.[17] (Satyrus was a Greek actor reputed to have tutored Demosthenes in the arts of stagecraft. Roscius was a first century BC comic actor who was a friend of Cicero.) Nell entered with relish into the bohemian world of the players but they decided that the teenager possessed more than just a delectable body. Somehow the decision was made to train her for the stage. Killigrew was on the lookout for talent and his son was currently a client of Rose Gwynn, so it seems likely that he was involved in what must at first have seemed an unlikely experiment. Nell was illiterate and, apart from her looks and her vivacious personality, she had nothing to commend her as a box office draw. But what she did possess was youth and determination. Under expert tutelage she mastered reading, dance and dramatic representation, and made her début in 1664 or 1665.

She was by no means an overnight sensation and her range was clearly limited by her age and lack of emotional experience. It was when Nell and Hart came together to create the 'gay couple' that something magical happened. They and their scriptwriters evolved a new convention which immediately caught the imagination of audiences. Like Beatrice and Benedick, the gay couple were a pair of lovers constantly engaged in verbal sparring but unlike Shakespeare's characters, the new *combatants d'amour* became standard roles developed from play to play and they reflected the loose nature of relationships currently admired by fashionable society. In *Much Ado about Nothing* marriage is the obvious end for the lovers but in *The Chances*, by the Duke of Buckingham, this is very specifically rejected. The gay couple resolve not to spoil things by commitment and the curtain descends on the lines, 'Now see the odds 'twixt married folks and friends: Our love begins just where their passion ends.'[18] Small wonder that Lady Castlemaine became a firm fan of Nell Gwynn.

Then, just as Nell's career was getting off the ground, tragedy struck. The Great Plague began its decimation of London's population and, on 5 June 1665, the theatres were closed. Along with most of the company, Nell fled to Oxford to be away from the contagion and close to the court. For sixteen months they were all out of work and fending for themselves as best they might. It is not difficult to decide how Nell must have kept body and soul together. In the autumn of 1666 the actors returned to the blackened wasteland that was the nation's capital. Fortunately the fire had not reached the theatre quarter beyond the city walls and Killigrew and Davenant were impatient to open their doors again. To help them Charles ordered several performances to be given at court before the ban could be lifted but, at the end of November, a public in sore need of diversion took their seats once more on the theatre benches. For the next few months Hart and Gwynn were the toast of the town. Lovers on and off stage, they were brilliant and happy, and in the aftermath of the recent tragedies the public were more receptive than ever to their talents. Dryden wrote plays specifically with the couple in mind, including *Secret Love, or The Maiden Queen*, with a plot supposedly suggested by the king himself. Pepys saw it on 2 March 1667 and was enraptured.

> . . . there is a comical part done by Nell, which is Florimell, that I can never hope ever to see the like done again, by man or woman. The king and Duke of York were at the play. But so great performance of a comical part was never, I believe, in the world before as Nell do this, both as a mad girl, then most and best of all when she comes in like a young gallant and hath the motions and carriage of a spark that ever I saw any man have.[19]

Nell was obviously stunning in a breeches role and her pert repartee and witty ad-libbing had the house in an uproar. She revelled in her popularity. But the idyll could not last.

Fame came too soon, too easily, and she could not handle it. In early July, Thomas Sackville, Lord Buckhurst, offered her £100 a year to be his mistress. Nell could scarcely believe her good fortune. At seventeen she had achieved what she had long hoped for – to be kept by one of the leading men in the land. Without stopping to think, she rushed headlong into the new relationship and turned her back on her stage friends. There was enough dash and danger about Buckhurst to sweep a young girl off her feet. He was probably the most dissolute of all the rakes in the royal entourage – a position for which there was much competition. With Rochester and Sedley he made a habit of drunken, loutish behaviour which amused their cronies and outraged citizens who were the victims of their pranks. These included running naked through the streets, shouting abuse and singing lewd songs, and urinating on protesters from the balcony of an inn. Captivated by her exciting and irreverent beau, Nell collected all her belongings from Drury Lane and went off to Buckhurst's country estate at Epsom.

Killigrew and Hart were, naturally, furious. They had lost their star attraction, and at a time when the theatre was having enough troubles already. In April John Lacy had overstepped the mark in a satirical play which attacked the court, 'with all imaginable wit and plainness about selling of places and doing everything for money'. Pepys thought it, 'the best that I ever saw at that house, being a great play and serious',[20] but the king was decidedly not amused. In the midst of the fiasco of the Dutch war, even he was sensitive to criticism. He threatened to close the playhouse down and was only with difficulty persuaded to relent. To cap that, Lacy fell ill with the pox and was thought to be at death's door.

It took Buckhurst six weeks to tire of his new mistress. Towards the end of August he sent her packing, telling her that she had got all she was going to get from him, and cruelly ridiculing her to his smart friends. Poor Nell returned to the Theatre Royal with her tail between her legs, to find, not surprisingly, that Hart wanted nothing to do with her and that all her former colleagues similarly shunned her. The hard-headed Killigrew, however, welcomed the prodigal's return and on 22 August she appeared as Cydaria, daughter of the Mexican ruler Montezuma, in a revival of Dryden's heroic tragedy, *The Indian Emperor*. Doubtless Killigrew hoped that Nell's return would pull in the crowds but she was hopelessly miscast in such a serious role and performed it, in Pepys' opinion, 'most basely'. It was months before Hart was prepared to act opposite his ex-lover. On 28 December the couple recreated their earlier success in *All Mistaken, or The Mad Couple*. Although 'but an ordinary play', it pleased Pepys because of the acting of the principals: 'Nell's and Hart's mad parts are most excellently done, but especially hers, which makes it a miracle to me to think how ill she do any serious part . . . and in a mad part do beyond all imitation almost'.[21]

Her temporary ostracism was her rival's opportunity. The counter-attraction to Nell was Moll Davis, the leading coquette of the Duke's company, and she made the most of having the field to herself. She could not match Nell in comedic skills and where Nell was spontaneous and witty, Moll was simply coarse. But she was the better dancer of the two. Richard Flecknoe, a second-rate poet, disapproved of the loose morals of theatre folk but, nevertheless, gave Moll credit for her talent:

> Who would not think to see thee dance so light,
> Thou wert all air? Or else all soul and spirit?

And when, later, Lely painted her portrait he showed her strumming a guitar (the newly fashionable instrument of the day). It was thoroughly characteristic of her that, at a performance at court, she cavorted herself so suggestively that, not only the queen, but also, astonishingly, Lady Castlemaine were affronted and left abruptly. Charles, by contrast, was captivated and began to take a closer interest in Moll. Some time in early January, perhaps Twelfth Night, a few of the ladies of the court along with the young Duke of Monmouth put on their own performance of *The Indian Emperor* and some of the professional actors were invited to attend. According to Pepys' informant, the amateurs acquitted themselves poorly but the play was not the main focus of attention. Everyone watched the king as he ogled Moll Davis, and they observed that Lady Castlemaine passed the evening in stony-faced silence. Shortly after this it was common knowledge that Charles had set up the actress in a house in Suffolk Street, off Pall Mall, and that she had left the Duke's Men.

This must be understood in terms of profoundly political and personal events in the life of the king. Clarendon's dismissal had upset the mechanism of government, and the manner of his dismissal must have troubled even Charles' well-armoured conscience. Other ministers followed the chancellor out of office, to be replaced by new men and, so far from initiating clear-cut, progressive policies, the council became the battleground between Buckingham and Arlington and their respective supporters. Furthermore, Charles trusted neither of these men with the central issues of foreign affairs and conducted, through Madame, his own negotiations in a spirit of frenzied confidentiality. By March 1668, he was having to justify his actions to an anxious sister:

> I perceive you are very much alarmed at my condition and at the cabals which are growing here. I do take your concern for me very kindly and thank you for the counsel you give me but I do not think you have so much cause to fear as you seem to do in your letter . . . I will not deny but that naturally I am more lazy than I ought to be but you are very ill informed if you do not know that my treasury and, indeed, all my other affairs are in as good a method as our understandings can put them to . . . I assure you that my lord of Buckingham does not govern affairs here. I do not doubt but my Lord Clarendon and some of his friends here will discredit me and my affairs as much as they can but . . . you would not doubt but he would be glad things should not go on smoothly now he is out of affairs . . .[22]

It is not difficult to discern the reality beneath Charles' insistence that all was well and any suggestions to the contrary merely the work of vindictive gossips. Insecurity, anxiety and duplicity were at the very heart of national life and Charles was in competition with the very men who were supposed to be his principal advisers.

His personal relations were in no less turmoil. Barbara Villiers' charms had faded and, though still under her spell, he felt no passion for her. He still pined for Frances Stuart, and Henrietta and Pepys both heard rumours that he was trying to entice her back to court – rumours which he refuted when writing to his sister. Catherine's barrenness was a constant anxiety. Only recently the court had repaired once again to Tunbridge Wells where the queen hopefully took the waters. She had learned by now how to play the role of impresario and used her visits to the spa town to preside over all manner of gay diversions. The comte de Gramont, French traveller and gossip, heartily approved:

> The Queen even surpassed her usual attentions in inventing and supporting entertainments: she endeavoured to increase the natural ease and freedom of Tunbridge, by dispensing with, rather than requiring, those ceremonies that were due to her presence; and, confining in the bottom of her heart that grief and uneasiness she could not overcome . . .[23]

Courtiers hugely enjoyed these holidays. Away from the cramped conditions of Whitehall there were novel delights to be had in the ballrooms, salons and summer fields. Catherine ordained that there should be dancing every day because the doctors recommended such exercise as a means of rendering the spa waters more efficacious. However, there were those who attributed any quickening of the birth rate to causes other than the properties of the healing springs:

> Never did love see his empire in a more flourishing condition than on this spot: those who were smitten before they came to it, felt a mighty augmentation of their flame; and those who seemed the least susceptible of love, laid aside their natural ferocity to act in a new character.[24]

Inevitably, Rochester described more crudely the uninhibited behaviour of young bucks, who

> With brawny back and legs and potent prick
> Who more substantially will cure thy wife
> And on her half-dead womb bestow new life.[25]

It must have been heart-rending for Catherine to witness the biological outcome of some of these holiday flings but she made every effort to turn the excursion into a merry affair and brought the acting companies down from London to entertain.

Charles, however, found it difficult to be diverted. It was now that Buckingham suggested to him the possibility of claiming that he had been married to the Duke of Monmouth's mother, and the king appeared to give the matter some consideration. Others about the court talked of finding some way to dissolve the king's marriage and there were even those who suggested that parliament might sanction Charles to live in bigamy. From all his cares and frustrations Charles sought solace in the arms of a variety of women, some of them actresses, the euphemism for their hiring being 'his majesty sent for her'. Pepys' indignation at this behaviour was not only on moral grounds; he was annoyed when talented ladies of the stage left their vocation for the royal bedroom and did not return (as was the case with Elizabeth Weaver in 1664). He was, however, concerned when playwrights ventured too close to home. In February 1668, Nell and Elizabeth Knepp spoke the prologue of *The Duke of Lerma*, a play, 'designed to reproach our king with his mistresses, that I was troubled for it and expected it should be interrupted; but it ended all well which saved all'.[26]

Most of Charles' liaisons were brief but he craved more satisfying female company and his relationship with Moll Davis lasted several years. In 1673 she presented Charles with his last illegitimate child, a daughter christened Mary Tudor. She enjoyed all the perks associated with her position, including her own carriage and footmen, and regularly importuned the indulgent king for more gifts. When the royal ardour eventually cooled Mistress Davis was left with a pension of £1,000 and an even finer house in St James's Square. Sometimes she performed her dances before the court, to the chagrin of the queen and Lady Castlemaine. Catherine had long since learned to live with the king's infidelities; not so Barbara. She now hit back.

It is ironic that those who preached the gospel of free love should often fall into the heresy of jealousy. Every new comedy that was staged carried further the exploration of the problems of love and matrimony. In *The Secret Love*, *The Mulberry Garden*, *An Evening's Love* and other plays the gay young couples discussed the difficulties of constancy, the unnatural restraints of the married state and the arrangements lovers might make to keep alive their feelings for each other. In the 'open' relationships advocated in these comedies men and women were regarded as equal and free and the assumption was that, thus liberated, they would no longer be in thrall to that possessiveness which leads to jealousy. It was a myth which took scant account of human nature, as Lady Castlemaine was about to demonstrate. Furious at being sidelined by a mere chit of an actress, she decided to pay her lover back in his own coin. She took up with Charles Hart. The actor was doubtless flattered by the attentions of the notorious lady and certainly enriched by them, receiving, as he did, many tokens of her affection. Charles' response was to seduce one of Barbara's maids. The relationship between king and mistress was becoming more sordid by the week and neither was able to stand back from it or halt its downward slide.

Barbara was not only offended by the king's association with 'common' women; she was also angry at Charles' reconciliation with the rival she thought she had disposed of. In March the Duchess of Richmond fell ill with smallpox. Pepys took the occasion to moralise: 'all do conclude she will be wholly spoiled, which is the greatest instance of the uncertainty of beauty that could be in this age; but, then, she hath had the benefit of it to be first married and to have kept it so long under the greatest temptations in the world from a king, and yet without the least imputation'.[27] Charles hastened to her bedside. All was forgiven and, when Frances recovered, she was readmitted to the queen's household. It tells us much about Charles' attitude towards women that when La Belle Stuart lost her looks he did not lose his interest in her. She and her husband were allotted some of the best lodgings at Whitehall, overlooking the waterfront on one side and the bowling green on the other. Frances remained a fixture at court throughout the remainder of the reign – and without the slightest breath of scandal attaching to her name. If Charles had been deeply hurt by her the previous year – as, indeed, he had – this was not just because she had resisted his sexual advances. It was because he had offered her genuine affection – what he often referred to as his 'friendship' (or so, at least, he persuaded himself) – and she had rejected it. He was genuinely overjoyed at having her company once more, so much so that, one May evening, on a sudden impulse, he jumped into a boat and rowed himself downriver to her house. There, finding the gate already locked, he scaled the wall in order to reach her. Her rehabilitation in his favour had nothing to do with her now welcoming him to her bed. He once boasted to Richmond when they were both in their cups that his lady had been much more amenable since her marriage but if this was a sexual innuendo, it was probably no more than wine-inspired braggadocio. The simple truth is that the king was, as ever, addicted to 'effeminate conversation'. He enjoyed the company of all sorts and conditions of women, just as he was openly friendly with a variety of men. One might almost say that he 'collected people'. It was for this 'unkingly' behaviour that he was so often censured. Some commentators, however, were more charitably disposed:

What . . . an angry philosopher would call lewdness [i.e. 'unseemly familiarity'] let frailer men call a warmth and sweetness of the blood, that would not be confined in the communicating of itself; an overflowing of good nature, of which he had such a stream that it would not be restrained within the banks of a crabbed and unsociable virtue.[28]

Barbara was not inclined to take such a generous view. She cared not a jot about the king's one-night stands but anything more serious threatened to loosen the hold she had on the royal purse strings. Hence her petulant response to leap into Hart's embrace. If she had ever felt deep affection for

Charles – and that must be doubted – she was now interested in nothing but wielding power over him. Sexual expertise had long since ceased to be the main weapon in her armoury; she now relied on sheer, naked force of personality. Pepys expressed succinctly the situation as it had developed by January 1669: 'Lady Castlemaine is in a higher command over the king than ever – not as a mistress, for she scorns him, but as a tyrant to command him.'[29]

The chorus of public complaint against Lady Castlemaine had by now risen to a crescendo. At Easter 1668 the first serious political disturbances to shake the City since the beginning of the reign had occurred and their target was the termagant who haughtily paraded herself around the streets of London and Westminster in her carriage and six. The Bawdy House Riots took place over three days at the end of March. Mobs, eventually numbering several thousand, descended on the capital's red light districts armed with 'iron bars, poleaxes, long staves and other weapons'. They were organised in almost military fashion and their prime targets were brothels, which they proceeded to tear down. The fury of the protesters, who came from a wide area in and around the capital, was fed by several grievances, moral and political, but they all seemed to fuse in the association of government with sexual promiscuity. Some of the slogans shouted by the marchers indicated that their next target was Whitehall, the biggest bawdy house of all. The agitation this caused at court inspired Pepys to one of his more amusing diary entries:

> And, Lord, to see the apprehensions this did give to all people at court, that presently order was given for all the soldiers, horse and foot, to be in arms! And forthwith alarms were beat by drum and trumpet throughout Westminster, and all to the colours and to horse, as if the French were coming into the town! So . . . I to Lincoln's Inn Fields . . . here we found these fields full of soldiers all in a body and my Lord Craven commanding of them and riding up and down to give orders like a madman.[30]

There was nothing humorous about the government's response. The riot was furiously suppressed, fifteen ringleaders were tried and four of them suffered the statutory punishment for treason. The king took the incident very seriously. Any such affray set him anxiously looking over his shoulder for signs of a repeat of 1642. As Pepys reflected, the lawbreakers were only giving expression to what many people thought. Charles must have been particularly alarmed by three satirical pamphlets, the first of which appeared on the streets within hours of the revolt being put down, and which linked its cause unequivocally with Lady Castlemaine.[31]

Pepys considered *The Poor Whores' Petition* 'not very witty but devilish severe against [Lady Castlemaine] and the king' and heard that the mistress was 'horribly vexed' at it. He saw its dissemination as proof of the looseness of the times and the 'disregard' in which people now held king, court and government.[32] It purported to be an appeal by all those prostitutes whose living had been jeopardised by the rioters to the one acknowledged as the leader of that profession, 'wherein your Ladyship hath great experience and for your diligence therein have arrived to high and eminent advancement for these last years'.

We . . . do implore your Honour to improve your interest, which (all know) is great, that some speedy relief may be afforded us to prevent our utter ruin and undoing. And that such a sure course may be taken with the ringleaders and abettors of these evil-disposed persons, that a stop may be put unto them before they come to your Honour's palace and bring contempt upon your worshipping of Venus, the great goddess whom we all adore.

The implied threat in those last words was enlarged upon, the petitioners solicitously urging strong action

that so your Ladyship may escape our present calamity, else we know not how soon it may be your Honour's own case. For, should your Eminence but once fall into these rough hands, you may expect no more favour than they have shown unto us poor inferior whores.[33]

While Londoners were still laughing over this audacious lampoon in tavern and coffee-house, the even more inflammatory *Gracious Answer of the most Illustrious Lady of Pleasure, the Countess of Castlemaine* came off the secret press. It purported to be Barbara's indignant response to the riot and her promise of support to the petitioners. It drew attention to all those aspects of the mistress's life for which she was most profoundly hated – her wealth, her power over the king, her loose morals, her Catholicism and her association with the more notorious rakes. The *Gracious Answer* fell short of explicit criticism of the king – but only just. The patroness of the whores received with gratitude the homage of the sisterhood acknowledging that it was but her due.

For, on Shrove Tuesday last splendidly did we appear upon the theatre at Whitehall, being to amazement wonderfully decked with jewels and diamonds, which the subjects of this kingdom have paid for. We have been also serene and illustrious ever since the day that Mars [the king] was so instrumental to restore our goddess Venus to her temple and worship, where, by special grant, we quickly became a famous lady, and, as a reward of our devotion, soon created the right honourable the Countess of Castlemaine . . . we have satisfied ourself with the delights of Venus and in our husband's absence we have had a numerous offspring (who are bountifully and nobly provided for).

The fictitious Lady Castlemaine promised financial aid to the dispossessed prostitutes from the national purse. She assured them of the highest protection for the plying of their trade:

doubt not of having what countenance the authority of Holy Mother Church can give you. And for the increase of our practice, the master of our revels shall give licence for the setting up as many playhouses as his holiness the pope hath holidays in his calendar, that the civil youth of the City may be debauched and trained up in looseness and ignorance, whereby the Roman religion may with ease be established in court, church, city and nation, the most effectual means for the accomplishment of our designs.

There followed implied criticisms of parliament for voting taxes to the king while failing to make adequate provision for the rebuilding of the part of London devastated by the Great Fire. Thus was Lady Castlemaine associated with a shopping basket of the realm's major grievances.

Heartily loathed by the king's subjects and replaced in his bed by younger women, she would have needed the insouciance of a *grande dame* coupled with the insensitivity of carved marble not to be aware of her vulnerability. But she was faced with a more immediate threat in the intrigues of Charles' leading ministers. Buckingham had once more turned against her and was allied with Arlington in seeking her downfall. Following the removal of Clarendon, they were still involved in weeding out everyone not of their party who exercised any influence with the king. Into this category fell people as disparate as the Duke of Ormonde, Sir William Coventry, highly respected councillor and Speaker of the Commons, who was a threat because 'he was too honest to engage in the designs into which the court was resolved to go'[34] – and the Countess of Castlemaine. The feuding took several forms.

In order to win valuable friends, Barbara cultivated the Duke of York, whose father-in-law she had recently helped to destroy. She went further and sought to win the favour of Louis XIV by insinuating herself into the diplomatic process. She entertained his ambassador, the Marquis Charles Colbert de Croissy and provided him with inside information. Louis set great store by his secret correspondence with Charles via Madame but that did not prevent him developing all other available intelligence services. In April 1669 he conveyed to Colbert his satisfaction with the agent's progress:

The king . . . is most impressed with the unreserved frankness with which [Lady Castlemaine] revealed to you that the King of England was well aware that Lord Arlington had no wish for a French alliance but that the king was resolved to reach it in spite of any obstacles which this minister might put in the way. His majesty sets great store on the counsel of this lady and since you add that she seemed to you very well disposed to such an alliance and you believe she can put more pressure on King Charles to effect this end than any other person, his majesty wishes you to cultivate this good beginning with her.[35]

If king, minister, ambassador or mistress believed that their proceedings were successfully masked in secrecy they were deceiving themselves. Even as Colbert was receiving his master's plaudits Pepys was learning from a court contact the general drift of foreign policy, in which erstwhile members of the old Louvre party were still very much active:

> . . . it is brought almost to effect, [through] the late endeavours of the Duke of York and Duchess, the queen mother and my Lord St Albans, together with some of the contrary faction [as] my Lord Arlington, that for a sum of money we shall enter into a league with the King of France . . . and that this sum of money will so help the king as that he will not need the parliament, and that, in that regard, it will be forwarded by the Duke of Buckingham and his faction, who dread the parliament . . . My Lady Castlemaine is instrumental in this matter . . .[36]

It was not difficult to discern Charles' inclination towards a French alliance, nor his dislike of parliament (he managed to do without it from May 1668 to October 1669), and any intelligent observer could guess that the king hoped for generous French subsidies to buy him that political independence he craved. What was unclear was the exact nature of any proposed agreement with France, and that was because each of the principal players had his own agenda. Arlington favoured a treaty that would not tie England into Louis' war with the Dutch. Buckingham had his eyes firmly fixed on the financial advantages of any deal. Charles wanted to ally himself with the most powerful king in Christendom, to be revenged upon the Dutch, and to remain personally in charge of all negotiations. He was prepared to make lavish promises to his brother monarch, promises which had to be cloaked from his ministers. Above all, he kept well concealed from Buckingham his ace of trumps – his willingness to declare himself a Catholic as an extra incentive to Louis to provide support. Thus, the situation throughout the closing years of the decade was one of complete confusion and duplicity. A score or so of principals were engaged in Anglo-French relations and few of them knew what the others were doing. It is very unlikely that, however much she busied herself and tried to impress Colbert with her influence over the king, that Barbara Villiers had much to do with the formulation of policy.

In political terms she often appeared to be more important than she was. When Charles was confronted with the issue of Barbara's 'interference', he retorted that no woman shared his political councils, save one: the duchesse d'Orléans.

It was in her high-profile personal intrigues and vendettas that Lady Castlemaine made the greatest – usually disastrous – impact. As a prime means of attacking or ridiculing enemies the playhouse was the equivalent of today's tabloid press. A knowing clientele expected to discern references to personalities and events of the moment and propagandists were not slow to take advantage of this. Buckingham wrote a comedy to lampoon Coventry and, though the king banned its performance, it served its purpose in that it provoked Sir William into issuing a challenge to the duke, for which he was subsequently sent to the Tower. Hearing the news, Barbara immediately went to harangue the king. How could he suffer Buckingham to exercise so much power over him? Did he not realise that this was precisely the kind of action that made him look ridiculous? Charles was unmoved and, within days, Coventry had joined the procession of able servants forced out of office by Buckingham. But Barbara was in no position to accuse Charles of bringing public humiliation upon himself. She, too, used the theatre in her own petty rivalries. She bribed the actress Catherine Corey to mimic Lady Harvey, one of Buckingham's associates, on stage. The minister's faction was outraged and Catherine was arrested. Barbara remonstrated and Charles ordered the woman's release. More than that, he demanded a repeat performance. By this time, however, the enemy had regrouped. They hired a crowd to pelt the actress with oranges. The performance degenerated into a riot while king and mistress beat a hurried retreat. Tragedy and farce were seldom far apart in the Whitehall repertoire.

Meanwhile Hart and Gwynn were back in harness again as the gay couple and the year 1668–9 witnessed their greatest triumphs. Killigrew capitalised on their box office success by featuring them in play after play. *Secret Love, The Surprizal, All Mistaken, The English Monsieur* and *Flora's Vagaries* played to packed houses and enjoyed long runs. The Theatre Royal company also staged revivals of earlier plays which could be adapted to suit the new stars. But the climax of Nell's career, in the summer of 1669, came in a tragedy, albeit one which trod the margin of self-parody in its extravagant exploitation of heroic convention. *Tyrannic Love, or The Royal Martyr* told the story of the sufferings of St Catherine for her faith and was designed by Dryden as a compliment to the queen. Like some modern 'exposé' journalism, which takes a high moral tone while, at the same time, drooling over titillating detail, this play ostensibly advocated virtue and religious constancy but also gave the audience their expected ration of sex and violence. Thus, the pit enjoyed seeing known whores such as Nell and Margaret Hughes (who played the saint and was known to be the mistress of Prince Rupert) in the roles of high-minded virgins. The piece ended in a welter of gore and some of its language was unequivocally eroto-masochistic, as when the evil emperor, Maximin, melodramatically ordered his soldiers to turn the torture wheel slowly.

> That by degrees her tender breasts may feel
> First the rough razings of the pointed steel.
> Her paps then let the bearded tenters stake,
> And on each hook a gory gobbet take,
> Till, the upper flesh by piecemeal torn away,
> Her beating heart shall to the sun display.

But it was Nell who yanked the carpet out from beneath any serious pretensions *Tyrannic Love* may have had. Having, in the character of Maximin's daughter Valeria, dramatically stabbed herself to death, she leaped up as a soldier was solemnly bearing her body from the stage with lines which must have brought the house down:

> Hold! Are you mad, you damned, confounded dog?
> I am to rise and speak the epilogue.

She then lampooned the piece which had just been performed as

> . . . a godly, out of fashion play:
> A play which if you dare but twice sit out,
> You'll all be slandered and be thought devout.

Then, slipping completely out of character, she presented herself as 'the ghost of poor departed Nelly', and in comically appalling rhyme explained,

> Here Nelly lies, who, though she lived a slattern,
> Yet died a princess, acting in St Cather'n.[37]

The words may have been intended as Nell's farewell to the stage for she was about to take up her new vocation. She had several times been 'sent for' but now she became the king's acknowledged mistress. Or one of them, for Charles maintained his association with Moll Davis and, doubtless, enjoyed having at his beck both rival beauties. This elevation of common women to the official status of royal companions was something of a departure for Charles. He was no Don Giovanni, indiscriminately adding to his catalogue of conquests, '*contadine, cameriere, cittadine, contesse, baronesse, marchesine, principesse*'. Though he did, indeed, like the don, couple with women of every rank, he had until now always made a distinction. Actresses, servants, prostitutes were all very well for casual sex but *mistresses* had to be women with a certain amount of breeding. Even now, Moll and Nell were kept apart from the life of the court and not provided with rooms at Whitehall. Nor were they ever granted titles of nobility. Charles, in fact, set a fashion among courtiers, who now all wanted to be seen abroad with stage beauties. This was a distinct disadvantage for the acting companies. Dryden had to put off the opening of *The Conquest of Granada, Part I* because, although his actors were ready, some of their counterparts were indisposed with a 'sickness' as a result of which 'nine whole months are lost'.

One of the pregnant ladies was Nell, who gave birth to a son on 8 May 1670. He was baptised with the name of Charles and a delightful story is told of how, six years later, his mother manoeuvred the king into granting the boy a title. When Charles called one day Nell yelled from the doorway, 'Come here, you little bastard, and say hello to your father!' When the king remonstrated with her about this harsh mode of address, Nell quickly replied that she did not know how else to refer to the brat, since 'Your Majesty has given me no other name by which I may call him'. Soon afterwards the child received the name Charles Beauclerk and the titles Baron Heddington and Earl of Burford. Eventually he would become Duke of St Albans. Nell was initially provided with the obligatory fine carriage and a house in Lincoln's Inn Fields. Subsequently she was relocated in Pall Mall, so that Charles could walk across St James's Park to her gate. One more move, in 1671, brought her to number 79, where she remained for the rest of her life.

It is not difficult to see what attracted Charles to his actresses and to Nell in particular. They were artless creatures with no education or refinement but they had mixed with members of the 'quality' and their talents for observation and mimicry meant that they could mingle in society without embarrassing their companions. Yet they were not caught up in the petty squabbles, footling intrigues and frenzied place-seeking of the court set and could indulge in the luxury of detached mockery. There was about Nell an audacious irreverence which either charmed or scandalised those who met her. A visitor to court summed her up very neatly: 'She is young, indiscreet, confident, wild and of an agreeable humour; she sings, she dances, she acts her part with a good grace.'[38] By comparison many of the Whitehall ladies appeared vapid, languid creatures. Nell and Moll also had the advantage of being comparatively cheap. Their expectations were nothing like as high as Castlemaine's. A fashionable town house, an impressive equipage, gowns *à la mode* and some showy jewellery fulfilled most of their desires. Above all, they had little understanding of or interest in politics.

> Hard by Pall Mall lives a wench called Nell.
> King Charles the Second he kept her.
> She hath got a trick to handle his p——,

But never lays hands on his sceptre.
All matters of state from her soul she does hate,
And leave to the politic bitches.
The whore's in the right, for 'tis her delight
To be scratching just [i.e. only] where it itches.[39]

One thing Moll and Nell shared with all those women who were important to Charles Stuart: they were strong. Although their self-assurance and stamina showed itself in other ways, these were essentially the same qualities as those demonstrated by Henrietta Maria, Christabella Wyndham, Jane Lane, Lucy Walter, Henrietta d'Orléans, Barbara Villiers, *et al.* They were survivors who had pulled themselves up by their own shoelaces and asserted themselves in a man's world by using to the best advantage those gifts with which nature had endowed them. Having come from humble origins, they enjoyed a measure of public indulgence, though, of course, a certain jealousy went with the territory, as one anonymous satirist warned the king:

Look back and see the people mad with rage
To see the bitch in so high equipage,
And every day they do the monster see
They let ten thousand curses fall on thee.[40]

Even to Pepys, who had once stolen pleasurable kisses from her, Nell Gwynn became a 'jade' and a 'bold, merry slut'.

Charles' actresses were diversions from tedious affairs of state. Lady Castlemaine blundered into affairs of state for her own ends. It was reserved for the surviving female members of the king's own family to play central roles in affairs of state and both his mother and sister were involved in the single most important diplomatic event of the reign – the Secret Treaty of Dover.

CHAPTER 10

Secrets

When Henrietta Maria left England in the summer of the plague year she regarded it as her main responsibility to ease relations between her son and her nephew. In August, Louis XIV was driven to her residence at Colombes, ostensibly to bid her farewell before she left to take the waters at Bourbon but, in reality, to discuss possible means of bringing England and Holland to the conference table so that France would not be obliged to enter the conflict on the side of her northern ally. For an hour or more they were closeted alone in the queen mother's bedchamber. Then, they were joined by Minette and more time passed before the trusted Lord St Albans and the abbé Montagu (of whom more anon) were admitted to their deliberations. No one outside this intimate group knew what was discussed, and Lord Holles, Charles' ambassador, was particularly incensed about being kept in the dark. Afterwards, he pestered Henrietta Maria to know what had transpired but she would tell him nothing and he immediately wrote an angry report to his master complaining that he was snubbed by Louis, mistrusted by the English king's own mother and abused by French royal servants. Over the following years there would be several diplomats and politicians who believed, with very good reason, that the Stuart family made their own international policy with scant reference to their advisers and representatives.

In France Minette and her mother (often referred to as 'Mam' in the correspondence between brother and sister) monitored the changing situation closely. Henrietta Maria often visited her daughter at Saint-Cloud and Minette as frequently had herself driven over to Colombe, the palace where she had grown up and where Henrietta Maria still lived. Although Louis only went to war reluctantly and half-heartedly with his cousin in January 1666, life was, nevertheless, uncomfortable for the ladies. Minette was eager to go to the French king to patch up relations but Henrietta Maria, who had many years' experience of the Bourbon court, concluded that the time was not yet right. 'I found by the letter the queen writ me . . . that mediations of that kind were not seasonable at this time,' Charles told his sister.[41] But the queen mother did not abandon her role as mediator. In April it was she who took the initiative, organising a conference at

Saint-Germain to free France from embarrassment by negotiating peace between England and the Dutch Republic. This came to nothing, the Dutch knowing themselves to have the upper hand, but Henrietta Maria and her intimate adviser, Lord St Albans, did not cease their endeavours. In October they persuaded Charles to seek an armistice and when the Dutch again proved obdurate Louis regarded this as releasing him from his treaty obligations to them. He was now prepared to discuss peace terms with England – but only in secret.

In 1667 the Earl of Essex, a member of Charles' council, was travelling through France and paid a courtesy call on the aged queen mother. He found her involved in some pretty unscrupulous dealing with some Irish papists who were seeking military and financial aid from King Louis and offering to deliver their land into his hands. Essex was appalled:

. . . he found the queen was in her inclination and advices true to her son's interest but he was amazed to see that a woman who, in a drawing room was the liveliest woman of the age and had a vivacity of imagination that surpassed all who came near her, yet, after all her practice in affairs, had so little either of judgement or conduct and he did not wonder at the miscarriage of the late king's councils, since she had such a share in them.[42]

Once again affairs of state became family affairs. The only people who knew anything about the negotiations were Charles, Louis, Henrietta Maria, Henrietta, St Albans, the French foreign minister and the ambassador, Ravigny. All Charles' councillors were kept in the dark until they could be presented with a *fait accompli*. This did not mean that those who felt they were being bypassed did not have their suspicions. The fact that private emissaries went back and forth across the Channel and that the visits to Colombe of King Louis and Madame often coincided were marked by those who were prone to jealousy and could be dangerous: the duc d'Orléans and the Duke of Buckingham.

By 1669 the political landscape of Europe had changed again. The Sun King had embarked upon his long career of military conquest and the first country over which he had cast a shadow was the Spanish Netherlands, to which he laid dubious claim in the name of his wife, daughter of the late king of Spain. In alarm, the Dutch had hastened to form a defensive alliance with England and Sweden – a Protestant league against the aggressive forces of Catholicism. It was Louis' intention to break this compact and teach the Calvinist republic a lesson. For that he would need the help of the English navy. He knew that Charles was eager for a return match against the Dutch and thirsting to avenge the humiliation of 1667, and he also knew that Charles was readily bribable.

Charles was very good at spending money – on his own pleasures, on enhancing the monarchy (he had grandiose plans for Whitehall and subsequently abandoned them in favour of a brand new palace at Winchester), on national development (for example by enlarging and improving the navy). What he was not very good at was inspiring his subjects to share his dreams and ambitions. In his basic understanding of his role Charles differed little from his father: as divinely ordained head of state he knew what was best for his people and he resented the interference of parliament and the power it exerted through the granting or withholding of taxation. The words Dryden put into the mouth of King Boabdelin in *The Conquest of Granada* were an obvious statement of Charles' views, though he would have been careful, whatever he thought, not to refer to his subjects as bestial:

> See what the many-headed beast demands.
> Cursed is that king whose honour's in their hands.
> In senates, either they too slowly grant
> Or saucily refuse to aid my want.

He blamed parliamentary parsimony and delays for the failure of the war effort and he resented having his determination to exercise religious toleration blocked. But because he was not, like his father, a man who held fast to principles, he resorted to gaining his objectives by devious methods. It is precisely because he told lies and half-truths and said different things to different people that it is difficult, now, to discover what convictions, if any, lay beneath his actions.

In no area is this more true than that of religion. Theological and spiritual issues held no interest for him and he was impatient with piety and moral earnestness. He certainly respected men who stood by their beliefs, as he showed in his well-known relations with the Reverend Thomas Ken. On a visit to Winchester Charles demanded that the clergyman's house be made available to Nell Gwynn but Ken staunchly refused to receive a woman of ill repute beneath his roof. The following year Charles appointed him Bishop of Bath and Wells, saying that no one should have the post but 'the little black fellow that refused his lodging to poor Nelly'. However, he never felt under any compulsion to follow such examples of godly living and he prided himself on his ability to sleep through sermons. Inasmuch as any religion appealed to him it was the easygoing, undemanding Catholicism of the French court which was a close ally of absolutist monarchy.

His mother was as passionate as ever to see her elder son embrace the true faith, and for the most pressing of reasons: she believed Charles' immortal soul was in peril as long as he persisted in adhering to Protestant heresy. She had failed with two of her children and she was tireless in embracing those remaining with her possessive piety. Henrietta, the only one to whom she was close, had been devoutly Catholic from childhood.

James was not far from the fold and she did, in fact, live long enough to receive word of his conversion. But Charles was almost as stubborn as his father in his public adherence to the Church of England – though for different reasons. He knew how ingrained hatred of Catholicism was among a people who still celebrated their deliverance from the Armada and the Gunpowder Plotters and who regularly burned the pope in effigy. Nor could he be ignorant of the suspicions they entertained about the Stuarts' attitude towards those issues which had torn the country apart in the 1640s. A satirical poem in circulation in the 1670s declared how provoking it was:

> To see 'Dei gratia' written on the throne
> And the king's wicked life say God there is none;
> That he should be styled 'Defender o' the Faith',
> Who believes not a word the word of God saith;
> That the duke should turn papist and that church defy
> For which his own father a martyr did die.
> Though he changed his religion I hope he's so civil
> Not to think his own father is gone to the devil.[43]

It would have been political suicide openly to embrace the hated religion of Rome.

However, that did not mean that the possibility of his doing so was bereft of political advantage. Louis XIV was intent on becoming the temporal leader of Catholic Europe, the crusader whose endeavours were blessed by God because he extirpated heresy from his own dominions and sought to do the same in those counties he conquered or with which he was allied. The potential reconversion of England was, thus, important to him and that gave Charles the only real advantage he had in his dealings with the French king. He played the religious card with cynical skill. In so doing he left his advisers, his family and later historians with complete uncertainty about what, if anything, he did really believe.

Minette was as eager as her mother for her brother's spiritual wellbeing and the return of his realm to papal obedience. By now Henrietta Maria's health was failing and Minette took the maintenance of contact between the kings entirely on her own shoulders. She worked tirelessly at the super-diplomatic role allotted to her. In truth, she had little else to which she could devote herself with equal enthusiasm. Hers was a wretched life. Her health was always delicate and her three pregnancies between 1661 and 1669 were considerable ordeals for her, the more so since she felt nothing but contempt for her husband. While Monsieur regarded himself as free to carry on his affairs, he was passionately jealous of Henrietta's indulgence in the flirtations which were an inevitable part of the life of the French court. Among the young bucks of Versailles and the Louvre amorous rivalries made Minette's life a misery. Armand, comte de Guiche, was a handsome devil and a considerable wit, the flower of French chivalry and a courtier extraordinaire, over whom many a maiden swooned. Mme de Sévigné, whose letters give such fascinating insight into the life of the Bourbon court, wrote, of him, 'I would have loved him passionately if he had loved me but a little.'[44] The young man did declare himself to be more than a little in love with Madame and she was ill advised enough to encourage him. This provoked the fury, not only of her husband, but also of another aspirant, the marquis de Vardes, and it was he who drew the king's attention to the 'affair' and had Guiche despatched to the garrison at distant Nancy.

Not unnaturally, Henrietta turned against Vardes and he responded by launching a vendetta against her. She suffered in silence for several months but eventually the jealous aristocrat went too far. Speaking loudly among a group of people in the queen's chambers, he remarked to his friend Philippe, chevalier de Lorraine, who pointed out the charms of one of Madame's ladies, 'I wonder you bother about her when you can easily have the mistress.' Henrietta went straight to the king, demanding that Vardes be punished for his insolence. She also wrote to her mother and brother. Her letter to Charles was quite peremptory in its tone:

> . . . it is a thing of such importance to me that the whole of the rest of my life may be affected by it. If it is not settled as I wish it to be, it will be a scandal that any private citizen should have been able to defy me and have the king's support; but if it is, it will be a warning to everyone in future not to dare to attack me . . . this now makes me request you to send a letter to the king in which you tell him that although you do not doubt that he will give me all the satisfaction possible in this affair . . . yet you interest yourself in it so much on account of the affection you have for me that you cannot prevent yourself from asking him to do me justice . . .[45]

To a king accustomed to receiving frequent abuse this may well have seemed like a storm in a teacup but he probably did do as his sister had asked. Louis, however, did not need his brother monarch's intervention to persuade him to oblige his beloved sister-in-law. His treatment of Vardes was cruel in the extreme and vividly displayed the regard he held for Minette. He dismissed the miscreant into distant obscurity in the Camargue for nineteen years, two of which the marquis spent in prison. But Minette's triumph was a shallow one; every display of the king's favour deepened the duc d'Orléans' resentment of his wife's popularity. Vardes' cronies were not disposed to let the matter rest. In 1667, the chevalier de Lorraine played upon Orléans' all-embracing sexuality to strike up an affair with him and the duke became totally besotted with the beautiful and vicious young man. One summer's day Monsieur turned up at the château of Villers-Cotterets, near Soissons, where Henrietta was recuperating from her latest illness under the watchful eye of her mother. His first activity was to rearrange the furniture in preparation for the arrival of his new 'friend'. This act was annoying in itself but even more distressing for what it symbolised. Lorraine moved in and immediately set about making himself master of the household. Under this malign influence husband and wife became even more thoroughly estranged. Henrietta enjoyed some relief at the end of the year when the Duke of Monmouth, Charles' eldest son, arrived at the French court to be 'polished'. She took her nephew under her wing and rapidly established a pleasant rapport with him. But this only made matrimonial relations worse. The duke's jealousy, fanned by Lorraine, had by now reached paranoid proportions. He whisked his wife off to Villers-Cotterets in the middle of winter where the old château, unprepared for their visit, was freezing and quite unsuitable for anyone of a delicate constitution. Six months later a further twist in this sordid domestic saga revealed just how completely Monsieur was under Lorraine's spell. When an affair came to light between the chevalier and one of Henrietta's maids of honour the duke flew into a rage – but not with Lorraine. It was Henrietta who felt the force of her husband's fury and her attendant who was summarily dismissed, while Monsieur's lover was more firmly entrenched than ever. And when the duke's own almoner, Daniel de Cosnac, Bishop of Valence, produced incontrovertible evidence of Lorraine's guilt in the form of letters, which not only declared ardent love but poured scorn on Monsieur, he too was angrily dismissed and ordered to return to his diocese.

This was the appalling situation from which Minette sought diversion by immersing herself in the high politics of the Louvre and Whitehall. In January 1669 Charles decided the time was right to introduce the religious issue into the negotiations. He went to his brother's quarters and there, according to James' later recollection, with tears in his eyes he announced his earnest desire to be reconciled to Rome and to declare his allegiance openly. The only other people present were Arlington, Lord Arundell and Sir Thomas Clifford (a client of Arlington and a recent addition to the council), Catholics all. They were, of course, sworn to secrecy. Buckingham, who would have been furious at any suggestion of a Catholic plot, realised that something was afoot and, through an intermediary, remonstrated with Madame. She professed herself shocked that he should believe that King Louis would contemplate not involving the duke fully in any important business between the two countries. Meanwhile, Charles made his correspondence with his sister more secure by writing in cipher and, in April, he enjoined her,

> It will be good that you write sometimes to Buckingham in general terms [so] that he may not suspect that there is farther negotiations than

what he knows of, but pray have a care you do not say anything to him which may make him think that I have employed anybody to Louis, which he is to know nothing of, because by the messenger he may suspect that there is something of Catholic interest in the case, which is a matter he must not be acquainted with. Therefore, you must have a great care not to say the least thing that may make him suspect anything of it.[46]

It is very revealing of the king's character that this was written at the same time that he was appeasing Buckingham by proceeding against those remaining councillors of the 'old school', Ormonde and Coventry. After his brush with the minister Sir William was relieved of all his posts, and the earl was summoned back from Ireland to be dismissed from his position as lord-lieutenant. Nor was it only Buckingham whom Charles was deceiving; he could be just as furtive with his sister. When she expressed concern over the removal of the two councillors (perhaps agreeing with Pepys that 'the Duke of Buckingham will be so flushed that he will not stop at anything'),[47] Charles fobbed her off with vague excuses: Ormonde had not fallen from favour; there were 'other considerations . . . too long for a letter' for replacing him; and Coventry had been a 'troublesome man'.

The negotiations during the next few months which culminated in the Secret Treaty of Dover comprehensively covered a range of sensitive topics: a combined invasion of the Dutch Republic; the return of Charles' dominions to the Roman faith; the provision of French money and, if necessary, troops to enforce the change of national religion. Carried through, they would have either created a Catholic Stuart dynasty with autocratic powers such as Charles I had dreamed of or they would have plunged the kingdoms back into civil war. The question that has plagued historians is how sincere Charles was over the religious issue. He may have revelled in the vision of a realm forcefully united in religion under the control of a parliament-free sovereign but he knew his people well enough to be aware that that vision could never become reality. He would love to have been an autocrat after the model of Louis, commanding his subjects in everything, including matters of belief, but he knew, as he told the French ambassador in 1665, 'I have to humour my people and my parliament. They have made great efforts to help me and I am bound to consider them and not to do anything that might give them cause for complaint.' Only one thing is certain: Charles wanted Louis to believe that he was serious and that meant ensuring that his mother and sister entertained no doubts.

The principal couriers chosen for this highly sensitive correspondence were men known and trusted by the family. Henry, Lord Arundell of Wardour was an elderly courtier and diplomat who also happened to be

Henrietta Maria's master of the horse. His companion was Walter Montagu, the equally venerable abbot of St Martin de Pontoise and almoner to Henrietta Maria. He was reared on intrigue, having been an agent for Buckingham's father and later for Charles II during the years of exile; a man as practised at slipping in and out of countries as he was at passing, unannounced, through palace offices and bedchambers. These aged servants were of Henrietta Maria's generation and shared a devotion to her as fervent as their adherence to Catholicism.

It was a comfort to the queen mother and her daughter to have such trusted men as their go-betweens in the vital mission on which they were now engaged. For that is what it must have seemed to them to be. At long last, after all the tragic years, they were helping to bring to pass God's vindication of his holy cause. The rising up of heretics and traitors against the Lord's anointed, the martyrdom of a sainted husband and father, the wilderness time of lonely vigil when they had had nothing to sustain them but their faith – all these things were now behind them and they had lived to witness the imminent return of the British kingdoms to Catholic Christendom under Stuart rule. Such reflections will have done much to brighten days that were otherwise drear and nerve-racked. At Saint-Cloud the chevalier de Lorraine was more insufferable than ever and Henrietta was having to cope with another pregnancy. During the last stages she was bedridden for weeks at a time. Her mother came over from Saint-Cloud as often as she could but her health, too, was failing. Mother and daughter spent several hours together on 13 August and four days later Henrietta was delivered of a daughter. The queen mother was too pain-racked to make the effort to visit her latest grandchild. On the last night of the month she took a large dose of the opiate prescribed by her physicians. She went to sleep and never woke. The great matriarch of the Stuart family was dead.

The queen mother was laid to rest alongside her Bourbon ancestors in the church of St Denis, near Paris, and the funeral oration was, appropriately, given by her friend, Jacques-Bénigne Bossuet. Bossuet was the leading French preacher of the day, a staunch upholder of autocracy and, more significantly in the particular circumstances, an ardent anti-Protestant polemicist. In England the court went into mourning but life – and politics – had to go on and there was no slackening of pace in the progress towards a clandestine understanding with the French king. For her part, Henrietta worked even more zealously to achieve what she knew had been her mother's dearest wish. She mastered all the intricacies of European diplomacy and she also, throughout the autumn, summoned Bossuet to Saint-Cloud to seek his advice on their religious implications. Nine days after Henrietta Maria's funeral, Minette wrote a long, well-reasoned letter to her brother, 'to let you know my opinion and what I have been able to see in this business'.

It is a piece of *realpolitik* based on the glorification of her brother's reign and the restitution of the Catholic faith throughout his dominions. First of all she disposes of the argument that England's best interests lie in maintaining friendship with the Dutch to prevent France becoming too powerful:

> But the matter takes on a different aspect, firstly because you have need of France to ensure the success of the design about R[eligion] and there is very little likelihood of your obtaining what you desire from the king except on condition that you enter into a league with him against Holland. I think you must take this resolution and when you have thought it well over you will find that, besides the intention of R, your glory and your profit will coincide in this design. Indeed, what is there more glorious and more profitable than to extend the confines of your kingdom beyond the sea and to become supreme in commerce, which is what your people most passionately desire and what will probably never occur so long as the Republic of Holland exists?

What is proposed is nothing less than the redrawing of the world map. The little Protestant republic is to be demolished and its land, ports and overseas possessions distributed between the usurpers.

There is, of course, a potential canker in this radiant and fragrant blossom and one which the writer knows her streetwise brother to be well aware of: once Louis' power, territory and maritime opportunities have been dramatically enhanced, what is to prevent him turning his hostile attentions on his former ally? Henrietta disposes of this fear by pointing out that Charles will have enhanced naval supremacy and the use of continental ports from which to keep a close eye on French ambitions. Furthermore, France's neighbour states will be very wary of her expansion and ever ready to league with England to contain her. What is interesting here is not the somewhat shaky arguments advanced to bolster a policy of naked aggression but the absence of the religious argument. Henrietta does not suggest that, once England had been reconciled to Rome, Louis would be obliged to maintain his friendship with her.

The reason for this omission is that the crucial issue in the negotiations had come to be the timing of Charles' declaration of his conversion. That brings us back to the question of his sincerity. First and foremost for him religion was a lever for prising from Louis the support he wanted. He would not make a public declaration before he had received that support. And afterwards? Well, he would wait and see. His display of eagerness for the principle coupled with caution about the means had already succeeded in putting Louis in an ambiguous position. If he was being expected to fund the reconversion of Britain he wanted to be sure of achieving the objective. It would not at all suit his foreign policy designs to tie up men and gold across the Channel in a long and costly war. Thus he, too, appreciated the necessity of waiting for the psychological moment.

In her letter Henrietta tacitly accepts her brother's timetable: the best opportunity for carrying out the religious programme will come *after* the war:

This war is not likely to be of long duration if the right measures are taken and, far from injuring the design you have touching R, it will, perhaps, give you the means of executing it with greater certainty and ease . . . having a pretext for keeping up troops outside your kingdom to protect your conquests, the thought alone of these troops, which for greater safety could be composed of foreigners and would be practically in sight of England, could keep [your country] in check and render parliament more amenable than it has been accustomed to be.

Here we have Henrietta Maria's daughter writing. During the Civil War the old queen had raised men and materiel abroad to help her husband bring to heel the traitorous, heretical rabble of parliament. Now Minette was calmly advising her brother to employ mercenaries against his own people in order to impose his religion upon them. She has a further cunning suggestion to make: when Charles sends an army across the Channel to participate in the invasion of Holland why does he not ensure that he distributes military command to men who, if they stayed at home, might oppose him on the religious issue? Thus, 'the two designs, that is to say that of R and that of the Dutch war, could be executed at the same time'.[48] It was as well for Charles that the glorious vision of a swift and brilliant victory assumed in this letter never became reality. Had it done so and had he then attempted to turn back the clock to the days before Henry VIII, Cranmer and Thomas Cromwell, he might have ended up sharing his father's fate or, at least, being harried back into exile.

The events of the next few months have many of the characteristics of a Cold War spy movie – sex, bribery, intercepted messages, interrogation, clandestine meetings and the knock on the door in the middle of the night. Henrietta's private life became tautly interwoven with affairs of state as the time for finalising a treaty drew nearer, and the complications of her domestic situation almost scuppered that treaty altogether. At the diplomatic level hard bargaining stumbled forward throughout the autumn and winter of 1669–70, dragging heavy chains of mutual suspicion, deliberate procrastination and irreconcilable interests. One matter which did become clear was that if the treaty was to remain secret it would be necessary for Madame to carry out the final negotiations. If English and French plenipotentiaries were locked together in earnest debate for several days it would be obvious that something important was afoot but what could be more natural than that Charles and his sister, who had not met for nine years, should spend some quality time together? This accorded with the royal siblings' dearest wishes. In their correspondence they had often made plans to meet but those plans had always been frustrated either by Henrietta's health or the pressures of national and international politics. Now that her two brothers were all that remained of her family Minette was even more desperate to see them both. Yet it was precisely the possibility of this reunion that was called in doubt by the sordid complications of Monsieur and Madame's relationships.

The sequence of violence, retaliation and revenge began in October when Minette wrote to Cosnac, still confined to his bishopric at Valence. Lorraine's arrogant and domineering behaviour had at last become intolerable and she asked her old friend to bring her certain letters in his possession which would discredit the chevalier and with which she hoped to encompass his downfall. Cosnac knew that he was under surveillance and it was with considerable trepidation that he donned a disguise and made the forbidden journey to Paris. Unfortunately he fell ill in some cheap lodging in the *quartier* Saint-Denis. A doctor was called to his bedside, recognised him and betrayed him to the authorities. Suspecting that his cover was blown, Cosnac dragged himself into an adjacent closet and got rid of all incriminating documents in the privy. Scarcely had he done so when the police burst in and carried him off to the nearest jail clad only in his dressing gown and underwear. Their excuse was that they believed him to be a forger who was on the wanted list. They ransacked his room and found one tiny piece of paper he had overlooked. It was a note from Suzanne-Charlotte de St-Chaumont, governess to the Orléans' children, whom Henrietta had used as an intermediary. While the bishop was despatched once more into exile, Monsieur gleefully dismissed Mme de St-Chaumont. A tearful Henrietta, seconded by the English ambassador, complained bitterly to Charles and he made representations to Louis about the disgraceful treatment being meted out to his sister and her suite at the instigation of the chevalier de Lorraine.

The French king, in the middle of delicate negotiations with his cousin, was put in the difficult position of intervening in a domestic fracas between his brother and his wife. Furthermore, the complaint arrived at the same time as the latest proposals from England – proposals which were so extreme as to make Louis wonder just how serious his brother monarch was. He watched for an excuse to take action against the chevalier de Lorraine and thus please Charles. The arrogant young man was not long in offering an opportunity. Cheated, as he thought, out of some revenues he believed should have come to him, he made some injudicious remarks about the king and was immediately arrested. The duc d'Orléans flew into a frenzy, grovelling before the king and even begging Madame to intercede on the chevalier's behalf. When his brother proved inflexible the duke flounced off to Villers-Cotterets taking his wife with him and vowing that he would never set foot in the court again. That scarcely bothered Louis but he was annoyed when letters to Orléans from his haughty

Adonis were intercepted urging the duke to remain steadfast in his opposition to the king. That earned the chevalier an immediate transfer to the Château d'If, the awesome island prison off Marseilles which would later be given worldwide notoriety by Dumas in *The Count of Monte Cristo*. The gauge needle of Monsieur's wrath swung into the red and, as always, his wife felt the force of it.

All this happened at the very time that Louis and Charles wanted to make arrangements for Henrietta's visit to England. Most of the log jams impeding agreement had, by dint of long days of discussion among the ministers and ambassadors party to the secret and even longer nights spent in drafting and redrafting sections of the treaty, been shifted. Both sides were eager to get everything signed, sealed and settled. The longer the final steps were delayed, the more chance there was of the secret getting out. But everything was dependent on Henrietta being able to make the journey, and that was dependent on Monsieur giving his consent, for even King Louis was not prepared to override the rights a husband had over his wife. It was not just the treatment of his boyfriend that stuck in Orléans' throat. The chevalier had his own espionage system and had learned something of the reason behind Henrietta's proposed trip to England. This intelligence he, of course, passed to the duke, who was furious that, yet again, he had been left out of the king's counsels and treated as a mere cipher. As well as requests travelling through official, diplomatic channels, Charles, James and Lord St Albans all wrote directly to the duke asking him to allow the duchess to visit her brother. These messages duly arrived at Villers-Cotterets but for several days Henrietta dared not pass them on to her husband. It was mid-February before Monsieur had sufficiently cooled down to make an approach possible. His brother urged him to return to court and as an inducement eased the chevalier's conditions of detention. The duke and duchess drove back to Paris – Monsieur was bored with his frozen country estate anyway – but he absolutely refused to allow Madame to cross the Channel unless his lover was restored to him. Since Louis was not prepared to humiliate himself by making that concession there was a state of stalemate.

If anything, Orléans' resolve was strengthened by the return to court. Everyone made a great fuss of Henrietta and sympathised with her over her husband's brutish treatment. Every afternoon the king spent time with her in private discussing affairs of national importance to which he – the king's brother and the man who would have to act as regent in the event of anything happening to Louis – was not privy. Everywhere he looked he was confronted by his wife's popularity and his own inadequacy. It is scarcely surprising that he focused his resentment on Henrietta by openly insulting her at every opportunity and refusing her the thing she most ardently desired – reunion with what was left of her own family. The programme Louis was working to entailed the conclusion of the treaty in

April. He was taking the court on progress into the Netherlands to inspect the territory he had conquered in the recent campaign and the plan was for Madame and her train to slip across the Channel from Dunkirk. Monsieur put every possible obstacle in the way of his brother's designs.

He declined to join the northern progress. Then he said that he and his wife *would* go but that she was to stay in French territory. Days later he yielded so far as to agree to accompany Madame on a brief visit to Dover. Every ounce of Charles' diplomatic tact was needed to suggest that the duke's presence would not be appropriate. Orléans eventually swallowed that and consented to his wife paying a short visit to Dover. Charles pointed out that a tiny fishing village was hardly the most suitable rendezvous for so exalted a personage as the sister-in-law of the King of France and that it was essential that Madame be received with all honours at Whitehall. At that Orléans dug his heels in: it was Dover or nothing – and only for three days. With that Charles and Louis had to be content. Even then, if one source 'close to the throne' is to be believed, Monsieur tried to scupper the plan by forcing himself on his wife every night in the hope that she would become pregnant and, therefore, unfit to travel.

Louis and his court, packed into scores of coaches and accompanied by an army of 30,000 to impress his new subjects, left Paris on 18 April. The journey turned into an ordeal for everyone concerned, though the accounts of it make humorous reading now. The weather was vile and the roads in places almost unusable. When they reached the Sambre the elegant lords and ladies in their fine coaches found that the river had burst its banks and that the only bridge had been swept away. Flood water swirled around them and all was confusion. The queen squealed hysterically that they were all going to be drowned. When equerries discovered a very modest farmhouse that would afford the royal party some shelter her majesty flatly refused to be lodged in such a hovel. When she had been persuaded that a night on bare boards was preferable to one spent cooped up in her carriage she almost stuck in the mud on her way to the building. Then, when a very basic meal was served, she turned her nose up at it, changing her mind only when the king and the rest of the party had heartily attacked the humble fare and there was nothing left. She might have imagined that, after this, things could only get better but she had not reckoned on trying to sleep with other women – and men – round a smoky fire with the sounds and smells of animals in adjacent accommodation filling the air. The news, brought to the king at four in the morning, that the bridge had been repaired at last put an end to a night of torment.

Unpleasant though the journey was for ladies not accustomed to such hardship, to a semi-invalid such as Henrietta it was truly purgatorial. The jolting, slithering progress of her coach used up all her strength and each night she retired, often able to take no more than a little milk. As for Monsieur, he positively gloated at her discomfort, observing on one occasion that the trip would probably be the death of her. When news arrived that all was ready aboard the English fleet to carry her across the Channel, he made a last-ditch effort to prevent her departure. This time Louis ordered him to stop his obstruction; Madame was going to England at his specific request and he would brook no opposition. Charles, meanwhile, had rushed to sea at the earliest opportunity, eager to meet his sister in mid-Channel, but contrary winds had forced him back to Gravesend, from where he rode to Dover. On 16 May 1670 brother and sister were at long last emotionally reunited aboard the English flagship as it glided into the harbour. As Charles escorted Henrietta to the rooms that had been prepared for her in the old castle overlooking the port, he can scarcely have failed to notice with alarm how much she had changed. The sixteen-year-old girl he had said goodbye to in 1661 had not been robust but her liveliness had well concealed her essential frailty. Now he was confronted by a prematurely aged woman of twenty-five.

Monsieur was persuaded to grant his wife an extension of her leave of absence and she was able to spend seventeen days with her brothers and their closest attendants, including Queen Catherine, whom she had never met but about whom Charles had often written, and her own erstwhile lady of the bedcamber, Frances, Duchess of Richmond. Although the resources of the capital were not available, Charles went to considerable lengths to entertain his sister. The Duke's Men were brought down to act for her; there was a banquet to mark the king's birthday; and further amusements were offered aboard Charles' flagship when he proudly took her to sea to show off his navy. The king's affection for his sole remaining female relative was genuine and obvious. The French ambassador, Colbert, declared, 'she has much more power over the king, her brother, than any other person in the world',[49] and included in that all-embracing statement were Charles' current mistresses.

But the main purpose of the visit was the treaty and this occupied brother and sister for the first few days of Henrietta's stay. The central clauses concerned the details about the coming conflict and the means by which Charles (and, hopefully, in time Britain) was to return to papal allegiance. Command in the war was divided between the two sovereigns: Charles would contribute 6,000 men to Louis' land force and have charge of the naval expedition comprising fifty English and forty French capital ships. In order to enable Charles to make his religious declaration the French king would provide 2 million livres (£1 = approx. 13 livres) in two instalments and, if necessary, 6,000 troops. What the treaty did not establish was when these events would take place. The opening of hostilities was left to Louis to decide, *after* Charles had made his declaration, and Charles was to make his declaration 'as soon as the welfare of his kingdom will permit', a deliciously slippery phrase. What Charles had succeeded in securing from his cousin was an open cheque, not only in cash terms but also in terms of diplomatic support. He had tied the greatest power in Europe to his regime and if at any time Louis should turn against him Charles could invoke their secret religious agreement. As to his declaration being a prelude to his entering the Dutch war, he very neatly got round that some months later. He had Buckingham conclude an *official* treaty with France. Its terms were almost exactly the same as those of the secret treaty but, since they were for public consumption, they made no mention of religion. Thus, Charles ended up committing himself to a combined war against the Dutch Republic with no religious strings attached. Before Minette's departure the secret treaty had been ratified by both sides.

All too soon the day of her return to France arrived. Charles and James accompanied her aboard her ship on 2 June and sailed some distance with her. The king showered his sister with presents, including 2,000 crowns for her to have a memorial chapel built for their mother at her favourite convent at Chaillot. According to the oft-reprinted romantic story, Henrietta, wanting to give something in return, called for her jewel box. It was brought by one of her ladies, a young, dark-haired, green-eyed Breton girl by the name of Louise de Keroualle. Minette invited her brother to select any jewel of his choice. Smiling on the young woman he said that she was the only precious object he desired. Perhaps Minette would leave her as a going-away present. Was it a jest to lighten the time of parting or was Charles' libido active even at such a sad moment? The anecdote, if true, might lead us to imagine that Charles was noticing Louise for the first time, which was certainly not the case. Anyone with the king's eye for a pretty face would have been struck by this lively and intelligent twenty-year-old daughter of an impoverished Breton aristocrat. The young woman may have had a special attraction for him precisely because she was a great favourite of Minette's. The Frances Stuart incident suggests that brother and sister had similar tastes in people. In whatever tone the request was made, Henrietta laughingly refused it, saying that she was responsible to the girl's parents for her safety. When the time for goodbyes arrived many tears were shed on both sides. Three times Charles walked across the deck to descend to the boat which was to take him to his yacht. Three times he ran back to embrace his sister. But, at last, he left.

With this brief interlude of happiness and the sense of something achieved behind her, Henrietta returned to her Bourbon relatives. Back at the French court nothing had changed; everyone loved Madame except her husband. The widespread adulation she received and the expressions of the king's gratitude heaped fresh coals on Monsieur's jealousy. He took his wife back to Saint-Cloud at the first opportunity and the old domestic misery resumed. She had one more task to perform for her English friends, and that was to inform Sir Thomas Clifford that she had urged her brother to grant him and Arlington fresh honours for their part in the treaty

making. Then she bent all her concentration on coping with her physical
and psychological distress.

The afternoon of 29 June was very hot and she drank some iced water
flavoured with chicory. Immediately she collapsed in excruciating pain
and, much to the consternation of her attendants, cried out that she had
been poisoned. Doctors were summoned and she was prescribed an
emetic. To calm her fears of foul play, Monsieur ordered some of her
women to drink from his wife's cup, which they did without suffering ill
effects, but this did nothing to remove Henrietta's conviction that she
was about to die at the hands of a murderer. Given all that she had
suffered in recent years, her suspicions were understandable. In fact, it
was the ulcer which had long plagued her that had brought on this attack.
After hours of useless ministrations by the physicians, Orléans was
sufficiently alarmed to send word to his brother, and the king and queen
immediately came from Versailles. They were joined by other court
notables until Madame's chamber was thronged with the cream of
French society.

One of those who attended Madame was the remarkable Marie-
Madeleine, comtesse de Lafayette. A friend of Racine and Corneille, she
was a leading figure in the Parisian literary scene and one of the first
French lady novelists. She wrote a first-hand account of the moving events
of the next few hours. As we read her words we need to keep in mind the
fact that she was a mistress of the affecting story.

> The king, seeing that all the signs indicated that there was no hope, said
> his farewells with tears in his eyes. She implored him not to weep, for
> that was moving her [to tears] also and she told him that the first news
> he would receive the next day would be of her death . . . The English
> ambassador [Ralph Montagu] arrived . . . As soon as she saw him she
> spoke to him about the king her brother and the sorrow that her death
> would bring him. She had spoken of this often in the early stages of her
> illness and she [now] begged him to assure the king that he was losing
> the one who loved him best in all the world. Then the ambassador asked
> her if she had been poisoned (or if she had earlier claimed to be
> poisoned; I am not sure which). [The conversation was in English which
> explains why the writer could not be certain on this crucial point.] But I
> do know that she insisted that he say nothing of this to the king her
> brother, for it would only deepen his grief and he must not even
> contemplate revenge. King Louis was in no way involved and her
> brother must under no circumstances blame him.

> Later that night she asked to see her husband. He came and embraced
> her and now seemed genuinely moved but she sent him away, saying that
> his presence disturbed her and that she wished only to think of God. Soon

after midnight Bossuet arrived and it was he who comforted her and, as far as possible, eased her passage into the next world.

. . . she responded to him clearly, as though she were not ill, all the time holding the crucifix to her lips. Only death made her abandon it. Her strength ebbed and she let it fall. Her speech faded at almost the same instant that life itself fled. Her agony lasted but a moment and, after two or three convulsive movements of her mouth, she died at half past two in the morning and nine hours after her final affliction had begun.[50]

Henrietta, duchesse d'Orléans, had just passed her twenty-sixth birthday.

Charles was distraught. As Burnet observed, 'few things ever went near his heart' but Henrietta's death afflicted him even more than his brother Henry's almost a decade before. He shut himself up in his bedchamber to grieve in solitude and did not emerge for several days. The depth of his feelings surprised many at court but the king recognised the truth of little Minette's words that he had lost someone who loved him deeply and had dedicated herself to his welfare.

The messenger who brought the ambassador's report on the events at Saint-Cloud and who travelled non-stop to break the sad news in person was Sir Thomas Armstrong, a royal servant high in the king's favour whose fortunes were destined to change tragically. Throughout the exile Armstrong had been one of the many royalists who suffered much in person and fortune for the Stuarts. He had travelled back and forth carrying intelligence and cash for Charles and been thrice imprisoned. At the Restoration he had been knighted by a grateful sovereign and given a captaincy in the king's guards. Yet, some time in the 1670s he was deprived of his offices, became a close supporter of the Duke of Monmouth (seen by many as a Protestant rival to the Duke of York as heir to the throne), was involved in intrigues against the king and his brother and suffered a traitor's death after a travesty of a trial during which Charles insisted, with breathtaking dishonesty, that years before Armstrong had attempted to assassinate him on Cromwell's orders.

We can only speculate about what turned a devoted subject against the king and what caused Charles' trust in Armstrong to turn to bitter hatred. However, a few facts may point us in the right direction and certainly help us to understand the thickening clouds of disaffection and contempt which gathered round Charles in the second half of his reign. Thomas was born in 1624, in the Netherlands. His father was a serving officer in the army sent over by James I to fight for his Protestant son-in-law, the Elector Palatine, against Catholic forces. His mother may have been Dutch. Armstrong grew up with profound anti-Catholic convictions. On Henrietta's death he waited upon the ambassador, Ralph Montagu, and discussed with him the latest distressing events. Montagu is unlikely to have revealed to Armstrong the news he had recently received from

Madame (and of which he strongly disapproved) of the secret Anglo-French agreement to wage war on the Dutch but he certainly shared his conviction that the king's sister had been murdered. On leaving Paris, Armstrong only broke his urgent journey to stop briefly at Saint-Cloud in order to gaze for a last time upon Madame, whose demise had much affected him. Arrived at Whitehall, did he add his own accusations of French perfidy to the official report from the ambassador? In the next few emotionally charged days he must have watched for the king's reaction and been disappointed – perhaps even disgusted – by it.

All manner of rumours were soon circulating in both Paris and London about the death of the Stuart princess. Orléans' enemies suggested that he had smeared the rim of his wife's cup with a toxic potion sent him for the purpose by the chevalier de Lorraine. They drew attention to the fact that, in recent weeks, Monsieur had been heard prophesying Henrietta's imminent demise. All this was very alarming for Louis – and Charles. It threatened the treaty they had spent so much time concluding, and, therefore, all their foreign ambitions. Louis wrote immediately to offer Charles his condolences and to assure him that the most thorough investigation into his sister's death would be set in motion and that if poison was as much as suspected no effort would be spared to track down and punish the perpetrator. He ordered a thorough post-mortem and this was carried out by several leading physicians in a specially prepared auditorium where more than a hundred interested (or just morbid) spectators could be accommodated. The verdict was that death was due to a choleric disorder. (Modern medical analysis based on the available evidence has suggested that Minette died of peritonitis following the perforation of an ulcer.) Inevitably, not everyone believed the official line and Montagu was among those who suspected a cover-up. Charles, however, declared himself fully satisfied with the report brought to him from Paris and assured Louis that the tragedy had not impaired their friendship. Those close to him noticed that he seemed much more concerned about recovering the letters he had written to Henrietta before they could fall into the hands of her un-grief-stricken widower. As for Armstrong, Charles ordered him not to mention his suspicions to anyone. To someone already disposed to Francophobia and anti-Catholicism such a 'weak' and cynical response can have done little to undergird respect for the king. A few years later Montagu was openly contemptuous of Charles, a circumstance Barbara Villiers tried to use to her advantage (see below, p. 302). He and Armstrong both committed themselves to the cause of the Protestant Duke of Monmouth.

In the short term, all the frenzied clandestine diplomacy, the hard bargaining and the deception of ministers and diplomats – everything that had helped to shorten Minette's life – produced for Charles nothing but fresh humiliations. The war which was confidently expected to bring the conspirator-kings swift and glorious triumph began in March 1672. Less than two years later Charles was obliged to sue for an ignominious peace. Louis had made some territorial gains but the Dutch had protected Amsterdam by opening the sluices and flooding the surrounding land. Neighbouring states, alarmed at France's spreading boundaries, had joined in the war and Charles' critics could, with some justification, claim that he had been dragged into an expensive conflict merely to further the aggrandisement of the Bourbon monarchy. Meanwhile at sea the only major engagement had been the battle of Southwold Bay, technically a draw but in effect a Dutch victory since it prevented the allies gaining control of the Narrow Seas and demonstrated that the two navies could not work together. Another unforeseen result was the emergence of Charles' nephew, William of Orange, as the saviour of his beleaguered nation and a formidable player in the European political game. The young man to whom Charles had always behaved as a patronising uncle became his country's military leader and was voted hereditary stadtholder.

At home matters went just as badly. As a first step – or, at least, a perceived first step – towards the revelation of his conversion Charles issued a Declaration of Indulgence which lifted all penal laws against Catholics and Nonconformists. This coincided with the opening of hostilities and lasted much less time than the conflict. When there was no quick victory and, therefore, no spoils of war to offset the cost of military action the king had to call parliament. The heir to the throne had, by now, openly declared his conversion and anti-popery was stronger than ever. It was obvious to the government and their supporters that the staunch Anglican majority in both houses would demand the rescinding of the declaration. In the event they went further: they passed a Test Act which provided that every person holding office in government or the armed forces was to take an oath to the king as head of the Church in England, to receive Holy Communion according to the Church of England rite, and specifically to abjure the doctrine of transubstantiation. If Charles had ever toyed with the idea of offering his allegiance to Rome this decisive action by the national assembly banished it from his mind for ever. In a later session of parliament in 1675 he affirmed 'hand on heart' his commitment to the national Church, from which, as he promised, 'I will never depart'.

Even as he spoke the words the secret Treaty of Dover was still in force, committing him to a diametrically opposed course of action and Louis still intended to hold him to his obligation. Charles might have been forced to make peace with the Dutch but the French king knew that, behind the façade of international diplomacy, his brother monarch was eager to maintain the amity between them. Unfortunately they had lost their private go-between. However, a replacement for Minette was not long in appearing. The death of the duchesse d'Orléans put little Louise de Keroualle out of a job. Charles and Louis managed to find her fresh employment.

CHAPTER 11

A Changeling King

A colony of French possess the court . . .
I' the sacred ear tyrannic arts they croak,
Pervert his mind, his good intentions choke,
Tell him of golden Indies, fairy lands,
Leviathans and absolute commands.
Thus, fairy-like, the king they steal away
And in his place a Louis changeling lay.[51]

Thus wrote the satirist John Ayloffe, whose utter contempt for the
Frenchified tone of Charles' court and politics led him later into treason
and a traitor's death. The arrival of Louise de Keroualle at Whitehall
marked a change in the household and government of the British king, or
perhaps it would be better to say that it accelerated a change that was
already under way. For pictorial evidence of this we may compare the
portraits of fashionable beauties before and after 1670. The voluptuous
languor of Barbara Villiers, who set the mode in the early days of the
reign, gives place to a new look in the 1670s. Masses of curls replace loose
hair and ringlets; heads no longer rest wearily on hands; eyes are alert,
intelligent, questioning instead of heavy-lidded and bed-ready; more use
is made of allegorical props and backgrounds. Paris had come to London
in the person of the king's new woman. A decade before, Pepys had
disapproved of Princess Henrietta's coiffure – 'her dressing of herself with
her hair frizzed short up to her ears, did make her seem so much the less to
me'[52] – but now all ladies of the *haut monde* rushed to embrace the
hairstyle and dress that the king obviously found so appealing.

Louise was to have an influence which went far beyond the world of
fashion and that makes it important to understand the circumstances which
brought her to the Stuart court in the first place. The jewel box story has
all the appearance of a popular, romantic myth created or embroidered
after the event to explain Louise's appearance as a result of the king's
readiness to become infatuated with every pretty woman who came within
his ken. It is part of the killjoy historian's lot to cast doubt on such simple
and attractive explanations of momentous events. Louise was the elder

270

daughter of Guillaume de Penancoet, comte de Keroualle, whose estates were in the region of Brest. He had court connections, and Sir Richard Browne, who was English resident in Paris from 1641 to 1660, knew the family well and thought highly of them. Browne's son-in-law, John Evelyn, who met Louise's parents in 1675, was also impressed: 'He seemed a soldierly person and a good fellow, as the Bretons generally are. His lady had been very handsome and seems a shrewd, understanding woman.'[53] For the Keroualles it was an important achievement getting their girl placed in the Orléans household and this was a major step towards securing for her a wealthy marriage or, possibly, the position of mistress to some prince of the blood. The likelihood is that Louise had had affairs before her entry into English history and her name was linked by gossips with various noble scions.

She was back in England within three months of her mistress's death but exactly who instigated the move is not altogether clear. Burnet attributed the whole scheme to Buckingham who had noticed Charles' interest in the woman and thought that he could use her in the same way that he had tried to use La Belle Stuart – to displace Lady Castlemaine. According to this version, the duke suggested to Charles that it would be a kindness to take care of some of Henrietta's servants. He then went to Louis and convinced him that 'he could never reckon himself sure of the king but by giving him a mistress that should be true to his interests'.[54] The same story was going the rounds of the diplomatic corps in Paris. The Duke of Savoy's ambassador reported, 'it is thought that the plan is to make her mistress to the King of Great Britain. [Buckingham] would like to dethrone Lady Castlemaine, who is his enemy and his most Christian majesty would not be sorry to see the position filled by one of his subjects, for it is said the ladies have great influence over the mind of the King of England.'[55] It was even being said that Buckingham still had ambitions to replace Queen Catherine and had selected Louise for this honour.

There is no doubt that the duke was the executive agent in this business but that need not mean that he was its originator. When he was sent over to France in the wake of Henrietta's death it was to negotiate a 'bogus' treaty with Louis. As the chief minister not trusted with the secret Treaty of Dover he was made to go through the charade of reaching an Anglo-French accord which, with the exception of the religious clause, was identical to the one already concluded. The king, his Catholic ministers and Louis were all highly amused to have Buckingham supposedly engaged in hard bargaining with his French counterpart over a treaty whose details had already been agreed. May it not be that he was also duped into believing that he had 'discovered' Louise de Keroualle and that it had already been arranged that she was to develop further that close relationship between the two kings begun by Minette? Some contemporaries believed that it was Henrietta's dying wish that Charles should invite Louise to join his household and that theory certainly fits better with the continuity of close relations between the courts in London and Paris. It also disposes of the problem presented by the ill-feeling between Louise and Buckingham. Had the lady been beholden to the duke as her sponsor she might have been expected to use her influence in his interests. As it was, she loathed him and the enmity was heartily reciprocated. It may even be that the duke went cold on the matchmaking mission before it was concluded. Having been appointed to convey Louise across the Channel, he abandoned her at Dieppe and caught the first available ship to England by himself. Louise was left stranded until Ralph Montagu sent word to London and Arlington despatched a barge to collect her.

Another possible explanation is that the stratagem originated entirely in the Louvre and that Louise was designated as the Trojan horse which would ensure that Charles kept the French alliance at the centre of his political thinking. Louis knew that his brother monarch was a slippery customer who needed closer supervision than his diplomats or pensioned English officials could provide. Lady Castlemaine had very limited value. She helped Louis' ambassadors only when it was in her own interests to do so and, in any case, her long reign seemed to be coming to an end. The glaringly obvious solution, if it could be managed, would be to replace the countess with someone whose loyalty to the French Crown was not in question. When, in the days immediately following her return, Henrietta had her regular meetings with Louis, when they discussed in great detail the situation in England, would they not have considered the placing of a close confidante at Whitehall who could report directly to Madame? And after Madame's sudden and unexpected death would it not have seemed sensible to stick, in essence, to the same plan?

In support of this interpretation we have Charles' own conduct. He certainly did not behave as though Mlle de Keroualle was the new mistress he had been excitedly expecting for several weeks. Louise's arrival as a new maid of honour for the queen made an immediate impact. When Evelyn saw her for the first time on 4 November she was already 'that famed beauty', though he was immune to her charms, her 'childish simple and baby face' not appealing to him.[56] Others were not so impervious and Louise was turning many heads about the court. However, the king was not, as yet, pursuing her very ardently. Although he often spent time with the young beauty, several months passed before eager eyes observed him going to her room. Colbert, the French ambassador, was disappointed that she was being slow in flaunting her charms and delighted when he was able to report to his master, in September 1671, that the lady had been overcome with an attack of nausea at an embassy function. The war minister, Louvois, was less inclined to clutch at straws and urged Colbert to be cautious in his interpretation of Louise's indisposition. King Louis, he remarked in his reply, was very surprised at the news because 'her conduct while she was here and since she has been in England gave no grounds for belief that such good fortune would befall her so soon'. The ambassador was charged to keep an even closer eye on the relationship between Charles and Louise.[57] The minister was right to be sceptical; Mlle de Keroualle was not pregnant. And one very good reason for that was that Charles was a very mediocre lover. If women did not thrust themselves into his arms or were not thrust there by one of his pimps he found it difficult to make the running by himself.

And Louise, for her part, was not a 'pushover'. She was a proud young woman with a great deal of self-respect. Belonging as she did to a family that had come down in the world it is not surprising that one of the commonest criticisms of her alluded to her haughtiness. She was conscious of her noble lineage and often referred to her kinship with several of the noble houses of France. She also made the grand assumption that she represented the superior culture of a magnificent superpower. It was not only in elegance that Paris led the world. In 1667 a notorious French publication had calmly asserted Louis' right to large swathes of European territory, 'the patrimony and former heritage of French princes . . . possessed by Charlemagne as King of France'. Louis' court claimed to represent the summit of Christian civilisation, and who, visiting the incomparable spectacle of Versailles, still a-building with total disregard for cost, could doubt that this was so?

And lovemaking, as Louise had become familiar with it, was as intricate and elaborate an art form as the designing of the great palace's parterres and watercourses or its glittering mirrored salons.

> The courtier, male and female, dresses up everything, from their bodies to their ways of speech, and sexuality is no exception; for them love-making is a ritual with tactical moves, progressive phases, fulfilment, and retreat. This explains why one of La Rochefoucauld's maxims asserts that nobody would fall in love if one hadn't heard about it. Obviously, the sexual impulse as such needs no previous notice to make its demands; its plain urge marks its distinction from love, which means whatever a period may fancy to embellish lust.[58]

The mores of the English court must have come as something of a shock to this creature raised in the rarefied atmosphere of Bourbon palaces and is enough in itself to explain the slow pace of her surrender to King Charles.

Yet there was another consideration which weighed with her and that was her desire for an 'honourable estate'. We need not dismiss this as calculating ambition. Louise understood from her years in French court circles that there were two respectable titles which could be held by the king's women: 'wife' and '*maîtresse en titre*'. In 1670 both positions were occupied. There can be little doubt that she would have preferred to have stepped into Catherine's shoes. In 1673, when the queen fell ill again, Dr Frazier diagnosed (incorrectly, as it turned out) consumption. Colbert reported home in some disgust that Mlle de Keroualle was indelicate enough to go about the court discussing, from morn till night, Catherine's 'mortal' affliction, the wish, presumably, being father to the thought.

There was still the possibility that Charles might find another way of untying his marriage. Divorce was once again in the air. Only a few months earlier Charles had taken a very close personal interest in the passage through parliament of a mould-breaking piece of legislation. John Manners, Baron Roos, brought a private bill into the Lords to enable him to remarry. He had earlier obtained a separation through the ecclesiastical courts but now, having unexpectedly become heir to the Earldom of Rutland, he wanted to be able to sire a legitimate heir. Since all legal opinion up to this point was based on belief in the indissolubility of marriage, the 1670 debate raised fundamental issues and took on the nature of a *cause célèbre*. Charles, for the first time, became a regular attender of their lordships' chamber and let it be known that he was on Roos' side. This clearly had an influence on the outcome and the bill scraped through. This not only opened the way for privileged people to use parliament to escape from unwanted marriages, it also suggested a possible means of providing a legitimate heir to the throne. In 1669 Queen Catherine had suffered what was probably her second miscarriage. Earlier pregnancy hopes had always been dashed and now it became clear that she would never conceive again. Speculation was rife that Charles might find a way to take a new, fertile bride and several advisers, indeed, urged him to do so.

Several courses of action were proposed, some more seriously than others. One was that Catherine might be prevailed upon to retire to a convent. Devout as she was, she had by now become so accustomed to the gaiety of her husband's court that the prospect of cloistered seclusion had no appeal for her. A much wilder scheme, suggested, apparently, by Buckingham, was that her majesty might simply be abducted and shipped off incognito to one of the Indies plantations where she would live a comfortable life and never be heard of again, it being given out that she had deserted her husband. Whether or not the plan was put forward as a joke, Charles, to his credit, was horrified by it. He said that it would be monstrous for a woman to be so ill used simply because she was his wife and barren. Some of the queen's attendants seem to have taken the threat of kidnap seriously. Her personal security was tightened and she was advised not to go abroad without a sizeable escort. With such ideas and rumours in circulation, the appearance of another pretty woman in the king's life encouraged people to put two and two together and make at least five.

Speculation would have added to Louise's uncertainty. Should she wait until the queen's fate had been decided or accept that Charles would never be able to bring himself to cast his wife aside unkindly? The possibility of following Lady Castlemaine's career path had no attractions for her. The model she had in her mind for royal mistress was Françoise-Athénaïs, Marquise de Montespan, the bewitching woman (some believed literally so, for the story was widely believed that she had come by her good fortune as the result of a compact with the devil) who had been Louis XIV's lover for three years and already borne him two children. Mme de Montespan's position at court was more conventional than that of Lady Castlemaine in England. She had no need to set herself up in ostentatious rivalry to the queen. The two ladies frequently appeared together on state occasions and habitually shared the same coach. To be sure, brave clergy thundered against this royal bigamy but the Sun King regarded it as just one expression of his superiority over ordinary mortals. And Louis' mistress possessed a dignity which Barbara Villiers notoriously lacked. She did not gleefully tumble into bed with courtiers, actors and servants. If Louise allowed herself to be groomed for Charles II's mistress she took time to know exactly what it was she was letting herself in for.

Of course, she was not entirely in charge of her own destiny. As the stalking horse of the pro-French faction she was taken through her paces not only by Colbert but also by Arlington. As the months slipped past and Louis was growing impatient to embroil England in war with the Dutch, her mentors left her in no doubt that if she could not help them to achieve their designs they would find someone who could. Royal mistresses were now attaining greater political significance. Buckingham relied principally on Nell Gwynn to enhance his influence with the king and this obliged Arlington to involve Louise de Keroualle in his own fortunes. He made his position quite clear to Colbert in the autumn of 1671:

> although his majesty is not disposed to communicate his affairs to women, nevertheless, as they can on occasion injure those whom they hate and in that way ruin much business, it was better for all good servants of the king that his attraction is to her whose humour is not mischievous and who is a lady, rather than to comediennes and the like on whom no honest man can rely, by whose means the Duke of Buckingham was always trying to entice the king in order to draw him away from all his court and monopolise him . . .[59]

The tensions and contradictions at the heart of Charles' government made intrigue inevitable. There was an unresolved and unresolvable conflict between royal and parliamentary power. The king was set on a foreign policy course that was out of sympathy with majority feeling in the country. He had secrets from his ministers and he encouraged their rivalries. Religious rifts widened as a vengeful royalist-Anglican parliamentary majority resisted every attempt to achieve a measure of toleration. Agents from abroad bribed ministers, MPs and courtiers to act in their interest. It was not only France who bought influence; William of Orange was just as determined to activate Protestant and anti-French sentiment. Since the fall of Clarendon and the old guard, government had, ostensibly, been in the hands of the so-called Cabal – Clifford, Arlington, Buckingham, Ashley and Lauderdale – but they were no 'cabinet'. They were simply those members of the council whom Charles consulted most frequently and, as we have seen, they were more likely to behave as individuals, shifting in and out of alliances and factions, than to act in concert. But the political instability of the 1660s was as nothing compared with that of the years to come – years that would inevitably involve everyone – man or woman – who had influence with the king.

It was Arlington who brought about the installation of his protégée, Louise de Keroualle, as *maîtresse en titre*. The setting might have been designed specifically for the purpose. In 1666 the earl had bought the Euston estate just south of Thetford, on the Norfolk–Suffolk border, and here he set about building a magnificent mansion in the latest – French – style. The reason for choosing the site was simple. Twice a year, in spring and autumn, king and court went to Newmarket for the racing, and Newmarket was only about twenty-five miles from Euston. Here Arlington could entertain his sovereign in style, for, as John Evelyn observed, his lordship was 'given to no expensive vice but building and to have all things rich, polite and princely'.[60] The house was completed in 1670 and the following year its proud owner was ready to receive his master there. During the October race meeting several important guests, including Mlle de Keroualle and, fortunately for us, Evelyn, stayed at Euston. The king spent much of the time at Newmarket with Nell, now heavily pregnant with his second child, but went to Euston

> almost every second day with the duke, who commonly returned again to Newmarket. But the king lay often here . . . It was universally reported that the fair lady was bedded one of these nights and the stocking flung, after the manner of a married bride. I acknowledge she was for the most part in her undress all day and that there was fondness and toying with that young wanton . . .[61]

Going about *déshabillé* was a sign of social superiority and, together with the mock marriage, indicated, to Louise at least, that she was *officially* the king's number two woman. Her position was enhanced when it soon became obvious that she was pregnant. Nine months after their first sexual encounter Louise presented the king with yet another bastard son. Queen Catherine accepted the situation with good grace.

Indeed, there was even some suggestion that she had encouraged Louise to submit to Charles before the Newmarket charade. It probably made him easier to live with; Charles' usual good humour was, doubtless, less in evidence when he was being balked of his prey and Catherine found the Frenchwoman's company more endurable than Lady Castlemaine's. The queen and the new mistress actually got on well together, partly because Louise was genuinely devout and also because she did not try to outshine her majesty. The new *ménage à trois* at the heart of national life was very much *à la façon française*, according to which each woman understood her role and did not try to upstage the other. Louise may have been a very proud woman but she brought a certain dignity to the royal household which was greatly at variance with the vulgar ostentation of Barbara Villiers. She threw her own, extremely lavish, parties but at court occasions she made no attempt to outshine the queen, unlike Lady Castlemaine, who attended one ball festooned with £40,000 worth of jewellery and had recently taken to going about in a carriage with no fewer than eight horses.

Catherine had by now become the perfect consort – perfect, that is, for a king like Charles. At state occasions she behaved with a fitting dignity. With her husband she received ambassadors, hosted dinners and balls, presided over Garter ceremonies and appeared on all occasions where her presence was expected, except religious worship, which she performed quietly with her own household. It has sometimes been suggested that Charles treated his wife very badly but this is to judge by the standards of a different age. In fact, he held Catherine in high regard and behaved towards her with unfailing courtesy. If we leave aside Charles' numerous amours, we can say that he cared for Catherine more than many aristocratic husbands of the time cared for their wives. She was simply one of his women and while she could not give him what his more exciting bedfellows gave, she occupied a place in his life that none of them could occupy. He often discussed important matters with her, as when he invited Evelyn into the queen's bedchamber and together all three of them pored over designs for the rebuilding of London after the fire. The diarist had a less happy interview with Catherine in March 1671 and formed a poor opinion of her taste. Evelyn had discovered an exceptionally talented young Anglo-Dutch wood-carver and was eager to commend him to their majesties. The artist had carved in relief an elaborate crucifix based upon a painting by Tintoretto comprising over a hundred figures and Evelyn arranged for Charles to see it. The king

> was astonished at the curiosity of it and, having considered it a long time ... he commanded it should be immediately carried to the queen's side to show her majesty ...

Servants, accordingly, manhandled the heavy and awkward piece of sculpture along passages and up stairways and came at last to Catherine's bedchamber. There, husband and wife admired the piece together and Gibbon was, doubtless, congratulating himself on the prospect of an important sale.

> ... but when his majesty was gone, a French peddling woman, one Mme de Bordes [one of the queen's dressers] that used to bring petticoats, and fans, and baubles out of France to the ladies, began to find faults with several things in the work, which she understood no more than an ass or a monkey . . .

The irritated Evelyn had the piece carried away before it could be made to suffer any more indignities, 'finding the queen so much governed by an ignorant French woman'. Thus, 'this incomparable artist had the labour only for his pains'.[62] Fortunately 'this incomparable artist' did not have to wait long for recognition. Grinling Gibbons became the most famous craftsman in wood of that, or any other, age and was patronised by the king and many of the fashionable élite. The fact that the queen was prepared to bow to the opinion of a junior member of her suite indicates not only Catherine's lack of confidence in things aesthetic, but also the influence – one might almost say the tyranny – of French taste.

Catherine understood her role as 'mother' of the court. She left intrigue to the mistresses and no ambassadors pestered her to exercise influence over her husband. In fact, she physically distanced herself from her husband's gamesome friends. Her own chapel was at St James's Palace and, when in residence at Whitehall, she daily resorted thither with her suite to hear mass and to celebrate the multitudinous Catholic festivals. Most of her household officials had their quarters at Somerset House, so that she had to spend much of her time there and, as the 1670s wore on, this became increasingly her home. She retained her rooms in Whitehall and never failed to accompany her husband to Newmarket, Windsor and other progress destinations but, in effect, she left Louise de Kerouaille to hold sway over the gay life of Whitehall.

By no means did this involve abdication of her position at important social and diplomatic functions, such as the reception and entertainment of her new sister-in-law. Anne, Duchess of York, died in 1671 and James, after a leisurely fashion, began casting around for a replacement. He was determined to have a Catholic princess and the choice eventually narrowed down to the fifteen-year-old Mary of Modena of the House of Este. The girl had several advantages in the duke's eyes. She was young and reputedly beautiful – excellent stock from which to breed a line of kings. She was devout and had hoped to be allowed to retire into a nunnery. It was the pope who had personally urged her to 'sacrifice' herself for the reconversion of England and Scotland. Mary was also the choice of Louis XIV, who saw her as forging yet another link between himself and Charles (Modena was a client state of France and Mary's mother was a cousin of the late Cardinal Mazarin) and promised a dowry of 400,000 crowns. Supremely indifferent to public opinion, James scrambled the marriage through in September 1673 while parliament lay prorogued and his bride arrived in November. (One of the first actions of the reconvened assembly in October was to call for the proxy marriage to be declared void.) For the final stage of her journey Mary was brought by night from Gravesend to Whitehall stairs shielded from prying eyes by darkness and riverine mist.

There was one person who knew what it was like to leave friends and family and come as a Stuart wife to a hostile, heretic country. Catherine had little cause to love the woman who would probably achieve what she had found impossible, producing an heir to the throne, but she was sympathetic to little Mary and took charge sensitively of her welcome over the ensuing weeks. As part of the court's Christmas festivities she brought into the country troupes of Italian actors and musicians and introduced to (largely unreceptive) English audiences both Italian opera and the *commedia dell'arte*, including the celeberated Tiberio Fiorillo, interpreter of the role of Scaramouche. Catherine was mindful, also, of the interests of the stepdaughters of the new Duchess of York and specially commissioned *Calisto, or The Chaste Nymph*, with parts written for young Mary and Anne. This was nothing less than an attempt to revive the court masque, which had long since fallen out of fashion. Catherine employed one of the minor, but popular dramatists of the day, John Crowne, and gave him precise instructions. The piece was to be written for seven ladies of whom only two were to appear in men's attire and it was to be a refined entertainment with no hint of bawdry. In this nostalgic harking back to the 1630s the queen was deliberately taking on what she considered the debased taste of her husband's court and showing that the stage could be used for propagating wholesome morals and elevated ideals.

Though Catherine held aloof from the cruder humour of the court wits and the loutish behaviour of the Whitehall rowdies, she was no dowdy, prudish matron. She continued to set a tone of gaiety and even spontaneity. In the late 1660s masquerading had become all the fashion. The royals and their intimates would go about the town in plain hackney chairs, heavily disguised, and call unannounced on unsuspecting friends who would not know who they were obliged to entertain. On one occasion Catherine's disguise was so good that her chairman went off without her and she had to make her way back to the palace in a hired coach or, as some versions of the story had it, in a cart. We have seen the entertainments she arranged at Tunbridge Wells and a similar holiday atmosphere pervaded the regular excursions to Newmarket. In October 1670 the queen decided that it would be rather fun to go to a country fair at Audley End, posing as 'ordinary people'. She and the Duchesses of Buckingham and Richmond with only three gentlemen for escort dressed up in what they thought to be suitably rustic attire and set out riding carthorses. The adventure did not turn out as they had planned.

They had all so overdone it in their disguise and looked so much more like antiques than country folk that, as soon as they came to the fair, the people began to go after them . . . the queen going to a booth to buy a pair of yellow stockings 'for her sweetheart' and Sir Bernard [Gascoign] asking for a pair of gloves stitched with blue 'for his sweetheart', they were soon by their gibberish found to be strangers, which drew a bigger flock about them.

When the queen was recognised, the party beat an undignified retreat to their horses but were still followed a long distance by a crowd eager 'to get as much gape as they could'. 'Thus,' a local chronicler reported, 'was a merry frolic turned into a penance.'[63]

It was not the relationship between Louise and the queen which excited interest among court commentators. What aroused critics of the regime to anxiety, anger and contempt were the antics of the triumvirate of the king's mistresses. For Louise soon discovered, as Catherine and Barbara had discovered before her, that Charles had no concept of fidelity. His latest conquest might think of herself as *maîtresse en titre* and have a clear idea of what she understood that title to imply but Charles played to a different set of rules – ones of his own devising. He continued to have one-night stands with creatures smuggled up the privy stairs by Chiffinch but, publicly and more importantly, he maintained his liaisons with Barbara and Nell. This domestic relationship of the King of England with three bickering, bitchy rival whores was a constant source of comment, ranging from wicked satire to angry denunciation.

Evelyn described a scene which, two centuries later, caught the fancy of a genre painter (Plate 3). As he was walking with the king through St James's Park, his companion became suddenly distracted by a familiar figure leaning over her garden wall: 'I both saw and heard a very familiar discourse between [the king] and Mrs Nellie, as they called an impudent comedienne, she looking out of her garden on a terrace at the top of the wall and [he] standing on the green walk under it. I was heartily sorry at this scene. Thence the king walked to the Duchess of Cleveland's [Barbara's new title – see p. 283], another lady of pleasure and curse of our nation.'[64]

John Ayloffe was much more biting. In 'Britannia and Rawleigh' he depicted Britannia, the spirit of the nation, being roundly abused by her enemies:

> . . . a confused murmur rose
> Of French, Scots, Irish (all my mortal foes).
> Some English, too, disguised (Oh shame) I spied,
> Led up by the wise son-in-law of Hyde [the Duke of York].
> With fury drunk, like bacchanals they roar,
> 'Down with that common Magna Charta whore!'
> With joint consent on helpless me they flew,
> And from my Charles to a base goal me drew,
> My reverend head exposed to scorn and shame,
> To boys, bawds, whores and made a public game.
> Frequent addresses to my Charles I send
> And to his care did my sad state commend.
> But his fair soul, transformed by that French dame,
> Had lost all sense of honour, justice, fame.
> Like a tame spinster in 's seraglio sits,
> Besieged by 's whores, buffoons and bastard chits.

The most extraordinary image in that diatribe is 'a tame spinster'. Charles is not portrayed in the harem as a macho sultan, surrounded by obedient concubines, ready to do his bidding. Rather he has become 'womanised' by feminine company. He is a weak crone whose will and energy have been sapped; one who,

> Lulled in security, rolling in lust
> Resigns his crown to angel Carwell's trust.[65]

('Carwell' was the common way that 'Keroualle' was rendered into English by people who could not cope or did not choose to cope with the French pronunciation.) The king's sexual activity was often seen, not as evidence of masculine vigour, but as submission to lust and the provokers of that lust. Indeed, in bawdy balladry his very potency was not infrequently called in question:

> This you'd believe, had I but time to tell ye,
> The pain it costs to poor laborious Nelly,
> While she employs hands, fingers, lips and thighs
> E'er she can raise the member she enjoys.[66]

In the eyes of such critics Charles has become emasculated by over-indulgence in what Ormonde had called years before, 'effeminate conversation'. One adjective often used to describe him was 'easy'. It was a word with many shades of meaning. An easy person was relaxed and approachable but he might also be fond of ease and averse to taking pains. Then again, he could be a pathetic creature, credulous, compliant and easily manipulated or dominated. The full range of the word was applied at various times to the king and it was in his love of female company that many observers detected both the symptom and the cause of his character disease.

Nor was it only in the coffee-houses and gossip alleys of the capital that the king's subjects spoke of him with scorn as a weakling under the thumb of his womenfolk. There is a pleasant story of Louise being waylaid in her coach near Bagshot by Old Mobb, a notorious highwayman. Glowering from the window at the blackguard who was waving a pistol at her, she tried to bluff it out. 'Do you know who I am?' she demanded haughtily. 'Yes, Madam,' the bandit replied. 'I know you to be the greatest whore in the kingdom and that you are maintained at the public charge . . . and that the king himself is your slave. But . . . a gentleman collector is a greater man upon the road and much more absolute than his majesty is at court. You may say now, Madam, that a single highwayman has exercised his authority where Charles the Second of England has often begged a favour and thought himself fortunate to obtain it at the expense of his treasure.'[67]

For four years the king divided most of his attention between his wife and his three mistresses. Only very gradually did Louise raise her profile at Whitehall. She would not compete with the queen and she disdained to be seen in open competition with Barbara Villiers. She concentrated on becoming the fashion guru of the age, the arbiter of style. Her allotted quarters at the end of the Stone Gallery, between the queen's apartments and the privy garden, were much closer to the heart of the palace than Lady Castlemaine's accommodation. In the 1670s there was a considerable amount of rebuilding at Whitehall and Louise seems to have profited from each rearrangement. Eventually, she occupied some forty rooms, all furnished and furbished by the king at considerable expense. She delighted to show off her exquisitely appointed chambers to visitors. Even Evelyn allowed himself to be impressed with their luxurious appurtenances, all in the latest fashion, such as large Gobelins tapestries representing Louis XIV's principal residences, ebulliently lacquered cabinets and screens displaying the current fascination with orientalia, sconces and candelabra of massy silver and some of the finest paintings from the royal collection. But he could not forbear to draw a moral: 'Lord, what contentment can there be in the riches and splendour of this world, purchased with vice and dishonour?'[68]

Yet, for all Louise de Keroualle's emerging eminence at court, beyond the walls of Whitehall Barbara Villiers continued to dominate the social scene. She was the leading celebrity of the day; the wicked but fascinating woman who never failed to draw a crowd whenever she ventured forth in her magnificent equipage and it was her liaisons and extravagant behaviour that attracted the attention of London gossips. She certainly gave them plenty to chatter about. But fascinated as people were, their assessment of Lady Castlemaine was increasingly hostile. It was in the aftermath of the Bawdy House Riots and the attendant canards and lampoons that Charles came to appreciate just how much of a PR liability Lady Castlemaine was. Somehow she had to be distanced from the day-to-day life of the palace. There was, of course, no chance that she would go quietly. She could only be induced to accept a change in her status by bribes – massive bribes. The extent of the pay-off she received over the next four years is truly breathtaking. In 1668 Charles borrowed £8,000 from his banker to acquire Berkshire House, recently vacated by Clarendon, and made a present of it to his mistress. This fine mansion close by St James's Palace had extensive grounds running northwards to Piccadilly. Whether it would have been in itself a sufficient inducement for Barbara to take the hint and give up her palace apartments we cannot know but the opportunity to rub Hyde's nose publicly in his defeat could not be resisted. She moved into her attractive new residence straight away but did not stay there for long. Such a prime site in the heart of the fashionable part of town offered excellent opportunities for speculative building. Within two years she demolished the mansion, sold off what she could for construction materials, divided part of the grounds into individual plots, and with some of the profit built for herself a new abode, Cleveland House.

The name drew constant attention to the new title she acquired in 1670. On 3 August, when the king had barely recovered from the death of Henrietta, and doubtless after much badgering, he raised Barbara to the dignities of Duchess of Cleveland, Countess of Southampton and Baroness Nonsuch. To support her new style he gave her, in addition to various cash grants, the palace and park of Nonsuch in Surrey. This Renaissance extravaganza set amidst elaborate groves, fountains, walks and bowers, and surrounded by 2,000 acres of parkland, had been begun (but never finished) by Henry VIII regardless of cost. Latterly it had belonged to Henrietta Maria. Now, following her death, it had reverted to the Crown. Barbara lost no time in asset-stripping her latest acquisition. The pleasure grounds and deer park were let out as farmland and everything from the building that could be sold was sold (for around £7,000). The remaining shell was left to the mercies of time. The duchess has often been condemned for this piece of 'vandalism', which smacks more of 1970s ruthless property speculation than of 1670s estate building, but, in truth, Nonsuch was doomed before Lady Cleveland got her rapacious hands on it. Loathed and threatened with demolition by Mary Tudor but loved by Elizabeth, it had had a chequered history. To the Stuarts it had been nothing but an antiquated white elephant and James had built himself a smaller lodge in the park for his hunting expeditions. His grandson had no use for it and was probably glad to be rid of it. It could have had a worse ultimate fate than being part of the pay-off of a superannuated mistress.

It would be tedious to trawl through all the booty Barbara accumulated over the years and impossible to come up with a definitive figure. Her biographer offers the following list, which is not inclusive of the steady flow of income from rents in Surrey, Cornwall, Gloucestershire, Huntingdonshire and Ireland, the sale of offices and douceurs from ambassadors and ministers:

Timber and Building materials from Nonsuch	£7,000
From the Customs	£10,000 p.a
From the excise on beer and ale	£10,000 p.a
From the Post Office	£4,700 p.a
From the Excise	£15,000 p.a
„ „ „	£7,000
From wine licences	£5,500 p.a
From Sir Henry Wood's estate	£40,000
„ „ „ „ „	£4,000[69]

Impressive it may be; adequate for the needs of this impulsive, obsessive creature it was not. Every penny she received trickled through her fingers like sand. Her two commanding vices were gambling and men. Most evenings found her at the tables and she was reputed to have lost as much as £20,000 at a sitting.

Her sexuality could never be curbed. What began as a net to ensnare wealthy lovers ended up entrapping her entirely. Lurid, gross and scandalous though many of the rhymes about her were, it was difficult for them to exaggerate her insatiable lasciviousness.

> The number can never be reckoned;
> She's fucked with great and small,
> From good King Charles the Second
> To honest Jacob Hall [a tightrope performer].[70]

In 1671 she added to the list an up-and-coming playwright who was also one of the handsomest men in London. William Wycherley, currently studying at the Inner Temple, had just scored a hit with his first play, *Love in a Wood*, which had introduced to the King's Theatre a new level of indelicacy. Barbara was taken with it and with its author and eager to discover whether the libidinous impulses he committed to paper were ones he surrendered to in real life. According to the oft-told tale, she called some suggestive remark to him as their carriages passed in the street and he responded by turning round and pursuing her to suggest they meet at the theatre that afternoon. Beyond this, the story of their relationship is obscured by salacious anecdotes: they share a fantasy relationship in which she steals to his lodgings disguised as a country maid, wearing a straw hat and wooden pattens. Early one morning the king, acting on information received, comes to a house in Pall Mall where the couple have spent the night. He passes Wycherley on the staircase and, going into the bedroom, discovers the duchess. He asks what she is doing there and she replies that she is at her Lenten devotions. To this Charles quickly responds, 'Ah, yes, I've just bumped into your confessor.'

Perhaps Wycherley was recalling Barbara's frenzied lovemaking in a scene from *The Plain Dealer*, in which the lusty Olivia, in her darkened chamber, thrusts herself upon Fidelia (masquerading as a man), her rival for the love of Captain Manly, who, unknown to her, is concealed in the gloom:

OLIVIA: Where are thy lips? Here, take the dumb and best welcomes – kisses and embraces. 'Tis not a time for idle words . . . Come, we are alone! Now the word is only satisfaction, and defend not thyself.

MANLY: How's this? Wuh! She makes love like a devil in a play, and in this darkness which conceals her angel's face, if I were apt to be afraid, I should think her a devil.
[*Fidelia avoids Olivia*]

OLIVIA: Nay, you are a coward. What, are you afraid of the fierceness of my love?

FIDELIA: Yes, Madam, lest its violence might presage its change and I must needs be afraid you would leave me quickly who could desert so brave a gentleman as Manly.

OLIVIA: Oh, name not his name, for in a time of stolen joys, as this is, the filthy name of husband were not a more allaying sound.[71]

What is beyond doubt is that Barbara's support helped to launch the dramatist's career. She was generous to him and it was thanks to her that he produced three other notable plays between 1672 and 1676. She provided him with an entrée to the court and to the world of aristocratic wits. Charles took to Wycherley and offered him a post as tutor to one of his sons but before he could assume his duties he became enamoured of a rich nobleman's widow. Had the rest of his life followed upon this fortunate beginning, he would have lived at ease and probably given the stage more proof of his talent. Sadly, ill health and debts subsequently overwhelmed him. By that time his doting patroness was no longer on hand to rescue him.

On 16 July 1672, two weeks before Louise's baby was born, the Duchess of Cleveland gave birth to her last child, a daughter christened Barbara. This time there could be no question of claiming royal paternity for the bastard. The father was the latest of the duchess's virile young bravos, a soldier by the name of John Churchill, better known to history by his later title of Duke of Marlborough. Churchill, nine years his mistress's junior, was already a dedicated soldier with battle honours to his credit and Barbara found it thrilling to be escorted by this brave, already well known, martial figure. He was the latest in her collection of celebrities, which included aristocrats, courtiers, an actor, a popular entertainer, a playwright and, of course, a king. However, in Churchill she seems to have met her match. This fearless soldier was not a whit in awe of her. Though personable and charming, he remained firmly in charge of their relationship. He came to her in wintertime, between campaigning seasons and he did not come fawning, pleading for favours. She had to wait for him. It was for her, perhaps, a novel experience. Churchill was mentally as well as physically strong; more of a man than most of her other lovers, including the king, and she was bowled over by him. He took from her whatever she had to give and offered little in return. But Barbara thrived on it. There was nothing she would not have done for her brave soldier. She showered him with gifts, including a cash payment of £5,000. Her other associates would have frittered away such a sum in a matter of days. The prudent Churchill invested it to purchase an annuity. It provided the basis for the immense fortune he would build up.

Barbara was also looking to the future. She had six children to provide for and she set about her task with her usual energy and lack of scruple. She was determined that her sons and daughters should not have to fend for themselves as she had had to do when little more than a child. The memory of her own early insecurity was still vivid; in all probability it haunted her. Barbara Villiers had inherited a famous name and little else. She would see to it that her offspring would become a formidable dynasty with titles, money to support them and assured places in society. Before her children reached puberty their futures were being planned. The five whom Charles acknowledged as his own (Henry was added to the list in 1672) all received peerages and the boys were in time elevated to the highest rank of nobility (here I give their ultimate titles). Henry, Duke of Grafton, was at the age of nine married to Arlington's only child, the five-year-old Isabella. George received the extinct title of Northumberland and his mother tried for years to have him married to Betty, the infant daughter of the last Percy duke and the richest heiress in England. At the age of twenty-one he selected his own bride – the daughter of a provincial poulterer. Anne was eleven when plans were set afoot to marry her to Thomas, Lord Dacre, created Earl of Sussex for the purpose and provided by the king with a dowry of £20,000. At the same time (1673) nine-year-old Charlotte was allocated Sir Edward Lee, who now became Earl of Lichfield and was similarly recompensed. Only little Barbara was unable to benefit from this gushing royal bounty. She bore the name of Fitzroy but, since she was manifestly not his daughter, Charles declined to provide for her. The Duchess of Cleveland lacked the resources to see the child set up in the same style as her siblings but she could undoubtedly have done better for her than the £1,000 she set aside for her youngest daughter. This money was used to place her in a French convent where she grew up as Sister Benedicta and eventually became Prioress of Pontoise. The holy regimen could not, however, totally eradicate the effect of Villiers genes; she bore an illegitimate child in 1691.

It was in the shameless intrigue surrounding the matrimonial negotiations for her eldest son, Charles, Duke of Southampton, that Barbara's skills and temper are seen in the clearest light. Sir Henry Wood, a lifelong Stuart servant and one-time treasurer to Henrietta Maria, had by a combination of manipulation and frugality amassed a considerable fortune. At the age of sixty-seven he sired his only child, a daughter called Mary, who became sole heiress to his extensive Suffolk estate. Lady Cleveland coveted the £4,000 annual income from the Wood lands, not just for her son at some future date, but for herself in the present. Thus, a marriage contract was drawn up on behalf of little Charles and Mary (aged eight and seven respectively). Its principal object was to tie the Lee fortune to the house of Villiers. Mary was pledged to marry either Charles or George Fitzroy at the age of sixteen, at which time the king would dower her with estates worth an extra £2,000 p.a. If Mary, at that time, rejected the arrangement £2,000 was to be paid to the disappointed suitor. Meanwhile, after her seventy-four-year-old father's death Mary was to be brought up by her own family. As an inducement Barbara pledged her influence to support the candidacy of Sir Henry's brother, Thomas, to the bishopric of Lichfield and Coventry and he was duly 'elected'. (He was later suspended from office by the archbishop for dereliction of duty.) It all seemed, by the standards of the day, a fair and equitable arrangement. But anyone who imagined that the Duchess of Cleveland would wait upon the whim of a teenage girl did not know the lady. As soon as Sir Henry died, she had Mary snatched and immediately married to her eldest son. Then she claimed administration of the estate in his name. And when Mary's aunt protested at the sheer effrontery of Lady Cleveland's behaviour she was met with the haughty rebuff, 'I wonder that so inconsiderable a person as you will contend with a lady of my quality.' The Woods began litigation and the complexities of the case kept lawyers happily engaged for over a generation but, as a peeress in her own right and someone close to the king, Barbara was, for all practical purposes, above the law.[72]

Louise de Keroualle was not prepared to stand idly by while all these goodies were being handed out to her rival. When her son was born in July 1672 he was named Charles Lennox because the king was not eager to acknowledge the boy as his. If ever he listened to his choristers when they sang the daily offices he will have heard them, on the twenty-seventh evening of the month, intone the words from Psalm 127,

> Lo, children and the fruit of the womb are an
> heritage and gift that cometh from the Lord . . .
> Happy is the man that hath his quiver full of them.

But he may well have felt that his own quiver was, by now, quite full enough. He gave Louise a £10,000 pension and probably hoped that she would be satisfied. Barbara was clamouring incessantly for privileges for her children. It was enough to give a man a headache. But, of course, Louise could not allow herself to be outfaced by Barbara, either for her own sake or for the sake of her son. Nothing less than a ducal coronet would do for her, too. Her technique was not to pester the king and rant at him. Instead, she demonstrated, on every possible occasion, the nobility and refinement of her own person, which contrasted so markedly with Lady Cleveland's brashness and vulgarity. However unpopular 'Carwell' was in the outside world, she brought a fresh, sophisticated but lively contribution to the life of the court. Her entertainments, whether private dinners and suppers or large guest-list affairs, were talked of for weeks afterwards. In July 1673 she excelled herself with a Thameside ball. Crowds flocked to see the gaily dressed ladies and gentlemen dancing beneath the 'fairy' lights glowing in the trees and a large contingent of privileged guests enjoyed a sumptuous banquet served in barges moored on the water.

It may be no coincidence that, less than a month after this, Louise was appointed as lady of the bedchamber (without Catherine's prior agreement) and at the same time raised to the peerage as Baroness Petersfield, Countess of Fareham and Duchess of Portsmouth. Since she was a French subject Charles had to apply to Louis for permission to enable her to change her nationality – permission which was, of course, readily given. But the connection with France was not broken. When, in 1675, Charles Lennox, his royal parentage by now acknowledged, was similarly ennobled, he received both British and French titles. In fact, the honours bestowed on the king's youngest son indicated dramatically the esteem in which he and his mother were now held. He was created Duke of Richmond and also Duke of Lennox in the Scottish peerage. At the same time Louis XIV was persuaded to confer on him the title of duc d'Aubigny. All these dukedoms were entitlements of the Stuart family, having last been carried by Charles Stuart, Duke of Richmond. The young man who had eloped with the delectable Frances in 1667 had died while on embassy in Denmark in December 1672. There was, therefore, a great deal of significance, emotional and otherwise, to the honours selected for Louise's son.

She also scored a victory over the Duchess of Cleveland in the matter of precedence. It became a matter of great personal pride to both women which of the sons was highest on the list of royal dukes. Both sent word to the lord treasurer, who had to sign the dockets approving the issue of patents, requesting him to process their applications first. The poor man was in a quandary, knowing that whatever he did would bring down upon his head the wrath of one of the mistresses. He hurried to the king for advice. Charles, who was no more eager than his official to assume responsibility, advised the man to work on the principle of first come, first served. Louise, who had the good fortune to be on hand, won the race, which meant that the Duke of Richmond would always take precedence over Barbara's boys. The treasurer completed the formalities – and then rushed off to Bath before the storm broke.

Meanwhile Charles' basic political dilemma had not changed; it had just become more acute. 'Can't live with 'em; can't live without 'em', thus he might well have characterised his relationship with both his French allies and his parliament. In foreign affairs he still favoured France and at home he still hoped to spread the blanket of toleration over the fires of religious discord. Neither of these objectives played well in parliament. Unfortunately, the House of Commons and Louis XIV were the twin sources of the income he needed to run his court and government. But neither provided him with sufficient cash to make himself independent of the other. He had to go on wooing both. As with his rival mistresses, he had to listen to their mutual complaints and try to keep them both happy. From time to time they both irritated him. Louis' territorial aggression made him the pariah of Europe, and an embarrassing ally. As for parliament, whenever they assembled they would insist on imposing restrictions on the monarchy that threatened to make Charles king in name only. The time was long past when he might have stood firm for a consistent programme to strengthen the Crown. He was locked into subterfuge and intrigue.

Early in 1674 the Venetian ambassador gave a concise assessment of the state of royal government: 'The king calls a cabinet council for the purpose of not listening to it and the ministers hold forth in it so as not to be understood.'[73] Even though the Cabal had been a ministry in name rather than fact, its collapse left a vacuum in which the king and his advisers floated freely, their relative positions constantly changing in response to the foreign situation and the demands of parliament. Arlington was a busted flush, thanks to the débâcle of the war at sea and the knives thrust by 'colleagues' into his unprotected back. The Test Act removed from office the Duke of York, who resigned his admiralship, and Lord Clifford, who ceased to be lord treasurer and one of Charles' closest confidants. The latter was a broken man. Enforced retirement into private life following the failure of the Dutch war sent him into a deep depression. Evelyn went to visit him at Tunbridge Wells and found him 'grieved to the heart . . . for, though he carried with him music and people to divert him . . . I found he was struggling in his mind and, being of a rough and ambitious nature, could not long brook the necessity he had brought on himself . . .' Within a couple of weeks he was dead. According to popular report a servant found him hanged from the bed tester by his own cravat and, though he cut his master down, the poor man did not long survive. Evelyn heard that Clifford's last words were, 'Well, let men say what they will, there is a God, a just God, above.'[74] Had Charles been prepared to heed it, this might have served as a prophetic warning to seek out some principles and beliefs to which he could adhere and so achieve a measure of dignity even at such a late stage in the reign.

He would also have saved himself much grief if he had considered the judgement of the French ambassador a few weeks later: 'a discarded minister, who is very ill-conditioned and clever, left perfectly free to act and speak, seems to me much to be feared in this country'.[75] Colbert was referring to Ashley, now Lord Shaftesbury, whom Charles had ignominiously dismissed from the lord chancellorship. The resentment of the sacked minister was boundless. He set himself to oppose in parliament the policies of the court and to raise a standard around which malcontents could gather. What then appeared no more than the emergence of just another faction had greater historical significance. Shaftesbury's defection can now be recognised as the beginning of an organised parliamentary opposition party. One of those who associated himself with Shaftesbury was the mercurial Duke of Buckingham. Another figure who was seen entering the crowded political arena was the Duke of Monmouth. Charles was certainly more fond of the young man than he was of his own brother and this encouraged many observers to believe that he might be persuaded to change the arrangements for the succession. The Duke of York's unpopularity had risen since his marriage to Mary of Modena had threatened the country with the establishment of a papist dynasty. The twenty-four-year-old Duke of Monmouth was meanwhile making a distinguished military career for himself on the continent and his popularity in the country was growing. He was the king's eldest illegitimate son and he was Protestant. An increasing number of political activists were seriously looking to the future and asking themselves 'What if?' Someone else determined to play a part in the shaping of that future was currently awaiting his cue to come on stage. Ralph Montagu, the ambassador to Paris, had just brought off a great matrimonial coup by securing the extremely rich widow of the Earl of Northumberland and was ready to use his new wealth and his French connections to destabilise the government and advance his own interests.

The man appointed to fill the vacancy left by Lord Treasurer Clifford was Sir Thomas Osborne, immediately created Viscount Danby, and, a year later, Earl of Danby. Everyone who knew Osborne assumed that this must be a stopgap measure. He was profoundly cynical, a man 'never overburdened with principles',[76] and was known to be a creature of the out-of-favour Buckingham. But he soon showed himself to be well provided with qualities invaluable to a politician: 'he had a peculiar way to make his friends depend on him and to believe he was true to them. He was a positive and undertaking man, so he gave the king great ease, by assuring him all things would go according to his mind in the next session of parliament. And when his hopes failed him he had always some excuse ready to put the miscarriage upon.'[77] Danby speedily attained the position of first minister, although he never enjoyed the freedom of action that Clarendon had assumed. The politics of the 1670s was more complex than that of the early 1660s and was made more so by Charles' secrecy and duplicity. While he was content to leave most of the bread-and-butter politics to Danby, he never completely took the minister into his confidence and might, at any moment, go behind his back.

The frantic game of musical chairs being played by all Charles' advisers meant, inevitably, that any man or woman who had a degree of influence over the king was drawn into the political action. That definitely included the royal mistresses. But not, for the time being, Barbara Villiers. She removed herself from the centre of affairs. She was in her mid-thirties and, though her appetites had not faded, her charms had. John Churchill left her in 1675, having delved to the bottom of her purse. Diplomatic gossip reckoned that he had had over £100,000 from her in one way or another. Extravagance and heavy gambling losses ate hungrily into her lifestyle and Charles was no longer prepared to restock her financial larder. When she discovered that she could not keep up Cleveland House or go about in society with her accustomed *élan* she was faced with a hard decision: she could either proudly strive to keep up appearances or take herself off to some place where her rather reduced circumstances would attract less attention. In the autumn of 1676 she travelled to Paris. It is difficult to imagine Lady Cleveland turning her back on intrigue but, if she tried to, she failed. Intrigue was waiting to confront her in the person of the ambitious and ruthless ambassador, Ralph Montagu (see below p. 302).

At Whitehall, meanwhile, Danby lost no time in courting Louise de Keroualle. The easiest way to do this was to ensure that all payments to her from the royal purse were made promptly, something that his predecessor had certainly not regarded as a priority. In return Louise became a conduit to the king for the minister's ideas and policies. Since it was a cornerstone of Danby's counsel that Charles would underestimate at his peril the depth of anti-French feeling in the country, Louise would not appear to be an obvious ally. Colbert was certainly unable to understand her Francophobia. Reporting to Paris he opined that she must either be harbouring a grudge or acting out of sheer caprice. Whatever the French ambassador said, the world at large remained convinced that Louise was merely a creature of Louis XIV. The common bruit around the court was that the new mistress was devoid of principles and would, as one shrew remarked, sell anyone for 500 guineas. This was probably true, but it was not the whole truth.

Louise de Keroualle's besetting sin was pride and that determined her to be her own woman. Just as she sometimes made herself look ridiculous by wearing mourning when some foreign princeling died with whom she claimed kinship, so she determined not to be manipulated by French agents. Her own interests came first and she milked her privileged position assiduously, knowing full well that it might not be permanent. Through her contacts at the French court she was aware of changes in Louis' domestic arrangements: as the decade wore on, Mme de Montespan was being eased out of her position at the Louvre by Mme de Maintenon, the erstwhile nurse to her children. There was a certain appropriateness about the alliance of Louise and Danby. Both had attained the social and political summit from starting positions well down the mountain. Both possessed the arriviste's insecurity-based pride. Evelyn, contrasting Danby with Clifford, found him 'of a more haughty and far less obliging nature . . . a man of excellent natural parts but nothing generous or grateful'.[78] Louise, like Danby, was dependent upon, and could not take for granted, the king's pleasure. Minister and mistress needed each other.

Nell Gwynn, by contrast, was apolitical and not afflicted with her rival's hauteur. Part of her attraction to Charles was her relaxed, 'non PC' irreverence. When she formed associations with members of the council it was on the basis of personality rather than policy or even self-interest. She was drawn to Buckingham because, like her, he was fun-loving, ebullient and no respecter of persons. Her friendship was very useful to the duke. As someone who found it hard to restrain his passions and who, therefore, was accustomed to finding himself in and out of royal favour, it was valuable for him to have an advocate with ready access to the king. Charles also was pleased to have a go-between, for, though it was frequently necessary for him to distance himself from the scapegrace duke, he maintained warm feelings for his old friend. Nell was never admitted to residence in the palace but Charles often visited her in Pall Mall. She could not throw the glittering parties which were Louise's speciality but she sometimes entertained the king to dinner or supper and invitations to such intimate occasions were eagerly sought by political aspirants. Just how useful Nell could be to her friends was demonstrated in 1677, when Buckingham found himself in the Tower for his latest indiscretion. Mistress Gwynn interceded on his behalf and then visited the duke in prison to explain the best way of getting back into Charles' good books. Buckingham took her advice and was set at liberty within days.

Nell was as constant in her animosities as in her friendships. Naturally Louise – 'Squintabella' or the 'weeping willow' (Louise was often reduced to tears by the rival's witty barbs) as she called the *maîtresse en titre* – was her principal target. The irrepressible Nell was utterly merciless in puncturing the Frenchwoman's pride – no difficult feat, considering Nell's gift for mimicry and Louise's widespread unpopularity. No biography of the cockney girl is complete without repetition of the story of the waylaying of Nell's coach by a group of rowdies who mistook her elegant equipage for that of Louise. She thrust her head out of the window and called to her attackers, 'Have a care; I'm the Protestant whore!' Other performances were less spontaneous. The chevalier de Rohan, scion of a very ancient Breton family, fell foul of the French king because of an intrigue involving Hortense, duchesse Mazarin, was stripped of his court offices and exiled to his Normandy estates. There, the disgruntled aristocrat was foolish enough to become involved in a minor rising against the Crown, for which he paid with his head. Hearing the news, Louise, who claimed, with dubious genealogical evidence, to be related to the unfortunate chevalier, went into mourning for him. The following day, Nell appeared at court similarly clothed. When asked why, she made a display of histrionic grief. 'The Cham of Tartary is dead!' she wailed, 'and he was as close to me as the chevalier de Rohan was to the Duchess of Portsmouth.' Once again, Louise was humiliated and the king was highly amused. It was useless for the victim to demand that Charles control the escapades of his London slut: as he once told a po-faced high-ranking official, he would not deny himself such diversions for any man or woman living.

Such squibs might be considered harmless fun but they often had political overtones. One example occurred in September 1677 when Danby's career was in the balance. He was genuinely alarmed to hear that when the king dined with Buckingham and his cronies at Mistress Gwynn's house their hostess kept the company amused with an impersonation of Lady Danby. It was agreed by those in the know that this was a bad omen and the earl took it seriously enough to send a message via an intermediary who was to say that the mistress was behaving badly to someone who had always shown her kindness and was astonished to see her succouring the king's 'enemies'.

Louise remained close to Danby as long as he was in power and there is no doubt that she discussed matters of state with Charles on the minister's behalf. We should be careful not to attach too much significance to this. In his indecision and confusion about his relations with foreign powers and parliament Charles was prepared to listen to almost anyone but he kept his own counsel and he who had secrets from his officials was not likely to be completely open with his women. Halifax went so far as to describe Charles as having three kinds of adviser, 'ministers of the council, ministers of the cabinet and ministers of the ruelle [or ladies' salon]'.[79] By the time Danby came to power the means of gaining the king's attention was well established. 'His aversion to formality made him dislike a serious discourse, if very long, except it was mixed with something to entertain him.'[80] One of the ways of sweetening the pill was to involve the reigning mistress. Lord Danby and Lady Portsmouth slipped very easily into this pattern.

Louise did not master the intricacies of policy; her influence, such as it was, lay in supporting or denigrating individuals. The possibilities for corruption, for selling her intercessory skills, were considerable and Louise, like Barbara, had no hesitation about charging for her services. This does not mean that cupidity was her only motivation in matters political, as her involvement in the career of Arthur Capel, Earl of Essex, demonstrates. In 1672, Capel succeeded Ormonde as lord-lieutenant of Ireland. This notoriously difficult sphere of royal service was rendered more so by the interference of court favourites who habitually regarded the province as a milch cow providing a stream of land grants, commercial revenues and lucrative offices. Essex proved a conscientious deputy who set himself to purge the administration of irregularities and govern in the best interests of the inhabitants. Therefore, he rapidly accumulated enemies at home, enemies who had the king's ear. His friends urged him to apply to the Duchess of Portsmouth to neutralise the influence of malicious tongues but the earl disdained such backstairs politics. 'By no means will I fix my reliance and dependence upon little people,' he responded to his advisers. 'To make any such [people] friends so as to be useful or a support to me will necessarily oblige me to be assistant to them in finding out money or other advantages for their qualifications and, if once I should begin, there would be no end to it.'[81] It was an accurate assessment but one on which it was politically inept to act.

Essex pursued his high-minded way, among other things balking the Duchess of Cleveland's claim to Phoenix Park, traditionally the preserve of the king's representative. Despite his entreaties, his friends at Whitehall worked on his behalf and, for a while, they had the Duchess of Portsmouth's support, given, it would seem, freely and not in response to massive bribes. No real blame can be attached to her for what happened next. Essex's main opponent was Richard Price, Earl of Ranelagh, a highly plausible man who had secured the office of chancellor of the Irish exchequer, out of the revenues of which he paid Louise a pension. Ranelagh came up with a gimcrack scheme which would make the province self-financing and provide the king with substantial funds for the renovation of Windsor Castle, on which he embarked in 1674. Essex refused to endorse the project but Charles was blind to anything but the possibility of adding to his revenue. When Ranelagh returned to Ireland the finances soon tumbled into chaos. Essex refused to endorse the accounts. Charles, whom Ranelagh had made sure received his cut, ordered him to do so. Now, the lieutenant-governor's friends reported that Danby, Louise and Ranelagh had pledged themselves to have Essex removed and replaced by Monmouth. It was a feasible plot. Charles doted on his eldest son and the Irish job would have been a suitably high-profile office for him. However, it seems to have been no more than a rumour, for when Essex was dismissed in 1677, Charles had the good sense to reinstate Ormonde. As for Louise, she had a financial interest in Ranelagh's success but it is doubtful whether anything she could have said would have swayed Charles one way or the other; he was hoodwinked by the Ranelagh faction.

The most serious outcome of the whole affair was that the king had turned another honest man against him. Essex returned to throw in his lot with Shaftesbury and Buckingham. Ormonde was left to clear up the mess of the Irish finances and an action was eventually brought against Ranelagh and his accomplices for the alleged misappropriation of £76,000. By an order in council, the undertakers were instructed to go to Ireland to answer to the lord-lieutenant and to abide by his ruling, while, at the same time, Danby would take care of any prosecution that was necessary through the English courts.[82] However, the sordid affair came too close to the king and the case was dropped. Ormonde was no less principled than Essex but he was sufficient of a realist to know that it was advisable to look after the interests of the royal mistresses. When it came to payments to be made out of the Irish revenues he made sure that Barbara, Louise and Nell came well up the pecking order.

But now the royal ladies of pleasure had another rival, and a formidable one at that. At the end of 1675 the most celebrated woman in Europe had ridden into London clad in man's attire. As the news spread, the capital was agog to see this beautiful, outrageous creature whose notoriety had gone before her, thanks to her own highly coloured published memoirs. Evelyn remarked, 'all the world knows her story'. No one was more anxious than the king to make the acquaintance of this ravishing siren – or rather to renew acquaintance. For the new centre of attraction was none other than Hortense Mancini, duchesse Mazarin, the lively girl he had wanted for a bride sixteen years before.

Hortense had grown into a remarkable woman in many ways. Far from taming her wild, free spirit, hard experience had added resourcefulness, calculation, cultural awareness and an intelligent inquisitiveness about everything around her. It was not that she deliberately flouted the conventions that society imposed on women; she simply did not recognise them. Other women might dream of the liberty and adventure society only permitted to men:

> Oh, could I change my sex, but 'tis in vain
> To wish myself or think to be a man,
> Like that wild creature, I would madly rove
> Through all the fields of gallantry and love,
> Heighten the pleasures of the day and night,
> Dissolve in joys and surfeit with delight,
> Not tamely, like a woman, wish and pray,
> And sigh my precious minutes all away.[83]

Hortense lived the dream, her love of cross-dressing an outward sign of her bisexuality. Having escaped from the prison house of her marriage to the crazed, jealous duc Mazarin, she spent eight years wandering southern France and Italy, driven by her needs to keep out of her husband's clutches, to find lovers to support her lavish lifestyle and to enjoy the sensory and intellectual pleasures of the world around her. In June 1675, her current protector and provider, the duc de Savoie, died and his widow, understandably, was not enthusiastic about continuing to offer hospitality to the shameless Hortense. News of her predicament reached Paris and, specifically, the ears of the ambassador, Ralph Montagu.

The clarity with which he saw the possibilities presented by Hortense suggests that he had already devised the strategy by which he planned to attain power: discrediting or undermining those close to the king in order to place himself and his friends about the royal person. Dangling new mistresses before Charles was a proven way for courtiers and politicians to enhance their standing with him and in the duchesse Mazarin Montagu had the perfect bait. She was no fresh, young novelty with whom the king might find a few nights of pleasure. She was an old flame, a mature yet stunning 'Roman' beauty, well versed in the arts of the bedroom but, above all, she was a sexual icon about whom men across Europe fantasised. That, Montagu calculated, would make her irresistible to the king. He would want her for his harem and, once there, she would have little difficulty in displacing Louise de Keroualle and those who relied on the influence of the *maîtresse en titre*.

Hortense's cover was that she was visiting her distant kinswoman, Mary of Modena. Though it is doubtful whether anyone at court took this at face value, it gave her access to the Duke of York's establishment and, thus, an entrée to royal society. She struck up a particularly close friendship with Anne, Duchess of Sussex, Charles' wilful daughter by Barbara Villiers. Anne, expecting her first child, was confined to her rooms (her mother's old quarters) at Whitehall and there Hortense frequently called upon her. This was very convenient for Charles, who had every good reason for visiting his daughter. Whatever the Duchess of Portsmouth might suspect, she had no grounds for protesting or going into hysterics. By April, royal watchers were convinced that Hortense had got her hooks into the king. The French ambassador reported that, 'though the affair has been conducted so far with some secrecy, it is likely that this growing passion will take the first place in the heart of that prince'.[84]

Hortense's primary objective in allowing herself to be manipulated by Montagu (now joined in the intrigue by Arlington, who had hopes of ousting Danby and regaining his former position) was financial. Duc Mazarin had frozen all his wife's assets, including a pension paid by Louis XIV, and she hoped that Charles would exert pressure on the French king to get her funds released. She threw herself on Charles' mercy as a damsel in distress and, of course, he succumbed. He dipped deep into his purse for her and he did send messages to his brother monarch on her behalf.

Hortense had no political agenda apart from commending her backers to the king but she could not avoid becoming a political figure. The French ambassador was inevitably concerned about the implications for Anglo-French relations of this new love in the king's life. The ideal solution, from his point of view, would have been for Hortense to return to France but duc Mazarin's absolute intransigence in demanding the duchess's return in abject submission and Louis' reluctance to intervene between husband and wife rendered this impossible. He urged a reluctant Louis to make some generous gesture towards the duchesse Mazarin, lest she should retaliate by souring Charles' mind against France. By the summer of 1676 he was very concerned that Louise de Keroualle had been ousted from first place in the king's heart. In August he reported to Paris on a very affecting encounter:

> I went to see Madame de Portsmouth. She opened her heart to me in the presence of two of her maids . . . [She] explained to me what grief the frequent visits of the King of England to Madame de Sussex cause her every day. The two girls remained propped against the wall with downcast eyes. Their mistress let loose a torrent of tears. Sobs and sighs interrupted her speech. Indeed, I have never beheld a sadder or more touching sight.[85]

Louise was experiencing the distress she had inflicted on Catherine. Now it was her turn to be the 'little wife', treated with courtesy and consideration but watching another share with Charles the moments of intimacy and passion that had once been hers.

Well might she be tearful. Everything she had achieved – wealth, social position, the grudging respect of everyone at court, influence – depended on the king's continued interest in her. Without it, she would be defenceless in a nation where she was thoroughly hated. Her only recourse would be to follow her predecessor into humiliating exile. But there was more to her despondency than that. She was aware that Hortense outshone her in every sphere. Her rival's pedigree was impeccable. She was obviously an exciting lover. Even in matters of culture and taste the newcomer was a challenge. Hortense could not boast a houseful of elegant furniture and works of art but she had established a salon to which the leaders of fashionable London flocked. The literary lion Charles, sieur de St-Évremond, who had made his home in England since arousing Louis XIV's displeasure, was devoted to her and regularly brought to her table dramatists, artists, wits and members of the intelligentsia. There they held learned conversations and never failed to enjoy the most sumptuous fare and delicacies brought over from France by Galet, the duchess's chef. Not only was Hortense wildly unconventional in her private life, she was also highly civilised. To the poet and playwright Aphra Behn it seemed that the duchess represented the possibilities of womanhood in all their fullness. Dedicating her story *The History of the Nun or the Fair Vow-breaker* to Hortense, she affirmed, 'how infinitely one of your own sex adores you'. To Louise, who did not adore her, it must have seemed that the infuriating Hortense excelled at everything and was always the centre of attraction. When she was with the court at Newmarket she was invariably up early and trying the fieriest horses over the gallops. On at least one occasion she provided morning strollers in St James's Park with a rare spectacle. She and the Countess of Sussex went out 'with drawn swords under their night gowns, which they drew out and made several fine passes with, to the admiration of several men that was lookers on in the park'.[86]

For eighteen months or so London society was diverted by the rivalry between the two 'French whores'. But what was amusing to courtiers was of growing interest and concern to politicians and diplomats. Honoré de Courtin, the French ambassador, was under instructions to bring the feud to an end lest it should lead to the emergence of serious factions which would provide rallying points for pro- and anti-French activists. Courtin claimed to have effected a *rapprochement* by means of a simple ruse. With the aid of accomplices he managed to bring both ladies to his supper table without either knowing that the other would be present. He then locked them by themselves in a small room and did not release them until they had begun to be civil to each other. The story is very suspect and, if it did take place, it is unlikely that the truce lasted very long.

In fact, it was entirely due to Hortense's exotic behaviour that the petticoat combat eventually came to an end. Early in 1667 Charles grew alarmed at the influence Hortense was having on his daughter, Anne. The young countess was completely besotted with her friend and was almost certainly in a lesbian relationship with her. When the Earl of Sussex ordered his wife to come with him to their country estate, she flew into hysterics, vowing that nothing should separate her from the woman she loved. The king insisted that she leave the capital and sulkily Anne went off to Hurstmonceux. Once there, she would do nothing but lie on her pillows repeatedly kissing a portrait miniature of the duchess.

The thought of Hortense in sexual dalliance with his own daughter was an interesting challenge to the broad-minded king. He who had chuckled at the humiliation of outraged fathers and cuckolded husbands when acted out on the stage or the living theatre of the royal court was now confronted with the reality in his own family. Suddenly it may not have seemed quite so funny. But Hortense's lack of restraint displayed itself in other ways that he found annoying. He had always expected his mistresses to be faithful or, at least, discreet. The duchesse Mazarin was neither. She had never regarded herself as tied to any man and did not intend to make an exception for the King of England. Her husband had failed to imprison her in his own house or in a convent and she would not allow Charles to place her under emotional duress. When he remonstrated with her about her affairs she took no notice. It was inevitable that she would eventually go a lover too far and when she became attached to the young Prince of Monaco, who was on an extended visit to England, Charles' patience snapped. There was a row and the king even revoked Hortense's pension, though only for a short while. The grand passion – Charles' last – came to an end. He and Hortense remained friends – and, doubtless, were occasionally something more than friends. Louise de Keroualle thankfully took up once more the reins of power at Whitehall.

In August 1678 the French and Dutch signed a peace treaty at Nijmegen and this was followed by the cessation of hostilities between Louis and all his other foes. It was a state of affairs Charles had long hoped for and his ministers had worked for. By no means did universal peace solve all the king's problems but it did help to lessen the tension under which he lived. He was still broke, parliament was still hostile and Louis was still wielding the financial stick and carrot by which he kept Charles dependent on himself. But, for the time being at least, Charles' problems seemed less pressing and he buried his head in the sand of his pleasures. The court went off for its summer holiday at Windsor and after that there was the prospect of the autumn meeting at Newmarket to look forward to. The king left Danby in charge at Whitehall while he fished and walked and gave himself to rural pursuits. Other men worried about the significance of heavenly omens. In recent months a new comet had been seen and there had been eclipses of both the sun and moon. Andrew Marvell wrote to a friend that there was abroad a widespread sense of foreboding, 'as if some great, and I hope good thing were to be expected'.[87] The king did not appear to share this apprehension.

If that was so, he was woefully wrong. Just over the horizon lay slander, forgery, blackmail, perjury, murder and the collapse of the government.

CHAPTER 12

This Is The Time

The series of storms that deluged the nation in 1678–9 sent Danby to the Tower, exiled the Duke of York to France, faced the queen with a charge of homicide, resigned the Duchess of Cleveland to a life of obscurity, caused the Duchess of Portsmouth to have her bags packed in readiness for sudden flight and almost swept away the dynasty. But storms do not emerge for no reason out of the clear blue air. The charged clouds of the Popish Plot that massed in the later months of 1678 had been building for years. They were made up of the same resentments that had plunged the country into war a generation earlier: indignation at the threat of an imposed religion; fear that parliament was being undermined by the king; conviction that the monarchy was being undermined by parliament; mutual mistrust between the sovereign and the representatives of his people. As in 1641, an organised anti-court 'party' had emerged in parliament and if they did not provoke a military insurrection it was not because anger was not deep or widespread enough but because the horror of civil war was firmly imprinted on men's minds.

For years criticism had found outlets in parliamentary debates, printed satires, scurrilous ballads and the tittle-tattle of tavern and coffee-house but it had changed nothing. For all that the politically aware populace could see, the Stuarts paid no heed to hints or direct complaints; they were set determinedly on the path to the creation of an autocratic Catholic state. It seemed to many that this could only have the most dire consequences. The satire, *A Dialogue between Two Horses*, probably written by Andrew Marvell, used the conceit of the animals in two equestrian statues of Charles I and Charles II meeting up and discussing the shortcomings of their respective masters. It ended in prophetic vein:

> If speech from brute animals in Rome's first age
> Prodigious events did surely presage,
> That shall come to pass all mankind may swear
> Which two inanimate horses declare.
> But I should have told you, before the jades parted,
> Both galloped to Whitehall and there horribly farted,

Which monarchy's downfall portended much more
Than all that the beasts had spoken before.
If the Delphick Sybills oracular speeches,
As learned men say, came out of their breeches,
Why might not our horses, since words are but wind,
Have the spirit of prophecy likewise behind?
Though tyrants make laws which they strictly proclaim
To conceal their own crimes and cover their shame,
Yet the beasts of the field or the stones in the wall
Will publish their faults and prophesy their fall.
When they take from the people the freedom of words,
They teach them the sooner to fall to their swords.[88]

By 1678 it was not only Marvell who sensed lurid lights and the growling of distant thunder in the political sky. The demand for change was tumultuous, as a popular song clamorously stated:

Would you send Kate to Portugal,
Great James to be a cardinal.
And make Prince Rupert admiral?
    This is the time!

Would you turn Danby out of doors,
Banish rebels and French whores,
The worser sort of common shores [sewers]?
    This is the time!

Would you make our sovereign disabuse,
And make the parliament of use,
Not to be changed like dirty shoes?
    This is the time!

Would you once more bless the nation
By changing Portsmouth's vocation,
And find one fit for procreation?
    This is the time!

Would you turn papists from the queen,
Cloister up fulsome Mazarine [Hortense Mancini],
Once more make Charles great again?
    This is the time![89]

Charles felt the first raindrops of the impending tempest in July and may have regarded them as little more than an inconvenient shower.

301

They took the form of a long and bitter complaint from Lady Cleveland in Paris about Ralph Montagu. She was incandescent with rage at the antics of the ambassador. When the two of them had met up in the French capital they had started an affair (neither the first nor the last there for either of them) during which Montagu had tried to draw the king's ex-mistress into his political intrigues. She was certainly not averse to this – until the summer of 1678. Then, they had a falling-out and, with all the viciousness of which they were capable, each tried to destroy the other. Barbara made a short visit to London, and Montagu, fearful of what she might reveal to the king, sought to undermine Charles' confidence in her, by sending to him some of her love letters which he had either intercepted or bought. The ploy obviously worked for Charles dismissed his mistress of sixteen years with the words, 'Madam, all that I ask of you, for your own sake, is live so for the future as to make the least noise you can, and I care not who you love.' For Charles all passion was spent; he had, at last, shaken himself free and his 'Frankly, my dear, I don't give a damn' attitude must have come as quite a shock. But that was as nothing compared to the horrors that confronted her on her return to Paris.

She discovered hitherto unsuspected depths to Montagu's malice. The town was buzzing with the news of a delicious scandal: as soon as the Duchess of Cleveland's back was turned, her seventeen-year-old daughter, Anne Fitzroy, Countess of Sussex, had immediately jumped into the bed Mama had just vacated. In truth, Anne was a chip off the old block. She had left her husband, had various other liaisons, including her infatuation with Hortense, and been sent over to Paris for her mother to supervise her moral upbringing! Her fling with Montagu was un-doubtedly six of one and half a dozen of the other but it admirably served the ambassador's purpose of rubbing salt in Barbara's wounds. However, her plight was very much worse, as she realised as soon as she learned what else the libertine had been up to in her absence. Montagu had gone to King Louis and sought his aid in his private war with the duchess. He gave a highly coloured account of Lady Cleveland's indiscretions and, claiming to speak for his own master, demanded that Barbara's latest lover, the chevalier de Châtillon, be banished and that the Lady Anne should be removed from her mother's care. He suggested that the French king might recommend to his brother monarch that Barbara's financial lifeline be cut. It is difficult not to feel that Barbara Villiers and Ralph Montagu thoroughly deserved each other.

In a panic of self-preservation and revenge the duchess wrote to Charles, revealing Montagu's schemes in the most lurid detail she could devise. She made no bones about denouncing, 'this ill man, who in his heart, I know, hates you and were it for his interest would ruin you, too, if he could'. Montagu, she averred, was a man who has neither conscience nor honour and has several times told me that in his heart he despised you and your brother; and that he wished with all his heart that the parliament would send you both to travel, for you were a dull, governable fool and the duke a wilful fool . . . you always chose a greater beast to govern you.

The ambassador's plan, Lady Cleveland revealed, was to send to Whitehall an astrologer who was in his own pay to warn the king of dire disaster unless he expelled Danby and the Duchess of Portsmouth from his presence. Montagu would then insinuate himself into the position of secretary of state. That, as he had told Barbara, was to be a mere stepping stone:

And when I have it I will be damned if I do not quickly get to be lord treasurer, and then you and your children shall find such a friend as never was. As for the king, I will find a way to furnish him so easily with money for his pocket and his wenches that we will quickly . . . lead the king by the nose.

Lady Cleveland was swift to distance herself from these schemes:

I told him that I thanked him but that I would not meddle in any such thing, and that, for my part, I had no malice to my Lady Portsmouth or the treasurer and, therefore, I would never be in any plot to destroy them; but that I found the character the world gave him was true – which was that the devil was not more designing than he was. And that I wondered at it; for that sure all these things working in his brains must make him very uneasy and would at last make him mad.[90]

The letter is very revealing about both Charles and Lady Cleveland. It exposes the unscrupulous way she had become accustomed to harassing the king out of motives of self-interest and how susceptible he was to female influence. Charles' deep respect for women shaded into unmanly malleability, as his ministers so often complained. In this case Barbara had played the cards of helpless woman and outraged mother in an alien environment. The strategy worked. When Montagu rushed back to Whitehall to put his side of the case to the king he was denied an audience and was informed by underlings that he had been deprived of all his offices.

Ralph Montagu was not the sort of man to accept defeat and retire into private life, his tail between his legs. Indeed, in disgrace he proved himself more dangerous than he had been when sitting in a foreign capital devising plots. He set in motion another plan to bring down Danby. The first step was to get himself elected to parliament where he would have a secure base from which to mount his attack. Opposition to the administration had become clamorous and, as an MP, Montagu could claim immunity from prosecution for anything he said within the chamber. The evidence he possessed to lay before the Commons was dynamite. It consisted of letters sent to Louis XIV by Danby, at the king's insistence, asking for secret subsidies to aid the French war effort and promising to prorogue parliament if they ever sought to pursue a foreign policy inimical to France. The first use he made of these documents was attempted blackmail. He demanded the office of secretary of state in return for his silence. Danby refused to put himself in his enemy's power and tried to circumvent any damaging revelation by ordering the seizure of Montagu's papers. This confrontation failed because the House of Commons, as the ex-ambassador had calculated, stuck by its member and instructed that the evidence should be examined at Westminster, not Whitehall.

Now the guard dog of secrecy which had protected the king's affairs for so long turned to bite him. Knowing little, the Commons suspected much and were prepared to believe anything. For instance, what was Charles proposing to do with the £300,000 p.a. he had negotiated from Louis?

... it was generally believed that the design was to keep up and model the army now raised, reckoning there would be money enough to pay them till the nation should be brought under a military government. And the opinion of this prevailed so that Lord Danby became the most hated minister that had ever been about the king. All people said now they saw the secret of that high favour he had been so long in and the black designs that he was contriving.[91]

Danby was impeached on 21 December. The following week Charles prorogued and, subsequently, dissolved a parliament which had sat for eighteen sessions since its election in 1660. The minister's fate hung in the balance. Only five months before he had buttressed his position by marrying his daughter to 'Don Carlos', Earl of Plymouth, Charles' son by Catherine Pegge. It remained to be seen whether the king would stand by his relative or bow to popular demand for his dismissal and even his death on a charge of high treason.

It was not only Charles who was in a dilemma. Louise's name was constantly linked with Danby's in public expressions of denigration. A courtier writing home with the latest news in December opined that the prorogation of parliament was the only way to save Danby,

who, with the Duchess of Portsmouth, made it their whole and daily business to persuade the king to it. She was so zealous that, if I am not misinformed, she was on her knees to the king for several days to prorogue them ...[92]

As the weeks passed, Louise had some hard thinking to do about their business relationship. The new French ambassador, Paul Barrillon, who was hand-in-glove with Montagu, was urging her to drop the minister, as were Ranelagh and his friends who, of course, had their own reasons for wanting Danby brought down. The mistress had to calculate whether to distance herself from the accused or whether, if she abandoned him to his enemies, she might be their next target.

Louise had every reason to be alarmed, for the storm had now broken in full fury. Through the dark days of autumn and winter, court and government had to contend with public panic and anti-Catholic feeling of an intensity not felt since the days of the Armada and with an organised opposition capable of taking full advantage of the prevailing mood. The notorious Popish Plot (see p. 307) aimed to sweep away the highest in the land in a torrent of libels, lies and innuendo but the more politically perceptive realised that the alliance of political dissidents in the Green Ribbon Clubs were potentially more destructive in the long term. This amorphous association was formed by Shaftesbury and Buckingham as a private club in the days after the government's attempt, in January 1676, to close down the coffee-houses or, at least, inhibit political discussion in them. They brought together members of parliament, merchants, City fathers, Nonconformist activists and sympathisers from the country, all of whom were opposed to the administration for one reason or another. The proliferation of the clubs worried the government, who set informers to spy on their activities. The report of one of these agents in the early days of 1679 gives a fairly clear idea of the Green Ribbon 'programme':

> The Green Ribbon men meet at Starkie's and Cotten's booksellers within Temple Bar and thence go to their clubs where the ordinary discourses are: that the nation is sold to the French, that at Whitehall they look one way and act another, that, whatever is pretended, popery and arbitrary government is intended, that a parliament is not to come again if they at Whitehall can live without it and, if any be suffered to sit, it must be in effect a French parliament or be none, for all is governed by the Duchess of Portsmouth, the Duke of York, the lord treasurer and the French ambassador, who all often meet the king at her lodgings and what is there agreed is next to be put in execution.[93]

Most of these suspicions, in contrast to the plethora of extravagant rumours scudding round the capital, were well founded. If Charles could have dispensed with parliament, then, like his father, he would have done so. That would only have been possible with French financial support and he would not have hesitated to make his Catholic declaration to buy that support. Of course, he was in no position to do any of these things so he pursued that pragmatic policy his mother had urged on her husband throughout the crisis years of telling every political group what it wanted to hear and making 'heartfelt' promises to those whose support he needed. Since the Green Ribbon men were generally so well informed and since they had friends in the Whitehall corridors of power, there is no reason to doubt their conviction that Louise de Keroualle had an important part to play in the king's inner councils nor that her chambers had become the venue for a kind of resurrected Somerset House junto.

However, what was exciting everyone beyond the huddles of the opposition clubmen were the 'revelations' of Titus Oates, Israel Tonge and their confederates. Given the extent of anti-Catholic paranoia in the country, it was, perhaps, almost inevitable that, in the absence of a genuine conspiracy against the Crown, one would be invented. Once invented, it would be sure to be believed. The whole of Europe was fiercely divided on the religious issue. The so-called 'wars of religion' may have come to an end but that did not eradicate minority communities of all persuasions nor prevent governments clamping down on those communities. The English parliament made repeated attempts (usually frustrated by the court party) to increase the restrictions on Catholics, most of whom were quietly loyal to king and country. If any objection was raised to such persecution, its defenders only needed to point across the Channel to what was happening in France. Louis XIV regarded his Huguenot subjects as potential rebels and took increasingly harsh measures against the Protestant minority. He pulled down their chapels, offered six *livres* to every Huguenot who converted and, when these measures failed to produce speedy results, he set in train the *dragonnades*, the billeting of dragoons on Protestant citizens for the purpose of inflicting upon them unspeakable atrocities. England's politico-religious agitators had constantly in mind the French bogeyman, whose activities were daily reported by travellers, diplomats and the trickle of Huguenots fleeing from oppression. If the Catholic autocrat thus treated his own people, how would he behave if Britain ever became a mere client state? It is against this wider background that we have to understand the panic caused by the Popish Plot, when,

> The world ran mad and each distempered brain
> Did strange and different frenzies entertain.
> Here politic mischiefs, there ambition swayed;
> The credulous rest were fool and coward made.[94]

Queen Catherine was among those who had to bear the brunt of common suspicion and hatred. Although she was allowed to exercise her religion, a watch was kept on her chapels in St James's Palace and Somerset House to make sure that no Englishmen resorted thither and, at one time, soldiers raided the warehouse above the queen's stables in search of popish books. She was frequently met with displays of sullen resentment when she travelled away from the capital. On a visit to Bath in 1676, her presence was pointedly ignored by the authorities through whose territory she passed. The king was furious. He rounded on the sheriffs of Berkshire and Wiltshire for their dereliction of duty and informed them that, as they had failed to pay their respects on the queen's outward journey, they would make good their omission when her majesty was on her return to London – and he sent the details of her itinerary so that they would have no excuse for failing to comply.

It was on the morning of 13 August 1678, as Charles was setting out for his routine stroll in the park, that he was approached by a certain Christopher Kirkby, with whom he had a slight acquaintance. The man was obviously agitated and when the king asked why, he replied that he feared assassins lay in wait to shoot his majesty. Plots and rumours of plots were scarcely new to Charles and he replied with some nonchalance that if Kirkby had something important to tell him they would discuss it when he returned from his walk. Such was the low-key beginning of the Popish Plot. Like some monstrous, parasitic weed, it would grow with alarming speed, soon outstripping the power of its propagators to halt its devastating progress. The king regained the palace in safety, having encountered nothing untoward and, that evening, he summoned the prophet of doom to explain himself. The story Kirkby told was the one in which he had been schooled by Tonge and Oates, the one a rabid and unscrupulous religious extremist and the other a rootless, inadequate man who had turned to crime as a means of giving his life some meaning. He told a garbled story of a widespread conspiracy backed by French gold to remove Charles, place his brother on the throne and force the nation into the waiting arms of Rome. The king listened courteously, believed not a word of it but referred Kirkby to Danby and went off to Windsor to relax.

When the lord treasurer interviewed Kirkby and Tonge he demanded documentary evidence to support their alarmist allegations. Oates was swift to oblige. He produced forged letters purporting to link the English Jesuit community and members of the queen's household with a raft of schemes to kill the king. Murderers stood in wait to poison him, stab him or shoot him and French troops were ready to take ship for Ireland as a staging post for the invasion of England. To add weight to his assertions, Oates took an oath before a highly respected London magistrate, Sir Edmund Berry Godfrey (Burnet said that he 'was esteemed the best justice of peace in England'). Danby, meanwhile, reposed as little trust as his master in the informers and, had it not been for the conspirators' first piece of good fortune, the matter might have been dropped. Some of Oates' 'evidence' found its way into the Duke of York's hands and he, smelling a *Protestant* plot, insisted on a full enquiry by the council. Oates and Tonge had now reached the point of no return. If they were to avoid the dire penalties meted out to perjurers, they had to stick to their story through thick and thin, continuing to embellish it with new 'facts' and allegations against more and more prominent people.

It was while the council were mulling over this evidence that the event occurred which lifted the affair out of the realm of in camera discussion and into the public domain. It was an event which seemed to authenticate the plotters' testimony and which spread throughout the capital panic news of a violent Catholic uprising. On 12 October, Sir Edmund Berry Godfrey went missing. What followed was later described graphically and with forensic accuracy by Bishop Burnet, who was an eyewitness. On the night of 17 October, the magistrate's body

> was found in a ditch about a mile out of the town, near St Pancras church. His sword was thrust through him but no blood was on his clothes or about him. His shoes were clean. His money was in his pocket. But nothing was about his neck, and a mark was all around it, an inch broad, which showed he was strangled. His breast was, likewise, all over marked with bruises and his neck was broken . . . There were many drops of white wax lights on his breeches, which he never used himself and, since only persons of quality or priests use those lights, this made all people conclude in whose hands he must have been . . . it was [clear that] he was first strangled and then carried to that place, where his sword was thrust through his dead body.[95]

The perpetrators of this brutal murder were never discovered and it remains one of the great unsolved mysteries of British criminological history.

If the conspirators were not themselves responsible for it, it was another and a most stupendous piece of luck for them, for now, however sceptical king and councillors might remain, people at large were disposed to swallow the Popish Plot hook, line and sinker. Parliament demanded that court and council be utterly purged of Catholics (though they exempted the queen's household) and that James should be removed from any position of influence. They even tried to make London and its environs a papist-free zone. Known and suspected Catholics were mercilessly harried. A bonfire was made of popish books in New Palace Yard. The Commons cellars were searched for a latter-day Guy Fawkes. The most bizarre rumours flew around the capital and not a few had to do with the king's women: Sir Edmund had got the Duchess of Portsmouth with child and, therefore, had to be silenced; the magistrate had been murdered in Somerset House where the queen had walked three times exultantly round his dead body and the duchess had spat on his face; the lord chief justice had issued a warrant against Lady Portsmouth for being privy to Sir Edmund's death; the 'French whore' was about to flee the country, either with Danby or the king; etc., etc.[96]

Fortune continued to smile on the plotters. Among the court personnel at whom they pointed the finger was a man who actually had been involved in clandestine correspondence with foreign Catholic agencies. Edward Coleman was a zealous convert to the faith and had become the secretary to Mary of Modena. 'A vain, meddling man of shallow intellect . . . inordinate conceit and strong ambition',[97] his pallid features and sunken eyes giving him an appearance of pious austerity, he had, a few years before, tried to interest French and papal agencies in funding attempts to have the restrictions against British Catholics eased. Now his lodgings were searched, his papers confiscated and he was arrested. At his trial Oates perjured himself up to the hilt, giving lurid details of a scheme involving Coleman and Sir George Wakeman, the queen's physician, to poison the king. Coleman was duly executed and Wakeman was detained pending trial. Small wonder that the Commons overwhelmingly supported a motion declaring their conviction that 'there hath been and still is a damnable and hellish plot contrived and carried on by the popish recusants for the assassinating . . . of the king, and for subverting the government, and rooting out and destroying the Protestant religion'.[98]

La calumnia was now doing its work with appalling efficiency. Flickering fires of accusation and suspicion ran through the City streets, turning neighbours into informers and inoffensive citizens into suspects. In mid-December the latest to be singed was Covent Garden goldsmith, Miles Prance. He was thrown into Newgate's foulest cell and loaded with chains in the hope that he would confess to complicity in Godfrey's murder. The terrified man was ready to grasp at any straw to save himself, so that when the conspirators smuggled some papers in to him he readily saw what was required of him. He begged an audience with the Earl of Shaftesbury and revealed what he 'knew' about the magistrate's death. His evidence implicated three members of the Somerset House staff and, though when taken before king and council his nerve failed him and he recanted, he subsequently returned to his original story, with the result that the three wretches were condemned and hanged. The king claimed that he signed the death warrants of these and other condemned men reluctantly and 'with tears in my eyes'.

These were terrifying days for the queen. She was deprived of some of her most loyal servants and witnessed other members of her household dragged off to prison. She was booed and hissed when she went out in her carriage and was eventually forced to remain at home. At the height of the frenzy the House of Commons demanded that she be packed off back to Portugal, although the Lords vetoed the proposal. And Oates had taken the final plunge by insisting to parliament, 'I do accuse the queen for conspiring the death of the king.' An outraged Charles ordered Oates to be confined at Whitehall but later had to respond to a parliamentary protest and set him at liberty. Catherine bore her trials with considerable fortitude.

Her main source of comfort was the unfailing support of her husband, as she confessed in her letters to her brother, the Prince Regent, Dom Pedro. Charles and Catherine might be a semi-attached couple who saw less of each other than in former years and Charles might derive more pleasure from the company of other women but he had never failed to render the respect and honour which were the queen's due. Now, in a time of crisis, these served as a platform on which he built a new edifice of genuine affection. Certainly there was a degree of self-preservation in his defence of the queen: if those closest to the Crown were allowed to topple, what might become of the Crown itself? Certainly family pride was involved, as it was when Charles insisted on the right of his brother to succeed him, although he had little confidence in James' ability. But the basis of his support for the beleaguered queen was that chivalrous consideration and loyalty he had always shown, uniquely, to women and which the Earl of Newcastle had instilled into him as a child. Charles indicated his attitude in his own letter to Catherine's brother:

We doubt not but that your Highness hath already heard of the unhappy reflection that hath lately been raised against our dear consort, the queen and do believe your Highness hath taken a sensible part with us in that indignation wherewith we have resented the same. We brought the matter (as soon as it was known) into our council board, and the reception which it there had we are sure will not sound unpleasing to your Highness, because it gave satisfaction to us and did let the queen clearly see that all was done for her present vindication which the time would permit. But this misfortune arising while the [parliament] of our kingdom were assembled, who by their constitution may take cognisance of whatever happens of an extraordinary nature, [Pedro was much more absolute in his dominions, even though he ruled as regent for his feeble-minded brother] they drew enquiry before them. [They] . . . found motives to reject the complaint and, instead of favouring the accusation, the time was only spent in magnifying her virtues . . .[99]

Dom Pedro was not mollified. He reflected angrily that 'the Diocletian persecution was nothing to this of the parliament of England'.[100] He sent over a highly placed dignitary of his court, the marquis de Arouches, to convey Catherine back to her homeland, where, he had decided, she should spend her remaining days in the Sacramento convent, close by his palace.

The Stuart monarchy was now facing its greatest crisis since 1641. The king and those closest to him were under siege from all sides and would need nerves of steel to survive. Elections to the new parliament, which convened in March, produced a House of Commons in which opponents of the regime were even more numerous than before. They immediately resumed the attack on Danby. Charles tried his utmost to save the minister. In return for Danby's voluntary resignation, the king granted him a full pardon, and was present in person to see the Great Seal attached to it. At the same time he raised the ex-treasurer to the marquisate. If this was a defiant gesture of loyalty, it was also an act of self-preservation. Charles knew, as his father had known, that every concession weakened the monarchy and it was during this crisis that Charles II came closest to the stubbornness that had characterised Charles I. His attitude was captured by Dryden in his play *Troilus and Cressida*, which had its first performance in April and related, in scarcely veiled terms, to the current political situation. Urging his brother to disembarrass himself of a woman for his own safety, Hector says,

> If parting from a mistress can procure
> A nation's happiness, show me that prince
> Who dares to trust his future fame so far
> To stand the shock of annals, blotted thus:
> *He sold his country for a woman's love.*

To which Troilus staunchly replies,

> And what are they that I should give up her
> To make them happy? Let me tell you, Brother,
> The public is the lees of vulgar slaves:
> Slaves, with the minds of slaves.

Though he would never have used such language, Charles held the Commons in similar contempt. If they demanded the sacrifice of a minister, a mistress or a wife, he would – he must – stand firm. He assured Danby that he would not allow the 'malicious prosecution of the parliament' to proceed. But proceed it did. The House of Lords tried to rescue the fallen minister by demanding his banishment but the lower house would have none of it. Danby was despatched to the Tower and, while legal arguments were raging, Charles once again prorogued parliament and subsequently dissolved it. In sharp contrast to its predecessor, this 'first exclusion parliament' lasted little more than four months. Charles had fallen back on his father's tactic of trying to dispense with an assembly that was getting too big for its boots.

To save friends and close advisers he used every conceivable trick, short of giving the demonstrative representatives what they wanted. In March, Shaftesbury introduced an Exclusion Bill into the upper chamber, which sought to remove James from the line of succession. The earl's supporters, who now began to be identified by their enemies as 'Whigs', after the extremist, Presbyterian rebels of an earlier day, failed to carry the motion but they now had not only a cause – Protestant succession – but a choice of figureheads. Some favoured William, Prince of Orange, who had recently married James' elder daughter, Mary. Others were for recognising the claim of Charles' eldest illegitimate son, the Duke of Monmouth. Around the beginning of the year, there had, indeed, been a determined pamphlet campaign aimed at proving that the king had, in fact, been married to Lucy Walter, Monmouth's mother. Charles not only denied this, he denied it with all the force at his disposal. He made a solemn declaration to his intimate advisers, repeated it in full council, personally wrote and signed a document declaring 'in the presence of Almighty God, that I never gave nor made any contract of marriage, nor was married to any woman whatsoever, but to my present wife Queen Catherine now living'. Finally he published the disavowal for all to read in the *London Gazette*. At the same time Charles tried to placate the opposition by giving Shaftesbury and some of his friends positions in a newly formed government. To ease the tension he also sent the Duke and Duchess of York abroad.

For both Charles and Catherine this was their most abysmal crisis. It was also their finest hour. Driven together, they supported and drew strength from each other. When Charles refused the easy way out of nominating Monmouth as his legitimate heir it was in the full realisation that to let parliament settle the Crown upon a head of their choosing would be to betray everything that the monarchy stood for. But he also had Catherine in mind and his vehement denial of a contract with Lucy was also a vehement affirmation of the solidity of his marriage. Catherine responded warmly. She, too, shunned the chance to run away from a distressing situation. Instead of obeying her brother's command to return home she was adamant that she would stay at her husband's side. This decision was made more difficult for her by the hectoring of the marquis de Arouches, who accused her, in front of the court, of disloyalty to her family and nation, and by angry letters from Dom Pedro. The queen was struck to the heart and complained bitterly to her brother of his ambassador's behaviour:

... he speaks to me in terms so different from those my replies merit that he gives me cause for pain ... and because I fear he may dare to write to you in the same doubtful manner as that in which he dared to speak in my presence, I am obliged to give this explanation, that the truth may be clearly known.

I have no need of praise from the marquis but it is very degrading that you doubt me. The king will speak on my behalf [as will] as many as know me, who know that there is no-one on earth whom I value more highly than the Prince of Portugal, my brother. By the chastisement of God, I have been forced to give evidence of the truth of what I did not

The Key to the Rehearsal.

A famous moment in the King's theatre: Nell Gwyn as Valeria in Dryden's *Tyrannic Love*, springs from her death bed to speak the epilogue. (*Frontispiece to section entitled The Works of His Grace George Villiers, Duke of Buckingham, in Two Volumes*, 1715)

St James's Park in the time of Charles II, *c.*1720.
In this panorama by Johannes Kip, St James's Palace can be seen on the left,
beyond which (*top right*) can be seen the Whitehall Palace complex.

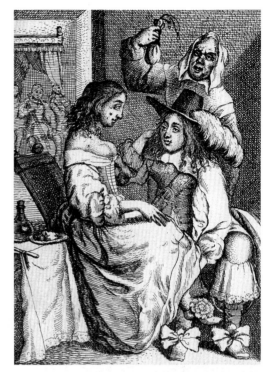

(*Above right*)
A Carolean gallant being
robbed in a London brothel.

(*Below right*) 79 Pall Mall –
the home of Nell Gwyn in 1820.

A Choice Collection of Books
being the Library of the late
famous Unborn Doctor, are
to be put to Sale this Day, and
to continue untill all be Sold,
at Mr. L___ 's Auction in the
North West Corner of Middle
Moorfields. Catalogues may
be had at most of the eminent
Booksellers in the four Quarters
of Moorfeilds Gratis. the Books
may be Seen before or at the
time of Sale.

Sutton Nicholls excudit

Come Sirs, and view this famous Library,
'Tis pity Learning should discourag'd be :
Here's Bookes (that is, if they were but well Sold)
I will maintain't are worth their weight in Gold.

**THE
COMPLEAT
AUCTIONER.**

Then bid apace, and break me out of hand :
Ne'er cry you don't the Subject understand :
For this I'll say - howe'er the Case may hit,
Whoever buys of me. - I teach 'em Wit.

There was no literary censorship in late 17th century England.
This itinerant bookseller offers his customers pornography
as well as medical treatises and works of fiction.

pope-burning procession. These events grew in number and elaborateness during the reign and were an outlet for the intense anti-Catholicism felt in many parts of the country.

The Coffee-House –
new phenomenon in the 1660s, where
vs, gossip and political satire were shared,
the consternation of the government.

(*Left*) Stage set for *The Empre[ss]
of Morroco* as performed by th[e]
Duke's Company in 1673.

Frances Stuart as Britannia.
This famous beauty, who mercif[ully]
evaded Charles' amorous approac[hes]
was the model for this medal
celebrating the Peace of Breda, 1[667]
and for the new copper coinag[e]
introduced around the same tim[e]

Whitehall Palace from St James's Park, clearly showing the grand staircase built for Barbara Villiers, (Duchess of Cleveland). Note the carriage and six, presumably belonging to the King's mistress. Painted by Hendrick Danckerts *c.* 1630–80.

Henrietta Maria as a widow, painted by William Faithorne.

think had been doubted. But it is your minister who has done these services to you and me and forces me to demonstrations such as no slanders whatever laid upon me by mine enemies compelled me to do till now . . . It seems you are practising to take away my life with pure grief. . .[101]

King and queen both extended their protection to others threatened by the general hysteria. When parliament obliged Catherine to shear her entourage of all but a handful of papists, one of the ladies she elected to keep was Lady Portsmouth. It was a magnanimous gesture motivated by a love for her husband which was stronger than her resentment of the exhibitionist rivalry with which Louise lorded it at Whitehall. In July, Sir George Wakeman, Catherine's physician, came up for trial. Every other judicial proceeding against men fingered by Oates and Co. had ended in conviction and the anti-court party confidently expected another show trial which would keep the Popish Plot bandwagon rolling. Charles had other ideas. The claws of bigotry and mass hysteria were reaching out towards the queen and had to be slapped down hard. He took a leaf from the conspirators' book. They had been manipulating the courts and undermining justice for their own ends; he would do the same. His first manoeuvre was to have Wakeman's accusers brought before the council. Throughout two long sessions Oates and his accomplice, William Bedloe, were quizzed as to the evidence they had implicating the queen. It amounted to very little but Charles was not content to score a partial victory; he was set on discrediting the plotters and weakening their political opposition. He made sure that Wakeman was provided with full details of the case against him and that the chief prosecution witnesses were brought into court and available for cross-examination. It is almost certain, also, that the king leaned on Lord Chief Justice Scroggs, the presiding judge, for that unscrupulous and belligerent anti-papist who had been a tower of strength to the Oates camp in previous trials now made a complete U-turn. (His interruptions and summations were notoriously peppered with such remarks as 'This is a religion that quite unhinges all piety, all morality . . . They eat their God, they kill their king and saint the murderer.') He warned the jury not to be swayed by plots and rumours of plots and not to deprive a man of his life without clear and unassailable evidence. The twelve good men and true took the hint and acquitted Wakeman.

It was the first setback the plotters had encountered and the government hoped that the tide had turned, but matters were destined to get worse before they got better. Now it was the Duke of Monmouth's cook who laid fresh information before Shaftesbury concerning members of Catherine's chaplaincy team, supposedly implicated in one of the many foiled attempts on the king's life. The earl demanded the right to interrogate the queen. This Charles angrily refused and then demonstrated his support for his wife by frequent visits to Somerset House, often staying with her for most of the night. But the royal couple were desperately worried and contingency plans were made for Catherine's speedy departure for Portugal if this became necessary. Then, as if things were not bad enough, Charles, who prided himself on his strong constitution, fell suddenly ill. The vultures immediately gathered. James and Monmouth rushed back to court and their supporters were ready to contest the succession. The king made a quick recovery but the scare had underlined for all concerned the urgency of deciding the succession. Charles sent the two contenders away again and also took advantage of a surge of popularity to dismiss Shaftesbury. A few weeks later he repented of this step and offered the Whig leader another post but Shaftesbury responded that he would only accept if the king withdrew support from both his brother and his wife, conditions which were, of course, quite unacceptable.

It really did seem to many that '41 is come again'. Crown and parliament were at loggerheads and the country was dividing along politico-religious lines. In February 1679 there was a riot in the King's Theatre provoked by Monmouth's supporters. Charles angrily closed the playhouse for several weeks but that chastening did not prevent a further tumult in the summer when 'many swords were drawn'. It wanted only a charismatic leader, a Pym or a Cromwell, for open rebellion to break out. Over the next year Charles put off the recall of parliament no fewer than seven times, while desperately appealing to Louis for funds that would enable him to 'subsist'. Opposition leaders were furious and resorted to other measures – pamphlets and petitions – to make their demands known. The Duke of Monmouth, daily increasing in popularity, chafed at his exile and was encouraged in his ambitions by supporters at home. At the end of November he could stand the inactivity no longer. Without permission he returned to London and was secretly lodged in Shaftesbury's house. The news leaked out and the citizens lit bonfires and rang their bells in jubilant welcome. Charles was furious at having the delicate political balance he was trying to sustain so wantonly upset by his own son. He refused to see Monmouth, stripped him of all his offices and ordered him out of the country.

Among those who tried to pour oil on troubled waters was Nell Gwynn. She was Monmouth's friend and he was careful to cultivate her as a conduit to the king. This does not mean that she supported his claim to the throne. In fact she ridiculed him for it in her own irreverent way and called him 'Prince Perkin' (after one of the pretenders to Henry VII's throne). Nell, who had no great ambitions for her own sons, may well have considered Monmouth's claim presumptuous. After all, he had no more right to the Crown than any of Charles' other male bastards. But Nell's greatest motivation is likely to have been her loyalty to and affection for the king. She never wavered in her devotion and never engaged in any political intrigues. Now she did her best to reconcile father and son but even her wiles were on this occasion powerless to overcome Charles' anxiety-driven indignation. Monmouth was at a turning point. He could obey the king and win his way back into favour or make a concerted bid for popular support. He often came to Nell's house in Pall Mall and her advice was succinct: 'pack up and be gone', she said. But patient waiting was not in the young duke's nature and 'he gave himself fatally up to the Lord Shaftesbury's conduct, who put him on all the methods imaginable to make himself popular. He went round many parts of England, pretending it was for hunting and horse matches, many thousands coming together in most places to see him, so that this looked like the mustering up the force of the party.'[102] In fact, apparent success was an illusion. The rallying of enthusiasts and the merely curious to the duke's presence alarmed not only those who were, by conviction, loyal to the Crown, but also the rank and file of English men and women who caught the scent of civil war in the air.

While Catherine and Nell stuck close to the king, Louise cast around for political allies. It is difficult to follow her shifting allegiances in the months of the Popish Plot and its aftermath. She had certainly sent large sums of money to France to provide a cushion against any sudden flight that might be forced upon her but escape was a last resort. Remaining in her own luxurious lair at the centre of national life could not but involve her with the leading politicians who were seeking to manipulate events for personal and party advantage. The man who emerged as the leader of the ruling clique after the departure of Danby and Shaftesbury was Robert Spencer, Earl of Sunderland, a thoroughgoing *politique* adept at following the track of personal advantage through the thickets of political complexity. He drew around him a party of men – the 'Tories' – who identified with a strong monarchy, adherence to the Church of England and opposition to toleration. Since Sunderland needed close contact with Charles he naturally paid court to Lady Portsmouth. However, if she was to be a bridge between king and minister she had to be firmly fixed at both ends and, given the evasiveness and secrecy of the two men, this was seldom easy. Sunderland was actually in favour of striking some kind of a deal with William of Orange in order to combat the threat of Monmouth, and Louise seems to have supported this policy. At the same time she realised that Charles rejected tinkering with the accepted rules of hereditary succession and she knew that he was striving mightily for French support and freedom from the shackles of a Protestant parliament. Yet she was careful not to cut herself off entirely from the opposition, and for this she had a very personal reason.

The over-subtle Montagu, who was leader of a parliamentary group only tangentially connected with Shaftesbury, pointed out that exclusion could work to Louise's advantage. His scheme involved persuading Charles to pass over his brother's claim to the throne in return for an Act of Parliament which would grant him the right to nominate his own successor. He calculated that William, Monmouth and their supporters would all be bound to support this compromise. However, once the succession lay entirely in Charles' gift, those who had the greatest influence over him would, in effect, be the real kingmakers. And who most likely to be the dominant figure among his counsellors but the Duchess of Portsmouth? That being so, she would be able to persuade Charles to nominate her own son. Montagu had one more ace to lay before her: to secure the support of France young Charles Lennox, Duke of Richmond, could be offered as a husband to Louis XIV's natural daughter, the duchesse de Bourbon. Did Louise fall for this Byzantine strategy? Did she not realise that Charles the schemer could recognise a fellow practitioner when he saw one? Well, Montagu was, as we have already seen, extremely plausible and his plan awakened all Louise's hubristic ambitions.

Yet still she kept her options open. While contemplating a plan that would deprive James of his inheritance, she maintained close contact with the duke and was widely believed to be acting in his interests. She was, for example, among those who wrote urgently to him when Charles fell ill. The heir presumptive, while exiled from the centre of power, desperately needed her advocacy and remained in close contact with her. Their main intermediary was Louis Duras, Earl of Feversham (modern Faversham). Duras, the younger son of a great French family and nephew of the magnificent General Turenne, had a military and diplomatic career behind him and was a favourite of the Duke of York, who had complete trust in him. He came by his title as an indirect result of one of the most celebrated tragedies of the era. In 1655, Freeman Sondes, the wastrel younger son of Sir George Sondes, a fervent Kentish royalist impoverished by the war, despatched his sleeping elder brother with a cleaver and was subsequently hanged for the murder. The devastated Sir George was left childless and his grief was compounded soon after by the death of his wife. The following year he married a woman of the Villiers family, who eventually presented him with two daughters. Duras married the elder girl, and when his father-in-law was raised to the peerage, he secured the remainder to Sondes' estate and titles. The crisis of the late 1670s brought Feversham into the bosom of the Stuart family as a trusted adviser and confidant. In December 1679, he became Catherine's master of the horse and, a few months later, her lord chamberlain. He was precisely the kind of well-connected Frenchman to whom Louise naturally gravitated and the two worked closely together. So closely that, in the following spring, a Taunton goldsmith was indicted for saying that King Charles had no council but the Duchess of Portsmouth, the French ambassador, Lord Duras and Lord Lauderdale.[103]

The duchess had always advertised (and perhaps exaggerated) her influence with the king and, having seen off the challenge of Hortense

Mancini, she was more inclined than ever to emphasise her importance. Politicians were obliged to canvas her support but, if they were wise, they did so circumspectly, for she was now more widely hated than ever and Louise's friendship could be a double-edged sword. In a contemporary satire the duchess's ministerial allies are represented as saying,

> She is the strongest pillar of our hope,
> The surest friend of our brave Plot and pope.
> She is all power; she is all command.
> By her assistance we'll betray this land.[104]

Popular invective against Louise, encouraged by the lapsing of the Licensing Act in June 1679, reached new lavatorial depths:

> Portsmouth, that pocky bitch,
> A damned papistical drab,
> An ugly, deformed witch,
> Eaten up with the mange and scab.
>
> This French hag's pocky bum
> So powerful is of late,
> Although it's blind and dumb,
> It rules both Church and State.[105]

Just how determined her enemies were to remove her from the king's side became clear at the end of 1679, when the opposition launched a well-orchestrated attack aimed at bringing the duchess to trial. A tract entitled *Articles of High Treason and Other High Crimes and Misdemeanours against the Duchess of Portsmouth* was published in the New Year. It accused Louise of a whole raft of diabolical acts, including sending vast sums of money out of the country, protecting Lord Ranalegh from prosecution, causing the repeated prorogation of parliament, maintaining the 'accursed amity' between France and England, sneaking Catholic priests into the royal chambers, spreading a rumour that she and Charles were secretly married and that her son was the rightful heir to the throne, involvement in the Popish Plot, and attempting to poison the king with the aid of a French confectioner especially brought over for the purpose.[106] The opposition intended to proceed against the duchess by parliamentary impeachment and Charles' determination to thwart them was a major reason for his repeated prorogation of the assembly.

The determined attacks on the *maîtresse en titre* severely shook her and her allies. Sunderland now distanced himself from Louise and she abandoned the Duke of York. By the time parliament reconvened in October 1680, both mistress and minister had been wonderfully converted to the cause of exclusion. Louise had to proceed carefully. Through an intermediary she made contact with William, Baron Howard of Escrick, a radical parliamentarian but one who had already demonstrated chameleon qualities as a politician. The two held clandestine meetings at Whitehall to which, it was later claimed, the king was party. Exactly what was said at these tête-à-têtes will never be known but the flow of information must have been two-way; Louise probing the activities of Shaftesbury's party and Howard trying to determine whether Lady Portsmouth could bring Charles to accept the necessity for exclusion.

Louise obviously, through Howard, impressed the Whig leadership for when, in January, a motion was raised in parliament for her removal from court it gained no support and was quashed by the Whigs, who now believed that she might be useful to them. She seems to have convinced herself and her new allies that Charles had come round to the inevitability of keeping James off the throne. The fate of the second Exclusion Bill must, therefore, have been as much of a shock to her as all other parties and factions involved. Charles, his back to the wall, reacted with a resolution which took everyone by surprise. The bill easily passed all its stages in the lower chamber but when it was brought into the House of Lords the king attended all sessions of the debate and made his opposition quite clear. The peers rejected the Bill by thirty-three votes. A stunned Commons responded by offering Charles £600,000 in supply in return for exclusion but he firmly rejected the bribe and once more prorogued parliament. A week later came another dissolution.

Louise was now exposed as having no greater access to the king's innermost thoughts than anyone else and this led to her public humiliation. Now her political alliances crumbled. Sunderland was dismissed and other advisers who had favoured exclusion were removed from the council. Charles summoned parliament to meet on 21 March 1681, but not at Westminster. He deliberately removed MPs and peers from the influences of the capital and chose Oxford, that city always loyal to the Stuarts, for the next session. When he arrived to open it he was in uncompromising mood and he gave bystanders a very visual demonstration of this. The three travelling companions with him in his coach were Catherine, Louise and Nell.

CHAPTER 13

The Ra-ree Show

For those with long enough memories, the closing years of the reign may have seemed like a return to the 1630s. The king ruled without parliament – he simply ignored the Triennial Act, which had ordained that Lords and Commons must be summoned at least every three years. The realm was at peace with its neighbours – it had to be, for only by avoiding costly foreign entanglements could Charles escape the clutches of the tax-making body. Government policy became more reactionary – the king, who would never have inaugurated an autocratic regime, slipped easily into it because the nation seemed prepared to accept it and he allowed his agents progressively to remove radicals from positions of authority both nationally and locally. Crown and Mitre held sway once more as in the good old days of Charles I and Laud. At the centre of the quiescent nation domestic harmony prevailed in the court. The ageing king, sexual passion mostly spent, enjoyed the company of his women, his favoured male companions and his clutch of illegitimate sons and daughters, while a Tory administration handled administrative details.

Yet the surface calm was an illusion, just as it had been during the eleven years' tyranny of the king's father. Profound political problems had not been solved; they had merely been put on hold. This did not bother Charles. Only the practicalities of government concerned him, not political theory. He had won the battle over exclusion and he remained constant in supporting James' right to succeed him, although that sometimes involved the heartache of ostracising Monmouth, the unruly son for whom he retained a firm affection. If he doubted the Duke of York's ability to take over the juggling act he had performed for more than two decades he was determined to make no constitutional provision that might make things easier for him. *Le déluge* might come but it would be *après nous* and that was really all that mattered to Charles. What he and his ministers did in 1681–2 with the aid of the *maîtresse en titre* was to thrust the cork firmly into the bottle of Whiggery and dissent, but the liquor was still fermenting.

Charles might have been forgiven a degree of optimism in the summer of 1681, for at Oxford, in March, he had acted speedily, decisively, cleverly and with complete success to confound his enemies. Fresh elections in February had shown the Whigs to be as strong as ever. Partisan ballad-writers and satirists were even more prolific. Though Louise de Keroualle had shifted her political position, her association with the Duke of York and the 'triple-crowned monster' of Rome had, by now, become a standard convention in pamphlets and lampoons. The writer of 'A Satire on Court Ladies' directed his venom at members of the York–Portsmouth circle, as he conceived it. 'Oglethorpe' and 'Lucy' were avowed supporters of James, and their wives were bosom companions of Louise. The 'Beast', of course, is Rome.

> Speak out, then, Muse, and all the vices tell
> With which our countries, court and cities swell.
> Though Oglethorpe, bold Lucy and the Beast
> Are stately pillars of York's interest,
> Yet still we'll curse the monster who'd enslave
> Our free-born souls and make's own brother's grave.
> Though Portsmouth have strong ruffians she can trust
> As well to serve her malice as her lust,
> Yet still she's slavish, prostrate, false and foul,
> Destroys our prince's honour, health and soul.[107]

But some writers went a great deal further. Not content to attack the evil influences at court, they aimed at Charles himself, accusing him of autocratic tendencies and prophesying that the end of Stuart ambitions was to set up a Catholic tyranny. Stephen College, carpenter by trade but by avocation a public speaker and writer of numerous violent attacks on Romanists, distributed his most popular ballad, 'The Ra-ree Show or The True Protestant Procession', in the weeks before parliament reassembled. In his somewhat confused allegory the king appears both as a tyrant determined to impose arbitrary rule and as a feeble, fairground huckster carrying on his back an absolutist ra-ree show (peep-show).

> ... What's past is not to come, with a hey, with a hey,
> Now safe is David's bum, with a ho,
> Then hey for Oxford , ho,
> Strong government Rar-ee show,
> With a hey, trany nony nony no.
>
> Rar-ee show is resolved, with a hey, with a hey,
> This is worse than dissolved, with a ho,
> [i.e., the king will try to go further than just dissolving parliament]
> May the mighty weight at's back

> Make's lecherous loins to crack,
> With a hey trany nony nony no.
>
> Methinks he seems to stagger, with a hey, with a hey,
> Who but now did so swagger, with a ho,
> God's fish, he's stuck i' the mire
> And all the fat's i' the fire.
> With a hey, trany nony nony no.

The versifier calls on Shaftesbury and his friends to 'pull down the rar-ee show'.

> And now you have freed the nation, with a hey, with a hey
> Cram in the convocation [the bishops], with a ho
> With pensioners all and some [those receiving French subsidies]
> Into this chest of Rome,
> With a hey trany nony nony no . . .
>
> Haloo, the hunt's begun, with a hey, with a hey,
> Like father, like son, with a ho . . .[108]

The hint that Charles II might be dealt with as his father had been dealt with was, of course, a dangerous one to make and it is not surprising that College was subsequently arrested for plotting the king's death but, at the time the ballad was written, it seemed, at least to optimists, that a strong curb was about to be placed on Stuart pretensions.

At Oxford the opposition certainly gave no ground. Charles offered a compromise on the succession: James was to take the throne but his political powers would be curbed by the presence of a Protestant regent. The proposition was full of holes, the largest being the character of James, who would not have accepted any limitation to his power. The Whigs dismissed the offer and brought in a third Exclusion Bill. This was crunch time. It would decide whether or not parliament had any role in deciding who should wear the crown and whether there was to be a religious qualification for monarchs in England, as there was in most Catholic countries. There could be no more evasive tactics and now, for the first time, Charles made his position crystal clear to Shaftesbury. And his determination.

> Let there be no delusion, I will not yield, nor will I be bullied. Men usually become more timid as they become older. It is the opposite with me, and for what may remain of my life I am determined that nothing will tarnish my reputation. I have law and reason and all right-thinking men on my side. I have the Church, and nothing will ever separate us.[109]

It would be agreeable to interpret the words as marking some kind of conversion; as showing that the seasoned pragmatist and master opportunist had, at last, found a principle on which he was prepared to take a stand. The firmness of his declaration might suggest that he would face a second exile or challenge parliament to mount a second rebellion rather than betray that principle. In reality, no such sea change had overtaken the king's character. If he affected a new bravado it was because, for the first time in almost three years, he came to the card table with a fistful of aces.

The first was a change in the public mood. The initial anti-Catholic fervour stirred up by Oates and his crew of informers, slanderers and perjurers had begun to give way to scepticism and alarm. People feared that a witch-hunt against supposed papist plotters might become the precursor to an attack on the monarchy which would lead to a resurgence of civil war. The Earl of Shaftesbury who, like the young lady of Riga, had cheerfully ridden the Popish Plot tiger, now looked as though he might share her fate.

> The shedding so much blood upon such doubtful evidence was like to have proved fatal to him who drove all these things on with the greatest fury; I mean the Earl of Shaftesbury himself. And the strange change that appeared over the nation with relation to the Duke [of York], from such an eager prosecution of the exclusion to an indecent courting and magnifying him . . . showed how little men could build on popular heats, which have their ebbings and flowings, and their hot and cold fits.[110]

Charles showed that he, too, could master the arts of propaganda. When he delivered his opening speech to parliament, on 21 March, he had it printed and distributed throughout the country. In it he exactly caught the mood of his war-wary subjects with a more-in-sorrow-than-in-anger reflection on the 'undutiful' behaviour of the last three parliaments and a strong asseveration of his commitment to Protestantism.

The reverse in national sentiment was accompanied by an economic upturn. European peace gave a boost to trade and an embargo on French imports came to an end in 1681. This brought a flood of luxury goods into the country and significantly added to the excise revenue.

However, what clinched Charles' ability to strike a new, independent pose was the success of his negotiations with Louis. Inspired as much by political considerations as by ideology, the French king was genuinely alarmed by the progress of the Whigs. He needed a government in England that was friendly and dependent. His ambassadors left him in no doubt about the overwhelming anti-French sentiment of the majority of Charles' subjects. If the Stuarts were removed or involved in a struggle for survival or obliged to fall in with the wishes of an over-powerful parliament this would unnecessarily complicate his own foreign policy. At the same time, he was quite unable to regard the opposition to Charles as simply a group of political malcontents; they were evil men in league with vile heretics and, just as he was engaged in a campaign of extirpation against his own Huguenots, so he felt that he must, in conscience, help a threatened brother monarch to exert the rights of religious absolutism against his own Protestant rabble. The tangible results of all this were an immediate payment of £40,000 and the promise of £115,000 p.a. for the next three years on condition that the English parliament did not meet during that period. Thus, when Charles came to Oxford he knew that, as long as he could avoid war or any other emergencies, his position was secure.

Unaware of the French deal, his enemies were caught completely off guard by the theatrical performance to which Charles treated them on 28 March. The Commons were labouring under some difficulty, having (deliberately?) been allocated somewhat restricted accommodation in the Schools. The king pleasantly agreed to move them into the Sheldonian Theatre on Monday the 28th. Accordingly, they were unhurriedly carrying on their business on Monday morning while awaiting their transfer to a more commodious venue. The Lords, meanwhile, were assembled in Christ Church hall. Thither came the king in a closed chair, his bearers slipping and stumbling in the street's frost-hardened ruts. Any passer-by, observing him dismount and enter the college, would readily have assumed that the bulky cloak in which he was enveloped was to protect him from the cold, though they might have wondered at the wrapped bundle he carried. As soon as he had taken his place on the throne, he ordered the Commons to be summoned. While Black Rod was about his business, Charles took off his cloak, revealing the state robes underneath. He removed the crown from its wrappings and placed it on his head. As the MPs filed in they were stunned by the sight before them. They were even more taken aback by what was probably the briefest speech ever made by a sovereign to the representatives of his people: 'All the world may see to what a point we are come. We are not likely to have a good end when the divisions at the beginning are such.' He declared the parliament dissolved, hurried out and immediately took coach for Windsor, leaving confusion and consternation behind him.

Now Charles was faced with the prospect of MPs returning to their shires and boroughs murmuring agin the government and stirring up discontent. To counteract this he immediately set about drafting another long declaration to be read in all churches a couple of weeks later. The sentiments he instructed clergy to express were blatantly dishonest and the royal promises to which they gave voice were lies. Having explained the king's disappointment with the ungracious behaviour of recent parliaments, it concluded,

But notwithstanding all this, let not the restless malice of ill men who are labouring to poison our people, some out of fondness for their old

323

beloved Commonwealth principles, and some out of anger at their being disappointed in the particular designs they had for the accomplishment of their own ambition and greatness, persuade any of our good subjects that we intend to lay aside the use of Parliaments. For we do still declare that no irregularities in Parliament shall ever make us out of love with Parliaments; which we look upon as the best method for healing the distempers of the kingdom, and the only means to preserve the monarchy in that due credit and respect which it ought to have both at home and abroad. And for this cause we are resolved, by the blessing of God, to have frequent Parliaments; and both in and out of Parliament to use our utmost endeavours to extirpate Popery and to redress all the grievances of our good subjects, and in all things to govern according to the laws of the kingdom.[111]

This outrageous exercise of flimflam worked superbly. Over the next few months a torrent of loyal addresses poured in from all corners of the king's realm. Town corporations, trade guilds, JPs, manorial authorities and even groups of apprentices fell over themselves to assure Charles of their devotion to him and his lawful heirs for ever.

Some biographers see in this evidence of Machiavellian cunning, political foresight and skilful planning of a preconceived programme. They suggest that Charles, who had long concealed his acumen behind a mask of indolence and hedonism, now revealed himself as a master political tactician who shaped events rather than being shaped by them. The truth is rather more complex. As Clarendon had long before observed, Charles certainly did possess intelligence and an acute understanding of men and events but was just too lazy to be proactive. He preferred to use other people's brains and talents. Just as he expected his women to entertain him in bed and declined to play the ardent, attentive, inventive lover, so he let his ministers govern without providing clear policy directives for them. He kept his own counsel, having long ago discovered that making politicians and diplomats guess what his plans and intentions might be left him with maximum room for manoeuvre. He had instincts rather than principles. He wanted to live as king with as few limitations as possible on his actions but that did not make him a dedicated autocrat. He would never have sacrificed everything for the sake of a high doctrine of kingship, like Charles I, and he would never have worked assiduously to make a potent reality of absolute monarchy, as did Louis XIV.

So, the king who appeared in 1681 with a ra-ree show on his back was not someone who had dramatically discarded the habits and attitudes of a lifetime. Burnet recalled that, in the early weeks of the new year, 'The king was now very uneasy. He saw he was despised all Europe over as a prince that had neither treasure nor power' and, for this reason, he opened negotiations with the opposition to find some acceptable compromise.[112] It was only when the French negotiations bore fruit that his cunning mind grasped the implications of a unique conjunction of favourable circumstances. He did not defend the succession out of love for his brother, or reverence for his murdered father, or fond memories of his dynastically ambitious mother, or a well-concealed desire for Catholicisation of his realm, or a belief in untrammelled monarchy. If the only price of survival had been giving in to the Whigs he would have paid it. As it was, he was quick-witted enough to see that he could dish the Whigs, get rid of an obnoxious parliament, defend himself and those close to him from further humiliation and be avenged on those who had treated him with barely disguised contempt for so long.

But that alone does not fully explain Charles' precipitate action on 28 March. There was about the escapade something of a desperate gamble. And it had a historical parallel. Almost forty years before, another dispute had arisen between king and parliament over issues of privilege. On that occasion Charles I had burst into the Commons chamber and tried to arrest five members. His humiliating failure was the prelude to his flight from London and jaw-jaw became war-war. The present king's father had been driven to that expedient by the Commons' threat to impeach his queen. Charles II was now motivated by a similar urgent need to protect those close to him from the anger of parliament, and specifically to keep his 'dearest Fubs', Louise de Keroualle, out of the Whigs' clutches.

It was precisely because the king had no programme and shared with no one the ideas that were in his mind that Lady Portsmouth was in real difficulties. Ever since 1678 she had found herself floundering in a sea of uncertainty, and moving awkwardly from political rock to political rock. She had ended up clinging to the exclusionists because she believed that Charles was prepared to do a deal with some of the opposition leaders if suitably face-saving arrangements could be made. But for a second time he had slammed the door in the faces of Shaftesbury and his allies. And this had left Lady Portsmouth discredited and friendless. York, Sunderland and Shaftesbury all felt to some degree betrayed. The last thing she now needed was to be named in a sensational treason trial.

That she was, was largely her own fault. In her insecurity she had employed one Edward Fitzharris, an Irish Catholic undercover agent, to find out what the Whigs might be hatching against her. It was he who had introduced her to Lord Howard of Escrick. In the malodorous underworld of plots, counter-plots, espionage and character assassination Fitzharris was very much at home and was prepared to make his repellent services available to the highest bidder. Having, at Louise's behest, insinuated himself into the counsels of the opposition, Fitzharris decided to enhance his value by fabricating evidence against them. He concocted a supposed Whig pamphlet, *The True Englishman Speaking Plain English in a Letter from a Friend to a Friend*, and planned to plant it on Howard. Thus, while the duchess was working for a *rapprochement* between king and parliament, her agent had decided to undermine the Whigs by 'revealing' a plot, not only to exclude James, but also to depose Charles. This would strengthen the king's hand and he would, doubtless, show his gratitude. Perjury and libel were in fashion; Oates and Co. had demonstrated how profitable this brand of criminality could be and Fitzharris thought that, he, too, could cash in on it. Unfortunately for him, he was betrayed by an accomplice, arrested and thrown into Newgate.

Once there, the prisoner immediately began singing a very different song. Now he offered to put his creative imagination at the disposal of the Whigs. The elaborate conspiracy theory he concocted in his overcrowded, typhus-ridden prison involved James, Danby and Louise, the murder of Godfrey and designs on the life of the king. Fitzharris' fabrications grew increasingly labyrinthine the more desperate his position became. He could only save himself if he was worth more alive than dead to one side or the other in the political conflict. Shaftesbury and his party had an interest in his survival – at least in the short term. They wanted to proceed by parliamentary impeachment so that they could retain control of his prosecution, for, whatever lies and half-truths Fitzharris spewed out, one thing was clear: he *had* had dealings with the Duchess of Portsmouth and, perhaps, directly with the king. Skilfully revealed before the bar of parliament, this could be political dynamite. By the same token, Charles wanted the accused to be swiftly tried in the criminal court – tried, sentenced and silenced for ever. He acted quickly. Fitzharris was moved from Newgate to the royal prison of the Tower. Charles instructed the prosecution to take place in King's Bench. This gave rise to a heated constitutional debate in the Oxford parliament about which court had precedence in treason cases. Balked by the royal party in the Lords, the Commons now passed a resolution 'that all those who concurred in any sort in trying Fitzharris in any other court were betrayers of the liberties of their country'.[113] This was the immediate background to the hurried termination of the 1681 parliament. The king's wild gamble came off. At one stroke he silenced the grumbling members and sent them all back to their homes. Whether he would have succeeded so completely had the parliament met, as usual, in Westminster is a matter for conjecture.

However, king and mistress were not yet out of the wood. Popular discontent might have lost its parliamentary focus: it had not lost its intensity. Interest now centred on the trial of Fitzharris, or rather on the trials of Oliver Plunket, Catholic Archbishop of Armagh, and Fitzharris, scheduled for 8 and 9 June respectively. Plunket was charged with plotting to bring a French and Irish army into England. It was, of course, nonsense but Charles, who had no animus against the archbishop, needed to establish confidence in the prosecution's false witnesses because they would also be giving evidence in the actions against Fitzharris and Whig leaders against whom he was now compiling a case. Lord Chief Justice Francis Pemberton presided on both occasions and a certain George Jeffreys made his first appearance as prosecutor in important show trials. They duly did their duty by the king. Fitzharris and Plunket were both executed on 1 July – public testimony to the even-handedness of Stuart corruption.

The delay is explained by the desire of royal agents to make maximum propaganda capital out of the prisoner in the Tower. They were instructed to discredit Shaftesbury and his allies and to accumulate evidence against them. To clear his brother, wife and mistress of the calumnies daily growing in intensity Charles had determined to mount a vigorous campaign against the Whig leadership. Royal agents visited Fitzharris in the Tower and held out the hope of a reprieve in return for a confession implicating certain targeted opponents of the regime. Fitzharris' new version of events named Howard as the author of the damaging pamphlet and other prominent Whigs as his aiders and abettors. Having obtained the confession, the government leaked it in the hope that the accused would flee and, thereby, demonstrate their guilt. Howard, advised by good friends who stood by him fearlessly, stayed at home and was arrested and taken to the Tower. The charges against him were patently absurd and their source was so unreliable that the courts refused to proceed against him and he was released after a couple of months.

The king did, however, manage to snatch another crumb of comfort from the judicial proceedings of the summer. Stephen College, the writer of 'The Ra-ree Show' and other vitriolic anti-court propaganda, was arrested on the day of Plunket's trial. He, too, was incarcerated in the Tower and cited for seditious words and actions. However, a London jury at the Old Bailey threw out the charge on the basis of insufficient evidence. The government were furious, declaring that Whig influence in the capital meant that the king was hard put to get justice there. They had College sent to Oxford for a new trial, where some of his offences were allegedly committed. There the usual tactics of perjured testimony, packed jury and browbeating were employed to achieve a verdict of guilty on a charge of encompassing the king's death, but it was clear that College was principally to be made an example of as an author of ballads and tracts against members of the royal circle. Jeffreys, again appearing for the prosecution, feigned indignation that a member of so humble a calling as the accused should presume to concern himself with affairs of state. 'God be thanked, we have a wise prince,' he observed, 'and God be thanked he hath wise counsellors about him and he and they know well enough how to do their own business, and not to need the advice of a joiner.'[114] College's fate was designed as a warning to any scribblers who might be tempted to put on record their disapproval of king, court and government.

It was not very effective. The flood of censure continued to rise, the tone of invective plaints and satires changing noticeably with the passing of the years. Witty squibs and bawdy verses gave place to unsubtle tirades and naked pornography. The nation was divided to an extent that it had not been since the 1640s. Some resented the 'troublemakers', a portmanteau word into which were stuffed Whigs, Nonconformists, republicans, supporters of rival claimants to the throne and all critics of the establishment. Others feared a resurgence of Catholicism, resented pro-French influences at court, were genuinely scandalised by the low moral tone set by the monarch's circle and looked to a Protestant succession which would do away with all religious, political and ethical ambiguities. That statement is, of course, an oversimplification; the polarisation of society was not complete. But, then, nor was it complete at the outbreak of the Civil War. Men and families took sides in 1642 for a variety of reasons and adhered with varying degrees of conviction and emotional commitment to 'King' or 'Parliament'. The fact that Charles II's reign did not end in another bloody conflict should not deceive us into believing that feelings were not running high. The literary (using that word in its broadest sense) output of Charles' autumn years and the government's attempts to stifle it are proof enough of a highly volatile atmosphere. Parliament had refused the council's request to renew the Licensing Act and the result, according to an, admittedly OTT, tirade by Lord Chief Justice Scroggs, was that the country was awash with inflammatory and seductive canards whose influence was undermining society:

> ... so fond are men in these days that, when they will deny their children a penny for bread, they will lay it out for a pamphlet. And it did so swarm and the temptations were so great that no man could keep twopence in his pocket because of the news.[115]

In lighter vein, a court wit made the same point, while, in fact, adding to the genre he affected to despise:

> Lampoons are grown tedious
> And damnable odious
> And now scarce worth the resenting . . .[116]

The king's women were the easiest targets for these attacks but Charles' mistresses by no means stood alone in the stocks of popular hatred. Lampoons against them both fed and fed off a disquieting fashionable misogyny. The changing role of women in society and their increasing prominence produced a vicious backlash, so that resentment of the court whores was often symptomatic of something deeper in the national psyche:

Of all the plagues with which this world abounds,
Our discords causes, wideners of our wounds,
Sure woman is the lewdest can be guessed.
Through woman mankind early ills did taste;
She was the world's first curse, will be the last.
To show what woman is, Heaven make Charles wise;
Some angel scale the blindness from his eyes.
Restored by miracle, he may believe
And seeing's follies, learn, though late, to live.
Why art thou poor, O King? Embezzling cunt,
That wide-mouthed, greedy monster, that has done't

Thus begins 'An Essay of Scandal' (1681), one of the more unrestrained examples of the genre. In it the author goes on to lash with his pen several named court ladies in a diatribe which has no party political bias: it snipes at both Whig and Tory leaders. But it is the familiar trio of Barbara, Nell and Louise who are his main targets:

Go visit Portsmouth fasting if thou darest,
(Which thou mayest, at the poor rate thou farest).
She'll with her noisome breath blast ev'n thy face,
Till thou, thyself, grow uglier than her grace.
Remove that costly dunghill from thy doors . . .

So much for Louise. The pleasantries directed at Barbara were no less lurid.

But from her den expel old ulcer quite.
She shines i'the dark, light rotten wood at night,
Dreads pepper [used to prevent decay in meat],
    penance, parliament and light.
Once with thy people's prayers resolve to join;
She's all the nation's nuisance, why not thine?

Nell, somewhat surprisingly, came in for fuller treatment.

Then next turn Nelly out of door,
That hare-brained, wrinkled, stopped-up whore,
Daily struck, stabbed, by half the pricks in town . . .
'Twas once, indeed, with her as 'twas with ore,
Uncoined, she was no public store,
Only Buckhurst's private whore.
But when that thou in wanton itch
With royal tarse had stamped her breech,

She grew a common, current bitch . . .
Kick her for her lewd cajoling
And bid her turn to her old trade of strolling.[117]

Pious indignation and insult merged into libel in such diatribes. Royal mistresses were routinely accused of bestowing their favours widely. While this was true of Barbara and Hortense, it certainly was not of Nell and Louise. The author of 'A Satire Upon the Mistresses' accused Charles of incest with his daughter, the Countess of Sussex. He dubbed the king a second Tarquin after the ancient Roman tyrant who was a byword for lechery and extravagance and was eventually exiled by his own people. He condemned Lady Portsmouth as a 'monster' whose example had set rolling a tidal wave which engulfed the whole nation in lust and debauchery. Politics and morality he saw as inextricably mixed, and he identified Catherine Crofts, the guardian of Charles' daughter, Mary Tudor, and Mary Knight, a famous singer and favourite at court, as both madams and party agents:

Next let us view the cock bawds of the court,
Kate Crofts and Knight contrivers of the sport,
Th'one for Shaftesbury, the other spy for Rome.
When things move thus, who may'nt pronounce our doom?
'Tis pity thus two factions for to see,
Not only linked in ills but lechery.[118]

The literary piece that carried this politico-sexual obsession to its bizarre illogical conclusion was a satirical heroic play entitled *Sodom* which told a fantasy story of a king living not a million miles away from Whitehall. Its premiss was simple: since woman was the arch-enemy who had emasculated the king, his court and government, the obvious solution was to banish the entire sex from the nation. The drama tells the story of how this transformation of society was carried out in the kingdom of Sodom, under the governance of its easygoing monarch, Bolloxinian, who, at the beginning of the play, declares his philosophy:

Thus in the zenith of my lust I reign:
I eat to swive and swive to eat again.

The king has a favourite mistress, Pockenello, but confines his sexual activity neither to her nor to her kind. He has several homosexual relationships and comes to prefer the company of young men (perhaps a reference to Charles' grandfather, James I). He graphically describes the reason for his preference:

330

> By oft fomenting, cunt so big doth swell
> That prick works there like clapper in a bell.
> All vacuum, no grasping flesh does hide
> Or hug, the brawny muscles of its side.

In a parody of Charles' attitude towards religious toleration, Bolloxinian issues a proclamation:

> Let conscience have its force of liberty.
> I do proclaim that buggery may be used
> Through all the land, so cunt be not abused.

Several openly pornographic scenes follow which bear out the promise of the play's prologue:

> It is the most debauched, heroic piece
> That e'er was wrote, what dare compare with this?
> Here's that will fit your fancy with delight.
> 'Twill tickle every vein and please your sight,
> Nay make your prick to have an appetite.

The new fashion takes on quickly, encouraged by the neighbouring monarch, Tarsehole of Gomorrah, and women are left to gain their satisfaction from dildos and animals. All, of course, ends in monumental disaster. An epidemic sweeps the land, the king has no new subjects to replenish the declining population and goes mad, hurling defiance at the gods, while vengeance falls from heaven.

> Kiss, rise up and dally,
> Frig, swive and rally,
> Curse, blaspheme and swear
> Those that will witness bear.
> For the Bollox singes
> Sodom off its hinges.
> Bugger, bugger, bugger
> All in a hugger-mugger.
> Fire doth descend.
> 'Tis too late to amend.[119]

Sodom was never performed and was probably never intended to be performed. Even in the licentious 1680s it would have been too 'hot', both morally and politically, for any public stage. But it provides for us a very revealing commentary on Restoration society's evaluation of itself. There was an obsession with sex and at the same time a revulsion from it. It was an age that knew itself to be decadent and realised that it was headed down a political cul-de-sac. It put the blame for many prevailing ills on to women – but also on to the king for being controlled by women. It was saying no more than the run of the mill satires and pamphlets were saying but it said it more pungently and, though it makes repugnant reading, it is, perhaps, only through such a piece of grotesque pornography that we can grasp something of the disgust and despair felt by many in 'Good King Charles' golden days'. At the same time we need to remind ourselves that this is a voice from the metropolis, from among those who considered themselves the sophisticated élite. There was another contemporary allegory, popular with a far greater number, that, while recognising the parlous state into which the nation had sunk, yet spoke a message of hope. It was called *The Pilgrim's Progress*.

Charles II emerged from the crisis years a changed man – older and, if not wiser, at least more ready to respond to the new opportunity to take charge of his political destiny. He was now in his fifties and, although his lifelong obsession with fitness had preserved his sound constitution, he was more prone to bouts of illness and was physically winding down. Mentally he was as acute as ever. It was in his emotional life that the alteration was most evident. Much of the passion which had found outlet in the eager pursuit of various pleasures was henceforth channelled into new courses. He was no longer the easygoing prince who shunned conflict whenever possible. Like many elderly people, he experienced bouts of bad temper and stubbornness. He and his ministers pursued his enemies with a venomous vigour that would once have seemed quite uncharacteristic and this, in turn, meant that he took a greater personal interest in day-to-day government (but see below, p. 341).

His relationship with Louise de Keroualle metamorphosed into something much more political. She appeared in the last years of the reign as the *grande dame* she had always wanted to be. She, too, had emerged toughened from the fire and was ready to become a royal consort in the French mould. All this was not immediately obvious in the summer of 1681. Louise had hastened to distance herself from Fitzharris as soon as he started to implicate her in his plots and Charles had rescued her by discrediting the Irishman and getting him quickly out of the way. But she had several bridges to repair if she was to regain any position of political influence. As he always did when his womenfolk came under attack, Charles stood staunchly by her. Together, they concocted a story that was at best only half true, for the consumption of the Duke of York, the French ambassador, William of Orange, the leading Tory politicians and all those whose co-operation they needed to overwhelm the Whigs and remain independent of parliament. According to their version of events, Louise's contact with the Whigs had been authorised by the king for the purpose of discovering their plans. Unfortunately, she had been duped by Shaftesbury's agents into believing that they were prepared to compromise on exclusion. As soon as she had discovered that they intended to impose severe restraints on the monarchy she had abandoned them. It is unlikely that the official story fooled anyone but all those who hoped to profit from the king's triumph over the opponents of excessive royal power were more than happy to swallow it.

Louise's closest allies were the 'Chits'. This was the contemptuous term (implying 'mere children') applied to a group of younger courtier politicians to whom the king turned during the exclusion crisis. Foremost among them were Laurence Hyde and Sidney Godolphin. The former was the second son of the Earl of Clarendon, who had died in 1674. He and his brother, Henry, had remained politically active after their father's disgrace but it was a long time before they enjoyed the king's confidence. During the exclusion crisis they staunchly supported their brother-in-law, the Duke of York. Godolphin had followed a conventional diplomatic career and had been involved in the clandestine negotiations between Charles and Louis XIV. With Sunderland, he and Laurence Hyde had become the king's leading councillors in 1679. It was largely thanks to Hyde's efforts that Louise and James were, not without difficulty, reconciled during the winter of 1681–2. Louise reciprocated by advancing his career and, at the end of 1682, Hyde received signal proof of his family's reinstatement when Charles bestowed upon him the earldom of Rochester, vacant since 1680 and formerly in the possession of his great friends, the Wilmots. It only remained for the king to forgive and restore Sunderland for the old administration of the duchess and her allies to be once more in command. Louise brought this about by the summer of 1682.

Effecting reconciliations was not easy. Charles had been deeply wounded by the events of the last few years and just as he was determined to be revenged on the Whig leadership, so he found it difficult to forgive and forget those like Sunderland who, he believed, had betrayed him. As for his brother, that uncompromising Catholic had become such an embarrassment that he was in no hurry to welcome him back to court. Louise had to tiptoe very gently around these delicate human relationships. However, with the patience, subtlety and gentle cajolery that only a woman could employ, it was Louise who brought into being the Tory 'cabinet' which constituted the government for the remainder of the reign. By the autumn of 1682 Ormonde, that seasoned politician, could assess the situation at Whitehall thus:

> Hyde is the best and honestest minister amongst us, though he is fain to comply with the Lady beyond what may be approved of . . . she is at this instant as powerful as ever, insomuch that there is no contending with her . . . nor do I think it would be for the service of the Crown that honest

men should make themselves useless to it by a vain and unreasonable opposition, since she cannot be removed. The next best is to make use of her credit to keep things as well as may be.[120]

Louise's supremacy was very public. She now presided over diplomatic receptions, a responsibility which had once been the queen's. When a Moroccan delegation arrived for discussions about Tangier, Catherine sat enthroned beside her husband for the formal audience but when, days later, a banquet 'of sweetmeats, music, etc' was given for the ambassador and his exotic suite Louise presided in her impressive dining chamber at Whitehall. Evelyn was intrigued to observe the behaviour of the Moors and seems to have been surprised to discover that these representatives of a different culture could behave with complete decorum:

> They drank a little milk and water but not a drop of wine. Also they drank of a sorbet and chocolate, did not look about nor stare on the ladies, or express the least of surprise, but with a courtly negligence in pace, countenance and whole behaviour, answering only to such questions as were asked, with a great deal of wit and gallantry . . .

Evelyn had rather sharper comment to make about the representatives of the host nation. The ambassador and his retinue were

> placed about a long table, a lady between two Moors . . . and most of these were the king's natural children, viz: the Lady Lichfield, Sussex, Duchess of Portsmouth, Nelly, etc., concubines and cattle of that sort, as splendid as jewels and excess of bravery [i.e. ostentatious finery] could make them.[121]

On this occasion the king turned up just as his colourful guests were leaving. He was obviously more than content to leave the presidency of such high-profile events to Louise. She was now deputising for him quite often, sometimes staying at the political centre of events while king and court retired to the country. Charles now spent as much time as possible away from the capital, much of it at Windsor, which was more secure, and Winchester where Christopher Wren was building him a new 160-room palace.

In the spring of 1682 Louise felt secure enough to pay a visit to France. Relations between the two royal courts were at an all-time high and she was promised a magnificent reception in Paris. She had several personal reasons for making the trip – family business, financial investments, inspection of her son's estate at Aubigny – but, above all, this was to be the apotheosis of ambition. She who had left her native land a dozen years before as a humble attendant to the duchesse d'Orléans was returning as an almost royal personage. Her journey was a triumphant progress. She and her impressive train sailed from Greenwich in an elaborately fitted out yacht and once ashore at Calais she was conveyed to the capital in a fleet of coaches bearing Charles' own insignia. Louis and his court received her and entertained her sumptuously and in return she threw balls and banquets as only she knew how. To show that celebrity had not completely turned her head, the duchess drove to Brittany to visit 'dear old mum and dad' and, while there, to redeem the pawned family estate. A final round of lavish partying in Paris and Versailles and she was ready to cross the Channel once more, weighed down with splendid gifts from the Sun King and his orbiting satellites. The king did not venture away from Windsor to meet her; that courtesy was reserved for family members and visiting royalty, but he did write a welcoming letter in which he affirmed, 'I should do myself wrong if I told you that I love you better than all the world besides, for . . . 'tis impossible to express the true passion and kindness I have for my dearest, dearest Fubs.'[122]

Catherine, too, was assured of her husband's affection, as she reported to her brother:

> I think he deserves something from you for the great protection he has shown me, and he continues to defend and protect me with so remarkable a show of goodwill that I find myself engaged by new obligations not to fail him in anything which I perceive to be due. And I am happy . . . I have everything that can give me complete satisfaction in this life, nor do I now wish to think I have reason to complain.[123]

Charles had, indeed, been assiduous in shielding his wife from her share of the calumnies showered upon his close circle in recent years. As had often been remarked with disapproval, he seemed more concerned to stand up for his womenfolk than for his ministers or, indeed, his realm. The last spectacular royal display of the reign was given in honour of Catherine's birthday and no expense was spared to ensure its success.

> . . . there was such a fireworks upon the Thames before Whitehall, with pageants of castles, forts and other devices of girandolas, serpents [species of fireworks], the king's and queen's arms and mottoes all represented in fire, as had not been seen in any age remembered here. That which was most remarkable was the several fires and skirmishes [brilliant displays] in the very water and now and then appearing above it, giving reports like muskets and cannon, with grenades and innumerable other devices. It is said this sole triumph cost 1,500 pounds, which was concluded with a ball, where all the ladies and gallants danced in the great hall. The court had not been so brave and rich in apparel since his majesty's restoration.[124]

335

As she looked out on the exploding shells mirrored in the glassy river and listened to the music and the cheering crowds, Catherine can scarcely have avoided being reminded of her splendid arrival by water at Whitehall almost a quarter of a century before. She will also have been looking forward to leaving this place, with its many unhappy memories, and Somerset House for her new home at Winchester. The court had spent all September in the palace which was still abuilding in Hampshire and the plan was to make it the permanent royal residence, an English Versailles. Catherine was very much taken up with the plans for the new building and with the excitement of agreeing the décor and ordering new furniture. Here, at last, she would share a home with Charles.

Pretty, witty Nelly also enjoyed these rural excursions and almost invariably accompanied the king when he was away from the capital. It was while visiting Winchester to survey the building works in 1681 or 1682 that the celebrated altercation occurred between Dr Thomas Ken and the king's agent who had come down to arrange accommodation for the royal entourage. Doubtless she would have been amused by the virtuous clergyman's refusal to allow 'a woman of ill repute' to be lodged in the prebendal house. Had it happened to her, Louise would have been reduced to angry tears and the stalwart Ken could have said goodbye to further preferment. Nell was subsequently provided with her own house at Winchester, to add to the ones she already owned at Newmarket and Windsor.

The social division among the mistresses was strictly maintained. Nell Gwynn never had quarters within any of the royal residences but the king always provided her with a pleasant house nearby. This meant that he had a haven whenever he wished to escape from the court. His visits to Nell and the simple pleasures she offered him (most of the money he gave her she spent on his entertainment) were a means of 'earthing' the king into the lives of ordinary people. And when she attended court functions he delighted in her irreverence towards the fine aristocrats and ladies of his entourage. No one could get away with pomposity when Nell was around.

One of the last images we have of Charles and Nell typifies their relationship. The winter of 1684 was very severe. In December, the Thames above London Bridge froze to a depth of several feet. This provided citizens with the opportunity for a frost fair. John Evelyn walked across from Westminster Stairs to the landing stage at Lambeth to dine with Archbishop Socroft and noted in passing 'whole streets of booths in which they roasted meat and had divers shops of wares, quite cross as in a town but coaches and carts and horses passed over.' As the bitter weather continued into February the river 'became a camp, ten thousands of people coaches, carts and all manner of sports continuing and increasing'. The hard winter was basically a disaster: 'miserable were the wants of poor people. Deer universally perished in most of the parks throughout England

and very much cattle.'[125] Shopkeepers, entrepreneurs and hucksters, however, grabbed the rare opportunity to attract custom, and pleasure seekers enjoyed the diversions offered by the ice. The king ordered a royal pavilion to be built on the frozen river and it was Nell who presided with him over the novel entertainments which they planned for courtiers and citizens.

Barbara Villiers, now in her forties, seems to have returned to London some time in 1684 and established herself in Arlington Street, off Piccadilly. Once again she had taken up with one of the more colourful and disreputable celebrities of the day. Cardell Goodman was a handsome reprobate who had managed to cram into thirty-odd years being expelled from home by his clergyman father, getting sent down from Cambridge for defacing a picture of the chancellor (the Duke of Monmouth), being dismissed for negligence from his position as page of the backstairs to the king, dissipating a substantial inheritance and dabbling in highway robbery before he discovered his true vocation as a lead actor with the King's Company. Such a good-looking and devil-may-care adventurer naturally appealed to the ladies, who fell over themselves to attract the man whose nickname was 'Scum'. The challenge was one Barbara could not resist. She had to show the ladies of the stage and the town that she could still outrun the field. She scooped Goodman up and the two lived the kind of tumultuous life to which Lady Cleveland had long become accustomed.

Charles welcomed her back to court from time to time and two incidents reveal that she maintained something of her old influence and insolence. When her lover was indicted for felony she extracted a pardon from Charles. Shortly after this, Catherine attended a performance at Drury Lane in which Goodman was starring. As was the custom, actors and audience waited until the royal party had taken their seats. The curtain duly rose and Goodman stepped forward to scan the boxes. 'Is my duchess come?' he demanded. Seeing that Barbara was not yet present, he swore roundly and declared, 'The play does not start until my lady is come.' Fortunately the duchess's arrival at that moment saved everyone from further embarrassment. We can only imagine the satisfaction this gave her as she made her formal obeisance to the queen.

By 1682 the king's 'top' women had settled into a pattern of life designed to provide him with maximum comfort and diversion. There was nothing inevitable about the choice of female companions who eventually became his intimates. Mistresses came and went but carnal liaisons became fewer and, after the domestic disruption caused by the whirlwind appearance of Hortense Mancini, membership of the top table was settled. Catherine, Louise and Nell between them met all the king's needs. Supplemented from time to time by the likes of Barbara and Hortense, these ladies were his friends, his best friends.

The king's taste for the country life had strengthened with the passing of the years but he now had political reasons for distancing himself from the capital. London was Whig territory (as, indeed, was Newmarket, which Charles also began to shun now) and the last years of the reign were spent in open warfare with the Whigs. A politically adroit commentator observed in the spring of 1681, ''Tis now come to a civil war, not with the sword but law.'[126] Charles was not content to pursue the small fry like Fitzharris; he, Louise and the Chits were bent on nothing less than the complete destruction of the opposition. Since they could not use parliament for their purposes and dared not use force, they had to rely on the lesser courts. If those were to achieve the required results the government had to ensure that they were peopled with pliant judges and juries. The legal proceedings of 1681–3 had nothing to do with justice and everything to do with politics. Both sides resorted to false testimony, packed juries, planted evidence and manipulation of court procedures, and victory went to the party that was most successful in these tactics.

Round one went to the Whigs. Lord Shaftesbury was arrested in July 1681 and kept in the Tower for four and a half months while the government tried to collect or manufacture evidence to support a charge of high treason. In November a grand jury was summoned to decide whether the prisoner had a case to answer. The chief justice and the attorney-general did their best but the jury had been packed by Whig sheriffs and they determined that there was insufficient evidence to place before a trial jury. While the king and his ministers fumed, London went wild: 'the bells rang, bonfires were made and such public rejoicing in the city that never such an insolent defiance of authority was seen'.[127] Jubilant party leaders caused a celebratory medal to be struck.

Charles felt betrayed and his temper was not improved when he discovered that, on Shaftesbury's being freed on bail, Monmouth was one of those who put up the necessary bond. The king might well have called to mind the scenes that had taken place in the City when the famous five had escaped his father's clutches. But 1681 was not 1642. The Crown had its supporters and success in the 'civil war with the law' was largely a question of martialling those supporters. This involved chicanery and the shameless application of royal power. The first major step taken by the government was interference with the elections to the City's common council the following summer, which resulted in the appointment of Tory sheriffs. That cleared the way for fresh proceedings against Shaftesbury. The earl immediately went into hiding and, before the end of the year, by now a very sick man, he fled to Holland. Within weeks he was dead.

But his movement had not expired with him. Clandestine plans had been a-hatching for months, involving potential risings in various localities and even assassination attempts on the king and his brother. Just how much danger the government was really in is problematic. The opposition was divided between Whig monarchists (who supported Monmouth), republicans, Protestant extremists and a broad spectrum of radicals. They would never have found a positive programme behind which they could unite but they could be a powerful negative force and if any of their extreme measures had been carried into effect the result might well have been political chaos.

Faced with this situation, Charles was in something of a dilemma. He had no compunction about using the machinery of informers, spies, suborned juries and partisan judges to purge the nation of all who sought to undermine royal power but he dreaded the thought of catching Monmouth in the net and having to make an appalling example of his son. Apart from his own emotional involvement, the public response to an act of filicide had also to be considered. He had already experienced a popular backlash from one alarming event involving Monmouth. The duke had been driving along Pall Mall with his friend Thomas Thynne in the latter's carriage. The conveyance came to a halt to allow Monmouth to alight and then continued on its way. Further down the road three horsemen stopped the carriage and one of them fired a blunderbuss in at the window, mortally wounding poor Thynne. It was a personal vendetta and the culprits were duly caught, tried and executed. However, the suspicion inevitably arose that this was a bungled attempt by the Duke of York's faction to get rid of the 'Protestant heir'. When the assassins were apprehended, Charles personally examined them in council, and after their condemnation he ordered that they should be put to death on the site of the murder so that they could publicly disavow any plot against Monmouth.

There was an air of desperation about the wayward duke and his friends. Time was not on their side. The king was ageing and would have no legitimate children. James was known to be obdurate in matters of religion. They had tried to displace him by peaceful, constitutional means. They had failed and now the opportunity to try again had been removed. There was no parliament, and heaven alone knew when and if there would ever be another. So they gathered their strength by holding meetings throughout the country and Monmouth went on his charismatic way drumming up popular support. For the first time the king was genuinely worried about his own safety. The monarch who prided himself on his accessibility to his people, who had walked daily in St James's Park for many years, suddenly became security conscious. He gratefully accepted the gift of some Swiss Guards from Louis XIV. He had several of the palace entrances bricked up. He spent more of his time away from Whitehall, preferring the strongly fortified Windsor Castle or, latterly, his new home at Winchester.

The government's response to Whig activity was a draconion use of prorogative power. They removed local JPs and replaced them with yesmen. Charles sacked eleven High Court judges in order to appoint in their places men who 'knew their duty'. Most notorious of these promotions was that of George Jeffreys, who became lord chief justice in 1683. But royal manipulation was not only applied to the judicial system. The government launched an all-out attack on local government. Wherever a case could be made against a town corporation for some indiscretion or alleged violation of its own constitution its charter was called in and a new one granted which incorporated more stringent royal control. It was in June 1683 that Charles got to taste the cherry on the cake. A judgment was given in King's Bench against the common council of London for certain technical misdemeanours. The mayor and aldermen were obliged to surrender the charter granted to them by William the Conqueror. At last the city that had defied Charles I and made the great revolution possible had been brought to heel. All this was combined with a more rigorous application of the laws against dissenters. It only remained for there to be some high-profile show trials for Whigs and radicals to be completely outmanoeuvred and undermined. The revelation of the supposed Rye House Plot provided the excuse for such trials.

Titus Oates and his cronies had made scapegoating and witch-hunts the height of fashion. Their lies and libels were eagerly circulated because there were always some political groups who could benefit from them. The Popish Plot had played into the hands of the Whigs. The conspiracy laid before the council by Josiah Keeling, 'a man of anabaptist sympathies and a decaying business',[128] in June 1683 was exactly what the Tory ministers were looking for. Keeling claimed that a plan to assassinate the royal brothers on their way back from Newmarket in March had failed only because Charles and James had set out earlier than expected. Within days the alleged ringleaders, including Lord Russell, Lord Essex and Sir Algernon Sidney, three of the most upright men in public life, found themselves in the Tower. There Essex, despairing of receiving justice, cut his throat. By chance (presumably) the king and his brother were at the Tower themselves, visiting the ordnance office, at that very time. One of the warders ran down to the wharf as they were embarking and broke the tragic news to them. Charles seemed genuinely distressed, though the suicide served to strengthen the case against Russell, which was heard on the same day.

Evelyn believed that Charles had no desire to exact the ultimate penalty from Essex, although 'he was altogether inexorable as to my Lord Russell and some of the rest'. The king was, indeed, determined to take some prominent scalps, partly from motives of revenge and partly to scare off Monmouth from any further involvement in anti-government plots. In this he showed himself quite impervious to public opinion,

few believing that they had any evil intention against his majesty or the church and some that they were cunningly drawn in by their enemies for not approving some late councils and management of affairs in relation to France, to popery, to the prosecution of the dissenters, etc.[129]

When Russell, whom Burnet called 'that great and good man', was brought to execution in Lincoln's Inn Fields a large crowd turned out to watch. Many wept. Some dipped handkerchiefs in his blood. Sidney was kept waiting till November for his ordeal. His trial was a travesty, even by seventeenth-century standards. George Jeffreys presided and the main prosecution witness was Lord Howard of Escrick, 'that monster of a man' (Evelyn), now making a reappearance in the courtroom. Howard was arrested as soon as the Rye House Plot was reported because of his prominent position in the Whig high command. It was not difficult for government agents to turn him. In order to save his own skin he fell over himself to give evidence against both Russell and Sidney. What made his crime so heinous in the eyes of many contemporaries was the fact that when he had been in trouble with the government in February 1682 it had been Sidney who had laboured hard for his release. Now it was solely on the strength of Howard's evidence that his saviour went to the block.

With the passing of Sidney it was almost as though a chapter had closed in Charles' life or, to use another metaphor, as though a wheel had come full circle. Sidney was the man who had, indirectly, brought Charles and Lucy Walter together by introducing her to the fashionable society of the Hague all those years ago. Now he was being deprived of life for his indirect connection with Lucy's son. Was it for this as well as his lifelong, unrepentant commitment to republicanism that the king required his extinction?

Or *was* it the king who was the driving force behind all this frenetic activity? He had always been more inclined to leniency than vindictiveness and it was his custom to allow trusted ministers to get on with the implementation of policy while he ignored it or interfered with it or changed it as and when he was moved to do so. Was it his minions who were, in fact, setting the pace in the closing years of the reign? In York, Sunderland, Rochester, Godolphin and Lady Portsmouth Charles had a formidable team and they worked together with a united political will – certainly as far as destroying the Whigs was concerned. James, after all he had suffered at their hands, was particularly set upon revenge. Whatever others might think of Sidney, he crowed at the 'rebel's' downfall. His execution, the duke wrote, 'besides the doing justice on so ill a man, will give the lie to the Whigs, who reported he was not to suffer'.[130]

York was, inevitably, interested in removing the threat of Monmouth or, at least, keeping his nephew on a very tight leash. There is much about the fanatical pursuance of party advantage in the last years of the reign that appears to have the stamp of the duke's character upon it. However, nobody understood him better than Charles and he knew full well that his blinkered brother could not be allowed too much control. In particular the siblings did not see eye to eye over Monmouth. The king swung between moods of extreme anger at his son's antics and generous forgiveness. Monmouth was arrested in 1682 and subsequently returned to favour. When another warrant was issued against him the following year he went into hiding but eventually surrendered himself to his father's mercy. Charles promised a pardon if Monmouth would make a clean breast to him in private of all he knew about the recent plots. He agreed, but refused point-blank to offer any abject apology to his uncle. At the same time James was demanding a written confession from the miscreant that would effectively undermine his reputation with the radicals. Charles was caught in the middle. With difficulty he persuaded Monmouth to provide the desired letter but, the following day, his son came to him in great agitation asking for the document back. It was a difficult interview. Charles, between anger and tears insisted, 'If you do not yield in this you will ruin me.' The meeting ended with Charles returning the letter but also banishing Monmouth from the court. It was the typical action of a man who tried to please everybody.

The only evidence of Charles' attitude towards his brother's ability as the future monarch comes from the reminiscence of a courtier-diplomat to whom the king unburdened himself during a stroll in the park some time in 1683. Charles, apparently, confided,

> . . . when I am dead and gone, I know not what my brother will do. I am much afraid that, when he comes to the crown, he will be obliged to travel again. And yet I will take care to leave my kingdoms to him in peace, wishing he may long keep them so. But this hath all of my fears, little of my hopes and less of my reason, and I am very much afraid that when my brother comes to the crown, he will be obliged again to leave his native soil.[131]

Charles did not allow York to set the tone of the government. One check upon the duke's influence was the Earl of Halifax. He had been a member of Shaftesbury's cabinet but parted company with him over exclusion. This did not mean that he was a supporter of the Duke of York, quite the opposite; as a firm Protestant, the thought of James gaining the throne was anathema to him. Halifax put his faith in Monmouth and it was largely due to the earl's efforts that the reconciliations of 1682 and 1683 were possible. James and Louise made continuous efforts to have Halifax removed from the council but all to no avail. Charles not only enjoyed the company of the witty and philosophical earl, he saw him as a useful moderate who could counterbalance the extremism of the Chits. In October 1682 he was appointed to the prestigious office of lord privy seal and, two years later, his position was strengthened when two of his nominees were appointed to the treasury commission and Rochester was eased out of power, first by being given the honorific title of lord president of the council, then by being made lord-lieutenant of Ireland. In the closing months of the reign Halifax was bold enough to broadcast in manuscript form his treatise on government, entitled *The Character of a Trimmer*, in which he urged the recall of parliament, the abandonment of blind allegiance to France and the jettisoning of the Duke of York.

If neither York nor Rochester had his hand firmly on the tiller, perhaps Lady Portsmouth did. It was said that no major business could be conducted without her and that when she was absent as a result of illness little government business got done. She certainly had a great deal of influence when it came to winning favours for friends and clients. In league with Rochester and Sunderland she was able to devise high Tory policies and communicate reactionary ideas to Charles in private. She was instrumental in having James restored to the command of the navy in defiance of the Test Act. This required an element of subterfuge. The duke could not be formally reinstated so Charles took control back into his own hands and appointed James to act as his deputy. But she was unable to maintain Rochester's power in the council or to undermine Halifax or to ensure the permanent exile of Monmouth.

In the spring of 1683 she made a serious blunder which could, at a stroke, have robbed her of that position she had so carefully built up. One of the worst rakes in France, Philippe de Vendôme, a cousin of the king and a nephew of Hortense Mancini, came on a visit to the English court. He was an arrogant young man who considered himself irresistible to women and had a track record which gave this boast some substance. He decided to direct his invincible charm at Lady Portsmouth. It may be that Charles was no longer providing adequately for Louise's sexual needs or that she was flattered by the attentions of someone from the gay world of Paris. Whatever the reason, she succumbed. When the whispers of gossip reached Charles his usual insouciance deserted him. Gone were the days when ceaseless flirtations, scandalous affairs and adulterous liaisons were the common coin of daily life for Charles, his friends and his mistresses. No longer could he shrug off with sophisticated nonchalance this betrayal by his dearest Fubs. Instead he reacted with the outraged fury of a cuckolded husband. He issued orders for Vendôme's immediate return to France and when that brash young man declined to remove himself, he was brought before the king, who told him to his face that if he was not aboard ship within forty-eight hours he would be placed under arrest and forcibly ejected from the country.

Louise was profoundly shaken, fearful and tearful. However influential she might be and however many political allies she might have, her position rested entirely on the king's favour. If ever she lost that, not a soul would come to her defence and the baying crowd outside the palace gates would pursue her all the way to the ship that would carry her into ignominious exile. She need not have worried. The king forgave her, accepting without question that she was more sinned against than sinning. The court watched to see if the *maîtresse en titre*'s influence had been severely dented. What they observed was Charles being more demonstrative than ever of his love for Louise, publicly embracing and fondling her as though he had been a moonstruck adolescent unable to keep his hands off the object of his desire. The king was infinitely relieved to have Fubs to himself again. He wanted domestic stability. He was too settled into a comfortable routine to allow a little infidelity to disturb the even tenor of his days. Louise's position as principal conduit between the king's private life and his government continued.

In the autumn of 1684, Louise fell seriously ill. It was reported that she thought herself to be dying and that, as a worried Charles sat at her bedside, she had made him promise never to abandon James. It is difficult to see why such a pledge should have been exacted. Charles' resolve over the succession had been made clear over and over again and the duke's peacock demeanour about the court was such that one wag commented that while parliament had decided that the duke should not reign after the king's death, the king had resolved that he should reign during his life. If there is any truth in the story it suggests that everything may not have been quite so cut and dried as it appeared to outsiders. A courtier confidently asserted that after the duchess's recovery, 'she is greater and more absolute than ever and, under her, the duke, my Lord Sunderland and Rochester direct and dispose of all things'.[132] Yet only a couple of months later, as the king lay dying, she had her bags packed, ready for a hurried departure to the haven of the French ambassador's house. This does not suggest that she had a perfect understanding with the heir to the throne.

It seems, then, that no one at Whitehall was all-powerful. There was no foursquare political edifice. Whatever temporary structures Charles' ministers and mistress threw up were built on the shifting sands of his secretive and changeable character.

At the turning of the year Charles was in pain from a leg that was either ulcerated or afflicted with gout. He attended Nell's by now traditional Christmas party but did not dance. Nor was he able to take his usual brisk daily exercise. He was reported to be 'pensive' and spent much of his time shut up in his laboratory. Declining health must have made him reflect deeply on his own fate and that of his realm. The story of his being accepted into the Roman Church at the eleventh hour is well known. There is also the possibility that, in the last weeks, his devious mind was still entertaining alternative thoughts about the succession. The royal brothers were perceived to be on less than amiable terms, perhaps because James could not conceal his eagerness to grasp the sceptre. Burnet tells a veiled story that he had from one of the king's ministers of Monmouth being brought clandestinely to the king by Louise's agency and going away again 'very pleased with his journey'. Sunderland, Godolphin and Louise were said to have persuaded Charles to send his brother to Scotland with the intention that, once parted, 'they would never meet again'. All this was and remains speculation. When Charles was suddenly bedridden on 2 February 1685 no new arrangements had been made which would in any way have disturbed the transfer of the Crown to the rightful successor by the normal laws of inheritance.

Death demands the observance of proprieties. Into the crowded bedchamber came ministers, clergy, doctors and close attendants. The king's sons – all except Monmouth – came to him for a final blessing. James, of course, was there, taking charge, making sure that everything went according to plan. Catherine came and remained long by her husband's side, until exhaustion and grief obliged her to withdraw. She felt dreadful at being unable to stay longer and sent her apologies. 'She begs my forgiveness?' Charles muttered. 'Rather should I seek hers.' The ladies of pleasure were kept well away but they were not far from the dying man's thoughts. He commended Barbara, Louise and Nell to his successor's care. Evelyn huffily remarked, 'I do not hear he said anything of the church or his people, now falling under the government of a prince suspected for his religion.' The diarist was not being unjust. Charles Stuart had no real concern for his country or his subjects. The circle of his affection had a small diameter but well within it – in fact at its very centre – there was a special place for all those women who had meant so much to him throughout a life that had seen many twists and turns of fortune. They had made him what he was – for good or ill – and without understanding that we do not understand him.

PART FOUR

CONCLUSIONS

The pale blood of the wizard at her touch
Took gayer colours, like an opal warmed.
She blamed herself for telling hearsay tales:
She shook from fear and for her fault she wept
Of petulancy; she called him lord and liege,
Her seer, her bard, her silver star of eve,
Her god, her Merlin, the one passionate love
Of her whole life . . .

For Merlin, overtalked and overworn,
Had yielded, told her all the charm, and slept.
Then in one moment, she put forth the charm
Of woven paces and of waving hands,
And in the hollow oak he lay as dead,
And lost to life and use and name and fame.
Then crying, 'I have made his glory mine',
And shrieking out 'O fool!', the harlot leaped
Adown the forest, and the thicket closed
Behind her, and the forest echoed, 'fool'.

Tennyson, *Idylls of the King*

CHAPTER 14

A Pair of Cards

'All' the king's women must logically include half his subjects. We would gain a seriously distorted impression if we treated Charles and the female members of his immediate circle in complete isolation from the attitudes towards women which were prevailing in society as a whole. Our conclusion, then, must try to set king and court in the wider context of the history of ideas, to identify the conventions governing male–female relations and the ways the king and his companions submitted to or rejected them. Western humanity has pilgrimaged from the sexual theology of Gregory the Great who asserted 'no sin is committed unless the flesh takes pleasure in it; but when the flesh begins to take pleasure, then sin is born and, if deliberate consent is given, sin is complete' to the modern orthodoxy that the pleasure principle is all and that restraint is a heresy against the freedom which is our 'right'. Throughout that arduous journey men and women have tried, with only limited success, to understand and truly value each other.

In the long evolution of the Arthurian legends the ambiguity about woman – or the ambiguity with which man regards woman – became starkly clear. In the guise of Morgan le Fay or Nymue or the Lady of the Lake or Vivien or Guinevere she appeared as both the saviour of Camelot and the agent of its downfall, the object of desire and of revulsion, the hapless victim to be defended by chivalrous champions and the witch encoiling innocent knights in her sorceries, the giver of Excalibur and the leech who sucked the magical power from the Round Table's fraternal fellowship. She was represented as both angel and devil. In Tennyson's treatment Vivien was the arch-betrayer, Eve and the serpent wrapped in one. She beguiled the magician, became his devoted pupil, then turned his charms upon him and tripped away triumphantly through the forest, crying, 'Fool!' The symbolism of the legend is blatant: in the very moment of submitting gladly and willingly to woman's sexual magic man despises himself and loathes the object of his desire. In appearing to dominate in the sex act, he becomes his partner's slave. Gratification and emasculation are inextricably entwined.

The versifiers of the Restoration court more than any other group of

English writers before or since gave powerful expression to this male affliction. Their pens were dipped in misogynistic bile and their lines smouldered with pornographic hatred. Traditionally, amorous poetry had been all about the exaltation of the mistress's virtues, the ardour of pursuit, the longing for consummation. Writers idolised 'love' and panted with ardent desire. Not so the cynics who haunted the court of Charles II. Their bitterness stripped the man–woman relationship of all romance, idealism and mystery. Coupling became a mere animal experience in which the man was ensnared, not so much by his own instinct, as by the allurements of the 'other'. In the satirical verses of the 1660s and 1670s women were castigated for presuming to choose where and whether to bestow their favours; for usurping sexual power which, by divine ordinance, belongs only to men. The sea change which had come over fashionable lyrics is well illustrated by contrasting the words of two jilted lovers. Michael Drayton, writing around 1620, accepted rejection with good grace.

> Since there's no help, come let us kiss and part,
> Nay, I have done: you get no more of me,
> And I am glad, yea, glad with all my heart,
> That thus so cleanly, I myself can free,
> Shake hands for ever, cancel all our vows,
> And when we meet at any time again,
> Be it not seen in either of our brows,
> That we one jot of former love retain.
> Now at the last gasp of Love's latest breath,
> When, his pulse failing, Passion speechless lies,
> When Faith is kneeling by his bed of death,
> And Innocence is closing up his eyes,
> Now, if thou wouldst, when all have given him over,
> From death to life thou might'st him yet recover.

There is nothing remotely gracious about Rochester, writing 'A ramble in St James's Park' on the other side of the Civil War–Restoration divide.

> May stinking vapour choke your womb
> Such as the men you dote upon!
> May your depraved appetite,
> That could in whiffling fools delight,
> Beget such frenzies in your mind
> You may go mad for the North wind,
> And fixing all your hopes upon't,
> To have him bluster in your cunt,
> Turn up your longing arse t'th'air
> And perish in a wild despair!

Neither example is unique of its time and type. Clearly, something radical had happened, at least in fashionable circles, to the way men treated and thought about women. We must seek some powerful cause which could produce the fury and violence of much Restoration satire – directed alike at women and at the king. It sprang from despair at the state of national life.

Margaret Cavendish, Duchess of Newcastle and wife of Charles' old tutor, was in no doubt where to lay the blame for the degeneration of society.

> Civil wars may be compared to a pair [i.e., a pack] of cards which, when they are made up in order, every several suit is by itself, as from one, two and three and so to the tenth card, which is like the commons in several degrees, in order, and the coat cards by themselves, which are the nobles. But factions, which are like gamesters when they play, setting life at the stake, shuffle them together, intermixing the nobles and commons, where loyalty is shuffled from the crown, duty from parents, tenderness from children, fidelity from masters, continencies from husbands and wives, truth from friends, from justice innocency, charity from misery. Chance plays and fortune draws the stakes.[1]

Every revolution is, in part, a sexual revolution. In the mid-seventeenth century, hundreds of families of the social élite lost their menfolk in battle, had their estates confiscated and spent longer or shorter spells in exile. The Restoration did not, with one wave of the wand, set all to rights. Property that had been seized or snapped up cheaply in a confused market could not revert automatically to its original ownership and the government shrank from legislation which would have alienated new landowners. Lawsuits begun in the 1660s dragged on for decades, even generations, often enriching only the lawyers. Society was radically disrupted for many years.

The effects on well-bred women and girls were tumultuous and often distressing. Orphaned or widowed or dowerless and finding themselves (whether at home or abroad) in a bewildering, alien environment, and bereft of the accoutrements of civilised life to which they were accustomed, they had to utilise whatever talents and charms nature had endowed them with. For many, the only way out of their plight was the obvious one of seeking a 'protector'. Often, as was the case with Lucy Walter, they ended up being passed from hand to hand as high-class whores. Lucy's name is known to us because of her relationship with the king but there were many who suffered the same fate and have disappeared in the dingy back alleys of history. They shared the insecure life of courtiers in exile, living as if there were no tomorrow, and, for some, there was not. They were kept until they became pregnant or until their lovers tired of them. They struggled to retain their looks, studied to learn the arts of seduction, sought abortions, suffered at the hands and tongues of rivals, intrigued and were intrigued against. To survive they had to be tough, coarse, manlike in their drinking, swearing and revelling in bawdy stories. It was only the fortunate and unscrupulous few, the 'aristocracy' of the profession, who made it into the company of the king's friends and who managed to hold places among the court hangers-on or, eventually, to achieve marriage to Carolean aristocrats who could restore them to the mainstream of respectability.

For such women the freedom from convention provided by a society in crisis was, at best, a mixed blessing. There were others for whom liberty meant the opportunity to develop skills and achieve a prominence which would in ordinary circumstances have been impossible. More widows and daughters than ever before took over businesses and managed estates. Several assumed positive roles in support of their families or of the cause they believed in. Margaret Cavendish was one such. She was a twenty-one-year-old maid of honour to Henrietta Maria when, in 1644, she accompanied her mistress into exile. In France she married the erudite and accomplished Marquess of Newcastle and travelled with him in his wanderings. Despite the fact that her husband was regarded as a very great traitor, Margaret returned to England and spent a year trying, unsuccessfully, to persuade the Protector's government to release income from some of the sequestered Newcastle estates. She was a lady of spirit as well as being something of a bluestocking and widely regarded as eccentric.

She clearly refused to accept the word 'impossible', for her next enterprise and the one which was to occupy most of the rest of her life involved her venturing into the male preserve of literature. Her post-Restoration output was prodigious. She wrote – *and had published* – poems, plays, essays, philosophical discourses and she considered no subject beyond the pale of her competence or legitimate enquiry. Many men of learning were affronted by her poaching in their coverts and when she expressed a desire to visit the Royal Society the committee of that body spent a long time in heated debate before a majority decided that she might be welcomed. Far from being cowed by male chauvinism, Margaret took it upon herself to challenge the observations of some of the leading experts and to forestall their objections:

They will, perhaps, think me an inconsiderable opposite because I am not of their sex . . . But if this should chance, the impartial world, I hope, will grant me so much justice as will declare them [i.e., the impartial world] to be patrons not only to truth but also to justice and equity, for which Heaven will grant them their reward and time will record their noble and worthy actions in the register of fame to be kept in everlasting memory.[2]

The strong-minded Lady Cavendish was one of the celebrities of the age. She eschewed the frivolous life of the court and did not in the slightest bother her head about fashion. Whenever she travelled it was in luxurious style and accompanied by a large retinue but her own clothes, though sumptuous, belonged to a bygone era. Because of her rare and unconventional appearances she caused a great stir whenever she did appear in public. In the spring of 1667, Pepys was all agog for a glimpse of her and several times went out of his way in the hope of seeing her. For several weeks he was frustrated by the crowds that congregated wherever she went, as though, he commented, she had been the Queen of Sweden (a shrewd comparison, for Christina was a woman of a very similar stamp and one who aroused a like curiosity in her travels around Europe):

> Thence Sir W. Pen and I in his coach, Tyburn way into the park, where a horrid dust and a number of coaches, without pleasure or order. That which we and almost all went for was to see my Lady Newcastle, which we could not, she being followed and crowded upon by coaches all the way she went, that nobody could come near her. Only I could see she was in a large black coach, adorned with silver instead of gold and so white curtains and everything black and white and herself in her cap, but other parts I could not make [out].[3]

More remarkable because more talented and starting without Margaret's social advantages was Aphra Behn, the first professional lady dramatist. She had already led a highly colourful life by the time she embarked on her literary career in 1667. She came from obscure merchant or, possibly, maritime stock and spent some of her earlier years in Surinam. Around 1664, when she was probably twenty-four, she married a Mr Behn, a London merchant of German extraction, but found herself widowed after a couple of years, when her husband succumbed to the plague. Now followed a brief but intriguing interlude, in which she was sent by Arlington to the Low Countries as a spy. Her employment in this mission may have been prompted by her facility with foreign languages but even so it suggests that she was recognised as a remarkable, resourceful woman and that she had influential contacts.

Aphra returned to London in dire straits, having received no payment for her services, a not uncommon predicament of government agents. She spent some time in prison for debt and wrote desperate letters to the king, begging for relief. There is no indication that he responded but Aphra did have influential friends and she seems to have endured only a few weeks' incarceration. She might have avoided even that unpleasantness had she been prepared to become the mistress of one of the gentlemen of the court but there is no indication that she was tempted to go down that road, either at the nadir of her fortunes or thereafter. She was, quite simply, not that kind of girl and the lustful braggarts of Whitehall quickly sensed that she had no place in their sexual diversions. Easy virtue was associated with the 'Frenchified' aristocracy who disdained moral restraint and the poor who could not afford it. Aphra came from the Protestant middle ranks of society whose daughters were brought up to be respectable.

However, she did have friends among the court wits and the literary circles in which they moved. Rochester, Dryden and Killigrew were among her supporters and it must have been thanks to them that the Duke's Men were induced to take the unusual step of accepting a play from Mrs Behn in 1670. *The Forced Marriage* was not entirely without precedent; one of Margaret Cavendish's dramas had already been performed (and dismissed by Pepys as 'the most silly thing that ever come upon a stage') and Katherine Philips, royalist wife of a parliamentary army officer, had translated Corneille's *Horace* and *La Mort de Pompée* which had been staged by the King's Men. It might seem that there was a certain inevitability about the emergence of the woman playwright and that, since the theatres had been opened up to actresses, it was only a matter of time before talented women writers joined the fellowship of the stage. That was not how most contemporaries viewed things. The actress, as we have seen, was little more than a sex object, hired to flaunt her body before the male members of the audience and to deliver titillating lines – lines written by men. It was considered unseemly that a woman should devise the bawdy plots and construct the explicit dialogue demanded by playhouse patrons. Aphra found it prudent to publish her more outrageous comedies anonymously but, even so, she could not avoid censure for daring to write for the public stage at all and for outdoing her male counterparts in the cynical and frank dealing with the sexual mores of fashionable society. But while her critics carped, the public clamoured for more. Aphra found herself in an invidious situation and bitterly resented it. In her introduction to the printed version of *Sir Patient Fancy* she complained,

The play had no other misfortune but that of coming out for a woman's. Had it been owned by a man, though the most dull, unthinking, rascally scribbler in town, it had been a most admirable play.

Members of her own sex, she suggested,

ought to have had good nature and justice enough to have attributed all its faults to the author's unhappiness who is forced to write for bread and not ashamed to own it, and consequently ought to write to please (if she can) an age which has given several proofs it was by this way of writing to be obliged, though it is a way too cheap for men of wit to pursue who write for glory, and a way even I despise as much below me.[4]

She might not have sold her body to make a living but she was obliged, or so she claimed, to prostitute her art.

This did not mean that she was, by nature, a prude nor that she took no pleasure in the earthy nature of her poems and dramatic dialogue. On the contrary, she used them to offer a woman's viewpoint on the battle of the sexes. She lampooned men's sexual inadequacy, their inconstancy and the dual morality with which they justified their dealings with women. In her poem 'The Disappointment', Lysander, having used all the arts of seduction, wears down Cloris' maidenly defences, only to discover that, when it comes to it, he is unable to perform. Who does he blame for this humiliation and frustration?

> His silent griefs swell up to storms,
> And not one god his fury spares;
> He cursed his birth, his fate, his stars;
> But more the shepherdess's charms,
> Whose soft, bewitching influence
> Had damned him to the hell of impotence.[5]

In her plays Aphra could not and did not shrink from giving the public what they wanted – bawdy scenes, sexual innuendo and political comment – but she refused to betray her sex. She exposed masculine weakness and extolled feminine virtues. *The Young King* (an early piece, though not staged till 1679, when it acquired fresh significance from the exclusion crisis) was, on the surface, an allegorical drama which delivered a commentary on the succession issue but it also entered a plea for the strength, wisdom and civilising influence of women. The story concerns Prince Orsames, kept from his throne because of a prophecy which declares that his reign will be short and bloody. His place is taken by his sister, Cleomena, an Amazonian figure who combines military prowess and statesmanship. Despite her wise governance, the ignorant mob clamour for a male ruler. The point the author makes is that, though men may be physically stronger, their very strength may betray them if they do not also espouse what she calls 'softness', a virtue mistakenly attributed only to women.

Aphra had a ready answer to the fashionable complaint that women exercised a usurped power over men. In a despairing tirade, 'A Poem Against Fruition', a contemporary had deplored the way women lured men with promises of bliss that proved illusory.

> Fruition shows the cheat and views 'em near.
> Then all their borrowed splendours plain appear
> And we what with much care we gain and skill
> An empty nothing find, or real ill.

The poet asks,

> Are we then masters or the slaves of things?
> Poor wretched vassals or terrestrial kings?

The answer is all too plain:

> Unsatisfied with beauteous nature's store,
> The universal monarch, man, is poor.

In her reply, Aphra exposes the flaw in the argument with supreme irony: if the sexual hedonist is enslaved, it is not by women but by his own libertinism. It is her own 'hapless sex' that is the victim of man's uncontrollable passion:

> Why do we deck, why do we dress
> For such a short-lived happiness?
> Why do we put attraction on,
> Since, either way, 'tis we must be undone.
>
> They fly if honour take our part,
> Our virtue drives 'em o'er the field.
> We lose 'em by too much desert,
> And, Oh! They fly us if we yield.
> Ye gods! Is there no charm in all the fair
> To fix this wild, this faithless wanderer?
>
> Man! Our great business and our aim,
> For whom we spread out fruitless snares,
> No sooner kindles the designing flame,
> But to the next bright object bears
> The trophies of his conquest and our shame.
> In constancy's the good supreme.
> The rest is airy notion, empty dream![6]

She made the point even more strongly in her enormously popular comedy, *The Revenge*. In this she took the theme of an old tragedy, *The Dutch Courtesan*, and made very significant alterations. The original was the sombre tale of a prostitute deserted by her lover, who avenged herself on him and his new mistress before finally being brought to justice and flogged. In Aphra's version the heroine, Corina, becomes a virtuous woman discarded by her lover, Wellman, in favour of a wealthy heiress. Disgraced and impoverished, Corina is forced to seek refuge in a brothel, where she is looked after without there being any question of her earning her keep in the traditional way. Various complications, disguisings and misunderstandings – the stock of Restoration comedy – occur before Corina and Wellman are reunited and he confesses that he is overwhelmed by the pure love of a good woman.

Aphra Behn was a woman struggling to maintain her place in a man's world. Her talents amply fitted her to occupy such a place but there were several ironies about her position. The dislocations of the time forced her into a literary career but also created the opportunity which enabled her to take it up. She was both praised and condemned for presuming to 'earn her bread' with her pen. She believed in the Protestant virtues of faithful monogamy based on mutual love but had to work within the lascivious conventions of the contemporary theatre, which scorned those very values. She lived and worked in fashionable circles where women were expected to ape the habits and attitudes of their menfolk but she managed, nevertheless, to be a voice for the interests of her own sex. Whether or not male members of her audience recognised it or took it to heart, there was a moral in Aphra's plays even though she had to wrap it up in the sensual trappings of libidinous convention. Hers was a stressful existence and it is scarcely to be wondered at that she found in lesbian relationships the fulfilment of her own emotional needs.

The Restoration theatre produced Britain's first female celebrities. At a time when all professions and vocations were closed to the 'inferior' sex and when the very idea of women having any place within the structures of power would have seemed to herald the collapse of the social order, actresses appeared on the public stage and rapidly gained their coteries of admirers. It would be a couple of hundred years before acting was regarded as a wholly respectable calling for women but the first significant male dyke had been breached and there was to be no going back. Nell Gwynn's is the only name now known to most people in connection with the revived theatre of Charles II's reign but that is only because of her subsequent story. Her acting career was very brief. Patrons who flocked to Drury Lane and Lincoln's Inn Fields in the 1660s and 1670s did so to see other stars. Rebecca Marshall, Elizabeth Boutell and Elizabeth Barry were among the box office draws of those years.

They offered audiences a new experience, a range of emotional expression which the best boy actors had never been able to achieve. Because genuine female talent was available playwrights were able to create more complex characters. They made such an impact on at least one viewer – Samuel Pepys – that he referred to some of the actresses in his diary by their stage personas. Thus Mary Betterton became 'Ianthe' and Hester Davenport 'Roxolana', after the characters they played in Davenant's *The Siege of Rhodes*. The popularity of the leading stage ladies and the growing demand to see them in major roles led to significant changes in the structure of plays. We have already seen the establishment of the 'gay couple' convention. Just as the Hollywood star system of the mid-twentieth century threw up romantic couples like Douglas Fairbanks and Mary Pickford, Humphrey Bogart and Lauren Bacall, so Restoration theatre managers gave their patrons the amorous sparring of Hart and Gwynn. Female parts became more rounded and this led to a new kind of 'coupling'. Actresses were no longer regarded just as foils for their male counterparts; they were antagonists in their own right. Heroines and villainesses fought out their rivalries on the boards. Davenant even wrote his own adaptation of *Macbeth* with an enlarged part for Lady Macduff as a virtuous foil for Lady Macbeth. The new variety of fictional represent-ations represented women as, if not equal to men, at least complementary. Good fiction always challenges stereotypes and, in London at least, the drama was doing just that.

For a few actresses popularity brought wealth and power. The best example of this is Elizabeth Barry. Her first appearances had been dismal failures but Rochester took her in hand and the combination of court patronage and her own strength of character lifted her, by 1680, to the position of first lady of the stage. She was a rarity in being a great tragedienne who could also carry off comedy parts with conviction. All the leading playwrights wrote especially for her and it is said that she created over a hundred roles during her long career. And for her it was a career. She had several lovers from among the court and the intelligentsia and could doubtless have lived very comfortably as a courtesan but she chose to work hard at her profession – and this devotion certainly paid off. She commanded higher wages than any other actress, and than some actors. While looking out diligently for her own interests, she became something of a shop steward within the company, always ready to stand up to the shareholders if she thought she and her colleagues were being exploited. Eventually, in 1695, she led a breakaway group and formed a new company, of which she was, for some years, the organising genius.

Oh King, this is my counsel unto thee and thy rulers and judges. Oh, hearken unto the light of Christ in your consciences that it may bear rule in your hearts, that you may judge for the Lord and oppression may be expelled in your dominions. Oh, that you would do justice and love mercy and walk humbly with the God of Heaven. Then would the Lord give you length of days and a long life, peace and plenty shall be in your dominions . . . joy and tranquillity shall be in your palaces. This shall you see and know to be accomplished if you will leave off oppressing the righteous and set the captive free.

The Trumpet of the Lord Sounded Forth Unto These Three Nations . . .
By one who is a sufferer for the testimony of Jesus in Newgate,
Hester Biddle[7]

Radical change was not confined to the microcosms of court and the capital. The words of an ardent Quaker pamphleteer quoted above remind us that the female revolution of the mid-seventeenth century was far from being confined to the women of fashionable London and Whitehall. It was a part of that larger but diverse, not to say confused, movement which Christopher Hill called 'a period of glorious flux and intellectual excitement, when, as Gerrard Winstanley put it, "the old world . . . is running up like parchment in the fire!"'.[8] When the monarchy was overthrown, when bishops were abolished, when families who had ruled their localities for generations were harried into exile, then it seemed that no political, social, religious or economic change was impossible. The years of war and constitutional experiment threw up numerous groups, all of which constructed their templates for a new order. Seekers, Ranters, Diggers, Levellers, Fifth Monarchists, Muggletonians, Baptists and Quakers were only the more easily identified of the visionary communities which emerged from the smoke of civil war. Beyond them and only partially observed amidst the confusion were myriad eccentric sects, cults and followers of self-styled prophets. In most of them women had their place among the body of ardent disciples. In some they were leaders.

In 1651 the Fifth Monarchist Mary Cary, in her *New and More Exact Mappe or Description of New Jerusalem's Glory*, declared, 'The time is coming when not only men but women shall prophesy; not only aged men but young men; not only superiors but inferiors; not only those that have university learning but those who have it not, even servants and handmaids'.[9] Her words were amply fulfilled over the next couple of decades and she, herself, raised the banner by publishing pamphlets and addressing meetings of spellbound disciples on her own brand of politico-religious apocalyptic. But Mary and women like her did not rise like Anadyomene from the foam of civil conflict. We have to look back to their mothers' and grandmothers' generations to see the accretion of layer upon layer of new ideas and ideals which challenged the traditional position of women in British society. Historians have become adept at digging down to the political and religious roots of the showdown between king and parliament. It was from those same roots that the suckers of female emancipation sprang.

Bible-embracing evangelical Christianity might seem a strange environment in which to look for the principles upon which radical propagandists would build their arguments for a realignment of the sexes. Had not St Paul laid down very strict rules governing the subordinate role of women? Indeed he had, and they were assiduously preached and taught in male-dominated, post-Reformation society. But in the New Testament those strictures were held in tension with other experiences of the early Church. God had poured out his spirit on 'all flesh' and that included women. Prophetesses and other prominent females had appeared, and the dominant spiritual message of the new faith was that there was no longer any distinction between Jew and Gentile, bond and free, man and woman, but all were 'one in Christ Jesus' (Galatians iii.28). It was to this that Protestant fringers looked to justify their proclamation of a new society. They could call on the evidence of political events in support of their convictions. Had not God raised up Elizabeth Tudor to be the sword-bearer of Protestant truth against the Spanish/Roman Antichrist? Was he not, as the British nations tumbled towards bloody strife, preparing the way for Armageddon and the rule of the saints? How could orthodox clergy be so blind as to stick to legalistic arguments about women being in all things and at all times silent in the presence of their superior menfolk? That was nothing less than a stifling of the Holy Spirit and must be resisted as the world moved into its last age.

As the years passed, more and more women joined the ranks of the literate and, in some instances because their time was less fully occupied than that of their husbands and fathers, they gave themselves to study of the scriptures, printed sermons and pamphlets. They flocked to hear itinerant preachers and the propagandists of new interpretations. And some felt themselves called to be the heralds urging people to 'prepare the way of the Lord'. Eleanor Touchet, Lady Davis (later Lady Douglas), was the daughter of the Irish peer, the Earl of Castlehaven, and born into an unruly family in which child abuse was common. Her brother was executed for homosexual practices in 1631. Her early life must have had much to do with the wild course of her later years. It was in 1625 that she was roused one morning by the prophet Daniel, announcing that the world would end in nineteen and a half years. The rest of her life was devoted to proclaiming judgement through pamphlets and impromptu preaching and foretelling dire national events. She denounced Charles I and his leading councillors and was obliged to flee to Holland to publish her prophecies. Those prophecies, like many examples of the genre ever since the pronouncements of the Delphic oracle, were cryptic, dense and (in her case) permeated with Bible quotes and autobiographical fragments:

> ... no inferior rack set upon in these days *Charles Stuart* his reign, as sometimes in *Caesar Augustus*, second of that monarchy, no small oppression, as the lineage of *David* a witness to it: closing it with these from her name, *Rachel's*, signifying a sheep, rendering *Charles* his soil for the golden fleece bearing the bell: so whom he hath joined of her lamentation, &c this *Jacob's* saying, *Some evil beast hath done it*, needs not ask *Whose coat party-coloured* also in pieces rent since our *British Union, &c*, not without cause of *weeping because they are not* . . .[10]

Eleanor's most celebrated escapade was the occupation of the episcopal throne in Lichfield Cathedral where she proclaimed herself the primate of all England. Not surprisingly, despite her social standing, this lady spent several spells in prison and was a source of constant embarrassment to her successive husbands.

If Lady Douglas' obscure rambling was a unique aberration we could safely dismiss it as having no significance. But as Edward Hyde observed in 1652, all England was 'alarmed and even half dead with prophecies'. People wanted some sort of explanation for the violent disturbances of the time and were ready to listen to men and women – but especially women – who offered answers – the more extreme the better, or so it seems. In 1641 the prognostications of Mother Shipton were published. This legendary and perhaps wholly fictitious Yorkshire woman of the early sixteenth century was reputed a kind of folk Nostradamus who foretold a sequence of major events. The core of her prophetic material was freely added to in a score of books and pamphlets throughout the later decades of the seventeenth century and it was not just simple, superstitious folk who took her messages seriously. Prince Rupert, on being told about the Great Fire of London, remarked that Mother Shipton's prophecy had come to pass.

Ecstatic women appeared all over Britain. When Oliver Cromwell moved to St Ives in 1631 he found the fenland town buzzing with the activities of a pedlar, Jane Hawkins, who

> . . . Having fallen into a rapture of ecstasy, has uttered strange things in verse which she could not confess she could ever make before or can do now in matters of divinity and state.

The local clergy took her seriously.

> . . . the vicar and Mr Wise, his curate and another scholar, sitting at the bed's feet and copying out the verses which the poor woman . . . did dictate, which amounting to some thousands, they had transcribed fair with intent to print them . . .[11]

The incident provides a clear demonstration of how such ecstatics obtained credibility. Jane's utterances could be dismissed as fraudulent or the babblings of an insane woman *or* they had to be accepted for what they claimed to be, pronouncements from on high. To those who believed or wanted to believe they carried their own authentication and men of the cloth who accepted them had no alternative but to become the devoted scribes of the handmaid of the Lord. Once the prophecies were endorsed by intelligent and godly men their widespread influence was assured.

The behaviour that found ready acceptance among some parish clergy was rife among members of the sects. Women did not have to be possessed of spectacular gifts to be accorded equality with men. John Bunyan had great difficulties with some of the female members of his Baptist congregation in Bedford throughout much of Charles II's reign. He resisted a determined movement to allow his sisters in Christ to minister in the congregation or even in separate women's meetings. His opposition was implacable but he acknowledged that he was 'like enough to run the gauntlet among [women] and to partake most smartly of the scourge of the tongues of some'.[12] Clearly, there were many Bedford Baptists who believed that Bunyan was being unreasonable and in some congregations women were allowed more latitude but the tinker-turned-minister insisted that if he yielded the point he would be no better than a Quaker or a Ranter.

For members of those sects, allowing women to exercise their gifts was not only a spiritual requirement, it was part of their programme of social justice. They were opposing a regime one of whose imperfections was the subjugation of one-half of humankind. In the more outlandish assemblies women preached, taught, served as missionaries, both at home and abroad, and shared in the government of local congregations and groups. They occupied a vital place in the life of such movements. Indeed, had it not been for women the Quaker movement would not have become so firmly established. Recent research has unearthed the names of over 300 female radical activists and claimed them as early heroines in the long battle for women's rights. In the new dispensation they strove to create, they certainly believed that spiritual equality of the sexes would be expressed in very visible ways. But it was essentially the religious imperative, based on a daring interpretation of Bible texts, that gave these bold, forthright women and their supporters unassailable sanction. It was as though they had been long imprisoned by convention and had suddenly discovered the key which would open the cell door. Being authorised and empowered by the Holy Spirit allowed them to break out from the control of husbands and fathers, and if their trances, fasts and ecstatic utterances carried conviction among their neighbours it was hard for their menfolk to silence them.

For the more radical communities it was a small step from women's partnership in government to sexual liberty. Those who wanted to break away from the traditional conventions had various motives and always put forward the most elevated of reasons. Quakers, for example, dispensed with the bride's promise to obey in the wedding ceremony on the grounds that submission to any earthly authority detracted from the allegiance believers owed only to God. Reformers were essentially rebelling against the obvious disadvantages of the status quo – loveless marriages, marriages contracted for financial gain or the consolidation or preservation of estates, widespread adultery, and the dual morality which underlay all these ills. Many sectarians accused the Church of failing women. Although it advocated monogamous relationships based on mutual affection and fidelity, its patriarchal system was seen by many as playing into the hands of unscrupulous parents and fortune hunters who used women and girls as pawns in their matrimonial games.

Yet, in matters of sex, motives are rarely pure and disinterested. When the Ranters insisted that God's elect could not sin and that free love was directed by the Holy Spirit, this was merely draping lust in pious garb. When zealots advocated female nudity as a means of outlawing the provocative dress fashionable after the Restoration one may doubt the sincerity of their righteous indignation. When a young woman worshipping in Whitehall Chapel threw off her clothes and streaked through the congregation, shouting 'Welcome the Resurrection!' we might suspect mere attention seeking. Among the varied solutions put forward by the daring new thinkers all were impracticable at that time and some were highly suspect. A Baptist lady, Mrs Attaway, urged the easy availability of divorce to men and women, an idea supported by many thinking people, including John Milton (though he only advocated this right for men). It was a proposal three centuries ahead of its time. A contrary way of dealing with the unhappiness of couples manacled together in monogamous misery was polygamy, a solution seriously advocated by some of the leading thinkers of the day. Significantly, what was proposed was that a man might have more than one wife – never the reverse.

Most of these fundamental social reforms were put forward, and in some cases adopted within closed communities, avowedly in the interests of both sexes, but it is difficult to see how women could have benefited from any of them. Until they achieved a degree of economic independence the vast majority of women would always be reliant on the male members of their families and it would, therefore, be the men who made the rules. As long as that was so, dual morality would prevail (whatever the established and Nonconformist churches taught about adultery). What is important is that sexual relationships, like all other social conventions, were being openly scrutinised as never before and that there was a real tension between conventional ethics and the achievement of a fairer society. That tension emerges in a story Margaret Cavendish wrote, called *The Matrimonial Agreement*. At first sight it appears to have a decidedly modern feminist ring to it. In this tale a gentleman of some means paid suit to a lady, pledging undying devotion and fidelity. For her, however, words were not enough; she demanded a written bond in which her husband agreed that if he broke his marriage vows she would not only be free to do the same but would be entitled to a portion of his estate suitable to her proper maintenance. In course of time the inevitable happened and the lady confronted her husband, who was obliged to abide by their agreement. But any suggestion that the author was advocating sexual equality was removed by the moral of the story which showed her to be still firmly tied to traditional attitudes:

Now jealousy and rage are her two bawds to corrupt her chastity, the one persuading her to be revenged, [the other] to show her husband she could take delight and have lovers as well as he. This makes her curl, paint, prune, dress, make feasts, plays, balls, masques, and have merry-meetings abroad, whereupon she began to find as much pleasure as her husband in variety and now begins to flatter him and to dissemble with him that she may play the whore more privately, finding a delight in obscurity, thinking that most sweet which is stolen. So they play, like children, at bo-peep in adultery and face it out with fair looks and smooth it over with sweet words and live with false hearts and die with large consciences.

The concluding bathetic sentence shows Margaret Cavendish clearly refusing the role of social crusader: 'But these, repenting when they died, made a fair end.'[13]

Lady Newcastle's story brings us back to the prevailing attitudes of the social élite in Restoration society. And it was 'restoration' that that society was all about – restoration of the monarchy and all the values and assumptions that the returning exiles and those who flocked to the Stuart court believed to have been the cement of the old order, before the nations had gone mad and plunged into an orgy of self-destruction. When, a hundred years after the event, Richard Brinsley Sheridan proclaimed, 'In Oliver Cromwell's time they were all precise, canting creatures and no sooner did Charles II come over than they turned gay rakes and libertines,' he gave expression to what had become a firmly established myth, and one that had less truth than most. During the Commonwealth and Protectorate, whatever repressive activities Puritan vigilantes might have been engaged in, there was a positive orgy of eccentric behaviour and unrestrained ideas. There was virtually no censorship and, as one commentator famously observed, it seemed that the world was turned upside down. It was Charles II's ministers and the Cavalier Parliament who were the reactionaries, intent on putting the clock back and clamping down on the freedom that had turned into licence. To a large extent they were successful. 'Property triumphed. Bishops returned to a state church, the universities and tithes survived. Women were put back into their place. The island of Great Bedlam became the island of Great Britain, God's confusion yielding place to God's order.'[14]

But any return to the old ways was not instantaneous and it was far from complete. There were aroused expectations and radical convictions that refused to be stuffed back into the box and securely locked up again. At the very end of the century no less a person than Daniel Defoe was arguing for more opportunities for women, confident, as he said, that 'had they the advantages of education equal to us, they would be guilty of less than ourselves'.[15] A feminist writer, Mary Astell, ventured into the pamphlet war on a variety of topical subjects. Mary is most remembered for proposing a scheme that never came to fruition to establish a kind of scholarly nunnery in which women might retire from the world to devote themselves to learning and piety. For this presumption she was roundly vilified. In some ways little had changed in a couple of generations. In 1659 a foreign treatise translated into English with the title, *The Learned Maid, or Whether a Maid may be a Scholar*, had been given a similarly rough reception.

Similar controversy attended the inflow of pornography into Britain. In January 1668, Pepys confided to his diary,

> . . . stopped at Martin's, my bookseller, where I saw the French book which I did think to have for my wife to translate, called, 'L'ecole des Filles', but when I came to look in it, it is the most bawdy, lewd book that ever I saw, rather worse than 'Puttana Errante', so that I was ashamed of reading it . . .[16]

Helot's *Ecole des filles* (1655) was one of several pornographic works of French and Italian origin which had been finding their way into England, where they had been eagerly translated, well over a decade before the king's return. Pepys was unable to resist the salacious tome. Three weeks later he was back at Martin's to buy it in plain binding, 'because I resolve, as soon as I have read it, to burn it, that it may not stand in the list of books, nor among them, to disgrace them if it should be found'. He bore it home and spent much of the next day at the office surreptitiously devouring it, squaring this with his conscience (even if he did not succeed in convincing the readers of his diary in later years) with the reflection that it was 'not amiss for a sober man once to read [it] over to inform himself in the villainy of the world'.[17] The *Ecole des filles*, which was publicly burned by the hangman in 1672, was obviously not the first such book that Pepys had read, since he could compare it with *Puttana Errante*, written in the style of Aretino, and available in French by 1660.

The undercover trade in such provocative literature went on under both the Cromwellian and Carolean regimes. During both it was officially outlawed but flourished because there was a steady demand and because censorship was lax. Pornography was even more readily available on the continent and members of the itinerant Stuart court of the 1650s – both men and women – were well versed in the latest examples to come off the presses. For many it had the added attraction of being anathema to the Puritans. By reading such material and assuming the loose sexual morals that it advocated, royalists could display their superiority over the 'canting hypocrites' currently in power in their homeland.

Pornography fed into the mind set of the leaders of Restoration society. It was, of course, exploitative and assertive of male aggression towards the opposite sex. It represented women as permissive, lustful and seductive. Every daughter of Eve, it suggested, was a whore at heart. There was, as there always is, a very thin dividing line between sexual excitement and loathing for those who provoked that excitement. The writers of the growing volume of anti-feminist satire in the 1660s and 1670s crossed that line.

Drawing on their own experience, on court gossip and on the relationships of the royal brothers with their procession of mistresses, they painted a picture of women as the representatives, if not the very embodiment, of the chaos that had overtaken British society. By usurping power they had thrown all into confusion. In what rapidly became an established verse genre, they vilifiy over and again 'that viler sex that damned us all'. They rage against the cruel trick of creation that has made woman necessary for the process of procreation, while, at the same time, using that trick as an excuse for their own irresistible sexual urge. They reiterate woman's inferiority:

> Whate'er was left unfit in the creation
> To make a toad, after its ugly fashion,
> Of scrapings from unfinished creatures had,
> Sure was the body of a woman made.[18]

Nor was it only the third-rate, pleasure-sated wits of the court who gave vent to sexist ire or despair. As remarked in the opening pages of this book, it was John Milton, in *Paradise Lost*, who pondered,

> O, why did God,
> Creator wise, that peopled highest heaven
> With spirits masculine, create at last
> This novelty on earth, this fair defect
> Of nature, and not fill the world at once
> With men as angels without feminine,
> Or find some other way to generate
> Mankind?[19]

And in *Hudibras* Samuel Butler begged leave to doubt whether these inferior beings actually possessed a soul.

Where was Charles in all this? Not, as has often been casually assumed, setting the tone of cynical hedonism expressively advocated by court poets. What incensed libidinous wits and solemn councillors alike was precisely that the king did not share their anti-feminism. Men who had supported the Stuart cause with their money and their blood, who had sacrificed lands and position, who had shared the discomforts and the shame of exile, and also those who had stayed at home and endured the humiliation of anti-monarchist triumphalism wanted above all else a king who was Protestant, powerful and politically adept. Their ideal ruler would give the strong lead which, as most of them grudgingly acknowledged, Cromwell had given but he would direct his talents to re-establishing and sustaining Charles I's polity of Crown and Mitre and purging the land of every vestige of politico-religious chaos. What they got was a king who was soft on his enemies, was committed to religious toleration, more than a little inclined to Catholicism, in the pocket of the French king *and* dominated by women. And it was that last weakness which for many observers was the *causa causans* of all the ills which beset the regime.

The staunchly royalist Evelyn regarded the third Stuart as a man who had tragically missed his moment of greatness, 'for never had king more glorious opportunities to have made himself, his people and all Europe happy'. The reason for this failure was, in the diarist's considered opinion, that Charles was 'an excellent prince, doubtless, had he been less addicted to women, which made him uneasy and always in want to supply their unmeasurable profusion'. Evelyn resented the siphoning off of royal bounty which should have been lavished on 'many indigent persons who had signally served both him and his father', and he lamented Charles' 'too easy nature' which allowed him to be manipulated by 'prophane wretches, who corrupted his otherwise sufficient parts'. The writer recalled the last time he had seen the king alive and could not forbear moralising:

I am never to forget the unexpressable luxury and prophaneness, gaming and all dissolution, and as it were total forgetfulness of God (it being Sunday evening) which, this day sennight I was witness of; the king, sitting and toying with his concubines, Portsmouth, Cleveland and Mazarin, &c, a French boy singing love songs in that glorious gallery, whilst about twenty of the great courtiers and other dissolute persons were at basset round a large table, a bank of at least 2,000 in gold before them ... it being a scene of utmost vanity ... six days after all was in the dust.[20]

We could dismiss this as sanctimonious preachifying if it were not supported by commentators who certainly did not share Evelyn's piety, some of whom might even have been among the gamblers in the royal apartments on that winter's night. Rochester, Buckingham and others who had taken the king's bread held him in disregard, if not contempt. And much of the reason was that Charles did not share their attitude towards women, who existed, in their view, to be used and abused at the whim of their masters. The key to his effeteness seemed to be his declining of this macho treatment of the opposite sex. One satirist identified Charles with Priapus, the Greek god of procreation:

The poor Priapus king led by the nose
Looks as one set up for to scare the crows.

Yet in the mimics of the spintrian sport*
Outdoes Tiberius and his goatish court.
In love's delights none did him ere excell;
Not Tereus with his sister Philomel.†
As they at Athens we at Dover meet,
And gentlier far the Orleans duchess treat.
What sad events attended on the same
We leave to the report of common fame.[21]

The poet, by an association of ideas, not only links Charles with all manner of sexual practices, but brings in Henrietta and the Secret Treaty of Dover to complete the catalogue of the king's disreputable acts.

Charles' critics were not slow in pointing out the contrast between him and more effective monarchs. The most obvious was Louis XIV, a real warrior king.

Thus, whilst the King of France with powerful arms
Frightens all Christendom with fresh alarms,
We in our glorious bacchanals dispose
The humble fate of a plebian nose.[22]

The allusion is to the unfortunate fate of Sir John Coventry, MP for Weymouth, who, in 1670, during a Commons debate on the taxation of theatres, made some disparaging remarks on the king's interest in actresses. A group of ruffians, acting, some believed, on royal orders, stopped Coventry's carriage, dragged him out and, in the ensuing brawl, slit his nose. It is very unlikely that Charles was behind the assault but he was known to be extremely sensitive to insults involving his lady friends and that was sufficient to lend credence to the rumour.

Ironically, he was also compared unfavourably with Queen Elizabeth.

A Tudor! A Tudor! We've had Stuarts enough.
None ever reigned like Old Bess in the ruff.[23]

Elizabeth was a woman but she lived in the collective memory as someone who had 'the heart and stomach of a king'. Poets looked back to hers as a golden age when the Crown provided inspiration to heroes who ventured forth triumphantly against the Catholic foe.

---

* 'spintrian sport' = male prostitution.
† According to the legend, Tereus, King of Thrace, raped his sister-in-law Philomela, daughter of the King of Athens, then cut out her tongue and imprisoned her in a castle to ensure her silence. The atrocity being discovered, Queen Procne and her sister murdered the king's son and served him up to Tereus at a feast.

> This isle was well reformed and gained renown,
> Whilst the brave Tudors wore th'imperial crown,
> But since the ill-got race of Stuarts came
> It has recoiled to popery and shame.
> Misguided monarchs, rarely wise or just,
> Tainted with pride or with impetuous lust.[24]

Frustration shudders through such lines. The follies of the king's father and grandfather had resulted in two decades of appalling carnage and political chaos. Notwithstanding that, loyal Britons had rallied to the royal standard, supported the cause when it seemed irredeemably lost, and given the Stuarts a second chance. Charles II had squandered this fund of royalist goodwill and it was his relationships with women that most glaringly showed up his shortcomings. Looking back through tinted spectacles over more than half a century, nostalgic poets observed the image of a Virgin Queen 'whose undiminished and uncorruptible sexuality bespoke the power of both the monarch and the nation . . . Charles, on the other hand, "spent" his erotic and political capital, his sexual extravagance degrading his masculine authority and making him . . . less than a woman, impotent, sterile, effeminate, homosexual.'[25]

Can we, with the benefit of historical perspective, say anything to modify the harsh judgement passed by many contemporaries, from bishops to rakes? We will certainly bring to our assessment the insights of our own age, an age which, adrift on a swirling sea of moral relativism, is less inclined to reach black and white verdicts. Whether or not that renders us more or less reliable tribunal members than our seventeenth-century ancestors is beside the point; we can only look at Charles II from where we stand.

He had grown up in a fairytale court and then been pitched out into the real world. Most of his formative years had been spent among ordinary people – both men and women – and he certainly got closer to his subjects than any other monarch before or since. He had had to pack away with the toys of childhood, the magic moments of irresponsible pleasure at his parents' glittering court and, as he met with soldiers, war widows and harassed local gentry who questioned the necessity of the conflict they were caught up in, he discarded the concept of semi-divine monarchy that carried Charles I stubbornly to death on a frosty winter's day. His mother's pragmatism, not to say downright duplicity, seemed to him a more effective political tool than the idealism of his father, or, for that matter, of the English fanatics who wielded the fatal axe, or the dour Scottish Presbyterians among whom he spent several gloomy months. The inattention to business which so frustrated Hyde was not simply the product of laziness: Charles found it increasingly difficult to stomach the preaching of yet another group of theorists – the ministers who wanted to mould him to their image of kingship. Survival through the uncertain years of exile was all about living from day to day. A cardboard king could not afford the luxury of principles. What appeared to many as an attitude of cynicism might more accurately be called non-idealism. Charles did not reject high principles – indeed, he always respected men who were motivated by strong beliefs. He simply did not see their relevance to himself. And in that, he had much in common with the indolent wits who were his companions before and after the Restoration and also with a wider constituency of his war-weary subjects.

However, he could not discard the influences of those who were close to him in his earliest years; their personalities and attitudes helped to form the future king's character matrix. Charles absorbed his father's unfailing courtesy and also something of his reserve. He never suffered from that shyness which was often misconstrued as aloofness in Charles I – quite the reverse – but he was able, when he wished, to distance himself from those around him and to assert that separateness necessary to princes. There was always a limit to the extent that he shared in the boisterousness of his carousing companions. Observers, who deplored the antics of the young louts which Charles seemed to find so amusing, acknowledged that he never shared in their bouts of heavy drinking and public rowdyism. He personally deplored the readiness of the young bloods to settle their disputes by crossing swords and more than once banished men from court for duelling. Thus, he was never a fully paid-up member of the macho Cavalier culture. This needs to be stressed because he was often accused of those excesses which were certainly characteristic of the court over which he presided but in which he did not fully share. Charles was never an unbridled libertine and to compare him with the likes of Tiberius was an absurd exaggeration. In no vice did he indulge to excess. Drinking, feasting, gambling – all these he enjoyed in moderation and if he often partied into the small hours, the other side of his regimen was an addiction to healthy exercise. He walked daily and frequently played tennis, went hunting and swimming.

It was much the same with his whoring. An innumerable cavalcade of women passed through his bedchamber. Most of them were low-class prostitutes procured for him by the likes of Taaffe and Chiffinch. Unlike the king's court ladies and actresses, they remain anonymous and that is precisely because Charles was discreet. Just as he never joined in tavern crawls with his cronies, so he did not visit in person the red light districts of continental cities. In other words, Charles behaved in this regard in the same way as many other European princes and there is no evidence that he was more sexually voracious than they. These casual, carnal encounters were just that and they tell us nothing about his significant relations with the opposite sex.

His relationship with his mother was fundamental. From his earliest memories of her until the day of her death Henrietta Maria exercised a strong influence over her favourite son. Though there were times when he ignored her advice and found her interference irksome, there were others when he sought her counsel or, through simple inertia, allowed her and the Louvre party to shape policy. The prince's earliest mentors, the Marquess of Newcastle and Christabella Wyndham, each in their way helped to fix his basic understanding of women. Newcastle impressed upon his charge a chivalrous attitude towards the opposite sex which was already becoming *passé* and Charles' nurse provided that demonstrative affection which his own mother was less free to show.

Courtesy and consideration always dominated his treatment of the women closest to him. This emerged over and again. His behaviour towards Lucy Walter was ultimately barbarous but the final rejection came only after a long, tumultuous relationship during which he had given her frequent proofs of his love and promised more than he was able to deliver. Her importunity and, perhaps, the political threat she was believed to represent, forced him to the final exigent but, even then, he could not bring himself to cast her off personally but had to act through intermediaries. Women were vital to Charles during the exile years. Not only did they satisfy his physical needs, they also bolstered his ego. At a time when everything he attempted turned to dust and ashes in his hands, they restored his faith in his manhood. As his letters to Jane Lane showed, Charles was always embarrassed at his inability to recompense them as he believed he should and this may have influenced his extravagance towards his mistresses as soon as he had the wherewithal to be generous. He felt gratitude and a sense of obligation towards his women for whatever each gave him. When Clarendon urged him to disentangle himself from Barbara Villiers the king replied that he had compromised her and could not abandon her. He was similarly unwilling to cast aside his barren wife, saying that it would be monstrous to treat her so unkindly simply because she was unfortunate enough not to be able to have children. And few things enraged Charles more than affronts to his female friends.

Inevitably, some women took advantage of Charles' easygoing nature. The two duchesses milked their relationship with the king to the last drop. They built up personal fortunes, accumulated titles for themselves and their offspring and became unbearably arrogant about their special relationship. They took money for obtaining offices and other signs of royal favour and they insinuated their clients into important positions. They participated in ministerial intrigues, and from as early as the 1650s (according to his correspondence with Jane Lane) Charles permitted his female intimates as well as members of his own family to offer advice. He saw nothing untoward about admitting them to his counsels. Mother, sisters, mistresses – he took them all into his confidence – to a certain extent. Never fully; no one enjoyed that privilege. However, it was the involvement of the king's women in affairs of state that so shocked political observers.

Yet, one indulgence was worse in the eyes of court watchers: the king *enjoyed* the company of women – lots of women. Indeed, he seemed at times actually to prefer female company. Charles surrounded himself with people who amused him. His regular entourage included wits, scientists, actors, philosophers and young bucks but always there were lively, beautiful women. The old convention of segregating the sexes into the two sides of the palace, the king's and the queen's, evaporated. The apartments of Charles and Catherine were separate but mistresses now had their own rooms, and those, like Nell Gwynn and Moll Davis, who did not were provided with houses nearby and came and went freely. The sexes mingled in a new, and to many observers a scandalous, way. This open nature of the court posed problems for ministers, ambassadors and all who aspired to influence or who had important business to conclude with the king. They had no alternative but to dance attendance on the king's friends, to give dinner parties for his women, to seek easy access to the mistresses' chambers where Charles was often to be found and to offer bribes to gain their intercession with him. The one thing they certainly could not afford to do was to fall out with these vital intermediaries. All this paying court to mere 'royal playthings' was humiliating for them.

There was an infuriating permanence about the king's women. Ministers came and went, often departing with their rivals' knives firmly embedded in their backs, ambassadors were recalled, sometimes in disgrace, and even longstanding cronies like Buckingham endured lengthy spells of disfavour, but Charles' female intimates were immovable. Nothing, it seemed, could prompt him to abandon them – not the desperate sadness of Catherine's childlessness (and it was a sadness to both husband and wife); not Barbara's constant bullying; not Frances' resistance to his advances; not the raging storm of unpopularity against Louise; not lampoons against Nell's vulgarity; nothing moved Charles to desert his role of protector. It was all immensely frustrating for those who believed, as most members of the establishment did believe, that politics was a man's game. Given the wider concerns about the unnatural usurpation of power by women in many walks of life, it is easy to see why the king's female companions became such an obvious target for those who suggested easy explanations for the ills besetting the realm.

Charles was at odds with the prevailing political correctness. He was always attracted by strong, feisty women. Those of his own family – Henrietta Maria, Mary, Henrietta – had all made their mark in a man's world, standing up to political enemies and enjoying the confidence of princes. The women he became attached to during and after his exile had surmounted huge family and personal difficulties in their upward scramble. Only Catherine of Braganza was not made of such stern stuff but she, too, proved herself to have the stamina which earned her her husband's affection. There was a shared suffering between all these women and the disinherited prince who regained his throne only after two decades of impecunious and humiliating wandering. Perhaps that was the real secret of the bond that existed between Charles and his close female companions. It was a bond which few contemporaries understood and most deplored.

We can comprehend it because we live in an age of greater sexual equality. The freedoms gained by seventeenth-century women were shortlived. As the upheavals of war and politico-religious dislocation receded into history, the old gender conventions reasserted themselves. Women were, for the most part, put back in their place. The ploughshares of social and philosophical change had not bitten deeply enough and the means of communication did not exist that could carry new ideas into every town and village of the British islands. Women had to wait for the more thoroughgoing revolutions of the twentieth century before they could begin to take their places alongside men. If we are right to regard our treatment of women as more civilised than that of our ancestors then we might be inclined to identify Charles II as a 'modern'. He was certainly weak. He was self-indulgent. He squandered his opportunities and was severely lacking in political foresight. But, ironically, we may judge to be most admirable that aspect of his behaviour which contemporaries considered most reprehensible – his treatment of women.

Notes

Introduction

1 John Evelyn, *Diary*, IV, p. 409 (6 February 1685).
2 Bishop Burnet's *History of His Own Time*, III, p. 502.
3 John Milton, *Paradise Lost*, Bk X, ll 888 ff.
4 C. Hill, *A Turbulent, Seditious and Factious People* (Oxford 1989), p. 4.
5 Evelyn, *Diary*, III, p. 302 (18 October 1666).

Part One

1 W.G. Day (ed.), *The Pepys Ballads* (Woodbridge, 1987), II p. 206.
2 Cf. R. Ollard, *The Image of the King* (1979), p. 172.
3 Clarendon, Edward, Earl of, *History of the Rebellion and Civil War in England* (Oxford, 1888 edn), IX, p. 19.
4 *Diary of Samuel Pepys*, ed. H.B. Wheatlay (1895), V, p. 161 (3 December 1665).
5 Cf. H.A. Wyndham, *A Family History* (Oxford, 1939), I, pp. 176–83.
6 Robert Herrick, *Poetical Works*, ed. F.W. Moorman (Oxford, 1921), p. 26.
7 Clarendon, *History of the Rebellion*, I, p. 167.
8 Ibid., VIII, p. 82.
9 Margaret Cavendish, *The Life of William Cavendish . . .* (1667), p. 5.
10 H. Ellis (ed.), *Original Letters, Illustrative of English History* (1824–46) 1st ser. III, pp. 288f.
11 *The Basilicon Doron of King James VI*, ed. J. Craigie (1944), p.75.
12 Bishop Burnet's *History of His Own Time* (Oxford, 1823), II, p. 177.
13 Ibid., I, p. 227.
14 Clarendon, Edward, Earl of, *The Life of Edward, Earl of Clarendon . . .* (Oxford, 1827), I, p. 51.
15 Clarendon, *History of the Rebellion*, VIII, p. 228.
16 Burnet, *History*, II, p. 52.
17 *The Basilicon Doron of King James VI*, p. 27.
18 J. Howell, *Epistolae Ho-elianae* (1645), p. 29. James Howell was

something of a secular vicar of Bray who commended himself in turn to Charles I, parliament, Cromwell and Charles II and whose literary output was both catholic and voluminous. His published collections of letters were undoubtedly partly fictional but, nevertheless, throw valuable light on the events and personalities of the age.

19   Carew's *Poems and Masque*, ed. Aurelian Townshend (Oxford, 1912), p. 93.
20   W. Prynne, *Histriomastix, The Player's Scourge or Actor's Tragedy* (1633), Garland reprint (New York, 1974), Preface To the Christian Reader.
21   *Commons Journals*, II, 134.
22   James I, letter to Archbishop Abbot, 1606, in David Wilkins, *Concilia Magnae Britanniae* . . . (1737), IV, p. 405.
23   Clarendon, *History of the Rebellion*, IV, p. 293.
24   Ibid., p. 296.
25   Ellis, *Original Letters*, 1st ser., IV, p. 2.
26   Clarendon, *History of the Rebellion*, IX, p. 18.
27   Ibid., VI, p. 390.
28   W.C. Abbot (ed.), *The Writings and Speeches of Oliver Cromwell*, (1937–47), I, p. 204.
29   *Calendar of State Papers Domestic of Charles I* (ed. J. Bruce and W.D. Hamilton 1859–97), hereafter referred to as Cal. S.P. Dom., XX, p. 262.
30   Clarendon, *History of the Rebellion*, VIII, p. 254n.
31   Ibid., IX, pp. 134, 135.
32   Ibid., p. 10.
33   *Mercurius Britannicus*, 90, cf. J. Raymond (ed.), *Making the News* (Moreton-in-the-Marsh, 1993), pp. 342–3.
34   Words of Endymion Porter, quoted in Richard Bulstrode, *Memoirs and Reflections upon the Reign and Government of Charles I and II* (1721), p. 137.
35   Clarendon, *History of the Rebellion*, VIII, p. 169.
36   Ibid., IX, p. 19.
37   Ibid.
38   Ibid.
39   Ibid.
40   Ibid.
41   Ibid., p. 53n.
42   Cal. S.P. Dom. Charles I, xx, p. 518. The letter, sent in cipher from Bridgwater, was signed with a code name but must have been sent by the governor or on his behalf.
43   Clarendon, *History of the Rebellion*, X, p. 4.
44   Pepys, *Diary*, V, pp. 24, 33 (24, 31 July 1665).
45   *State Papers Collected by Edward, Earl of Clarendon* (R. Scope and

T. Monkhouse, eds Oxford, 1767–86), II, p. 238.

46 Ibid., p. 307.
47 Clarendon, *History of the Rebellion*, I, p. 10.
48 Wyndham, *Family History*, I, p. 243.
49 'A Godly Warning to All Maidens', in Day (ed.), *Pepys Ballads*, I, p. 505.
50 Cf. William Gouge, *Of Domestical Duties* (1634).
51 C. Oman, *Henrietta Maria* (1936), p. 184.
52 *The English Works of Thomas Hobbes*, ed. W. Molesworth (1839–45), I, p. 186.
53 *State Papers of Clarendon*, II, p. 291.
54 *Dictionary of National Biography*.
55 *State Papers of Clarendon* II, p. 291.
56 Burnet, *History*, II, p. 94.
57 H.A.I. Fisher, *A History of Europe* (1952), p. 632.
58 H. Hantsche, *Die Geschichte Osterreichs* (Vienna, 1962), II, p. 560; E.N. Williams, *The Ancien Régime in Europe* (1970), p. 40.
59 Clarendon, *History of the Rebellion*, XI, p. 33.
60 Baronne d'Aulnoy, *Memoirs of the Court of England in 1675* (trans 1707), p. 95.
61 Clarendon, *History of the Rebellion*, XII, p. 1.
62 Ollard, *Image of the King*, p. 71.
63 Ephraim Pagit, *Christianographie, or a Description of the Sundry Sorts of Christians in the World* (1646 edn), I, p. 147.
64 Clarendon, *History of the Rebellion*, XII, p. 59.
65 *Correspondence of Sir Edward Nicholas, Secretary of State*, ed. G.F. Warner (Camden Society, 1886), I, p. 295.
66 Clarendon, *History of the Rebellion*, XII, p. 60.
67 Ibid., VIII, p. 30.
68 *Dictionary of National Biography*.
69 Clarendon, *History of the Rebellion*, XIII, p. 4.
70 Ibid, p. 6.
71 Abbott (ed.), *Writings and Speeches of Oliver Cromwell*, II, p. 302.
72 *State Papers of Clarendon*, II, p. 546.
73 Clarendon, *History of the Rebellion*, XIII, p. 62.
74 *State Papers of Clarendon*, II, p. 562.
75 J. Hughes (ed.), *The Boscobel Tracts: relating to the Escape of Charles the Second after the Battle of Worcester* (1830), p. 12.
76 Manuscripts of Allan George Finch, *Historical Manuscript Commission Reports*, I (1913), p. 65.
77 A. Bryant (ed.), *The Letters, Speeches and Declarations of King Charles II* (1968 edn), p. 25.
78 Ibid., p. 38.
79 Hughes (ed.), *Boscobel Tracts*, p. 76.

80 Ibid., p. 304.
81 Ibid., p. 307.
82 Ibid., p. 328.

Part Two

1 'Upon his Majesty's being made free of the City', *Poems and Letters of Andrew Marvell*, ed. H.M. Margoliouth (Oxford, 1927), I, p. 181.
2 Clarendon, *History of the Rebellion*, XIII, p. 107.
3 Quoted in C.R. Boxer, *The Dutch Seaborne Empire, 1600–1800* (1965), pp. 170–1.
4 Williams, *The Ancien Régime in Europe*, p. 138.
5 Burnet, *History*, II, pp. 463–4, Pepys, *Diary*, V, p. 161, IV, p. 299 (3 December 1665, 3 December 1664).
6 Clarendon, *History of the Rebellion*, XI, p. 65.
7 Ibid., XIV, p. 71.
8 *Mercurius Politicus* 8–15 January 1652, in Raymond (ed.), *Making the News*, p. 277.
9 *State Papers of Clarendon*, III, p. 170.
10 Ibid., p. 171.
11 Ibid.
12 Quoted in A.I. Dasent, *Private Life of Charles II* (1927), p. 29n.
13 S.R. Gardiner, *History of the Commonwealth and Protectorate* (1895–1901), III, p. 137.
14 T. Birch (ed.), *A Collection of the State Papers of John Thurloe*, (1742), V, p. 645.
15 Pepys, *Diary*, VI, p. 286 (26 April 1667).
16 Clarendon, *Life*, p. 205.
17 Pepys, *Diary*, VI, p. 288 (26 April 1667).
18 Bryant (ed.), *Letters of Charles II*, pp. 29–30.
19 *Correspondence of Sir Edward Nicholas*, ed. G.F. Warner (Camden Society, 1886), II, p. 109; Lord Hatton to Charles II, 20 October, 1654.
20 Bryant (ed.), *Letters of Charles II*, p. 31.
21 Clarendon, *History of the Rebellion*, XIV, p. 137.
22 Ibid., VIII, p. 268.
23 Birch (ed.), *State Papers of John Thurloe*, I, pp. 683–4.
24 *State Papers of Clarendon*, III, p. 298.
25 Clarendon, *History of the Rebellion*, XV, p. 121.
26 *State Papers of Clarendon*, III, p. 297.
27 Ibid., p. 387.
28 *The Political Works of Benedict de Spinoza*, trans. A.G. Wernham (Oxford, 1958), pp. 442–5; cf. M.R. Sommerville, *Sex and Subjection* (1995), p. 23.
29 Christopher Marlowe, *The Conquests of Tamburlaine*, Pt. I.

30 T. Crist (ed.), *Letters in Exile* (1974), p. 39.
31 Ibid., p. 19.
32 Ibid., p. 37; Thomas Carte, *Original Letters and Papers* (1739), II, p. 276.
33 Crist (ed.), *Letters in Exile*, p. 39.
34 Clarendon, *History of the Rebellion*, IV, p. 127.
35 Crist (ed.), *Letters in Exile*, p. 27.
36 *State Papers of Clarendon*, III, p. 382.
37 Ibid., p. 383.
38 Crist (ed.), *Letters in Exile*, p. 29.
39 Ibid., p. 31.
40 Carte, *Original Letters*, II, p. 157.
41 Crist (ed.), *Letters in Exile*, p. 39.
42 Ibid., p. 35.
43 Clarendon, *History of the Rebellion*, XVI, p. 58.
44 Ibid., p. 73.
45 Ibid., p. 141.
46 Bryant (ed.), *Letters of Charles II*, p. 58.
47 Quoted in M.A. Everett Green, *Lives of the Princesses of England* (Coburn, 1855), p. 262.
48 Burnet, *History*, I, p. 121n.
49 Clarendon, *History of the Rebellion*, XVI, pp. 74–5.
50 Ibid., pp. 111–12.
51 Mme de Lafayette, *Vie de la Princesse d'Angleterre*, ed. Marie Theresa Hipp (Geneva, 1967), p. 25.
52 Bryant (ed.), *Letters of Charles II*, p. 80,
53 Pepys, *Diary*, II, p. 92; III, p. 123 (31 August 1661, 15 May 1663).
54 Ibid., I, p. 294.
55 *The Letters of Philip, Second Earl of Chesterfield* (1835), p. 86.
56 Ibid., p. 97.
57 Cal. S.P. Dom., CC, p. 259.
58 W. Harris, *An Historical and Critical Account of the Life of Charles II* (1747), I, p. 281.
59 Clarendon, *History of the Rebellion*, XVI, pp. 194–7.
60 Ibid., p. 185.
61 Ibid., p. 247.
62 J. Evelyn, *Diary*, III, p. 246 (29 May 1660).
63 Bishop Burnet, *History*, I, p. 160.
64 Pepys, *Diary*, VI, p. 87 (1 December 1666).
65 Ibid., I, p. 200 (13 July 1660).
66 Quoted in Green, *Lives of the Princesses*, II, p. 311.
67 Ibid., p. 310.
68 Pepys, *Diary*, I, p. 256 (7 October 1660).
69 Burnet, *History*, II, p. 168.

70 *Continuation of the Life of Edward, Earl of Clarendon* (1759), p. 32.
71 Burnet, *History*, I, p. 170n.
72 Ibid., p. 171.
73 Ibid., p. 169.
74 Evelyn, *Diary*, III, p. 17 (17 October 1660).
75 Burnet, *History*, I, p. 162.
76 Ibid., p. 171.
77 Pepys, *Diary*, I, p. 310 (24 December 1660).
78 Ibid., p. 290 (22 November 1660).
79 Burnet, *History*, II, p. 172.
80 Cf. G.P. Gooch, *Louis XV: The Monarchy in Decline* (1956), p. 5.
81 J. Collier, *A Short View of the Profaneness and Immorality of the English Stage* . . . (1698; citation from the 1730 edn).
82 Pepys, *Diary*, I, pp. 280–1 (22 April 1661).
83 *Continuation of the Life of* . . . *Clarendon*, p. 366.
84 Pepys, *Diary*, II, p. 72 (27 July 1661).
85 Bryant (ed.), *Letters of Charles II*, pp. 116–17.
86 Burnet, *History*, II, p. 174.
87 Bryant (ed.), *Letters of Charles II*, pp. 126–7.
88 C.H. Hartmann, *Charles II and Madame* (1934), p. 43.
89 Bryant (ed.), *Letters of Charles II*, pp. 126–7.
90 Ibid., p. 127.
91 Letter of Lord Cornbury to the Marchioness of Worcester, 10 June 1662, *Historical Manuscript Commission Reports*, IX (1902), p. 52.
92 T.H. Lister, *Life and Administration of Edward, First Earl of Clarendon* (1838), III, p. 198.
93 Ibid., p. 228.
94 Hartmann, *Charles II and Madame*, pp. 50–1.
95 Lister, *Life* . . . *of Clarendon*, III, p. 202.
96 Halifax, *Complete Works*, ed. J.P. Kenyon (1969), pp. 252–4.
97 Burnet, *History*, II, p. 94.
98 Ibid., p. 255.
99 Ibid., I, p. 93.
100 The Duke of Buckingham, *Collected Poems* (1704), p. 156.
101 Burnet, *History*, II, p. 264.
102 Cf. J.H. Wilson, *Court Satires of the Restoration* (Columbus, 1976), p. xv.
103 Ibid., p. 39.
104 Pepys, *Diary*, III, p. 44 (17 February 1663).
105 Evelyn, *Diary*, II, p. 333 (23 August 1662).
106 Bryant (ed.), *Letters of Charles II,* p. 130.
107 Evelyn, *Diary*, III, p. 330 (14 August 1662).
108 Pepys, *Diary*, II, p. 331 (7 September 1662).
109 Ibid., p. 433 (31 December 1662).

110 Ibid., III, p. 44 (17 February 1663).
111 Hartmann, *Charles II and Madame*, p. 133.
112 Ibid., p. 147.
113 Pepys, *Diary*, VII, p. 200 (16 November 1667).
114 Burnet, *History*, II, p. 99.
115 Ibid.
116 Pepys, *Diary*, III, p. 133 (15 May 1663).
117 Lister, *Life . . . of Clarendon*, III, p. 244.
118 S. Thurley, *The Whitehall Palace Plan of 1670, London Topographical Society Publication, 153* (1998), p. 34.
119 Cf. Wilson, *Court Satires*, pp. 10–12.
120 *Historical MSS Commission*, Portland, III, p. 293. Cf. A. Andrews, *Royal Whore* (1971), p. 96.
121 *News from the Coffee House* (1667); cf. H. Weber, *Paper Bullets: Print and Kingship under Charles II* (Kentucky, 1996), p. 159.
122 Wilson, *Court Satires*, p. 11.
123 *New Satirical Ballad of the Licentiousness of the Times* (1679); cf. Weber, *Paper Bullets*, p. 160.
124 Ibid., p. 161.
125 J.J. Jusserand, *A French Ambassador at the Court of Charles II*, (1892), p. 144.
126 T. Hobbes, *Leviathan*, in *The English Works of Thomas Hobbes*, I, p. 135.
127 Rochester, 'Signor Dildoe', in *Poems on Affairs of State . . .*, I (1703), p. 189.
128 Pepys, *Diary*, VI, p. 274 (16 April 1667).
129 J. Lacy, 'Satire', in *Poems on Affairs of State*, I, pp. 425–8.
130 Halifax, *Complete Works*, p. 255.
131 J.R. Jones, *Charles II, Royal Politician* (1987), p. 190.
132 Pepys, *Diary*, VI, p. 399 (28 June 1667).
133 J. Sheffield, 'Essay on Satire', in *Poems on Affairs of State*, I, p. 136.
134 Hartmann, *Charles II and Madame*, p. 42.
135 Pepys, *Diary*, III, p. 209 (13 July 1663).
136 Halifax, *Complete Works*, pp. 252–3.
137 Pepys, *Diary*, III, p. 35 (8 February 1663).
138 Ibid., p. 330 (6 November 1663).
139 Jusserand, *French Ambassador*, p. 91.
140 Ibid., III, pp. 159, 246 (4 June, 11 August 1663).
141 Hartmann, *Charles II and Madame*, p. 81.
142 Ibid., p. 83.
143 Ibid., p. 87.
144 Ibid., p. 89.
145 Ibid., p. 100.
146 Edmund Waller, 'Upon the Golden Medal'.

147 Hartmann, *Charles II and Madame*, p. 37.
148 Ibid., p. 91.
149 Ibid., p. 57.
150 Ibid., pp. 111–12.
151 Ibid., p. 91.
152 Ibid., p. 155.
153 Andrew Marvell, 'Second Advice to a Painter', in *Poems on Affairs of State*, I, p. 44.
154 Jusserand, *French Ambassador*, pp. 170–1.
155 Hartmann, *Charles II and Madame*, pp. 147–8.
156 Ibid., p. 112.
157 *Continuation of the Life of . . . Clarendon*, p. 827.
158 Pepys, *Diary*, VI, p. 362 (13 June 1667).
159 Ibid.
160 Ibid., p. 286 (26 April 1667).
161 'Fourth Advice to a Painter', in *Poems on Affairs of State*, I, p. 146.
162 Sonya Wynne, 'The Mistresses of Charles II, and Restoration Court Politics 1660–85', Cambridge PhD thesis, 1996, p. 161. In assessing the political influence of Barbara Villiers and Louise de Keroualle I follow closely Ms Wynne's excellent research and analysis.
163 Ibid., p. 163.
164 *Poems and Letters of Andrew Marvell*, I, p. 201.
165 Pepys, *Diary*, VII, p. 39 (27 July 1667).
166 *Complete Works of John Wilmot, Earl of Rochester*, ed. D. Vieth (New Haven, 1968), pp. 61 and 135.
167 Burnet, *History*, II, p. 252.
168 Pepys, *Diary*, VI, p. 368 (14 July 1666).
169 *Poems on Affairs of State*, I, p. 253.
170 Pepys, *Diary*, VII, pp. 39 and 52 (27 and 30 July 1667).
171 Ibid., VII, p. 18 (12 July 1667)
172 Ibid., p. 76 (25 July 1667).
173 Ibid., p. 40 (27 July 1667).
174 M. Ingram, 'The Reform of Popular Culture? Sex and Marriage in Early Modern England', in *Popular Culture in Seventeenth Century England*, ed. B. Reay (1988), p. 157.
175 Pepys, *Diary*, VII, p. 40 (27 July 1667).
176 Ibid., p. 84 (27 August 1667).
177 Bryant (ed.), *Letters of Charles II*, p. 204.
178 Ibid., pp. 203–4.
179 H. Craik, *The Life of Edward, Earl of Clarendon* (1911), p. 303.

Part Three
1 Burnet, *History*, II, p. 263.
2 J. Collier, *A Short View*, Preface.

3 Ibid., p. 209.
4 *Dictionary of National Biography.*
5 Ibid.
6 A. Nicoll, *A History of English Drama* (1952), I, p. 343.
7 Jusserand, *French Ambassador*, p. 152.
8 Pepys, *Diary*, VII, p. 277 (11 January 1668).
9 Cf. E. Howe, *The First English Actresses* (Cambridge, 1992), pp. 25–6.
10 Ibid., p. 58.
11 Ibid., p. 34.
12 Ibid., pp. 62–3.
13 J. Collier, *A Short View*, p. 6.
14 *The Works of Mr Thomas Brown* (1707–8), II, p. 166.
15 Pepys, *Diary*, VII, p. 397 (7 April 1668).
16 Ibid., VI, pp. 144–5 (23 January 1667).
17 Evelyn, *Diary*, III, p. 345 (27 November 1662).
18 Cf. E. Howe, *First English Actresses*, p. 70.
19 Pepys, *Diary*, VI, p. 203 (2 March 1667).
20 Ibid., p. 273 (15 April 1667).
21 Ibid., VIII, p. 252 (28 December 1667).
22 Hartmann, *Charles II and Madame*, pp. 203–4.
23 *Memoirs of the Count de Gramont*, ed. A. Fea (1906), p. 286.
24 Ibid., pp. 286–7.
25 *Complete Poems of John Wilmot, Earl of Rochester*, ed. D.M. Vieth, (Yale 1968), p. 74.
26 Pepys, *Diary*, VII, pp. 330–1 (20 February 1668).
27 Ibid., p. 379 (26 March 1668).
28 Halifax, *Complete Works*, p. 265.
29 Burnet, *History*, II, p. 265.
30 Pepys, *Diary*, VII, p. 374 (24 March 1668).
31 For a fuller treatment of the Bawdy House or Messenger Riots cf. T. Harris, *London Crowds in the Reign of Charles II* (Cambridge, 1987), p. 82ff.
32 Pepys, *Diary*, II, p. 395 (6 April 1668).
33 *The Poor Whores' Petition to the most Splendid, Illustrious, Serene, and Eminent Lady of Pleasure, the Countess of Castlemayne, etc.* (1668).
34 Burnet, *History*, II, p. 265.
35 Cf. Andrews, *Royal Whore*, pp. 141–2.
36 Pepys, *Diary*, VIII, p. 308 (28 April 1669).
37 *The Works of John Dryden*, ed. H.T. Swedenberg, Jr., *et al.* (Berkeley, 1956), I, p. 38.
38 *Letters from the Marchioness de Sevigné to her Daughter the Countess de Grignan* (1764), p. 70.

39 *Poems on Affairs of State*, I, p. 420.
40 Ibid., p. 426.
41 Hartmann, *Charles II and Madame*, p. 178.
42 Burnet, *History*, II, p. 250.
43 *Poems and Letters of Andrew Marvell*, I, p. 192.
44 *Letters from the Marchioness de Sévigné*, p. 96.
45 Hartmann, *Charles II and Madame*, pp. 131–2.
46 Ibid., p. 245.
47 Pepys, *Diary*, VIII, p. 244 (4 March 1669).
48 Hartmann, *Charles II and Madame*, pp. 277–80.
49 Ibid., p. 315.
50 Mme de Lafayette, *Vie de la Princesse d'Angleterre*, p. 111ff.
51 'Britannia and Rawleigh', in *Poems and Letters of Andrew Marvell*, I, p. 185.
52 Pepys, *Diary*, I, p. 290 (22 November 1660).
53 Evelyn, *Diary*, IV, p. 66 (15 June 1675).
54 Burnet, *History*, II, p. 337.
55 Cf. P.W. Sergeant, *My Lady Castlemaine* (1912), p. 164.
56 Evelyn, *Diary*, III, p. 564 (4 November 1670).
57 Cf. Andrews, *Royal Whore*, p. 155.
58 J. Barzun, *From Dawn to Decadence* (2001), p. 290.
59 Cf. Andrews, *Royal Whore*, p. 154.
60 Evelyn, *Diary*, IV, p. 117 (10 September 1677).
61 Ibid., III, p. 589 (9 October 1671).
62 Ibid., p. 572 (1 March 1671).
63 J. Ives, *Selected Papers*, p. 39.
64 Evelyn, *Diary*, III, p. 573 (2 March 1671).
65 'Britannia Rawleigh' in *Poems and Letters of Andrew Marvell*, I, p. 187.
66 'The Duchess of Portsmouth's Pictures', in *Poems on Affairs of State*, I, p. 51.
67 Cf. A.I. Dasent, *The Private Life of Charles II* (1937), p. 196.
68 Evelyn, *Diary*, IV, p. 343 (4 October 1683).
69 Andrews, *Royal Whore*, pp. 166–7.
70 An anonymous lampoon, cf. Wilson, *Court Satires*.
71 William Wycherley, *The Plain Dealer*, Act IV, sc. ii.
72 Andrews, *Royal Whore*, pp. 157ff.
73 Cal. S.P. Venetian, 1673–5, p. 187.
74 Evelyn, *Diary*, IV, pp. 16–21 (30 July–18 August 1673).
75 *Dictionary of National Biography*, Anthony Ashly Cooper.
76 J. Miller, *Charles II* (1991), p. 224.
77 Burnet, *History*, II, p. 351.
78 Evelyn, *Diary*, IV, p. 21 (18 August 1673).
79 Halifax, *Complete Works*, p. 256.

80 Ibid., p. 257.
81 O. Airy and C.E. Pike, *Essex Papers, 1672–77* (Camden Society, new series, xlvii 1890), pp. 272, 265.
82 Cal. S.P. Dom., 1679–80, p. 21.
83 Cf. F.A. Nussbaum, *The Brink of All We Hate* (Lexington, 1984), p. 41.
84 Cf. C.H. Hartmann, *The Vagabond Duchess* (1926), p. 168.
85 Ibid., p. 190.
86 Cf. Andrews, *Royal Whore*, p. 179.
87 *Poems and Letters of Andrew Marvell*, II, p. 226.
88 Ibid. I, p. 196.
89 Cf. J. Mackay, *Catherine of Braganza* (1937), p. 199.
90 Cf. Andrews, *Royal Whore*, pp. 203–6.
91 Burnet, *History*, III, pp. 421–2.
92 Cal. S.P. Dom., 1679–80, p. 68.
93 Ibid., p. 21.
94 Aphra Behn, Poem to L'Estrange; cf. M. Duffy, *The Passionate Shepherdess* (1989), p. 181.
95 Burnet, *History*, III, p. 429.
96 Cal. S.P. Dom., 1679–80, p. 256.
97 *Dictionary of National Biography*.
98 *Commons Journal*, IX, 530, 31 October 1678.
99 Mackay, *Catherine*, p. 216.
100 Ibid., p. 219.
101 Cf. Mackay, *Catherine*, p. 226.
102 Burnet, *History*, III, p. 477.
103 Cal. S.P. Dom., 1679–80, p. 428.
104 'A Dialogue between Duke Lauderdale and Lord Danby', in *Poems on Affairs of State*, II, p. 117.
105 Ibid., pp. 290–1.
106 W. Scott (ed.), *A Collection of Scarce and Valuable Tracts* (1812), III, pp. 137ff. S.M. Wynne discusses the tract fully in her PhD thesis, 'The Mistresses of Charles II and Restoration Court Politics, 1660–85', pp. 231ff.
107 Wilson, *Court Satires*, pp. 36–7.
108 *Poems on Affairs of State*, II, pp. 428–31.
109 Cf. D. Ogg, *England in the Reign of Charles II* (Oxford, 1967), pp. 618–19.
110 Burnet, *History*, III, p. 499.
111 Bryant (ed.), *Letters of Charles II*, pp. 311–12.
112 Burnet, *History*, III, p. 496.
113 Ibid., p. 499.
114 Cf. Weber, *Paper Bullets*, p. 198.
115 Ibid., p. 172.

116 Wilson, *Court Satires*, p. 94.
117 Ibid., pp. 63–5.
118 *The Roxburghe Ballads*, ed. W. Chapell and J.W. Ebsworth (New York, 1966 edn) V, pp. 130–3.
119 The play is fully discussed in Weber, *Paper Bullets*, pp. 111–22.
120 Quoted in Wynne, 'The Mistresses of Charles II', p. 152.
121 Evelyn, *Diary*, IV, pp. 267–8 (24 January 1682).
122 Letters in Chichester Record Office, quoted by B. Masters, *The Mistresses of Charles II* (1979), p. 140.
123 Cf. Mackay, *Catherine of Braganza*, p. 230.
124 Evelyn, *Diary*, IV, p. 395 (15 November 1684).
125 Ibid., pp. 359–66 passim.
126 Cal. S.P. Dom., 1680–81, p. 660.
127 *Dictionary of National Biography*.
128 D'Ogg, *England*, p. 647.
129 Evelyn, *Diary*, IV, p. 322 (28 June 1683).
130 *Dictionary of National Biography*.
131 R. Bulstrode, *Memoirs and Reflections upon the Reign and Government of King Charles II* (1721), p. 424.
132 Quoted in Wynne, 'The Mistresses of Charles II', p. 158.

Part Four

1   P. Salzmann (ed.), *Early Modern Women's Writing* (Oxford, 2000), pp. 245–6.
2   Ibid., p. 241.
3   Pepys, *Diary*, VI, p. 299 (1 May 1667).
4   Cf. Duffy, *Passionate Shepherdess* (2001), pp. 166–7.
5   Salzmann, *Women's Writing*, p. 382.
6   'To Alexis in Answer to his Poem Against Fruition', cf. ibid., pp. 386, 435–6.
7   Ibid., p. 154.
8   Christopher Hill, *The World Turned Upside Down* (1972), p. 14.
9   Ibid., p. 322.
10   Salzmann, *Women's Writing*, p. 141.
11   Cal. S.P. Dom., Charles I, 1628–9, p. 530.
12   Cf. Christopher Hill, *A Turbulent, Seditious and Factious People* (Oxford, 1989), p. 300.
13   Salzmann, *Women's Writing*, p. 245.
14   Hill, *A Turbulent, Seditious and Factious People*, p. 379.
15   Daniel Defoe, *An Essay on Projects* (1697).
16   Pepys, *Diary*, VII, p. 279 (13 January 1668).
17   Ibid., pp. 310–11 (8–9 February 1668).
18   *Myzoginus, or A Satire Upon Women* (1682).
19   John Milton, *Paradise Lost*, Bk X, 11. 888ff.

20 Evelyn, *Diary*, IV, pp. 409–13 (6 February 1685).
21 'An Historical Poem', in *Poems and Letters of Andrew Marvell*, I, p. 202.
22 'Further Advice to a Painter', ibid., p. 169.
23 'Dialogue between Two Horses', ibid., p. 195.
24 'An Historical Poem', ibid., p. 202.
25 Weber, *Paper Bullets*, p. 125.

Bibliography

(The place of publication is London unless indicated to the contrary)

A battle between two lapdogs of the Utopian court, 1681
A dialogue between the Duchess of Cleveland and the Duchess of Portsmouth . . . , 1682
A dialogue between the Duchess of Portsmouth and Madam Gwin . . . , 1682
A pleasant dialogue betwixt two wanton ladies of pleasure . . . , 1685
Andrews, A., *The royal whore: Barbara Villiers . . .* , 1971
Anon, *Histoire Secrette de la Duchesse de Portsmouth*, 1690
Anon, *Secret History of the court and reign of Charles II*, 2 vols, 1792
Anon, *Secret History of the reigns of Charles II and James II*, 1690
Barbour, V., *Henry Bennett, Earl of Arlington . . .* , 1914
Baronne d'Aulnoy, *Memoirs of the Court in England in 1675*, 1707
Bevan, B., *Charles II's French Mistress, A biography of Louise de Keroualle*, 1972
Bevan, B., *Duchess Hortense,* 1987
Bevan, B., *Nell Gwynn*, 1969
Bloom, E.A. and L.D., *Satire's Persuasive Voice*, 1979
Browning, A., *Thos Osborne, Earl of Danby . . .* , 1951
Buckingham, George Duke of, *Collected Poems*, 1704
Bulstrode, R., *Memoirs and Reflections upon the Reign and Government of Charles I and Charles II,* 1721
Burnet, G. *History of his own Time*, Oxford, 1823
Calendar of State Papers Domestic of Charles I (ed. J. Bruce and W.D. Hamilton, 1859–97)
Calendar of State Papers Domestic of Charles II (ed. J. Bruce and W.D. Hamilton, 1859–97)
Calendar of State Papers Venetian (ed. G.C. Bentinck and A.B. Hinds, 1864)
Carlton, C., *Royal Mistresses*, 1990
Carswell, J., *The Porcupine: The Life of Algernon Sidney*, 1989
Carte, T., *Original Letters and Papers*, 1739
Cavendish, M., *The Life of William Cavendish . . .* , 1667

389

Chapman, H., *Great Villiers . . .* , 1949

Charles II, *Letters, Speeches and Declarations of King Charles II* (ed. A. Bryant, 1935)

Clarendon, Edward, Earl of, *Continuation of the Life of Edward, Earl of Clarendon,* Oxford, 1759

Clarendon, Edward, Earl of, *History of the Rebellion and Civil Wars in England,* Oxford (1888 edn)

Clarendon, Edward, Earl of, *State Papers collated by Edward, Earl of Clarendon,* Oxford, 1767–86

Clarendon, Edward, Earl of, *The Life of Edward, Earl of Clarendon . . .* , Oxford, 1827

Collier, J., *A Short View of the Profaness and Immorality of the English Stage,* 1698, 1730

Commons Journals 1803

Coote, S., *Royal Survivor: A Life of Charles II,* 1999

Correspondence of the Family of Hatton, 1601–1704 (ed. E.M. Thompson, Camden Soc., 1878)

Craik, H., *The Life of Edward, Earl of Clarendon,* 1911

Crist, T. (ed.), *Charles II to Lord Taaffe, Letters in Exile,* 1974

Cunningham, P., *The Story of Nell Gwyn 1903,* 1927

Dalrymple, J., *Memoirs of Great Britain and Ireland,* 1773

Dasent, A., *Nell Gwynne 1650–1687 . . .* , 1924

Dasent, A., *The Private Life of Charles II,* 1927

Davidson, L.C., *Catherine of Bragança,* 1908

Day, W.G. (ed.), *The Pepys Ballads,* 1987

de Sola, P.V., *Enthusiast in Wits – A Portrait of John Wilmot, Earl of Rochester, 1647–1680,* (1962 ed.)

Delpech, J., *The Duchess of Portsmouth,* 1953

Delpech, J., *Life and Times of the Duchess of Portsmouth* (trans. A. Lindsay), 1953

Dryden, J., *The Poems of John Dryden,* ed. J. Kinsley, Oxford, 1958

Duffy, M., *The Passionate Shepherdess, Aphra Behn, 1640–1689,* 1977

Dunlop, I., *Louis XIV,* 1999

Ellis, H., *Original Letters, Illustrative of English History,* 1824–46

Elsna, H., *Catherine of Bragança . . .* , 1967

Evelyn, J., *The Diary of John Evelyn* (ed. E.S. de Beer, Oxford, 1955)

Feiling, K., 'Henrietta Stuart, Duchess of Orleans, and the Origins of the Treaty of Dover', *English Historical Review,* XLV, 1932

Fraser, A., *King Charles II,* 1980

Fraser, A., *The Weaker Vessel,* 1984

Gardiner, S.R., *History of the Commonwealth and Protectorate,* 1895–1901

Gilmour, M., *The Great Lady . . .* , 1944

Gooch, G.P., *Louis XV: The Monarchy in Decline,* 1956

Gouge, W., *Of Domestical Duties,* 1634

Grant, Mrs Colquohoun, *Brittany to Whitehall; Life of Louise Reneé de Keroualle* . . . , 1909

Hamilton, A., *Memoirs of Comte de Gramont*, 1930

Hamilton, E., *Henrietta Maria*, 1976

Hamilton, E., *The Illustrious Lady* . . . , 1980

Harbage, A., *Thomas Killigrew, Cavalier Dramatist, 1612–1683*, 1930

Harris, F.R., *The Life of Edward Mountagu, 1st Earl Sandwich*, 1912

Harris, R.W., *Clarendon and the English Revolution*, 1983

Harris, T., 'The Bawdy House Riots of 1668', *Historical Journal*, XXXIX, 1986

Harris, T., *London Crowds in the Reign of Charles II: Propaganda and Politics from the Restoration to the Exclusion Crisis*, Cambridge, 1987

Harris, T., Seaward, P. and Goldie M. (eds), *The Politics of Religion in Restoration England*, Oxford, 1990

Harris, W., *An Historical and Critical Account of the Life of Charles II*, 1747

Hart, W.H., *A Memorial of Nell Gwynne, the Actress, and Thomas Otway, the Dramatist*, 1868

Hartmann, C.H., *Charles II and Madame*, 1934

Hartmann, C.H., *La Belle Stuart*, 1924

Hartmann, C.H., *The King's Friend*, 1951

Hartmann, C.H., *The Vagabond Duchess*, 1926

Hill C., *Some Intellectual Consequences of the English Revolution*, Madison, Wisconsin, 1980

Hill, C., *A Turbulent, Seditious and Factious People – John Bunyan and his Church*, Oxford, 1989

Hill, C., *The Century of Revolution, 1603–1714*, 1961

Hill, C., *The World Turned Upside Down: Radical Ideas During the English Revolution*, 1972

Historical MSS Commission Reports

Hobbes, T., *The English Works of Thomas Hobbes* (ed. W. Molesworth), 1839–45

Hobby, E., *Virtue of Necessity: English Women's Writings, 1649–88*, 1988

Hopkins, G., *Nell Gwynne – A Passionate Life*, 2000

Houston, A. and Pincus S, *A Nation Transformed: England After the Restoration*, Cambridge, 2002

Howe, E., *The First English Actresses, Women and Drama 1660–1700*, Cambridge, 1992

Howell, J., *Epistolae Ho-eliassae*, 1645

Huertas, M. de, *Louise de Kéroualle: presque reine d'Angleterre*, Paris, 1988

Hughes, J. (ed.), *The Boscobel Tracts: relating to the escape of Charles the Second after the Battle of Worcester*, Edinburgh and London, 1830

Hulton, R., 'The Making of the Secret Treaty of Dover', *Historical Journal* 1986, pp. 297–318

Hulton, R., *Charles II*, Oxford, 1991

Hulton, R., *Charles the Second, King of England, Scotland and Ireland*, Oxford, 1989

Hulton, R., *The Restoration: A Political and Religious History of England and Wales, 1658–1667*, Oxford, 1985

Hunt, L., ed., *Eroticism and the Body Politic*, Baltimore, 1991

Irwin, M.E., *Henrietta Anne*, 1937

James, M.E., *Society, Politics and Culture: Studies in Early Modern England*, Cambridge, 1986

Jenson, H.J., *The Sensational Restoration*, Indiana, 1996

Jones, J.R. (ed.), *The Restored Monarchy, 1660–1688*, 1979

Jones, J.R., *Charles II, Royal Politician*, 1987

Jones, J.R., *The First Whigs*, 1961

Jusserand, J.J., *A French ambassador at the court of Charles II . . .* , 1892

Justice, G.L. and Tinker, N. (eds.), *Women's Writing and the Circulation of Ideas: Manuscript Publication in England, 1550–1800*, Cambridge, 2002

Kenyon, J., *Robert Spencer, 1st Earl of Sunderland, 1641–1702*, 1958

Kenyon, J., *The Popish Plot*, 1972

Lafayette, Mme de, *Vie de la Princesse d'Angleterre*, (ed. M.T. Hipp), Geneva, 1967

Lister, T.H., *Life and Administration of Edward, First Earl of Clarendon*, 1838

Lord, George de F., *et al.*, ed., *Poems on Affairs of State: Augustan Satirical Verse, 1660–1714*, New Haven, 1963–75

Love, H. (ed.), *The Penguin Book of Restoration Verse*, 1968

Macgregor-Hastie, R., *Nell Gwyn*, 1987

Mackay, J., *Catherine of Braganza*, 1937

Macpherson, J., ed. *Original Papers Containing Secret History of Great Britain*, 2 vols, 1775

Magalotti, L., *Travels of Cosimo II, Grand Duke of Tuscany* (ed. J. Mauma, 1821)

Marshall, A., *Intelligence and Espionage in the Reign of Charles II*, Cambridge, 1994

Masters, B., *The Mistresses of Charles II*, 1979

Mazarin, Hortense de, *Memoirs of the Duchess of Mazarine*, (trans. P. Porter), 1676

Miller, J., 'Charles II and his Parliaments' in *Transactions of the Royal Historical Soc.*, 5th series, xxxii, 1982

Miller, J., *After the Civil Wars: English Politics and Government in the Reign of Charles II*, 2000

Miller, J., *Charles II*, 1991

Miller, J., *Popery and Politics in England, 1660–1688*, 1973

Montpensier, duchesse de, *Memoirs of Anne, Duchesse de Montpensier*, 1848

Murray, N., *Andrew Marvell: World Enough and Time*, 1999

Nicholas, E., *Correspondence of Sir Edward Nicholas, Secretary of State* (ed. G.F. Warner, Camden Society, 1866)

Nicoll, A., *A History of English Drama 1660–1900*, I, 1952

Nussbaum, F.A., *The Brink of All We Hate, English Satires on Women, 1660–1750*, Lexington, 1984

Ogg, D., *England in the Reign of Charles II*, Oxford, 1934

Ollard, R., *The Escape of Charles II*, 1966

Ollard, R., *The Image of the King*, 1979

Oman, C., *Henrietta Maria*, 1951

Parker, D., *Nell Gwyn*, 2000

Peck, L., *Court Patronage and Corruption in Early Stuart England*, Boston, 1990

Pepys, S., *The Diary of Samuel Pepys* (ed. M.B.Wheatley), 1895

Picard, L., *Restoration London*, 1997

Prior, M. (ed.), *Women in English Society 1500–1800*, 1985

Rawson, C. (ed.), *English Satire and the Satiric Tradition*, Oxford, 1984

Raymond, J. (ed.), *Making the News: An Anthology of the Newsbooks of Revolutionary England 1641–1660*, Moreton-in-the-Marsh, 1993

Reay, B. (ed.), *Popular Culture in Seventeenth-Century England*, 1988

Roberts, C., *Schemes and Undertakings: A Study of English Politics . . .* , Columbus, 1985

Roberts, C., *The Ladies, Female Patronage of Restoration Drama*, Oxford, 1989

Rochester, John, Earl of, *The Complete Poems of John Wilmot, Earl of Rochester*, (ed. D. Vieth, New Haven), 1968

Roxburghe Ballads (ed. W. Chapell and J.W. Ebsworth), New York, 1966

Salzman, P. (ed.), *Early Modern Women's Writing – an anthology 1560–1700*, Oxford, 2000

Savile, G., *Marquess of Halifax, Complete Works*, ed. J. Kenyon, 1969

Scott, G., *Lucy Walter, Wife or Mistress?*, 1947

Scott, J., *Algernon Sidney and the Restoration Crisis, 1677–1683*, Cambridge, 1991

Seaward, P., *The Cavalier Parliament and the Reconstruction of the Old Regime, 1661–1667*, Cambridge, 1989

Senior, D.P., *The King's Ladies . . .* , 1936

Sergeant, P., *My Lady Castlemaine*, 1912

Sevigné, Marchioness de, *Letters from the marchioness de Sevigné to her daughter, the countess de Grignan*, 1764

Smith, .D.L., *The Stuart Parliaments, 1603–1689*, 1999

Sommerville, M.R., *Sex and Subjection: Attitudes to Women . . .* , 1995

Sophia, Electress of Hanover, *Memoirs of Sophia, Electress of Hanover* (trans. H. Forester), 1888

Stanhope, Philip, Earl of Chesterfield, *Correspondence with various ladies*, 1930

Stone, L. *The Family, Sex and Marriage in England, 1500–1800*, 1977

The poore-whores' petition . . . , 1688

Thomas, K., *Religion and the Decline of Magic: Studies in Popular Beliefs in Sixteenth and Seventeenth Century England*, 1971

Thompson, R., *Unfit for Modest Ears*, 1979

Thormählen, M., *Rochester: The Poems in Context*, Cambridge, 1993

Thurley, S., *The Whitehall Palace Plan of 1670*, 1998

Thurloe, J., *A Collection of the State Papers of John Thurloe* (ed. T. Birch, 1742)

Todd, J., *The Secret Life of Aphra Behn*, 1996

Trease G., *Portrait of a Cavalier – William Cavendish, First Duke of Newcastle*, 1979

Weber, H.M., *Paper Bullets, Print and Kingship under Charles II*, Kentucky, 1996

Wilson, J.H. (ed.), *Court Satires of the Restoration*, Columbus, 1976

Wilson, J.H., *Court wits of the Restoration* . . . , Princeton, 1948

Wilson, J.H., *Nell Gwynn, Royal Mistress*, 1952

Winn, J.A., *John Dryden and His World*, Yale, 1987

Witcombe, D.T., *Charles II and the Cavalier House of Commons, 1663–1674*, Manchester, 1966

Wyndham, H.A., *A Family History*, Oxford, 1939

Wyndham, V., *The Protestant Duke*, 1976

Wynne, S., *The Mistresses of Charles II and Restoration Court Politics, 1660–85*, Cambridge Ph.D. thesis, 1996

Index

Index